Lecture Notes of the Institute for Computer Sciences, Social Informatics and Telecommunications Engineering 283

More information about this series at http://www.springer.com/series/8197

Vladimir Poulkov (Ed.)

Future Access Enablers for Ubiquitous and Intelligent Infrastructures

4th EAI International Conference, FABULOUS 2019
Sofia, Bulgaria, March 28–29, 2019
Proceedings

 Springer

Editor
Vladimir Poulkov
Department of Communication Networks
Technical University of Sofia
Sofia, Bulgaria

ISSN 1867-8211 ISSN 1867-822X (electronic)
Lecture Notes of the Institute for Computer Sciences, Social Informatics
and Telecommunications Engineering
ISBN 978-3-030-23975-6 ISBN 978-3-030-23976-3 (eBook)
https://doi.org/10.1007/978-3-030-23976-3

This Springer imprint is published by the registered company Springer Nature Switzerland AG
The registered company address is: Gewerbestrasse 11, 6330 Cham, Switzerland

A Note from the General Chairs

We are delighted to introduce the proceedings of the 2019 European Alliance for Innovation (EAI) International Conference on Future Access Enablers of Ubiquitous and Intelligent Infrastructures (FABULOUS 2019). This was the fourth edition of the conference, which was held in the beautiful city of Sofia, the capital of Bulgaria, under the theme "Globalization Through Advanced Digital Technologies." The event brings together experts, researchers, business innovators, and students to exchange knowledge and ideas on the newest digital and wireless technologies toward innovative and sustainable solutions for ubiquitous and intelligent communication infrastructures.

The technical program of FABULOUS 2019 featured 35 papers distributed over several sessions, as well as two plenary speaker presentations. The papers contain novel contributions on current key digital technologies, such as: 5G wireless communications, Internet of Things, artificial intelligence, cloud computing, big data, and virtual and augmented reality, which all have opened the field to novel application scenarios where physical presence is less relevant and communication is extended to human-to-human, human-to-machine, and machine-to-machine scenarios. Cities, roads, homes, and businesses have become intelligent information hubs, challenging the communication and societal norms and transforming their fundamental nature.

We would like to recognize the support of the Steering Committee chair, Imrich Chlamtach, from the University of Trento, Italy, and the invaluable effort put forth to making this event a strong platform for research discussions by: the Technical Program Committee chairs – Markus Rupp from the Technical University of Vienna, Austria, Octavian Fratu from Politehnica University of Bucharest, Romania, and Albena Mihovska from Aarhus University, Denmark; the publicity and social media chair: Georgi Iliev from the Technical University of Sofia, Bulgaria; the sponsorship and exhibits chair: Zlatka Valkova-Jarvis from the Technical University of Sofia, Bulgaria; the publications chair: Ernestina Cianca, from the University of Rome Tor Vergata, Italy; the local arrangements chair: Agata Manolova from the Technical University of Sofia, Bulgaria; the Web chair: Alexandru Vulpe from Politehnica University of Bucharest, Romania; and the conference manager: Andrea Piekova from EAI.

We believe that these conference proceedings of the high-quality scientific contributions presented at FABULOUS 2019 will stimulate and inspire early-stage and established researchers, manufacturers, policy and standardization makers, and educators on the road to digitalization toward innovative and sustainable solutions for ubiquitous and intelligent communication infrastructures.

May 2019

Vladimir Poulkov
Liljana Gavrilovska
Constantinos B. Papadias

Conference Organization

Steering Committee

Imrich Chlamtac   Bruno Kessler Professor University of Trento, Italy

Organizing Committee

General Chair and Co-chairs

Vladimir Poulkov   Technical University of Sofia, Bulgaria
Liljana Gavrilovska   Ss. Cyril and Methodius University, Skopje,
     Republic of Macedonia
Constantinos Papadias   Athens Information Technology, Athens, Greece

TPC Chair and Co-chairs

Markus Rupp   Technical University of Vienna, Austria
Octavian Fratu   Politehnica University of Bucharest, Romania
Albena Mihovska   Aarhus University, Denmark

Sponsorship and Exhibit Chair

Zlatka Valkova-Jarvis   Technical University of Sofia, Bulgaria

Local Chair

Agata Manolova   Technical University of Sofia, Bulgaria

Publicity and Social Media Chair

Georgi Iliev   Technical University of Sofia, Bulgaria

Publications Chair

Ernestina Cianca   University of Rome Tor Vergata, Italy

Web Chair

Alexandru Vulpe   Politehnica University of Bucharest, Romania

Technical Program Committee

Georgi Iliev   Technical University of Sofia, Bulgaria
Arianit Maraj   Telecom of Kosovo and AAB College
Venceslav Kafedziski   FEEIT Skopje, Republic of Macedonia
Marian Vladescu   Politehnica University of Bucharest, Romania

Marian Vlădescu	Politehnica University of Bucharest, Romania
Simona Halunga	Politehnica University of Bucharest, Romania
Pero Latkoski	Skopje, Republic of Macedonia
Sunny Sanyal	.
Carmen Voicu	Politehnica University of Bucharest, Romania
Pavlos Lazaridis	University of Huddersfield, UK
Vladimir Atanasovski	Ss. Cyril and Methodius University in Skopje, Republic of Macedonia
Vasile Bota	Technical University of Cluj-Napoca, Romania
Dragos Burileanu	Politehnica University of Bucharest, Romania
Zaharias Zaharis	Aristotle University of Thessaloniki, Greece
Marghescu Ion	University Politehnica of Bucharest, Romania
Nenad Filipovic	University of Kragujevac, Serbia
Doru Florin Chiper	Technical University Gheorghe Asachi Iasi, Romania
Alexandru Vulpe	Politehnica University of Bucharest, Romania
Nicolae Militaru	Politehnica University of Bucharest, Romania
Igor Radusinovic	University of Montenegro
Albena Mihovska	Aarhus University, Denmark
Onoriu Bradeanu	Vodafone Romania
Claudia Zenkova	.
Miroslav Voznak	Technical University of Ostrava, Czech Republic
Larysa Globa	.
Yannick Saouter	Lab-STICC
Lela Mirtskhulava	Ivane Javakhishvili Tbilisi State University/San Diego State University, Georgia/USA
Mohamed Amine Ferrag	Guelma University, Algeria
Hirley Alves	University of Oulu, Finland
Nicola Marchetti	CTVR

Contents

Healthcare/Wellness Applications

Anthropomorphic EMG-Driven
Prosthetic Hand

Ioan Coman[1], Ana-Maria Claudia Drăgulinescu[2(✉)], Doina Bucur[1],
Andrei Drăgulinescu[2], Simona Halunga[2], and Octavian Fratu[2]

[1] Medical Engineering Faculty, University Politehnica of Bucharest,
Bucharest, Romania
[2] Electronics, Telecommunications and Information Technology Faculty,
University Politehnica of Bucharest, Bucharest, Romania
amc.dragulinescu@gmail.com

Abstract. Hazards in industry, wars and serious medical reasons determined
the increase of the number of amputations and, thus, the need for designing
prosthetics that replace the missing segment by imitating its natural movements.
Research in prosthetics domain became, consequently, a primary activity both
for engineers and physicians. Due to structural and functional acclimation to the
complexity of human activities, one of the most difficult to approach limb of the
human body is the hand. This paper is aimed to design an anthropomorphic
prosthetic hand controlled based on surface electromyography sensors data
acquired from two important muscles: flexor pollicis longus muscle and flexor
digitorum profundus muscle. Another purpose of the paper consists in providing
two main functions of the prosthetic hand, prehension and fingers flexion.

Keywords: Anthropomorphic · EMG signals · Ehealth · Fingers flexion ·
Prehension · Prosthetic hand

1 Introduction

Vascular disease, as diabetes and peripheral arterial disease, trauma suffered due to
industry hazards and cancer are the main causes for amputation [1]. Human hand is a
very sophisticated component of the human body as its capabilities are complex and
all-important [2]. Without hands, the quality of human life is severely diminished. To
greet the needs of the persons affected by hand loss, different devices that try to imitate
the anatomy, properties and functionality of the human hand were proposed [3]. If one
hundred years ago, the prosthesis designed by Hosmer-Dorrance had reduced functionality (grabbing function) and was designed as a hook, the next prostheses developed usually in Russia and United States, especially after World War II, were
improved. Thus, more functions were added, the prostheses became lighter and patient-
molded [4]. With the advent and development of microprocessors and robotics, the
prostheses were further enhanced. The need for enhanced functions, aesthetics and
more comfortable devices intensified the research in electromyography and myoelectric
prosthetics [5]. Moreover, the 3D printing technology contributed to the design of
various lighter, cheaper and less time-consuming prostheses [6]. Atasoy et al. [3]

V. Poulkov (Ed.): FABULOUS 2019, LNICST 283, pp. 3–11, 2019.
https://doi.org/10.1007/978-3-030-23976-3_1

presented a mechanical design prosthetic hand having brushless DC motor and shape memory alloy (SMA) actuators to mimic the anatomy of the human hand. EMG signals were acquired through the MYO Armband device equipped with 8 surface EMG (electromyography) electrodes and the features were extracted using Wavelet Packet Transform (WPT), a method that decomposes a time signal into independent time-frequency signals known as packets and enables the localization (in time) of transitory events [3, 7]. The classification method used in [3] is based on neural networks and 7 hand postures and grasps are recognized with a success rate of 80% (when all subjects are trained for all data) and 95–98% when only one subject is trained for all seven events. In [6] a 3D-printed upper-extremity prosthesis equipped with pressure sensor is proposed and compared with Otto Bock myoelectric prosthesis from the point of view of functions, dexterity, cost, fabrication period and weight. Several tests were conducted: nine hole pegboard test, box & block test, hand strength measurement. The differences were minor in what concerns the first and the second test, but the hand strength of Otto Bock prosthesis was much greater than the one of the proposed prosthesis (13.6 kg vs. 5.9 kg). Also, due to some limitations, three out of five activities were not conducted by the patient wearing 3D-printed pressure-sensor prosthesis (to button, write, grip the small corn). With both prostheses, the patient succeeded in conducting the two other activities (to dress the socks, to transfer the paper cup). Kocejko et al. [8] proposed a hybrid solution comprising EMG and EEG (electroencephalogram) sensors along with an eye tracker with a use case for patients with whole arm amputation. The joints of the 3D-printed arm are controlled through eye tracking. The role of the eye tracker resides in capturing the point in 3D space towards which the user gazes in order to place the arm in the correct position. An EMG sensor placed on the trapezius muscle is used to prevent the undesired, false-triggered positioning of the arm at each changing of the gaze point. Unfortunately, in [8] the role of the EEG interface is not clearly defined. In [9], a two-finger prosthesis based on one EMG sensor is described. Mahanth et al. [9] implemented the 4 electronic circuits aimed to acquire, full-wave rectify, to integrate and to amplify the EMG signal used to drive the prothesis. The movement of the fingers was triggered by the exceeding of a threshold that discriminates between the inactivity of the muscles and the muscular activity. This approach, however, is not suitable for reaching the human fingers' dynamics. Sharmila and Ramachandran [10] propose a model for a prosthetic arm that contrives to classify two hand movements (fingers flexion and fingers extension) based on a single 3-electrodes EMG sensor whose signal is passed through several conditioning and amplification circuits (instrumentation amplifier, high pass filter, low pass filter, notch filter, DC coupling circuit). As features extracted from the EMG signal, Root Mean Square and Frequency Energy are mentioned. For classification, a Support Vector Machine and binary linear classifier were chosen in [10]. The success rate of the proposed model is 76.6%. In [11], a method was developed to distinguish between the movements of wrist, finger and the combined action of wrist and fingers. A double differential electrode unit consisting in four anoxic copper electrodes was realized and tested. The discrimination is made by means of two methods, depending on the deviation between low-frequency component of EMG signal and the high-frequency one that is small for a wrist action and high for the other two possible cases. Next, if the deviation is large, the second method discriminates between the two other actions.

In our work, an anthropomorphic EMG-driven prosthesis is proposed. The artificial hand is controlled by means of the signal acquired from two EMG surface sensors. Further, the paper is organized as follows: Sect. 2 comprises theoretical background related to electromyography, EMG sensors and signals, in Sect. 3 the experimental setup and conditions are presented, as well as the experimental results and discussions. Section 4 outlines conclusions, future improvements and research.

2 Electromyography, EMG Sensors and Signals

As regards hand anatomy and muscle activation, if an amputee misses the hand segment together with all muscles and tendons, the forearm muscles activity must be related to hand movements in order to develop an EMG-driven prosthetic hand. It is well known that, although a limb segment is missing, the brain continues to command muscle contraction when the subject intends to use his limb.

Electromyography represents a medical procedure that monitors the electrical activity in the muscle [12] and it is based on a phenomenon called electromechanical coupling in muscle [13]. Muscle cells or fibers generate an electrical potential (ranging from 50 μV to 30 mV) when they are electrically or neurologically activated [14]. There are two types of electromyography procedure. The clinical procedure called needle EMG is invasive and implies the use of a needle electrode that penetrates the skin. This method is the most accurate, providing fibre-level details of the physiology of the muscle. Needle EMG is necessary in medical and scientific studies to track and char-acterize pathological events and disorders that affect the muscle's motor units, that is, the motor neuron and the muscle fibers stimulated (or innervated) by this neuron [15]-[17].

Surface electromyography (sEMG) is a non-invasive method used to determine the electrical activity of the muscle. If needle EMG allows the monitoring of a motor unit at a time through the needle electrode, in order to obtain an objective quantification of the energy of the muscles using sEMG technique, several surface electrodes are needed. In this paper, sEMG will be employed, therefore, only surface EMG sensors will be described.

A surface EMG sensor consists in 2 or 3 surface electrodes and signal conditioning circuits. 2-electrode configuration provides a less stable signal – as it is affected by noise - compared to 3-electrode configuration [14]. For a 3-electrode sensor (Fig. 1), the electrodes are assigned and positioned as follows: MID (middle of the targeted muscle), END (at one end of the targeted muscle), GND (must be placed on an electrically neutral body area, usually a bony tissue [18], as the elbow). The size of the active area of the electrodes is crucial for the quality of the EMG signal while the distance that must separate the ground electrode from the other(s) electrode(s) is not so important [14].

Compared to other biopotential signals (EEG, ECG), the frequency range of EMG signal is very wide, in general, between 20 Hz and 2000 Hz [19] and for surface EMG signals, between 10 and 500 Hz. The amplitude of raw EMG signals ranges from 0 to 10 mV [20], thus being necessary to include amplifying circuits to provide a signal for further processing.

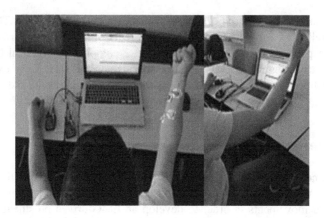

Fig. 1. 3-electrode EMG sensors position (MID - yellow, END - violet, GND in blue) (Color figure online)

3 Proposed Prosthetic Hand Architecture. Experimental Results

Figure 2 depicts the components of the proposed EMG-driven hand prosthesis. Two EMG sensors are attached to forearm's skin as emphasized in Fig. 1. EMG Sensor 1 is positioned such that it records the activity of the flexor pollicis longus muscle and EMG Sensor 2 is placed such that it provides EMG signal of both flexor digitorum profundus and superficialis muscles.

MCU-AU1 and MCU-AU2 are two complex units, each consisting in a micro-controller (MCU) and an EMG acquisition unit (AU). MCU-AU1 will acquire the EMG signal of flexor pollicis longus muscle and will control pollicis servomotor. MCU-AU2 will gather data from EMG Sensor 2 and will control the prosthetic fingers.

For our experimental setup, we chose Arduino Uno equipped with ATmega328P microcontroller and eHealth Shields v 2.0 (Fig. 2). To acquire an EMG signal, as eHealth shield allows the acquisition of at least ten human body parameters and signals, the jumper ECG/EMG next to Analog Inputs connector must be in EMG position, i.e., it must connect pins 2 and 3.

Each eHealth shield comprises an EMG connector for three EMG electrodes. Also, the shield includes signal amplifying, rectifying and smoothing circuits.

MID and END electrodes of each sensor are connected to the corresponding complex unit. Nevertheless, only one GND electrode should be used to avoid the ground loops, as they can provoke electrical shocks to the subject [21]. Consequently, the reference electrode (GND) will be shared by both eHealth shields through jumper wires.

The prosthetic fingers are controlled through five servomotors SG-90 that are calibrated to rotate between $0°–180°$. To calibrate them, we wrote a script that commands their rotation to pre-defined positions, as $0°$, $90°$ or $180°$.

The implementation has two stages:

- Signal acquisition and processing, decision-making. At this stage, the data acquired from two EMG sensors are sent through MATLAB software via serial ports of a computer to process the signals and extract the most important features that distinguish the motions proposed in this work: prehension, fingers flexion and relaxation. It is worth mentioning that the serial communication and MATLAB software are proposed only for prototyping. Generally, the proposed prosthetic hand should use wireless technology communications to send EMG samples to devices having high computational ability. Thus, the prosthesis will appoint the processing and decision-making tasks to devices as PC, tablet or smartphone that run a dedicated software application for supporting further processing.
- Prosthetic hand actuation. At this stage, the prototype is no longer connected to the serial ports of the computer, the parameters computed by MATLAB are sent to and used by microcontroller to provide the correct rotation of the servomotors, and, thus, the actuation of the prosthetic hand becomes dependent on the EMG signals parameters.

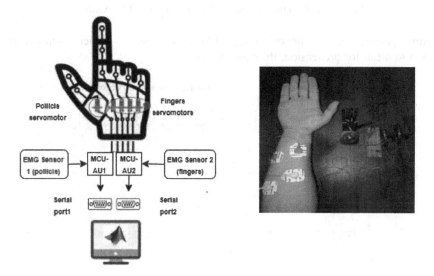

Fig. 2. Proposed architecture of prototype EMG-driven prosthesis (left) EMG signals acquisition setup (right)

Ten experiments were performed: prehension (1), relaxation (2), strongly flexing (3) and extending all fingers (4), extending (5) and flexing (6) all fingers, except the pollicis, flexing (7) and extending (8) the pollicis, lifting the arm in lateral at a 90° with respect to the body and hold the hand at 90° with respect to arm (9), lifting the arm at 90° in front of the body (10). Experiments (1)-(8) were doubled by asking the subject to perform the tasks both sustaining the hand on a table and standing up.

In Fig. 3, we represented the two EMG signals resulted during prehension and relaxation. For both cases, the mean values of the two signals are almost the same

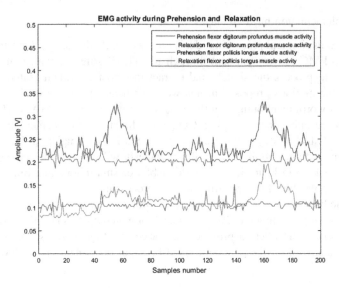

Fig. 3. EMG signals during two prehensions and relaxation

(flexor digitorum: 0.23 V, flexor pollicis: 0.11), but there is a higher deviation with respect to mean for prehension, than for relaxation.

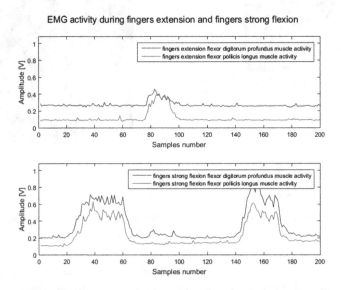

Fig. 4. EMG signals during all fingers extension (up) and two strong fingers flexions (down)

Figure 4 depicts the graphical results when the subject was asked to extend and strongly flex all fingers. One can notice that for fingers extension, the maxima of amplitude of pollicis muscle and flexor digitorum muscle have similar values, while for finger flexion the maxima hardly reach comparable values.

In what concerns, pollicis flexion, we noticed that, although the amplitude of pollicis muscle activity is significantly lower than that of flexor digitorum muscle activity, for the first one an increasing in amplitude corresponding to the flexion is observed, while the amplitude of the latter has a neglectable deviation from the mean. When slowly extending the pollicis (as a strong extension of the pollicis would have determined an extension of the other fingers), we noticed that the amplitude variation was inconclusive. In experiment (9), we observed a similar pattern for relaxation. Due to the position, arm muscles take over the sustaining effort and help to forearm relaxation.

In experiment (10), however, the muscles activity increases and extremely high values of the EMG amplitudes (around 2 V for pollicis muscle and 2.5 for flexor digitorum muscle) are obtained. When the subject was asked to stand up, very high values were obtained, too, and we could not describe a pattern.

4   Conclusions, Contributions Emphasis and Future Research

This paper reveals important methodological aspects concerning the EMG signals acquisition and offers an experimental setup for an EMG-controlled prosthetic hand.

As distinct from [3] in which SMA actuators were used, our prosthesis was 3D-printed. We acquired the signals using eHealth Shield, which, in our knowledge, in our paper, is the first time used for controlling a prosthesis. Unlike [9] and [10], we used two 3-electrodes EMG sensors and we reckoned with the role of each muscle group when choosing the position of each sensor on the forearm, thus succeeding in controlling separately the pollicis and the other four fingers of the artificial hand. Moreover, the correct positioning of the sensors and electrodes is explained and fig-ured, a detail that in similar articles misses. Also, it presents and emphasizes the patterns of the amplitude of EMG signals acquired from flexor digitorum muscles and flexor pollicis longus muscle. These patterns are aimed to distinguish fundamental hand movements as prehension, fingers flexion and extension, pollicis flexion and relaxation.

The present work, beside other papers, proposes the implementation of a hand prosthetic that may be able to appoint the processing stage to a higher computational ability device by sending in real-time the samples, through a communication tech-nology (Bluetooth Low Energy or LPWAN technologies) to a PC, tablet or smartphone that sends back to the prosthesis the decisions taken based on processed signal. This aspect is very important as the prosthesis must be energy-efficient.

In future, we will propose new methods to render finer hand movements. Also, we intend to design, implement and test a system that uses EMG signals not only to control the prosthesis, but also for controlling useful actuators in the context of Smart Home and Smart Car use cases dedicated to impaired people.

Acknowledgments. This work was supported by a grant of the Ministry of Innovation and Research, UEFISCDI, project number 33PCCDI/01.03.2018 within PNCDI III, Platform of multi-agent intelligent systems for water quality monitoring on Romanian sector of Danube and Danube Delta (MultiMonD2), and partially funded under contract no. 5Sol/2017 within PNCDI III, Integrated Software Platform for Mobile Malware Analysis (ToR-SIM).

References

1. Amputee statistics you ought to know. http://advancedamputees.com/amputee-statistics-you-ought-know. Accessed 06 June 2018
2. Clement, R.G.E., Bugler, K.E., Oliver, C.W.: Bionic prosthetic hands: a review of present technology and future aspirations. Surg. J. **9**, 336–340 (2011)
3. Atasoy, A., Kaya, E., Toptas, E., Kuchimov, S., Kaplanoglu, E., Ozkan, M.: 24 DOF EMG controlled hybrid actuated prosthetic hand. In: 2016 38th Annual International Conference of the IEEE Engineering in Medicine and Biology Society (EMBC), pp. 5059–5062 (2016)
4. Norton, K.M.: A brief history of prosthetics. inMotion Mag. **17**(7). www.amputee-coalition.org/resources/a-brief-history-of-prosthetics/. Accessed 20 Aug 2018
5. Zuo, K.J., Olson, J.R.: The evolution of functional hand replacement: From iron prostheses to hand transplantation. Plast. Surg. J. (Oakv) **2**(1), 44–51 (2014)
6. Lee, K.H., Bin, H., Ahn, S.Y., Kim, B.-O., Bok, S.-K., Wang, J.: Hand functions of myoelectric and 3D-printed pressure-sensored prosthetics: a comparative study. Ann. Rehabil. Med. **41**(5), 875–880 (2017)
7. García Plaza, E., Núñez López, P.J.: Application of the wavelet packet transform to vibration signals for surface roughness monitoring in CNC turning operations. Mech. Syst. Signal Process. **98**, 902–918 (2018)
8. Kocejko, T., Ruminski, J., Przystup, P., Polinski, A., Wtorek, J.: The role of EMG module in hybrid interface of prosthetic arm. In: 2017 10th International Conference on Human System Interactions (HSI), pp. 36–40 (2017)
9. Mahanth, G.N., Sachin, B.C., Kumar, J.S., Vinay, S.N., Sompur, V.P.: Design of prosthetic finger replacements using surface EMG signal acquisition. In: 2014 Texas Instruments India Educators' Conference (TIIEC), pp. 100–104 (2014)
10. Sharmila, K., Sarath, T.V., Ramachandran, K.I.: EMG controlled low cost prosthetic arm. In: 2016 IEEE Distributed Computing, VLSI, Electrical Circuits and Robotics (DISCOVER), pp. 169–172 (2016)
11. Kawano, T., Koganezawa, K.: A method of discriminating fingers and wrist action from surface EMG signals for controlling robotic or prosthetic forearm hand. In: 2016 IEEE International Conference on Advanced Intelligent Mechatronics (AIM), pp. 13–18 (2016)
12. Mills, K.R.: The basics of electromyography. J. Neurol. Neurosurg. Psychiatry **76**(Suppl. II), ii32–ii35 (2005)
13. Kumar, S., Mital, A. (eds.): Electromyography In Ergonomics. CRC Press, London (1996)
14. Vavrinsky, E., et al.: Electrode configuration for EMG measurements. In: The 8th International Conference on Advanced Semiconductor Devices and Microsystems, pp. 203–206 (2010)
15. Di, R.: Needle electromyography: basic concepts and patterns of abnormalities. Neurol. Clin. J. **30**(2), 429–456 (2012)
16. Loeb, G., Ghez, C.: The motor unit and the muscle action. In: Principles of Neural Science, p. 675 (2000)
17. Beneteau, A., Di Caterina, G., Petropoulakis, L., Soraghan, J.J.: Low-cost wireless surface EMG sensor using the MSP430 microcontroller. In: 2014 6th European Embedded Design in Education and Research Conference (EDERC), pp. 264–268 (2014)
18. Nishihara, K., Isho, T.: Location of electrodes in surface EMG. In: Schwartz, M. (ed.) EMG Methods for Evaluating Muscle and Nerve Function. IntechOpen. https://www.intechopen.com/books/emg-methods-for-evaluating-muscle-and-nerve-function/location-of-electrodes-in-surface-emg

19. Fauzani, N.J., et al.: Two electrodes system: Performance on ECG FECG and EMG detection. In: 2013 IEEE Student Conference on Research and Developement, pp. 506–510 (2013)
20. Nazmi, N., et al.: A review of classification techniques of EMG signals during isotonic and isometric contractions. Sens. (Basel) 16(8), 1304. http://doi.org/10.3390/s16081304E
21. Gordon, D., Robertson, E.: Electromyography: Recording. http://health.uottawa.ca/biomech/courses/apa4311/emg-p1.pps. Accessed 01 Sept 2018

Framework for Next Generation of Digital Healthcare Systems

Jovan Karamachoski[✉] and Liljana Gavrilovska

FEIT, University Ss. Cyril and Methodius in Skopje,
Skopje, Republic of Macedonia
jovankaramac@yahoo.com, liljana@feit.ukim.edu.mk

Abstract. The healthcare system is one of the most important segments of the modern society. The support of cost effective and reliable digital solutions, can enhance the health of the patients and improve the healthcare system as a whole. The evolution of the eHealth systems shows immense benefits from implementation of modern technologies (e.g. smartphones, 3G and 4G networks, IoT sensor networks) improving quality of life and increasing comfort. One of the last technological breakthrough, the Blockchain technology, is promising even better improvements in eHealth systems by enhancing the privacy and security protection, easing the usability of the IoT devices, predicting potential hazardous illnesses and leveraging the comfort of living. This paper proposes a generic framework for a novel eHealth system based on the Blockchain technology that complements the development of the future 5G services.

Keywords: eHealth · Blockchain · Framework for healthcare systems

1 Introduction

The healthcare system, together with the healthcare regulations can create significant impact on the comfort of the patients' life. It can also affect the health condition of the community as a whole. Modern healthcare system relays on digital technologies for gathering and storing patients' data, remotely diagnosing illnesses and monitoring vital signs. The digital technologies used to deliver medical care or monitor patients' health condition are known as telemedicine, telehealth or eHealth. The terms are used interchangeably. However, the last one points to the most modern Internet-based solutions. All of them exchange medical data through different telecommunication systems.

The development of the electronic healthcare systems for delivering medical care on a distance can be divided into pre-Internet and Internet-based electronic healthcare systems. The pre-Internet electronic healthcare systems are also referred as telemedicine systems. They focus on enabling the medical care on a remote sites, and/or on digitalization of the medical records.

The development of the Internet-based healthcare systems, known as eHealth systems, also passed through several generations. Each generation introduces a new subsystem or a feature, (e.g. cloud-based solutions, integration of 4G services, IoT devices, Blockchain, integration of 5G services). There are three existing Internet-based generations of eHealth systems developed until today.

© ICST Institute for Computer Sciences, Social Informatics and Telecommunications Engineering 2019
Published by Springer Nature Switzerland AG 2019. All Rights Reserved
V. Poulkov (Ed.): FABULOUS 2019, LNICST 283, pp. 12–24, 2019.
https://doi.org/10.1007/978-3-030-23976-3_2

In this paper we propose a novel generic framework for the next generation of eHealth systems, the fourth generation, with strong accent to the privacy, security, persistence and usability of data. It implements the most modern technologies, like Blockchain and Machine Learning, and provides enhanced comfort and users' mobility.

The paper is organized as follows. Section 2 presents the related work and Sect. 3 gives our definition of eHealth system generations and their characteristics. In Sect. 4 we are proposing the generic layered approach for building the next (fourth) generation of eHealth systems. Section 5 gives the direction for the future work and Sect. 6 concludes the paper.

2 Related Work

There are already some ongoing activities, both in academia and in companies, focusing on implementation of the Blockchain technology integrated with the IoT networks, for design of enhanced healthcare systems [1]. They try to deliver competitive solutions, despite the limitations of the current Blockchain technology. The main hook for this fusion is the privacy-by-design provided by the Blockchain technology. It might solve the most important privacy issues for the healthcare systems.

The Blockchain technology provides the access management capabilities for the patients. The authors in [2–5] propose access management protocols for medical data records, based on the Blockchain technology. The self-executable Smart contracts deployed on the Blockchain, can check credentials of the users, compare the authorization roles and privileges, change the scope of control based on patients' needs and execute any restrictive code to change a user privileges. The Blockchain ledger can record all input parameters, roles and privileges and can act as an arbiter for access management. Particular solutions for access management based on Blockchain technology can be adapted from other scenarios, such as IoT network access control mechanisms, presented in [6–8]. These solutions can provide enhanced automation in machine-to-machine type communication scenarios.

Another important aspect of the healthcare system design is the storage of medical data. As described in [1], the scalability issue regarding the storage capacity is immense in a large-scale scenarios. Current baseline Blockchains have poor storage capacity and are inappropriate for the healthcare system solutions. The academia offers several solutions, targeting the storage capacity. The authors in [9] propose general guide for architecture design and storage location. They stress the importance of the extensively distributed architecture for Blockchain based scenarios, in order to benefit from the decentralization of the procedures. Particular solutions can be found in [10–12]. The papers propose scalable data storage solutions, where the Blockchain acts as a ledger of data addresses, pointing out the location of the particular data.

The implementation of the Smart contracts in automatic or semi-automatic manner, will improve the machine-to-machine communications. Moreover, the implementation of the Artificial Intelligence (AI) agents capable to execute Machine Learning algorithms in the Blockchain networks can conduct predictive analysis. In practical healthcare systems these AI agents (Doctor-bots) can determine personalized diagnoses or predict illnesses or epidemics. The importance of the Internet of Robotic Things for the Ambient Assisted Living (AAL) in correlation with future Blockchain-based solutions can be found in [13]. The AAL is extremely important for the patients with dementia or Alzheimer's disease. Also the AAL solutions are tightly linked with smart home solutions. This enables many Blockchain-based smart home and smart city solutions to be implemented in the future eHealth systems [14–16].

3   Healthcare System Generations

The healthcare practice on a distance is present for centuries, but the development of the telemedicine, date back in the second half of the 20th century, after the initial development of the telemedicine system for health condition monitoring of the astro-nauts. Recent history of the telemedicine developments can be found in [17]. The first telemedicine projects were television and telephone based two-way communication systems that enabled consultation practices. Mainly bulky, pricey and very complex, these projects were not successful telemedicine solutions. After the initial phase, by the end of 20th century, the telemedicine systems started to be based on computers, servers and local network, basically used to digitalize the patients' data. Generally, these are the systems collocated in hospitals, built with intention to enhance the internal work-flow and inter-sector communication. They are mainly offline (Internet-less) systems. The main concern are the security of the communication and privacy of the patients' data. The lack of Internet access in these types of electronic healthcare systems decreases the privacy related concerns mainly because the systems are not spread among large number of institutions and the access to the data is physically protected. Also, the potential awareness of the patients' privacy was low.

At the end of the 20th century, with the development and deployment of the Internet, new type of telemedicine systems emerged [18], today known as eHealth systems. The eHealth systems are online Internet-based systems, where the entities from different healthcare institutions are connected and are able to share information, collaborate in real-time or access patients' information on a distance. The deployment of the Internet and the cost-effectiveness of the modern systems, spread the medical point-of-presence in every hospital, every office and even in each mobile device. The omnipresence of the eHealth systems and services, rises the awareness for privacy issues requiring further enhancements. There are several generations (phases) in development of the eHealth systems.

3.1   First Generation eHealth Systems

The first generation of eHealth systems is built from independent and isolated corporate networks, with data centers collocated in the hospitals, as presented in Fig. 1. These systems are dimensioned to store sufficient amount of medical records, with easily extensible capacity due to server modularity. They are following general client-server architecture focusing on the enhanced network protection. The supplied Internet access exposes the systems to potential attacks and rises privacy concerns. The maintenance of the corporate network is huge burden for the hospitals, since it requires skilled engineers and expensive equipment to maintain reliable network with strong security and privacy. The privacy management is guaranteed by the hospitals and patients don't have any control over their personal data or collected health related data.

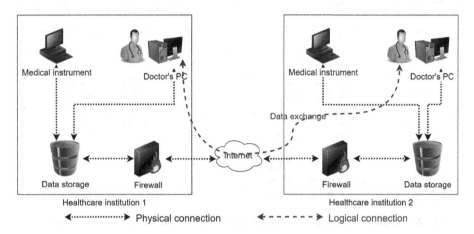

Fig. 1. Simplified communication procedure in first generation of eHealth systems

3.2 Second Generation eHealth Systems

The second generation of eHealth systems is characterized by introduction of cloud-based and IoT services (see Fig. 2). With the development of the cloud-based services, the eHealth systems were transformed from the hospital-centric to cloud-centric. The centralization of the system solutions, rises concerns for the privacy and security of the patients' data. This may decrease the expenditures of the hospitals for maintenance of the corporate network. However, the single point of access for this type of systems is potential bottleneck and makes it prone to attacks. Consequently it requires higher level of security, authentication and authorization measures are taken into account. Beside the concerns there are benefits from this type of systems. Mainly the cost effectiveness is the biggest benefit, but also the Government institutions can have greater insight in the patients' health status and the possibility to analyze the financial aspect of the healthcare system.

The introduction of the IoT nodes in the second generation of eHealth systems, provide the patients and the healthcare practitioners with better tool for monitoring of the patients' health status with higher precision and better comfort [19, 20]. The placement of the wireless health monitoring sensors on the patients' body for constant monitoring, supplies the healthcare practitioners with real-time data of the patients' health condition. The 3G data network access offers enhanced mobility in real-time monitoring protocols for any measured patient's parameter independently of the patients' location. The widespread high speed Internet access also offers more advanced services, such as remote surgery services on-the-go, home assistance for elder people, remote diagnostics, etc.

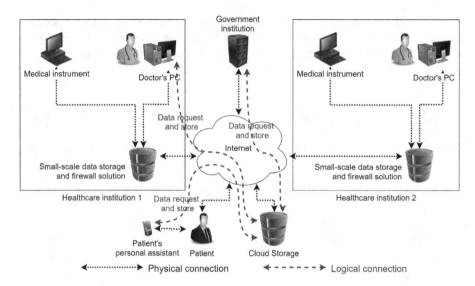

Fig. 2. Simplified communication procedure in second generation of eHealth systems

3.3 Third Generation eHealth Systems

The third generation of eHealth systems try to fix the growing privacy concerns, by introduction of the Blockchain technology in the system (see Fig. 3). The new environment witness continuous growth in number of mobile devices and application. With widespread high-speed Internet access, through Wi-Fi and 4G networks, the eHealth services can be delivered on a mobile device. These types of eHealth services are known as mHealth services. With the introduction of the Blockchain technology the patients can have full control of the auditability of the data. The patients can give temporal or permanent access to the healthcare practitioner by authorization through mobile application connected to the Blockchain. Other entities and governmental institutions can access the data if they are granted. The Blockchain acts as a ledger or third-party node to manage the access rights, as a complementary technology to the centralized cloud-based architecture. Several solutions are currently elaborated in [4, 21–23]. The main advantage of this generation of eHealth system over the previous ones is the user-centric approach for privacy management over the personal health related data. The implementation of the Blockchain technology solves the end-point privacy, but still have problem with privacy protection in the cloud. Moreover, there is a possibility of security attacks of stealing credentials or data from the end-user devices.

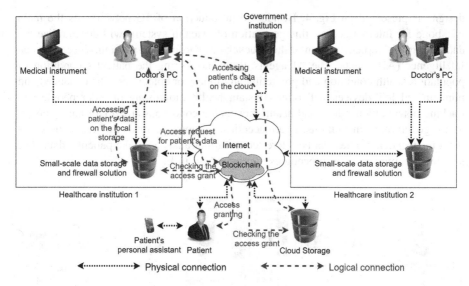

Fig. 3. Simplified communication procedure in third generation of eHealth systems

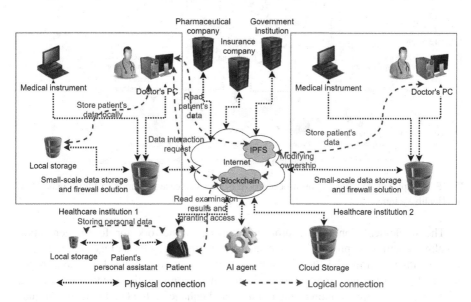

Fig. 4. Simplified communication procedures for basic use case scenario in fourth generation of eHealth systems

3.4 Fourth Generation eHealth Systems

The goal in this paper is to propose a generic framework for the next generation of eHealth systems. The fourth generation will have further improvements regarding the privacy, storage management, service availability, broader range of monitored health-related parameters, new business models, predictive analysis and even new architecture design, as presented on Fig. 4. Beside the introduction of 5G networks as the main backbone for Internet access, this generation of eHealth systems will decentralize the data storage by implementation of the Blockchain sharding and will introduce Artificial Intelligence (AI) agents. The AI agents allow monitoring the patient's condition or population health condition and predicting any illness or epidemics. The enhanced and miniaturized IoT devices will offer constant health monitoring of elder people and tracking potential hazardous and health threatening conditions at work or/and at home. Many government institutions, pharmaceutical companies, insurance companies and other independent bodies can be interested in further analysis of the patients' data. The simplified communication procedures, are presented in Fig. 5.

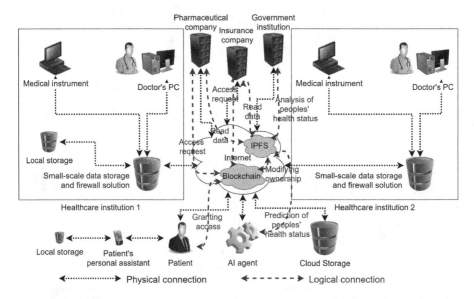

Fig. 5. Simplified communication procedures for other use case scenarios in fourth generation of eHealth systems

The implementation of the proposed generic framework for fourth generation eHealth system will provide advancement over the previous storage solutions, by implementing multimodal storage solution, without essential need of cloud-based databases. Also the new framework will offer more commodities for the patients and elder people by simplification of the usability and enhancing the Quality of Experience (QoE). The most important outcome will be the enhanced general population health. Contrary, the main disadvantage is the high complexity of the system for initial deployment due to small acceptance rate and the lack of understanding of the Blockchain technologies. After the initial deployment the system will be self-orchestrated due to deployed Smart contracts. The Smart contracts also provide the government's law framework to be implemented by a delegated entity.

4 Fourth Generation's Specifics

The generic framework for the future eHealth systems offers many advantages but also faces many problems towards the implementation phase. The specifics of the fourth generations of eHealth systems reflect on the overall layered eHealth system architecture, its entities and functionalities.

Layered Architecture. The proposed Layered structure of the next generation of eHealth systems is presented in Fig. 6. Based on the most recent technologies, the new system will offer enhanced privacy, data security, data persistence, user-centric data access management, predictive health analysis, new business models, etc.

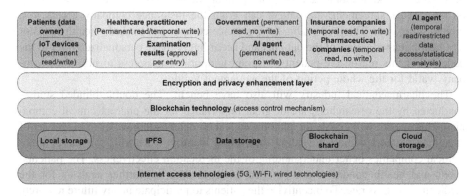

Fig. 6. Layered structure of the next generation eHealth system

The most important part of the architecture is the patient, or the data owner in the system. The Wallet address or more precisely the Blockchain public address presents the identity of the patient in this electronic system. The patient will have full control of its personal health data by use of mobile application. A Smart contracts, deployed on the Blockchain, will conduct the access restrictions set by the patients. The patient will be able to grant or revoke access rights on-the-go. By default, every data collected for the patient will be secured. Depending on the scenario, the patient can open selected data set and publically share it with relevant entities. Taking into account that any personal IoT device connected to the patient will collect large amount of data, it is convenient to give permanent data read and write permission to any IoT device attached on the patient body. The permission can be retracted in any time after the device is removed or there is no need for further data collection.

The healthcare practitioner will be another entity in the framework with main role to conduct medical protocols for the patient. The patient can choose to grant permanent or temporal data access to the doctor. The most convenient approach is the patient to choose a family doctor and grant him permanent data access, but he can also grant temporal access to any other doctor/specialist/emergency room doctor. In order to deter the doctor from entering data without patient's awareness, every entry of data by the doctor should be acknowledged by the patient.

New Use Cases and Business Models. The increased privacy will offer several new use cases and potential business cases. As a main advantage is the ability of the system to give the Governmental institutions a tool for monitoring of the health status of the nation. The openness of the data to the Government can increase the effectiveness of the healthcare system as a whole. By attaching AI agents to the eHealth system, the Governmental institutions can do predictive analysis for the expenditures of the healthcare system. Also, the AI agent can do predictive analysis per patient or per group of people, can suggest further treatment and predict illness or epidemics. The patient will give permanent data access to the Governmental institutions for full or restricted set of data, depending on the legislation.

The private sector, mainly the insurance companies, will be able to introduce new business cases like personalized insurance plan or adaptive insurance plans. Depending on the mutual agreement, the patient can grant the insurance company access to a limited set of data. This will enable the insurance company to track the health status or past health related issues of the patients and accordingly make personalized offer to the patient. For this reason the patient can grant temporal data access to insurance company, valid for the whole period of the agreement validity.

The pharmaceutical industry will also have benefit. The double-blinded studies conducted by the researchers, are of great importance for the pharmaceutical companies. This system will enable the pharmaceutical companies to have even bigger set of examined patients without revealing the patient identity. This will give the pharmaceutical companies better understanding of the medication effectiveness. The patients' habits and health condition can be used as input data for further analysis for the medication success rate. To incentivize the patients to participate in any future research, the pharmaceutical industry can pay for the data shared by the patients. This way the patients can monetize the collected data.

Introduced Intelligence - Smart Solutions. An independent public AI agents implemented in a form of Smart contract, can leverage the capabilities of the healthcare system. The AI agent will enable the system to predict possible pandemics or epidemics, but also can track patient's health and patient's habits and predict personalized health conditions. These AI agents can analyze the health condition of patients, without exposing the private data. The data set exposed to the AI agent can be negotiated or selected by the user. The access can be granted temporarily to a verified public AI agents. To incentivize the patient to share the personal data, the AI agent will pay the patient for the shared data. In order to be self-sustainable, an AI agent can sell the output data to independent researchers, can mint digital currency and can buy patients' data.

Enhanced Security. The entities involved in the communication will exchange data through the encryption and privacy enhancement layer. The anonymization introduced by the Blockchain is not sufficient to protect the patients' identity. This layer considers implementation of strong encryption in any information transaction and enhanced privacy protection tools, like TOR [24].

New Blockchain Types. The coordination of the procedures and execution of Smart contracts will be orchestrated by the Blockchain layer. Further analysis is required to determine which type of Blockchain will suite the eHealth system the most. The eHealth system based on a permissionless Blockchain will build trust from the openness of the code and procedures in the system. Also this will encourage the community to develop the whole system even further by fixing the issues, building applications and support the system. Contrary to the permissionless Blockchain, the permissioned Blockchain is relatively limiting solution that can still rise concerns regarding the privacy of the system. The perfect solution will be a combination of the advantages of both types of Blockchains. Generally speaking, the interfacing between the two distinct types of Blockchains will be great starting position.

Scalability and Storage Solutions. For future-proof next generation healthcare digital system, we are looking forward for a Blockchain solution that will solve the major scalability issue related to the data storage capacity of the whole system. As potential data storage solutions for the eHealth system we are proposing the use of local storage, IPFS (Inter-Planetary File System), Blockchain sharding and Cloud data storage.

Due to heavy data load of images and videos in the healthcare systems, but also the huge amount of IoT devices that are collecting patients' data, an offload from the Blockchain must take place. The local storage will be used by the patients and healthcare practitioners, as a fast access data storage. The data storage limitations of IoT device will be solved by periodical data offload to a dedicated local storage of the patient. The current version of IPFS offers slow but reliable data access, therefore the IPFS will be used to obtain redundancy of the data. The local storage and IPFS storage is not sufficient to withhold the traffic that is transiting through the eHealth system. Because of that, Blockchain sharding will split the data streams and offload the main Blockchain from the intensive data exchange. Further, the eHealth system will have optional cloud storage used as a cold storage for the patient data or will be used for compatibility reasons with the current system designs.

New Internet Access. The bottom of the layered structure is referring to the 5G, Wi-Fi and other wired broadband technologies as a main network solutions to provide Internet access to the users. The current deployment of 5G network will offer high speed mobile Internet access for the patient and more significant is that this technology will enable the healthcare practitioners to have continuous real-time monitoring of the patient parameters, by the deployed IoT devices. The Wi-Fi networks and other wired broadband network technologies will enable not only the healthcare practitioners but also the family members with tool for constant monitoring and assisted living for elder people.

5 Future Work

The development of Blockchain pave the path for future communication solutions with high level of security and privacy for the end users. Beside the existing healthcare solutions that are complemented with Blockchain technology to provide better privacy protection, this paper offers framework for broader use of Blockchain as a main technology for orchestration the future eHealth systems. The main future task would be the definition of the protocols for interaction between the entities in the eHealth system (patients, healthcare practitioners, governmental institutions, insurance companies, pharmaceutical companies and AI agents).

The most promising are the existing technologies, such as Ethereum (as permissionless technology) and Hyperledger (as permissioned technology). The performances analysis of the permissionless and the permissioned technologies, concerning the eHealth systems, will determine the platform for building the final solution. It must consider the existing IoT related Blockchain solutions as a starting point in definition of the interaction between the autonomous IoT devices in the eHealth system.

Future system solutions may focus on fragmented implementation of the proposed layered architecture. The first step will be to upgrade our current general purpose Smart contract on Ethereum platform and build an adapted Smart contract for an eHealth testbed. The current general purpose Smart contract offers write access management over the data, and it needs to be upgraded by procedures for read access management by implementation of encryption layer and plug-and-play functionalities for the IoT devices.

As a long-term imperative will be the implementation of the proposed forth generation eHealth system solution on a new Blockchain technology that will implement multi-dimensionality of the future Blockchains that natively solves the scalability issues, and provides high level of end-to-end security and privacy protection. The multi-dimensionality can be provided by sharding, clustering or offloading the data from the main Blockchain.

6 Conclusion

This paper proposes generic framework for the novel generation of eHealth systems based on the Blockchain technology. The reliability of the Blockchain technology is proven by the large amount of products that are already present on the market. The inherent liveness of the collected data and the persistence of the ledger-like Blockchain technology, makes it suitable for the eHealth systems. Foremost, the integration of the Blockchain technology in the eHealth systems will leverage the privacy of the patients while the implementation of the advanced cryptographic mechanisms will secure the overall communication and the data storage. We are foreseeing huge improvement in the usability and data management in the future eHealth systems. This will allow the immense health improvement of the population. The future work will be toward the definition of the system level functionalities and protocols, and building the future-proof eHealth system bottom up.

References

1. Karamachoski, J., Gavrilovska, L., Sefidanoski, A.: The fusion between Blockchain and IoT for healthcare systems. In: ETAI Conference, pp. 1–6 (2018)
2. Linn, L., Koo, M.: Blockchain for health data and its potential use in health IT and health care related research. In: ONC/NIST Use of Blockchain for Healthcare and Research Workshop, Gaithersburg, Maryland: USA. ONC/NIST (2016)

3. Schwerin, S., et al.: Medixain: Robust Blockchain Optimization Enabling Individual Medical Wallet Architecture (2017)
4. Ekblaw, A.C.: MedRec: blockchain for medical data access, permission management and trend analysis (2017)
5. Jesus, E.F., Chicarino, V.R., de Albuquerque, C.V., Rocha, A.A. de A.: A survey of how to use blockchain to secure internet of Things and the stalker attack. Secur. Commun. Netw. **2018** (2018). https://doi.org/10.1155/2018/9675050
6. Ouaddah, A., Abou Elkalam, A., Ait Ouahman, A.: FairAccess: a new Blockchain-based access control framework for the Internet of Things. Secur. Commun. Netw. **9**(18), 5943–5964 (2016). https://doi.org/10.1002/sec.1748
7. Bagchi, R.: Using blockchain technology and smart contracts for access management in IoT devices. Thesis, University of Helsinki (2017)
8. Dukkipati, C., Zhang, Y., Cheng, L.C.: Decentralized, blockchain based access control framework for the heterogeneous Internet of Things. In: Proceedings of the Third ACM Workshop on Attribute-Based Access Control, pp. 61–69 (2018). https://doi.org/10.1145/3180457.3180458
9. Liao, C.-F., Bao, S.-W., Cheng, C.-J., Chen, K.: On design issues and architectural styles for blockchain-driven IoT services. In: 2017 IEEE International Conference on Consumer Electronics-Taiwan (ICCE-TW), pp. 351–352 (2017). https://doi.org/10.1109/icce-china.2017.7991140
10. McConaghy, T., et al.: BigchainDB: a scalable blockchain database. White paper, BigChainDB (2016)
11. Yu, X.L., Xu, X., Liu, B.: EthDrive: a peer-to-peer data storage with provenance. CAiSE-Forum-DC, Germany (2017)
12. Shafagh, H., Burkhalter, L., Hithnawi, A., Duquennoy, S.: Towards blockchain-based auditable storage and sharing of IoT data. In: Proceedings of the 2017 on Cloud Computing Security Workshop, pp. 45–50 (2017). https://doi.org/10.1145/3140649.3140656
13. Vermesan, O., et al.: Internet of robotic things: converging sensing/actuating, hypoconnectivity, artificial intelligence and IoT Platforms (2017)
14. Dorri, A., Kanhere, S.S., Jurdak, R.: Towards an optimized blockchain for IoT. In: Proceedings of the Second International Conference on Internet-of-Things Design and Implementation, pp. 173–178 (2017). https://doi.org/10.1145/3054977.3055003
15. Sharma, P.K., Park, J.H.: Blockchain based hybrid network architecture for the smart city. Future Gener. Comput. Sys. **86**, 650–655 (2018). https://doi.org/10.1016/j.future.2018.04.060
16. Dustdar, S., Nastic, S., Scekic, O.: A novel vision of cyber-human smart city. In: 2016 Fourth IEEE Workshop on Hot Topics in Web Systems and Technologies (HotWeb), pp. 42–47 (2016). https://doi.org/10.1109/hotweb.2016.16
17. Zundel, K.M.: Telemedicine: history, applications, and impact on librarianship. Bull. Med. Libr. Assoc. **84**, 71 (1996)
18. Shirzadfar, H., Lotfi, F.: The evolution and transformation of telemedicine. Int. J. Biosens. Bioelectron. **3**(4), 303–306 (2017). https://doi.org/10.15406/ijbsbe.2017.03.00070
19. Chatterjee, P., Armentano, R.L.: Internet of Things for a smart and ubiquitous ehealth system. In: 2015 International Conference on Computational Intelligence and Communication Networks (CICN), pp. 903–907 (2015). https://doi.org/10.1109/cicn.2015.178
20. Ida, I.B., Jemai, A., Loukil, A.: A survey on security of IoT in the context of eHealth and clouds. In: 2016 11th International International Design and Test Symposium (IDT), pp. 25–30 (2016). https://doi.org/10.1109/idt.2016.7843009
21. Medicalchain Whitepaper 2.1. https://medicalchain.com/Medicalchain-Whitepaper-EN.pdf

22. Da Conceição, A.F., da Silva, F.S.C., Rocha, V., Locoro, A., Barguil, J.M.: Eletronic Health records using blockchain technology. arXiv preprint, arXiv:1804.10078 (2018)
23. McFarlane, C., Beer, M., Brown, J., Prendergast, N.: Patientory: A Healthcare Peer-to-Peer EMR Storage Network v1 (2017)
24. Syverson, P., Dingledine, R., Mathewson, N.: Tor: the second generation onion router. Usenix Security (2004)

ECG-Based Human Emotion Recognition Across Multiple Subjects

Desislava Nikolova[1], Petia Mihaylova[1], Agata Manolova[1(✉)] ⓘD,
and Petia Georgieva[2] ⓘD

[1] Technical University of Sofia, Sofia, Bulgaria
desislava.v.nikolova@gmail.com, mihaylova_p@yahoo.com,
amanolova@tu-sofia.bg
[2] DETI/IEETA, University of Aveiro, Aveiro, Portugal
petia@ua.pt

Abstract. Electrocardiogram (ECG) based affective computing is a new research field that aims to find correlates between human emotions and the registered ECG signals. Typically, emotion recognition systems are personalized, i.e. the discrimination models are subject-dependent. Building subject-independent models is a harder problem due to the high ECG variability between individuals. In this paper, we study the potential of two machine learning methods (Logistic Regression and Artificial Neural Network) to discriminate human emotional states across multiple subjects. The users were exposed to movies with different emotional content (neutral, fear, disgust) and their ECG activity was registered. Based on extracted features from the ECG recordings, the three emotional states were partially discriminated.

Keywords: ECG · Affective computing ·
Human emotion recognition · Machine learning ·
Artificial Neural Networks · Logistic Regression

1 Introduction

Emotions are part of any natural communication involving humans. Given the strong interface between affect and cognition on the one hand, and given the increasing versatility of computer agents on the other hand, the attempt to enable our computer tools to acknowledge affective phenomena rather than to remain blind to them appears desirable. They can be expressed through several channels and modalities. Facial expressions, gestures, postures, speech and intonation of voice are certainly those that are the most obvious. However, emotional information can also be found in many other modalities. For instance, it has been shown that there are different physiological states of the body corresponding to different emotions. Examples of such states are paralysis of muscles in case of fear, increase of heart rate for aroused emotions. They are generally

V. Poulkov (Ed.): FABULOUS 2019, LNICST 283, pp. 25–36, 2019.
https://doi.org/10.1007/978-3-030-23976-3_3

less perceivable by people unless an observer is close enough to the person that feels the emotion. However, these reactions could be easily recorded using specific sensors. Some of those physiological changes can also be directly perceived such as a sharp increase in blood pressure that would lead to a blush of the cheeks.

Currently different human computer interface (HCI) systems use physiological signals for classifying the human emotional state such as: electroencephalogram (EEG), electrocardiogram (ECG), electromyogram (EMG), electrooculogram (EoG), skin conductive resistance (SCR), skin temperature (ST), and respiration rate (RR). Among these, ECG and EMG are the most popular choices for developing portable, non-intrusive, reliable, and computationally efficient emotion recognition systems [1]. One of the advantages of recognizing emotions and feelings using ECG signal is that this is unconscious response, basic biological necessity of the human body, and therefore it is very difficult to falsify or conceal. The use for ECG in HCI for human emotion recognition would revolutionize applications in medicine, entertainment, educ0ation, safety, etc. Nevertheless there are many theoretical and practical challenges with regard to ECG-based emotion recognition methodology. For example the heart rate can increase when the person is feeling fear or excitement or arousal. Another challenge presented in this paper is how correct is the choice between subject-dependent or subject-independent classification procedure in the case of ECG emotion recognition.

The goal of this research work is to investigate the usability of the physiological ECG signal in affective computing. The rest of this paper is organized as follows. Section 2 describes introduces the recent advances in research on emotion recognition based on ECG signals. Section 3 provides a detailed overview of the proposed methodology. Section 4 presents the experimental results based on two methods: Logistic regression and Artificial Neural Networks. The last section discusses some of the challenges and opportunities in this field and identifies potential future directions.

The paper is organized as follow: In Sect. 2 the most common feature extraction methods used in ECG signal processing for emotions recognition are reviewed. In Sect. 3 is described the proposed research methodology. In Sect. 4 are presented the experimental results and finally in Sect. 5 the conclusions are drawn.

2   Related Work

The ECG signal processing to extract relevant features can be performed either in time or frequency domain. However, the combination of features from both time and frequency domains provides often better insight of the underlying characteristics of the ECG signal.

In [2–4] different binary classifiers are compared to recognize Joy and Sadness emotional states based on the frequency domain features Continuously Wavelet Transform (CWT) and Discrete Wavelet Transform (DWT).

In [5] Local Pattern Description (LPD) methods combined with k-Nearest Neighbour (kNN) classifier are applied to distinguish between three emotional states (Joy, Anger and Sadness).

The authors of [6] aim to assess five human emotions (happiness, disgust, fear, sadness, and neutral) using Hearth Rate Variability (HRV) features derived from the ECG. The emotions were induced via video clips on 20 healthy (23 years old) students. The ECG signals were acquired using 3 electrodes and were preprocessed using a 3rd order Butterworth filter to remove the noise and

Table 1. Overview of methods of ECG-based emotions recognition

Features	Feature selection method	Classifier
Continuously Wavelet	Binary Particle Swarm Transform Optimization	k-Nearest Neighbor (kNN)
	Hybrid Particle Swarm Optimization	
	Genetic Algorithms	Fisher classifier
Discrete Wavelet Transform (DWT)	Tabu Search Algorithm (TS)	kNN
		Linear Discriminant Analysis (LDA)
		Fisher classifier
Local Pattern Description	Local Binary Pattern	kNN
	Local Ternary Pattern	
Hurst	Rescaled Range Statistics	Bayesian Classifier
	Finite Variance Scaling	Regression Trees
	Higher Order Statistics	kNN
		Fuzzy kNN
Fast Fourier Transform (FFT)	Tabu search (TS)	Fisher Classifier
Statistical features		Adaptive Neuro-Fuzzy Inference System
		Support Vector Machine
Raw signal		Deep Learning (Convolutional & Recurrent Neural Networks)
Discrete Cosine Transform	Principal Component Analysis (PCA)	Probabilistic Neural Network
	LDA	
	Kernel PCA	

baseline wander. DWT was used to extract statistical features from the HRV signals. The kNN and Linear Discriminant Analysis (LDA) were applied to map the statistical features into corresponding emotions.

The affective computing system proposed in [7] distinguishes six emotions (happiness, sadness, fear, disgust, surprise and neutral) induced by audio visual stimuli. The Hurst features are computed based on Re-scaled Range Statistics (RRS), Finite Variance Scaling (FVS) methods and Higher Order statistics (HOS). Bayesian Classier, Regression Tree, kNN and Fuzzy kNN are comparatively studied classifiers for this task. The results demonstrate that RRS and FVS methods have similar classification accuracy, however the FVS and HOS combined features performed better for the classification of the six emotional states.

Recently [8] proposed a deep neural network (DNN) to decode human emotions directly from row ECG data. The motivation behind the deep learning architectures is that they are able to automatically extract relevant features that may be overlooked by human experts.

Table 1 summarizes common feature extraction methods used for ECG-based emotions recognition.

Based on these recent papers, we can conclude that there is a big diversity in feature selection methods and none is predominating over the others with better recognition rates or accuracy.

3   Proposed Methodology

The process for ECG-based emotion recognition consists of four steps - data collection, feature extraction, feature normalization (if necessary) and classification.

3.1   Data Collection

Data used in this study are provided by the Psychology department of University of Aveiro. 25 volunteers (10 males, 15 females) took part in the experiments. Electrocardiogram signals were recorded while each participant watched three different movies in distinct days. The movie contents were carefully selected in order to induce the following emotions:

- movie with Neutral emotional content
- movie with Fear emotional content
- movie with Disgust emotional content

75 ECG time series were collected corresponding to 3 movies with different emotional content for each of the 25 participants. The ECG signal was divided in four segments corresponding to the baseline period (before the movie start), pre-video, mid-video and last-video periods reflecting the assumption that the emotional intensity varies over the movie duration. The average duration of each segment is as follows:

- Baseline (4 min of preparation before the movie start) - 240 000 samples;
- pre-Video (first 5 min of the movie) - 300 000 samples;
- mid-Video (next 15 min of the movie) - 900 000 samples;
- last-Video (last left x min of the movie) - varying number of samples.

The statistical analysis has shown that the ECG signal collected during the pre-video and the mid-video periods have the highest discrimination capacity, therefore the emotion recognition was focused into these signal segments.

3.2   Feature Extraction

Typical ECG signal is illustrated in Fig. 1. Quantitative information, such as amplitude and latency, regarding the P-wave, T-wave and QRS-complex wave, are the main ECG characteristics based on which most emotion recognition systems are built.

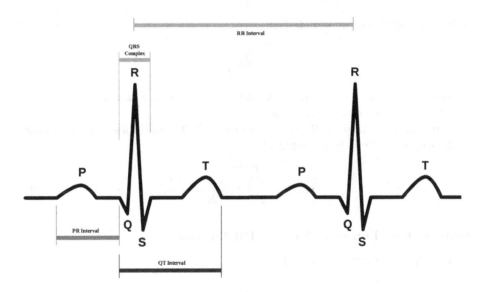

Fig. 1. ECG signal

In the present study the R peaks amplitude and the RR intervals (the number of samples between two R peaks) were extracted as primary quantities from the raw ECG signal. Based on them eight statistical features were computed, two of them related with the R peak amplitude, and six with the length of the RR intervals. The Length of the RR interval is the interval between successive R peaks. In Fig. 2 is illustrated the extraction of the R peaks from the complete ECG signal recorded during one movie. In Fig. 3 is presented a fragment of the same signal for a better visualization.

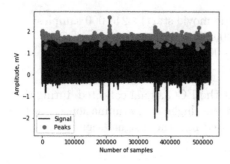 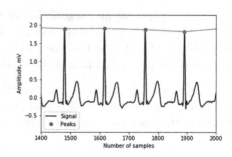

Fig. 2. ECG R peaks (Complete signal)   **Fig. 3.** ECG R peaks (Zoomed signal)

Features Based on R Peak Amplitude

The maximum amplitude of the R wave (measured in mV) is called "R peak amplitude", or just "R peak".

– *Average of R peak amplitude* $(\overline{A})$:

$$\overline{A} = \frac{\sum_{i=1}^{N} A_i}{N},\tag{1}$$

where A_i is the current R peak amplitude, N is the number of R peaks collected during one video segment.

– *Standard Deviation of R peak amplitude (StdA)* quantifies the amount of dispersion of the R peak amplitude:

$$StdA = \sqrt[2]{\frac{\sum_{i=1}^{N}(A_i - \overline{A})^2}{N}}.\tag{2}$$

Features Based on Length of the RR Intervals

– *Mean value of RR Intervals* $(\overline{I})$:

$$\overline{I} = \frac{\sum_{i=1}^{N} I_i}{N},\tag{3}$$

where I_i is the current length of the RR interval, N is the number of RR intervals collected during one video segment.

– *Beats per minute (BPM)*
Heart rate is the speed of the heartbeat measured by the number of contractions of the heart per minute. A normal resting heart rate for adults ranges from 60 to 100 beats a minute. The sum of the RR intervals along the axis divided by the number of intervals. Every minute contains 60 000 ms.

$$BPM = \frac{60000}{\overline{I}}.\tag{4}$$

- *Mean value of the RR Intervals absolute difference* $(\overline{I}_{abs})$:

$$\overline{I}_{abs} = \frac{\sum_{i=2}^{N} |I_i - I_{i-1}|}{N - 1}. \tag{5}$$

- *Square Root Mean Value of the RR intervals absolute difference* $(\overline{I}_{sqrt})$:
  The root mean square successive difference in heart period series is a time domain measure of heart period variability.

$$\overline{I}_{sqrt} = \frac{\sum_{i=2}^{N} \sqrt[2]{|I_i - I_{i-1}|}}{N - 1}. \tag{6}$$

- *Standard Deviation of RR intervals (StdR):*

$$StdR = \sqrt[2]{\frac{\sum_{i=1}^{N} (I_i - \overline{I})^2}{N}}. \tag{7}$$

- *Standard Deviation of the R intervals absolute difference (StdRdif):*

$$StdRdif = \sqrt[2]{\frac{\sum_{i=2}^{N} (I_i - I_{i-1})^2}{N - 1}}. \tag{8}$$

3.3 Normalization

Though the extracted features do not vary in significantly different ranges, we studied the classification performance both with normalized and not-normalized data sets. The following normalization was applied:

$$x_{norm} = \frac{x_{original} - mean(x_{vector})}{max(x_{vector}) - min(x_{vector})}. \tag{9}$$

The distribution of the eight normalized features with respect to the three classes (disgust, fear, neutral) and during the four video segments - baseline (4 min of preparation before the movie start), pre-video (first 5 min of the movie), mid-video (next 15 min of the movie), last-video (last 5 min of the movie) are illustrated in Fig. 4.

3.4 Classification

At the classification step, two classifiers - Logistic Regression (LR) and Artificial Neural Networks (ANN) - were compared. The results are discussed in the next section.

4 Experimental Results

The statistical analysis has shown that the pre-Video and mid-Video ECG temporal segments have the highest discrimination capacity, therefore the classifiers were provided with features extracted during these segments.

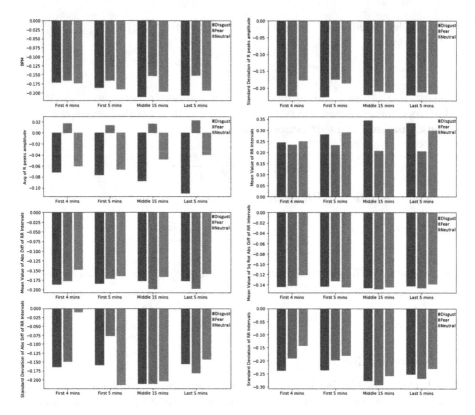

Fig. 4. Distribution of normalized features over classes (Disgust (in blue), Fear (in red), Neutral (in green)) and video segments (baseline, pre-, mid-, last-video) (Color figure online)

4.1 Logistic Regression

The performance of the Logistic Regression (LR) classifier in terms of accuracy on training and testing data was studied. LR behaves significantly better with non-normalized data, therefore only these results are shown on the next figures.

First, the convergence properties of the classifier were studied and the results are depicted in Figs. 5 and 6. For both time segments the accuracy converges after 40–50 iterations, however the testing accuracy with the pre-video ECG features is higher and closely follows the training accuracy.

Next, the optimal number of input features is assessed and the results are summarized in Figs. 7 and 8. The features are ordered based on their importance determined by the recursive feature elimination (RFE) method. The feature rank of importance is the the following: (0) Standard Deviation of R peaks amplitude, (1) Average of R peaks amplitude, (2) Beats per minute, (3) Standard Deviation of the absolute difference of RR intervals, (4) Standard Deviation of RR intervals, (5) Mean value of abs difference of RR Intervals, (6) Mean value of RR Intervals, (7) Mean Value of Square Root Abs difference of RR intervals. Note, that the

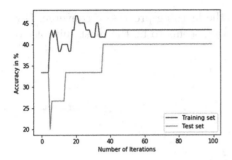

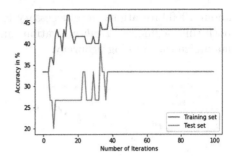

Fig. 5. LR performance vs. # of iterations for the pre-Video segment.

Fig. 6. LR performance vs.# of iterations for the mid-Video segment.

first five features (for the pre-video segment) and the first six features (for the mid-video segment) are sufficient to achieve the maximum test accuracy, which is the ultimate goal of the recognition model. Similarly to the previous study, the pre-video ECG features have better generalization properties (train and test performance are close enough).

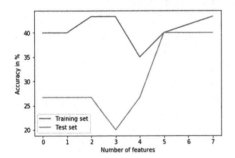

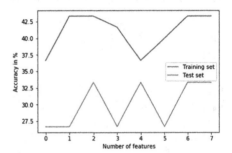

Fig. 7. LR performance vs. # of features for the pre-Video segment.

Fig. 8. LR performance vs. # of features for the mid-Video segment.

4.2 Artificial Neural Networks

Now the performance of the Artificial Neural Network (ANN) classifier in terms of accuracy on training and testing data was assessed. ANN architecture with only one hidden layer was considered as sufficient for this problem. In contrast to LR, ANN is more successful with normalized data, therefore only these results are shown on the next figures.

First, the convergence properties of the ANN classifier were studied for different choice of the activation functions (*ReLu, Sigmoid, Tanh*). As can be seen in Figs. 9 and 10, the ANN model largely outperforms the LR model (90 % training accuracy), however it is paid by a huge number of iterations (i.e. epochs), about 10000 iterations were necessary for the learning process to converge. For both time segments, *Tanh* activation function seems to be the most suitable to maximize the training accuracy.

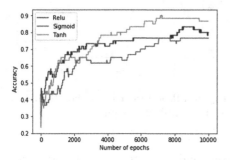

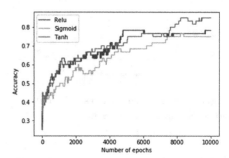

Fig. 9. ANN performance vs. # of itera-tions for the pre-Video segment

Fig. 10. ANN performance vs. # of iter-ations for the mid-Video segment

The search for the optimal number of nodes is summarized in Figs. 11 and 12. The final ANN architecture was fixed with 7 *Tanh* nodes.

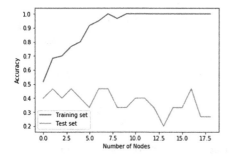

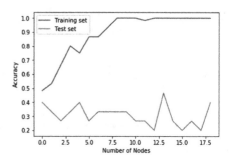

Fig. 11. ANN performance vs. # of nodes for the pre-Video segment

Fig. 12. ANN performance vs. # of nodes for the mid-Video segment

Note, the notorious overfitting ANN problem with the increasing number of hidden layer nodes. This problem was addressed by adding a regularization term in the cost function. The optimal value of the regularization parameter l2 (l2 = 3) was obtained after a grid search as shown in Figs. 13 and 14.

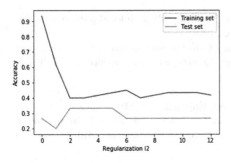

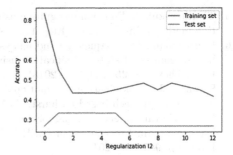

Fig. 13. ANN performance vs. regularization parameter l2 for the pre-Video segment

Fig. 14. ANN performance vs. regularization parameter l2 for the mid-Video segment

5   Conclusion

The goal of this paper was to built an ECG-based human emotion recognition system of three specific emotions (fear, disgust, neutral) across multiple subjects (25 volunteers, in particular). The system was trained with data from some of the participants (20 subjects) and then tested with data from the rest of the participants (5 subjects). This is a very challenging scenario, taking into account the significant ECG variability not only between subjects but also within different sessions with the same subject. Nevertheless, based on eight statistical features extracted from two major ECG characteristics - R peak amplitude and RR intervals we have obtained 40% testing accuracy with the LR classifier and 35% testing accuracy with the ANN classifier. These promising results suggest that the ECG modality may potentially be useful in affective computing if combined with other modalities such as physiological signals, facial expression, voice analysis.

Acknowledgements. This work was supported by European Regional Development Fund and the Operational Program "Science and Education for Smart Growth" under contract UNITe BG05M2OP001-1.001-0004-01 (2018–2023).

References

1. Konar, A., Chakraborty, A.: Emotion Recognition: A Pattern Analysis Approach. Wiley, Hoboken (2014)
2. Xu, Y.: A method of emotion recognition based on ECG signal. In: 2009 International Conference on Computational Intelligence and Natural Computing, pp. 202–205 (2009)
3. Min, H.: Analysis of affective ECG signals toward emotion I. Introduction ECG data collection III. ECG feature extraction. J. Electron. (China) 9–14 (2010)
4. Cai, J.: The research on emotion recognition from ECG signal. In: Proceedings of 2009 International Conference on Information Technology and Computer Science, ITCS 2009, pp. 497–500 (2009)

5. Tivatansakul, S.: Emotion recognition using ECG signals with local pattern description methods. Int. J. Affect. Eng. **15**, 51–61 (2016)
6. Murugappan, M.: Frequency band analysis of electrocardiogram (ECG) signals for human emotional state classification using discrete wavelet transform (DWT). J. Phys. Ther. Sci. **25**, 753–759 (2013)
7. Selvaraj, J.: Classification of emotional states from electrocardiogram signals: a non-linear approach based on hurst. BioMed. Eng. **12**, 44 (2013)
8. Keren, G.: End-to-end learning for dimensional emotion recognition from physiological signals. In: Proceedings of IEEE International Conference on Multimedia and Expo, pp. 985–990 (2017)

Wireless Smart Monitoring of Patient Health Data in a Hospital Setup

Alexander Bødker Andersen and Albena Mihovska[(✉)]

BTECH, Aarhus University, Herning, Denmark
201407929@post.au.dk, amihovska@btech.au.dk

Abstract. Monitoring of patient health data is an important part of the medical treatment of a patient. This paper studies how wireless smart technology for patient monitoring can be used and implemented in a hospital setup. The research focuses on the patients and the clinical perspective on how wireless monitoring of health data in the hospital can be utilized for support of mobility of the patients and for cost-efficiency of the patient pathway during hospitalization. Furthermore, is it investigated which strategic considerations should be made before developing and implementing the technology. It is proposed to design the wireless monitoring system in the hospital as a LPWAN network system with the DASH7 network protocol for data transmission as it would have the advantages of low cost, long range and low-energy consumption. The results indicate that patients will benefit from the implementation of a wireless monitoring system in terms of increased mobility at the hospital. Moreover, the clinical personnel could potentially achieve a decrease in workload and an improvement of the quality of treatments.

Keywords: Wireless monitoring · Healthcare · IoT

1 Introduction

The Danish healthcare system faces several challenges in the near future, such as rising expenses, an increasing amount of patients with long term and chronic diseases and an increasing workload for clinical personnel in the hospitals. Several national strategies and technologies are emerging as potential solutions to some of the challenges. The Danish healthcare system has a large focus on new emerging solutions such as the digitalization of data and workflows, smart IT systems and the Internet of Things. One of the areas that are rapidly advancing in new technologies is monitoring of patient health data, which is an important part of the diagnosis and treatment of patients in the hospital.

The project of modernizing the Danish hospitals is a part of the big visions and goals set by the Danish government, Danish Regions and the Local Government Denmark. The three institutions, in a collaboration, have made a national quality program [1–3]. The quality program is a framework developed for ensuring that the Danish healthcare system has a high level of quality in the treatment of patients and a balanced focus on activities, quality, results and costs. The national quality program has three overall goals:

© ICST Institute for Computer Sciences, Social Informatics and Telecommunications Engineering 2019
Published by Springer Nature Switzerland AG 2019. All Rights Reserved
V. Poulkov (Ed.): FABULOUS 2019, LNICST 283, pp. 37–48, 2019.
https://doi.org/10.1007/978-3-030-23976-3_4

- Improved state of health in the population;
- High patient experienced quality;
- Low costs per treated citizen.

An improved systematic use of health data with a focus on the management processes and the development of competencies is critical for an improved patient involvement [4]. Digitalization of data, procedures and workflows is part of the development and improvement of the Danish healthcare system. The digitalization of the healthcare system is underpinned by the implementation and use of information and communication technology (ICT). The use of ICT in the healthcare system is defined as e-health and has potential benefits for optimizing the processes and for improving the health data collection by, for example, tracking persons and objects in the hospital or smart monitoring of patients by wearable technology [5].

The monitoring is a continuous observation of a patient's vital signs, and it is necessary for a correct diagnosis. The traditional way of monitoring is manually using technology in form of devices that can monitor a specific vital sign of a patient. The device can, for example, be an electrocardiogram (ECG) for monitoring heart rhythms, a thermometer, for the measurement of a patient's temperature or inflatable pressure cuffs with a stethoscope to monitor the blood pressure. The monitored health data is assessed and analysed by clinical personnel such as medical doctors and nurses. The technology of patient monitoring has advanced in the recent years to include and obtain data from wearable sensors and devices, which can continuously and in real-time monitor and send the patient's data to the clinical personnel [6–8]. The remote monitoring has the advantage of providing vital health data related to a patient independently of a specific location [6].

Monitoring is a vital part of the treatment and diagnosis of patients and it is one of the areas that are in rapid development with new technologies emerging, such as the Internet of Things (IoT), smart technology and big data. The purpose of this research study was to identify key technical, ethical, and user aspects related to the successful acceptance and deployment of this technology on a wider scale.

This paper is further organized as follows. Section 2 describes the state-of-the-art in the area. Section 3 proposes the implementation model, which is based on DASH7 and LPWAN technologies. Section 4 analyzes the potential barriers for the implementation of the system. Section 5 concludes the paper.

2 Digitalization and Health Data

2.1 Digitalization in the Danish Healthcare System

Digitalization and digitization have become extensive and they are topics with a large focus in the Danish healthcare system. The Danish healthcare system is, in general, a front-runner in the use of digital health and the system is characterized by its large use of electronic communication and IT systems in hospitals. A new national strategy was launched by the Danish government, Danish Regions and Local Government Denmark in January 2018 and the strategy has the goals of high use of digital health data in a combination for both primary- and secondary user purposes. The primary user purpose is using digital data for direct care and treatment of patients and citizens, while the latter is using digital data for research, quality assurance and management in the healthcare sector [3].

Health data is systematically collected throughout the Danish healthcare system including in the hospitals and by the general practitioners. The large amount of data is an important part of the monitoring and treatment of patients and the data are saved in electronic health records, the national patient register and medication databases among others. The health data is transported across, both, the primary and the secondary sector as well across several departments and institutions such as hospitals, general practitioners, local authorities and home care services.

The Danish healthcare system has a large focus on the prevalence of IT standards for facilitating such data transportation through electronic communication [9]. The Danish healthcare system's high use of ICT, digital workflows and e-health, in general, secures a fully integrated use of digital health data. However, the Danish healthcare system seeks to improve the quality and efficiency of the offered healthcare services with a coherent collaboration across sectors and departments, while having a high focus on continuously improving the use of digital health [9].

2.2 Wireless Technologies for Smart Monitoring

A key requirement for a smart monitoring technology is that it is energy-efficient because most of the elements of such a network would be battery-driven devices. Narrowband technologies, such as Low Power Wide Area Networks (LPWAN) have been gaining a lot of attention for use in the above scenario because of their capability to provide a high energy-efficient transmission of small data packages with a high coverage at low costs [10]. The use and implementation of LPWAN in the Danish infrastructure and industries are in the early stage of progress. However, the technologies are emerging and it is predicted to have a high influence on the societies in the near future. There exists a broad range of different LPWAN technologies and operators - each with their individual advantages, features and limitations.

Some of the most well-known and important technologies for LPWAN are the following:

- Sigfox;
- NarrowBand-IoT;
- LoRaWAN;
- DASH7.

DASH7 technology has been explored by researchers to develop a radio-frequency identification (RFID) tracking system that places tags on beds, materials and equipment and makes it possible to locate either inventory or patients in a hospital environment. Such system has currently been implemented at Aarhus University Hospital (AUH) and is the largest RFID installation of this kind in the world, with 1.000 hospital beds and 300.000 pieces of material to be part of the tracking system with the availability of locating them wirelessly [11, 12].

DASH7 is based on the ISO/IEC 18000-7 international standard, which provides technical specifications on RFID devices and can be used in item management applications. It is suitable to describe the use and specifications on RFID devices operating at the 433-MHz frequency band. The low frequency enables a high propagation with penetration ability on multi-floored buildings and it operates with a low energy consumption. The DASH7 uses asynchronous communication and the network consists of gateways and endpoints. The gateways have the functionality of receiving data and processing it, whereas the endpoints are simpler devices, containing sensors that monitor the needed data and information. The endpoint is designed to be in a sleep mode, which enables the low energy consumption and allows for periodically receiving and sending data to the gateways.

DASH7 can be used as a wireless technology for facilitating and enabling of data transmissions to support effective patient care. DASH7 has a high reliability potential in a medical environment compared to Wi-Fi, Bluetooth and ZigBee as it is not suffering from interference problems while having the advantages of low power, long range and low cost [16].

2.3 Smart Monitoring of Patients Using the Internet of Things

Using a wearable monitoring technology, which can remotely monitor patients is a part of the term called 'smart technology'. The environment of using smart technology consists of objects that can exchange, store and process data and information applying the concept of IoT [16]. The possibilities of IoT in the healthcare industry fits the emerging challenge of an increasing number of patients with chronic and long-term diseases due to the fact that it can create value by providing different monitoring functions and application possibilities [7, 8, 16]. This is also supported by a rapid evolvement of wearable technology, such as computerized watches, sensors integrated in textiles and smart glasses. The trend is towards technology with minimized sizes and a higher possibility of monitoring biomedical data, including the vital signs of patients [17]. The use of wearable devices for monitoring is potentially making the treatment process more patient-centric hence making the individual patient possible of managing their own health data monitoring and giving the possibility of continuous ambulatory monitoring of vital signs with the advantages of enabling mobility and minimising interference with other activities [18].

Monitoring of Vital Biosignals. Monitoring of patients consists of several different monitoring technologies and devices since the human body is producing multiple various measurable vital biosignals. The signals can be bioelectrical or biochemical signs and the signals are monitored, analyzed and assessed for diagnosis and treatment of patients. Some of the most important vital biosignals are summarized in Table 1.

Table 1. Monitoring of vital biosignals (based on [12])

Vital biosignals	Description	Monitoring technology
ECG	Information of the cardiac electrical cycle shown as an ECG waveform. Used to analyse the cardiac rhythm, ischemic changes and to predict and treat acute myocardinal infarctions and coronary events	Electrodes used for transduce ionic current from the heart into electron current
Heart rate	Information about the physiologic status by indicating changes in the heart cycle	Data extraction from ECG or use of inertial sensors
Blood pressure	Indicating the pressure exerted by blood against the arterial wall. Provides information about the blood flow including systole and diastole. Can monitor hypertension and hypotension	Use of inflatable pressure cuffs with a stethoscope or sensors on the wrist
Blood oxygen saturation	Monitor oxygen level in the patient's blood. Used for detecting hypoxia	Photoplethysmography technology and pulse oximetry principles on a patient's finger
Body temperature	Balance between heat production and heat loss. Detection of too high or too low body temperature	Measurement of core and skin temperature by sensors

3 Impact of the Wireless Monitoring Technology Implementation in a Hospital Environment

The impact was evaluated for the case study of an implementation at AUH, Aarhus, Denmark, and relates to both types of potential users, namely, the patients and the medical personnel. The RFID tracking system at AUH uses small tags, which are attached to the materials or the staff's name badge.

3.1 Requirements for the Wireless Monitoring System

The users had a key role in identifying the technical requirements for the proposed architecture. For this purpose, questionnaires were carried out with both, patients and medical personnel. Additional interviews were carried out with selected medical personnel.

Patients Requirements. Changes in the vital biosignals of patients carry important information used for their treatment and diagnosis in the hospitals. The human body is producing multiple biosignals, which are used when clinical personnel assess the health condition of a given patient. In order to find out how using smart technology in wireless monitoring could affect the treatment of patients in the hospital, a questionnaire was conducted at AUH for the purpose of getting data on patients', and their relatives', the view on using wireless technology in the hospital and monitoring equipment in general. The questionnaire got a total of 10 respondents where the one half are women and the other half are men. The ages of the respondents are distributed in the ages from 18 to 75, where most of them are in the age categories 46–55 and 56–65. Three of the respondents have been hospitalized in the past two years and the remaining are either relatives or ambulant patients. The respondents were asked about their experience on using monitoring technology including a question whether they have felt inconvenience by the way they have been monitored and a question addressed to the potential limitation of their freedom of movement in the hospital.

The results from the questionnaire show that 100% of the respondents either strongly disagree or disagree on the statement of feeling inconvenience in the way they have been monitored.

Concerning the potentially limited freedom of movement because of monitoring equipment, 80% either strongly disagree or disagree and 20% agree on the statement. The answers regarding the current monitoring procedures and technologies at AUH indicates that the patients are satisfied with the monitoring as it is. Hence, the current technology is well-functioning and does not disturb or unsettle the patients.

However, when the respondents were asked if they would prefer higher freedom of movement when hospitalized, they answered with a higher distribution among the answers with 20% 'strongly disagree', 10% 'disagree', 40% were neutral and 30% agreed on the statement. This could indicate that some patients and their relatives would like to have an increased amount of freedom of movement in the hospital but it is not valid for all of them. The respondents were moreover asked about the idea of having the exact location of the patients visible continuously for the clinical personnel. The respondents were predominantly positive about the idea as 80% either agreed or strongly agreed on the statement of being fine with continuously being tracked and 20% were neutral. These results indicate that patients have no problem with the monitoring technology being able to inform the clinical personnel about the location at the hospital.

In addition, medical doctors were also interviewed, with regard to mobility of the patients at the Pediatric ward. An increased mobility based on use of wireless monitoring would be desired for the case of newborn babies during their transfer from to their parents and back again. Another potential hurdle with the current cable-based monitoring technology at the hospital is about patients in intensive care where the high amount of cables for monitoring technologies can trouble and disturb the treatment of patients. Further, patients would be more likely to be physically active when they are not inhibited by many wires around their body.

Medical Personnel. Interviews were carried out with medical doctors (MDs). The MDs could see potentials gains of the technology if, however, the monitoring will satisfy the requirements of being reliable, user-friendly and highly dependable for successfully using it in the treatment of patients. The interviews indicate that using wireless monitoring technology with a tracking function of hospitalized patients could improve the treatments in the hospital. Being able to continuously having the exact location of patients could potentially ease the tasks of the clinical personnel in terms of locating the patients in an easier way.

A tracking function could potentially make resource savings for the clinical personnel in the hospital, which is advantageous due to the challenges of rising expenses and the shortage of clinical personnel in the healthcare system.

Technical Requirements. The technical requirements can subdivided into functional and non-functional.

Functional Requirements

- The monitoring device shall monitor vital biosignals by sensors. The vital biosignals can be: blood pressure, heart rate, ECG, blood oxygen saturation or body temperature.
- The system shall include an alarm system. The alarm system notifies the clinical personnel if the measured values from the biosignals surpasses preset thresholds.
- The system shall send continuously the monitored data to the clinical personnel's equipment.
- The system shall have a tracking function where patients' location can be shown in case of the alarm system notifies the clinical personnel.

Non-Functional Requirements

- The monitoring technology shall be user-friendly and dependable.
- The data transfer from the monitoring system shall be reliable.
- The data transfer from the monitoring system shall be wireless.
- The monitoring system shall be designed according to the LPWAN protocol DASH7 and ISO 18000-7. The monitoring devices shall be operating at 433-MHz frequency band.

3.2 Proposed Wireless Monitoring Architecture

The proposed wireless monitoring architecture is shown in Fig. 1. It consists of the overall monitoring system and three entities, namely, Patient, Clinical personnel and Data storage.

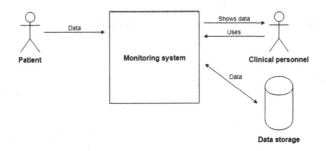

Fig. 1. Wireless monitoring architecture for hospital environment.

The Monitoring system shall be seen as a black box system consisting of all the sensors, connections, algorithms etc., which are part of the system. The entities are described below.

The Patient is a primary entity that interacts with the wireless monitoring system. The patient shall be interpreted as a human, in any age, being treated at the hospital.

The treatment of the patient can be acute, ambulant or regarding a hospitalization of the patient. The patient interacts with the monitoring system in terms of a monitoring or measurement of a vital biosignal, such as blood pressure, ECG, blood oxygen saturation or localisation of the patient. The monitoring enabled by sensors attached to the patient's skin.

The Clinical Personnel are the other primary entity of the monitoring system. The clinical personnel shall be interpreted as a human employed at the hospital and can have the function of a nurse, medical doctor or another clinical function. The clinical personnel interacts with the system in a double way. The first is when the personnel uses the monitoring system to measure and monitor the patients, which is an important part of their tasks and functions at the hospital. The interacting is double sided, because the system sends and shows the monitored data to the clinical personnel's equipment which is used for diagnosis and treatment of the patient.

The Data Storage is a secondary entity used for storage of the monitored data from the patients. The data storage is connected to the monitoring system and the monitored data gets transferred back and forth from the system.

The overall system architecture is shown in Fig. 2 and its different components are found and analyzed based on information from [13, 19]. The sensors are attached to the patients with specific on-body placements all dependent of, which biosignal being monitored and the condition of the patient. The sensor module can be measuring vital biosignals such as ECG, blood pressure, heart rate, body temperature, blood oxygen saturation or the sensor can provide the localisation of the patient. The sensors are endpoints in the DASH7 network that transmits the data asynchronously to the gateways.

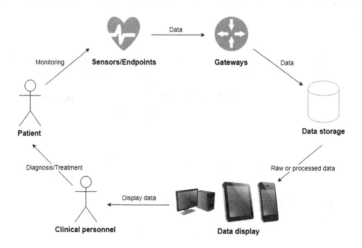

Fig. 2. Overall system architecture.

The gateway is a device, which continuously is listening for packets of data from the endpoints. The gateway receives the monitored data from the patients at transmit further in the hospital's network. The gateway can be installed as several devices throughout the hospital.

The data display component of the system architecture consist of the technology displaying the monitored and processed data from the patients. The data display can be designed in several ways dependent on the user and the setup in the hospital. The technology can be handheld, such as smartphones or tablets, and it can be stationary, such as computer screens or other screens. The data is transmitted by the data storage component and is either raw or processed dependent on which biosignal is being measured and what the purpose of the signal is.

4 Barriers to Real-Hospital Implementation and Deployment

4.1 Technical Barriers

The monitoring system has an extensive amount of components and different technical connections and the system faces several barriers that can potentially limit the clinical implementation of the monitoring system. The technological setup is in an early stage of the design and development process, that is why specifications of the wireless monitoring have to be carefully defined further for a successful implementation of the system.

One of the potential technical barriers is the design of the sensor module in the wireless monitoring system. The type of sensor used in the system depends on several aspects, including what kind of biosignal is being monitored as each signal can be measured with different kinds of electrodes and sensors. The sensors have to be resistant to motion artefacts, because one of the benefits of wireless monitoring is to have an increased patient mobility. The wireless sensor module moreover have to incorporate solutions to electromagnetic interference for getting reliable data. It is recommended to design the data storage and processing components with modern technologies and techniques such as machine learning, artificial intelligence or a clinical decision support system for a more successful use and implementation of the monitoring system. In that way, will the monitored data provide an even more informative information to the clinical personnel, which could potentially decrease the workload for the staff.

4.2 Compliance

Compliance is defined as "the ability of an individual or organisation to implement, manage and follow law, regulations, standards, guidelines, norms and similar normative directives" [20]. When a product is in compliance with the existing regulations and standards, it would have the advantage of fulfilling the requirements, which facilitates the deployment implementation. The healthcare sector has a large number of regulations and requirements for any technology aimed for medical use.

CE Marking. When developing technology to be used in the hospitals and in the healthcare sector in general it is required to investigate if the technology has to be classified as a medical device. By spring 2020, the classification of medical devices would follow the regulation "Medical Device Regulation 2017/745" (MDR) made by the European Parliament [21]. This classification process is key to the successful market implementation. According to Article 2 in MDR, the wireless monitoring technology can be defined as a medical device with the specific purpose of monitoring patients for treatment and diagnosis. Depending on the intended use of the technology and its inherent risks, it will be classified and divided in one out of four risk classes: I, IIa, IIb and III. The classification will be carried out according to Annex VIII in MDR. The Annex contains a set of classification rules, and by the intended use of the monitoring technology, it can be concluded that for our case, rule 10 applies. The technology consists of active devices intended for diagnosis and the monitoring of vital physiological parameters, and the nature of variations in the parameters could immediately result in danger to the patients (class IIb).

The classification as a medical device in class IIb means that AUH, or another manufacturer of the product, will have to demonstrate that the technology meets the requirements in the MDR by conducting a conformity assessment before CE marking the product and using it in the hospital.

The requirements in MDR consist of general safety and performance requirements such as clinical evidence and investigation, physical properties and performance characteristics. The manufacturer, furthermore, has to formulate technical documentation with specifications and models for the technology. For completing the process and satisfying the requirements of MDR, it is recommended to follow the harmonized standard [22]. The road to being in compliance with MDR and the harmonized standards can be a complex and expensive process, why it is recommended to make a collaboration with companies or consultants who are experts within the field of market medical devices in the healthcare sector.

Technical Compliance. Besides the harmonised standards and requirements of the MDR, due to the classification as a medical device, it is advisable to be in compliance with ISO/IEC 18000-7 and the DASH7 Alliance Protocol. The ISO/IEC 18000-7 standard describes the specifications and detailed technical description of air interface communication at 433 MHz, and the standard will be applicable in the development of the wireless monitoring system [23]. Using the DASH7 Alliance Protocol will be helpful in the development as it contains specifications and open source data. Being in compliance with ISO/IEC 18000-7 and the DASH7 protocol is advisable and can potentially ease the development of the technology and make of the technical requirements in the development specific.

The General Data Protection Regulation (GDPR) was introduced in May 2018 and it is a European regulation for data protection and privacy. The GDPR contains a set of requirements that each organization must comply with. Especially, healthcare organizations, such as the hospital, have a unique set of requirements since they are having a high use of health data and personal data collected from the patients. The wireless monitoring technology provides several kinds of data from the patients including personal genetic data and biometric data. Therefore, the manufacturer of the monitoring

technology required to facilitate cybersecurity capabilities and satisfy other requirements. It is largely recommended to incorporate and satisfy the requirements of GDPR
for a successful implementation of the technology. A large hospital, normally would
have a strong experience with handling health data and the relevant requirements in the
legislation.

5 Conclusion

This paper investigated how wireless monitoring technology could be used and
implemented in a large hospital in Denmark. A system concept based on the DASH7
protocol was proposed. The problem statement and research questions have been
focused on the patient and the clinical perspective of how the proposed system for
wireless monitoring of health data in the hospital could improve the patients' well-
being and treatment, while allowing for more cost-efficiency of the hospital operations.
The research was performed with a general deductive approach by a research design
consisting of a case study including the used data collection techniques, state-of-the art
analysis, interviews and a questionnaire. Several strategic considerations have to be
included in the development and implementation of the wireless monitoring system for
a successful process. Compliance with MDR, GDPR and other essential standards is a
critical requirement. It can be overall concluded that the use and implementation of a
wireless monitoring system could improve the monitoring of health data in the hospital.
There are several potential benefits with a clinical perspective, but the technology is in
a very early stage of the process and the topics have to be investigated further for a
more clear conclusion can be made.

References

1. Central Denmark Region: Inauguration of the new super-hospital in aarhus (2017). http://
   www.en.auh.dk/press-room/news-archive/2017/inauguration-of-the-new-superhospital-in-
   aarhus/. Accessed 02 Jan 2019
2. Danske Regioner: Pres på sundhedsvæsenet, Technical report, Danske Regioner (2015)
3. Healthcare Denmark: Danish digital health strategy 2018–2022 now available in English
   (2018). https://www.healthcaredenmark.dk/news/listnews/danish-digital-health-strategy-
   2018-2022-now-available-in-english/. Accessed 29 Dec 2018
4. Ministry of Health: Nationalt kvalitetsprogram for sundhedsområdet 2015–2018, Technical
   report, Ministry of Health, Denmark (2015)
5. The National eHealth Authority [2013], Making ehealth work, Technical report, The Danish
   Government, Local Government Denmark and Danish Regions
6. Omoogun, M., Ramsurrun, V., Guness, S., Seeam, P., Bellekens, X., Seeam, A.: Critical
   patient ehealth monitoring system using wearable sensors. In: 2017 1st International
   Conference on 'Next Generation Computing Applications (NextComp), pp. 169–174. IEEE
   (2017)
7. Kyriazakos, S., et al.: "eWALL: an open-source cloud-based eHealth platform for creating
   home caring environments for older adults living with chronic diseases or frailty. Wireless
   Pers. Commun. **97**, 1835 (2017). https://doi.org/10.1007/s11277-017-4656-7

8. Mihovska, A., et al.: Integration of sensing devices and the cloud for innovative e-Health applications. In: Velez, F.J., Derogarian Miyandoab, F. (eds.) Wearable Technologies and Wireless Body Sensor Networks for Healthcare, Chapter 11,, IET Publications (2019). expected April 2019
9. Ministry of Health: "Healthcare in Denmark - an Overview", Technical report, Ministry of Health, Denmark (2017)
10. Herlich, M., von Tüllenburg, F.: Introduction to narrowband communication (2018)
11. P 360 [n.d.]: Mere tid til patienterne: 300.000 enheder rfid-tagges på skejby. http://p360.dk/mere-tid-patienterne-300000-enheder-rfid-tagges-pa-skejby. Accessed 02 Jan 2019
12. Lyngsoe Systems [n.d.], 'World's largest rfid-based tracking installation of its kind'. https://www.lyngsoesystems.com/en/case-stories/auh-aarhus-university-hospital/. Accessed 02 Jan 2019
13. Weyn, M., Ergeerts, G., Berkvens, R., Wojciechowski, B., Tabakov, Y.: Dash7 alliance protocol 1.0: Low-power, mid-range sensor and actuator communication. In: 2015 IEEE Conference on 'Standards for Communications and Networking (CSCN), pp. 54–59. IEEE (2015)
14. Weyn, M., Ergeerts, G., Wante, L., Vercauteren, C., Hellinckx, P.: Survey of the dash7 alliance protocol for 433 mhz wireless sensor communication. Int. J. Distrib. Sens. Netw. 9 (12), 870430 (2013)
15. Park, A., Chang, H., Lee, K.J.: How to sustain smart connected hospital services: an experience from a pilot project on IoT-based healthcare services. Healthcare Inf. Res. 24(4), 387–393 (2018)
16. Yearp, A., Newell, D., Davies, P.,Wade, R., Sahandi, R.: Wireless remote patient monitoring system: Effects of interference. In: 2016 10th International Conference on Innovative Mobile and Internet Services in Ubiquitous Computing (IMIS), pp. 367–370. IEEE (2016)
17. Haghi, M., Thurow, K., Stoll, R.: Wearable devices in medical internet of things: scientific research and commercially available devices. Healthcare Inf. Res. 23(1), 4–15 (2017)
18. Dias, D., Paulo Silva Cunha, J.: Wearable health devices—vital sign monitoring, systems and technologies. Sensors 18(8), 2414 (2018)
19. Baig, M.M., GholamHosseini, H., Moqeem, A.A., Mirza, F., Lindén, M.: A systematic review of wearable patient monitoring systems–current challenges and opportu nities for clinical adoption. J. Med. Syst. 41(7), 115 (2017)
20. Tambo, T.: Compliance management, in 'Lecture, Aarhus University - BTECH' (2018)
21. European Commission [n.d.]: The new regulations on medical devices. https://ec.europa.eu/growth/sectors/medical-devices/regulatory-frameworkda. Accessed 06 Jan 2019
22. MHRA [n.d.]: An introductory guide to the medical device regulation (mdr) and the in vitro diagnostic medical device regulation (ivdr), Technical report, MHRA
23. International Organization for Standardization: ISO/IEC 18000-7: Information technology—radiofrequency identification for item management – parameters for active air interface communications at 433 mhz, Standard, International Organization for Standardization, Geneva, CH (2014)

Game and Multisensory Driven Ecosystem to an Active Lifestyle

Aristodemos Pnevmatikakis[1], Harm op den Akker[2,3],
Sofoklis Kyriazakos[4], Andrew Pomazanskyi[5],
and Albena Mihovska[4(✉)]

[1] Multimodal Signal Analytics Group, Athens Information Technology,
Athens, Greece
apne@ait.gr
[2] eHealth Group, Roessingh Research and Development,
Enschede, The Netherlands
H.opdenAkker@rrd.nl
[3] Biomedical Signals and Systems Group, University of Twente,
Enschede, The Netherlands
[4] BTECH, Aarhus University, Herning, Denmark
{sofoklis,amihovska}@btech.au.dk
[5] Nuromedia GmbH, Cologne, Germany
andrew.pomazanskyi@mgt.nuromedia.com

Abstract. The trends in healthcare are continuously evolving towards a virtually rich personalized experience that involves human-to-human (H2H), human-to-machine (H2M) and machine-to-machine (M2M) interactions. This article proposes a platform that fosters an ecosystem of games and applies them to real-life situations to motivate an active lifestyle in elderly and health-impacted adults. The platform facilitates behavioral change through numerous games and applications that contribute to active living by introducing awards that can be earned upon reaching goals and can be redeemed in other applications of the GOAL ecosystem. The platform consists of core functionalities (account management, virtual reward system and activity recognition); tools for social inclusion (the social marketplace) and tools for healthy behavior (the goal setting service and the motivational agent). Multisensory technology has been proposed as means to enhance the evaluation on the achieved degree of user motivation. The platform applications are interactive games functioning as GOAL Coin Generators and/or Spenders.

Keywords: Interactive games · Health and social inequities · Active lifestyle

1 Introduction

Failing health due to cognitive impairments, chronical diseases or simply advanced age, can seriously impact the lifestyle of the patients towards physically inactive one and social isolation. Gamification has been gaining momentum as a technology-based healthcare and training tool with the potential to motivate healthy and unhealthy individuals and reduce hospitalization and caregiving costs [1]. Existing virtual reality

V. Poulkov (Ed.): FABULOUS 2019, LNICST 283, pp. 49–58, 2019.
https://doi.org/10.1007/978-3-030-23976-3_5

(VR) games (e.g., Oculus Rift, HTC Vive, and PlayStation VR) already provide quite an immersive user experience, which is also a main user requirement when selecting a gaming application. Intelligent computer vision techniques have also been gaining strong research focus because of their potential to realize personalized applications based on human activity, object or scene recognition, of particular interest to the area of assisted living and eHealth, and even business modeling [2–5]. Such emerging technologies and platforms, are capable of sensing, digitization, transmission and replication of human-related information and can be seen as a first step towards a multisensory human-bond data communication (HBC) framework.

The field of promoting healthy lifestyles has exploded in recent years, with countless of tools and interventions generated in research labs and by commercial vendors alike. A key issue in each lifestyle- or behavior change tool is to enable motivation [6]. The user himself has to be motivated to change behavior – i.e. walk more, do physical or cognitive exercise, get out and socialize. There are many strategies towards increasing the user's motivation to comply with behavior change tools. These can be broadly categorized in those that aim to increase intrinsic motivation (using e.g., Social Cognitive Theory [7] or the Transtheoretical Model [8]) and those that provide extrinsic motivation. The GOAL platform focuses specifically on extrinsic motivation, by rewarding the user's good behavior with virtual (or real) rewards that are unrelated to the positive effects of the behavior itself. GOAL, thus, targets the less explored path of stimulating extrinsic motivation, by providing health benefits to the group most difficult to target and by using common health-behavior change tools.

In this context, enhancing the GOAL concept with advanced tools for capturing the multisensory information related to the user behavior and good feeling after getting a reward can increase the motivational impact with huge benefits for the individual's well-being.

The GOAL platform provides a set of services to integrated games and health apps. At the core of these are the physical measurements of activities of the individuals, which are enabled by smartphone or ambient sensors. Any physical activity application collaborating with the GOAL platform would obtain measurements from the sensors, would process them for the extraction of useful metadata and would report them to the GOAL platform. Optionally, the collected data can be visualized. Subsequent paragraphs, however, are indented.

Enriching the GOAL platform with multisensory communication via the Information and Communication Technology (ICT) infrastructure introduces new requirements to the provision of services in terms of delay, packet loss, computing, and cloud, encoding and other. Challenges are to establish the spatial-temporal constraints that determine the quality of the multisensory experience, and to develop coding, compression and transmission techniques that preserve the perceptual integrity of the multisensory signal thereby yielding a "natural" multisensory experience.

This paper is further organized to describe the main functionalities and implementation of the GOAL architecture, the physical activity measurements and the integration of multisensory features, and will focus on the expected impact, and possible integration with third-party applications.

2   Goal Architecture and Main Functionalities

The GOAL platform is an open middleware that can be integrated into apps and games. The platform has a server-based architecture and is inherently agnostic to device or platform of the applications or games that it integrates. The overall architecture is shown in Fig. 1. The platform supports a complete virtual reward system, in which applications function as coin generators, coin spenders or both. The platform provides generic, adaptive personalized goal-setting that apps and games can leverage to automatically provide the most relevant challenge to their users. An integrated motivational agent helps users to achieve their health-, or in-game goals. Finally, the platform includes a social marketplace that fosters social interactions among the GOAL community.

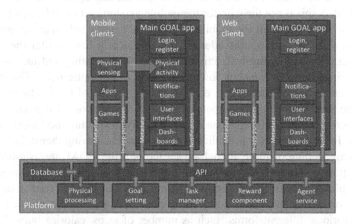

Fig. 1. High-level GOAL modular platform architecture.

2.1   Service Components

The platform has a server-based architecture and is inherently agnostic to the device or platform of the applications or games being integrated. The platform provides the following four major service components (see Fig. 1).

First of all, the platform provides account management and storage, as well as access to the user's virtual GOAL coin wallet. Integrated applications are categorized as coin generators or coin spenders, or can fulfill both of these roles simultaneously. Coin generators are those apps that stimulate healthy behavior and are allowed to award GOAL coins to the user, while coin spenders are games that allow spending coins.

Second, the platform provides a virtual market that stimulates social interaction among the users by allowing them to trade their earned coins for virtual goods or actions, but also for real-world gains. The platform provides the virtual marketplace, while users, developers, local business, or governmental organizations can provide the content. Third, the platform provides a generic goal-setting service to its connected apps, allowing, both, health applications and games to automatically set goals that are relevant for the individual users. The goal-setting component automatically learns to adjust to its users by observing their lifestyle or game-play behavior and fine-tuning daily, weekly, or long-term goals accordingly. Finally, a motivational agent, which is an artificially intelligent companion guides the users through their game-play and motivates healthy lifestyle behaviors. The companion is tightly integrated with the goal-setting services of the GOAL platform, ensuring that the lifestyle motivations are appropriate to the context of the user's real behavior.

2.2 Other Components

The main GOAL app component allows for the creation and management of the user profiles and acts as the main interaction point for the user to check the status of the earned and spent GOAL coins on, both, the web and mobile. While using the web, access to all the other components (other web apps) making up the platform would be readily provided, this is not the case for the mobile version. All GOAL apps need to be installed individually, and in the mobile version the main GOAL app also acts as the only GOAL software a new user interacts with. Hence, it has to offer the complete GOAL experience of the physical activity measurement, gaming and the social marketplace, by integrating at least cut-down versions of these applications. The interested users can then download more apps, enriching their version of the platform.

The automatic goal-setting component is a service component that automatically calculates personalized goals based on measured activities within the GOAL platform. These goals form the basis for providing rewards (upon achieving them), and form the target for provisioning of motivational advice through the GOAL motivational agent. The goal-setting component provides added functionality on top of all measured data in the GOAL platform, to which some form of progress can be attributed. Examples of data types, on which the goal-setting component operate, are the physical activity (including various different forms, such as number of steps, calories burned and distance), and the cognitive behavior (e.g., amount of time spent in cognitive games, or cognitive game scores). The goal-setting component is a key element for providing relevant and personalized rewards. Earlier work on goal setting in the daily physical activity was reported in [9].

The motivational agent is a personal assistant that provides motivational feedback, advice and a friendly listening ear to the users of the GOAL platform. From a technical point of view, the motivational agent is a loosely connected GOAL platform component, built "on-top-of" the basic GOAL services and grounded on user tailored persuasive-technology principles. The design of the motivational agent has been tailored to provide additional levels of adherence, motivation, and fun to the platform. Regarding the interaction, the motivational agent has two modes of operation with the end user, namely, the following:

- User Initiated (UI) Actions – The user, through a UI action, requests to start a dialogue with the agent. At this point, the motivational agent component compiles the user profile with a request of all latest data from the GOAL Platform. Then, based on integrated persuasive and behavioral change methodologies, it would reply back to the user's UI with a list of possible topics, indicating possible subjects for interaction.

- System Initiated Actions – The motivational agent component will periodically reconfigure and update the User Profile with the user's accumulative behavioral data (physical-, and cognitive activity). If the user is deviating too much from a predetermined goal, the agent will initiate an action – a motivational message (see, [10]) – that will be pushed to the most appropriate UI device available.

The social marketplace exposes the social aspects of the GOAL platform, where players can interact by asking for favors (e.g. "I would like my grandsons to visit me!") or challenging each other with tasks (e.g., "Which of my friends can walk the most steps in the coming week?"). The component includes a back-end component that collects and stores task data, allowing it to process the full lifetime of a task from the generation to the awarding of a winner. This is of particular interest for the tasks, where the winner is detected automatically. The front-end application exposes the functionality to create a task, views tasks, selects tasks to participate to and views the ongoing task statistics (e.g., current or final rankings).

The physical activity is measured and presented to the GOAL players by the health apps. The physical activity measurement is by nature split into two parts: the front-end (i.e. sensor connection) and the back-end (processing). The signal sensing is carried out on the mobile device, and involves (i) atmospheric pressure; (ii) acceleration (3 axes); (iii) step counter, the latter, when present is asynchronously firing step count integer, whenever there is a new step or group of steps; and (iv) GPS data (latitude, longitude, elevation). The processing performed on the captured signal at the mobile device involves the following:

- Activity intensity estimation and step counting from acceleration;
- Altitude change estimation from atmospheric pressure and step activity;
- Distance, speed and altitude change estimation from GPS data;
- Activity intensity estimation in terms of Metabolic Equivalent of Task (MET) and its characterization based upon the step rate, speed and elevation change, together with the GOAL player profile.

The MET is a measure of energy cost of different physical activities normalized by the duration of the activity and the weight of the person exercising it. It is defined as the ratio of metabolic rate (and therefore the rate of energy consumption) during a specific physical activity to the reference metabolic rate of resting. The GOAL platform utilizes gender and age related thresholds on MET to quantify the intensity of the exercise, as shown in Fig. 2 [11].

The GOAL platform estimates the energy expenditure as active MET-minutes (enumerating the energy expenditure of some activity over the resting energy expenditure). Active MET-minutes along with the more widespread number of steps are used by the platform to define the personalized goals for the different users. The physical activity measurement system of the platform produces the regular meta-data records every few seconds. This level of processing is not prohibitive for the mobile device, and allows a significant reduction of the volume of transferred data. The server physical activity component utilizes the regular meta-data for activity classification and then computes meta-data aggregations to be used for visualizations and long-term storage.

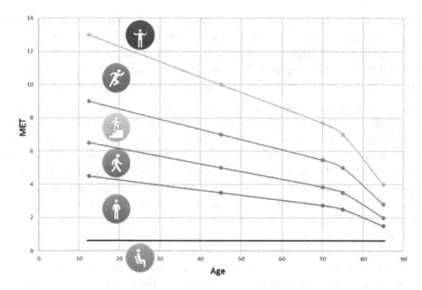

Fig. 2. MET-based intensity classification as a function of the age into idle, light, moderate, heavy, very heavy and extreme (that should not be maintained). Note, that for men the limits should be increased by roughly 15%, while for women they should be decreased by 15%.

3 Physical Activity Measurements

The physical activity measurements are an integral part of the platform, and it comes along with its own, feature-rich physical activity application, integrated within the mobile version of the GOAL main application. Although always there, the use of this integrated application is not mandatory. GOAL players can use other physical activity applications that communicate with the GOAL platform.

3.1 Physical Activity Measured from a Smartphone

The GOAL Physical Activity Application that comes with the GOAL Main Application utilizes the sensors of the smartphone to extract metadata, such as steps walked and stepping speed, floors climbed, distance, speed, elevation, energy consumed, active minutes. The Physical Activity Application can be accessed by clicking on the physical activity overview card of the main interface of the Main GOAL application as shown in Fig. 1. These metadata can be enriched with data registered by intelligent vision techniques and smart sensors, able to detect mood, degree of sweating and similar additional data that would provide vital information about the degree of user experience, which could be then rewarded by a higher value award in the GOAL platform. Such an approach would be vital to keeping high user motivation and determination to follow the activities. When the detected experience is below positive, it could be timely proposed to change the activity with a more rewarding one. An example of the metadata visualization on the mobile device is shown in Fig. 3. The physical activity tracking options can be reached as a category of the main GOAL application options.

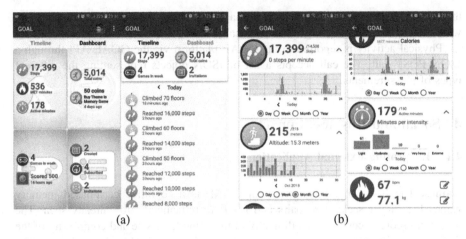

(a)   (b)

Fig. 3. GOAL metadata visualization. (a) Overview (dashboard and timeline views) and (b) physical activity details.

3.2 Physical Activity Measured from Smart Sensors

GOAL supports the integration from "3rd party" health applications. From the product perspective, commercial health apps could integrate their applications with the GOAL platform and report user's health and wellbeing data to the platform. In this way, users can continue using their preferred fitness tracker, food logging app, weight manager, relaxation app, etc. while benefitting from the additional motivation to use those apps through the GOAL platform. The GOAL Physical Activity Application utilizes the following sensors:

- Accelerometer: The average magnitude of acceleration is calculated in every reporting window.
- Android step counter: The steps accumulated in the reporting period are calculated, and from those the step rate, distance travelled and speed. In the absence of an Android step counter, the proprietary GOAL one is used. This utilizes directly the accelerometer samples.
- Barometer: The difference of elevation in the reporting period is estimated from the barometer reading. The barometer reading is only considered if the change is moderate and the current step rate is not zero, to filter out variations to the atmospheric pressure due to the changing weather.
- GPS: When outdoors, this yields a better estimation of the distance, speed and elevation.

Other physical activity applications can utilize sensors from the phone or from some third party hardware activity tracker. Here, an approach to capture multisensory information will allow for extracting novel contextual information in combination with information about the location, time, date, network, analytics and user settings. This would enable to customize an activity program to each user and increasing the rewarding experience on a personalized basis, and would enhance the functionality of the activity type classification with personalized features, which aims at identifying what the GOAL user is doing when physically active.

Physical activity is reported to the GOAL platform via the GOAL API through a JSON POST call. The call accepts a list of JSON objects representing the different types of measurements.

4   Social and Business Impact

4.1   Integrating External Applications

Games. The first game integrated with GOAL is a cognitive card-based memory game. The player seeks card pairs and needs to remember cards already seen. The maximum score depends on the difficulty of the game (grid size and complexity of the deck, i.e. the images depicted) as well as the number of mistakes the user does. The score is reported to GOAL, and the platform translates it to GOAL coins based on the goals being set for the particular user.

There are also game spending mechanisms integrated in the game: The user can chose to cheat (peak at the cards on the grid) for a number of GOAL coins. The user can also buy more decks with GOAL coins. This offers variety in the three levels of deck difficulty.

Physical Activity Apps. Two physical activity apps currently have been integrated with the platform. One implements the platform's physical sensing and displays the information to the user as shown in Fig. 2. As already explained, the user profile plays an important role on how the different physical measurements are processed into an understanding of the user's physical behavior.

The second physical activity application, the Activity Coach, reports daily physical activity as it is captured by a third-party system, (e.g., Fitbit). The current design of the Activity Coach app is able to show the user's current number of steps and allows for switching to detailed- or weekly overviews. The integration of the app with the GOAL platform will be executed in the way it is envisioned for third-party app developers to perform the integration. This means that the app will include the option for the user to link his "Activity Coach" account with a "GOAL Account", after which, data will be shared between the application and the GOAL API.

User Impact. The GOAL platform has two clearly distinct target users - those that play games, and those that develop them. The primary target population are the players, and the GOAL project focuses specifically on the subsection of players that is most at risk of adverse health effects – older adults. Lack of physical activity, decline in cognitive skills, and social isolation are all commonplace issues in the older adult population – issues that are targeted by the GOAL platform.

Impact on the Game Industry. The GOAL platform has the potential to provide benefits to the gaming industry in two different ways. On one hand, it is opening up new markets, in which health behavior of the end user plays a central role, therefore introducing leisure games to a number of new target groups by pro-viding new emerging experiences. On the other hand, the ability opens up to exploit the GOAL platform functionalities enhanced with multisensory context and introduce completely new business and revenue stream models. Over the past few years the market for mobile applications and games has shown a strong growth – at the same time over-saturating the market and creating a fierce competition. In order to stand out, developers seek for possibilities to provide some added value to their games in addition to unique art design and game-play. This is the gap that the GOAL platform can fill and address the demand. In fact, several developers already use different types of the reward systems, e.g. earning coins by playing partner games that the user can later spend on the gift cards, real products or paid apps. Nevertheless it is the first time that a platform connects to distinct areas – health applications and games (either physical or cognitive) with leisure gaming therefore having the potential of reaching a much larger user base.

5 Conclusion

A game-based multisensory approach carries an immense innovation potential to the traditional practices of support of active living of elderly and chronically ill patients. Besides the added value of a novel type of context that can be utilized to personalized applications and custom-tailored therapies, the proposed platform is a strong enabler of user motivation, which is still a crucial barrier to the successful deployment of eHeatlh therapies. Many research challenges lie ahead, requiring solutions allowing for the detection, sensory analysis and evaluation methodology, coding/decoding, synchro-nization, transmission, and reconstruction over the ICT infrastructure of complex data associated with the olfactory, gustatory and tactile experiences of a user. The authors believe that exploration of the integration of multisensory context with eHealth plat-forms will boost the user acceptance and speed up actual deployment.

References

1. Lee, C., Lee, K., Lee, D.: Mobile healthcare applications and gamification for sustained health maintenance. J. Sustain. 9(772) (2017). https://doi.org/10.3390/su9050772
2. Li, K., Sun, Sh., Wu, J., Zhao, X., Tan, M.: Real-time human-robot interaction for a service robot based on 3D human activity recognition and human-like decision mechanism. arXiv: 1802.00272 [cs.HC], Cornell University Library, February 2018
3. Manolova, A., Panev, S., Tonchev, K.: Human gaze tracking with an active multi-camera system. In: Cantoni, V., Dimov, D., Tistarelli, M. (eds.) BIOMET 2014. LNCS, vol. 8897, pp. 176–188. Springer, Cham (2014). https://doi.org/10.1007/978-3-319-13386-7_14
4. Tonchev, K., Lindgren, P., Manolova, A., Neshov, N., Poulkov, V.: Digitizing human behavior in business model innovation. Presented at GWS, May 2017. https://ieeexplore.ieee.org/stamp/stamp.jsp?tp=&arnumber=8300484
5. Kyriazakos, S., et al.: eWALL: an open-source cloud-based eHealth platform for creating home caring environments for older adults living with chronic diseases or frailty. Wirel. Pers. Commun. 97, 1835 (2017). https://doi.org/10.1007/s11277-017-4656-7
6. Pollak, K.I., et al.: Physician communication techniques and weight loss in adults: project CHAT. Am. J. Prev. Med. 39(4), 321–328 (2010)

7. Bandura, A.: Self-efficacy: toward a unifying theory of behavioral change. Psychol. Rev. **84** (2), 191–215 (1977). https://doi.org/10.1037/0033-295X.84.2.191
8. Prochaska, J.O., DiClemente, C.C.: Stages and processes of self-change of smoking toward an integrative model of change. J. Am. Psych. Assoc. **51**(3), 390–395 (1983)
9. Cabrita, M., op den Akker, H., Achterkamp, R., Hermens, H.J., Vollenbroek-Hutten, M.M. R.: Automated personalized goal-setting in an activity coaching application. Presented at 3rd International Conference on Sensor Networks (SensorNets2014). Lisbon, Portugal, pp. 389–396 (2014)
10. op den Akker, H., Cabrita, M., op den Akker, R., Jones, V.M., Hermens, H.J.: Tailored motivational message generation: a model and practical framework for real-time physical activity coaching. J. Biomed. Inform. **55**, 104–115 (2015)
11. McArdle, W.D., Katch, F.I., Katch, V.L.: Human energy expenditure during rest and physical activity. In: Exercise Physiology: Nutrition, Energy, and Human Performance, 7th edn., pp. 192–205. Lippincott Williams & Wilkins, Baltimore (2010)

EEG Signal Processing: Applying Deep Learning Methods to Identify and Classify Epilepsy Episodes

George Suciu[1]([⊠]) and Maria-Cristina Dițu[1,2]

[1] Beia Consult International, 16, Peroni Street, Bucharest, Romania
{george,maria.ditu}@beia.ro
[2] Faculty of Electronics, Telecommunications and Information Technology,
Politehnica University of Bucharest, 1-3, Iuliu Maniu Boulevard,
Bucharest, Romania

Abstract. Epilepsy is a chronic disease characterized by a deviation from the normal electrical activity of the brain leading to seizures caused by nerve impulses discharge. It is currently considered the fourth global neurological problem, being overcome only by diseases such as strokes. Moreover, according to the World Health Organization, nearly 50 million people suffer from epilepsy, with approximately 2.4 million patients annually diagnosed. It is worth mentioning that the elderly and children are the most exposed categories, but if the situation is considered, one of 26 people is likely to develop this condition at a point in life.

Through three gates, the network can also be used for larger data sequences. Moreover, given that the EEG signals are significantly more dynamic and not linear, an LSTM-based approach has, by definition, an advantage given by the ability to isolate different characteristics of brain activity. In the United States, for example, this condition can be found at 48 people out of 100,000.

Keywords: Epilepsy · EEG · Strokes

1 Introduction

Over the past few years, researchers have discovered that an epilepsy crisis does not occur suddenly but is manifested in a certain way a few minutes before the onset of clinical symptoms. The question was whether this state can be distinguished from the interictal one.

Crises can be controlled with medicines. However, for 25% of patients, crises cannot be controlled by available therapy. A method able to predict the next crisis would greatly improve their quality of life, paving the way for new therapeutic methods such as deep brain stimulation [1].

Electroencephalogram (EEG) is a test commonly used to diagnose epilepsy because the EEG signal contains important information about the electrical activity of the brain. Neuroscientists usually follow the visual signal and identify possible abnormalities. However, such an approach consumes time and is limited by potential impediments

© ICST Institute for Computer Sciences, Social Informatics and Telecommunications Engineering 2019
Published by Springer Nature Switzerland AG 2019. All Rights Reserved
V. Poulkov (Ed.): FABULOUS 2019, LNICST 283, pp. 59–66, 2019.
https://doi.org/10.1007/978-3-030-23976-3_6

such as involuntary movements of the body that may occur. Therefore, it is important to develop a system designed to identify and classify epilepsy episodes.

Over time, techniques applied to the pure EEG signal have been used to fragment it into shorter sequences.

The basic principle consists in taking the initial signal and dividing it into non-overlapping segments. Each segment is categorized according to the stage of the patient: before the crisis (precious), during the crisis (ictal) and after the crisis (postictal) [2].

Subsequently, each segment is passed through a module that extracts features of the EEG signal and eventually arrives in an LSTM network that classifies, based on the extracted features, the state of the patient.

The paper is organized as follows: Sect. 2 analyses related work, Sect. 3 describes the database used, while Sect. 4 presents the development of the system and Sect. 5 draws the conclusions and envisions future work.

2   Related Work

The presented paper aims to bring into attention the possibility of resolving a critical healthcare problem. eHealth and eCare solutions are two important subjects that will be probably given during the conference. Therefore, there the concept of an advanced algorithm that will predict and classify the epileptic seizures will be described.

Until now, several encephalogram-based algorithms have used linear and non-linear methods, yielding promising results. Linear predictions are based on frequency analysis. The emergence of the theory of linear dynamics has led to the development of different predictive methods such as dynamic training, the creation of models that simulate neural cells, Kolmogorov entropy [3].

In [4], 10 subjects were tested in the European database, aged between 15 and 57 years. The signals used were taken in two epilepsy centers in Portugal and France. For each patient, 22 invariant features were derived from six channels. Subsequently, these data were processed by a Butterworth filter at 50 Hz to eliminate distortions caused by AC power. The bandwidth is segmented, resulting in the following cases: delta (≤ 3 Hz), theta (4–7 Hz), alpha (8–13 Hz), beta (14–30 Hz) and gamma (>30 Hz).

Analyzing the variations within these frequencies has proven to be a good way of identifying neurological problems [5, 6].

The Fourier transform is applied so to a segmented signal, and then a sum of the resulting coefficients is achieved. For each patient, the dataset provided was divided into two parts: one that corresponds to the training of the SVM (Support Vector Machine) and another to perform the tests. SVM is currently one of the most important tools in the processing of signals based on deep learning. The SVM classifier can be described by the following formula:

$$K(x, y) = e^{-\frac{|x-y|^2}{2*\sigma^2}}$$
(1)

$$\sigma = \text{scale parameter}$$
$$x,\ y = \text{vectors}$$

Another approach considered was that based on spikes of EEG signals in patients with epilepsy. Spikes are sudden variations of easily distinguishable waves that last between 20 and 70 ms. In the study [7], they used data coming from the Center for the Study of Epilepsy at the University Hospital in Freiburg, Germany. The database contains information from 21 patients. The records can be divided into four stages: preictal, ictal, postictal, and interictal. They were sampled at the frequency of 256 Hz, and the A /D conversion was performed at a 16-bit resolution. Also, for EEG data processing, a low-pass filter between 0.5 and 120 Hz, as well as a notch filter with a frequency of 50 Hz were used. Let be a signal of the form x(k) = y(k) + z(k), where y(k) is an EEG signal with slow variations, and z(k) a signal with fast variations. After x(k) was filtered by means of OC (opening-closing) and CO (closing-opening), the resulting signal is y(k) represented by the following expression:

$$Y(k) = \frac{1}{2}[OC(x(k)) + CO(x(k))] \tag{2}$$

The steps for detecting spikes using a combination of OC and CO are as follows:

(1) Removing the transient signal from an EEG segment using OC and CO;
(2) Using the Eq. (2) to eliminate inappropriate amplitudes, resulting in a background signal y(k);
(3) Deduce the signal y(k) from the signal x(k).

The resulting effects indicate a gradual increase in the proximity of the next epilepsy crisis. Almost all existing methods for detecting epilepsy are based on feature extraction techniques.

In the paper [8], features such as Shannon's entropy, standard deviation, and energy were extracted, using the database available from the University of Bonn. An accuracy of 100% and 99.18% for A-E and AB-E cases was thus obtained. However, for the other sets, B-E, C-E, D-E, CD-E and ABCD-E, the percentage was 98.4%. In this study, the signals were analyzed using Dual-tree complex wavelet transform, the resulting coefficients being used to evaluate six characteristic parameters. Particular attention was paid to the phenomenon of over-engaging data that may occur. Also, the complexity of the proposed method was also considered, the largest being equivalent to O (N ^ 2logN) [9].

Another important area in the EEG analysis is given by the graphical representation of some purely theoretical traces. Therefore, graph theory introduced a new approach in studying the anatomical and functional features of the brain.

In paper [10], a non-linear system using an LSTM network was modeled. It was used the input u(k) to simulate and to analyze the behavior. After the network was trained, they concluded that the testing results are good enough. Therefore, by using a recurrent neural network, the study found that LSTM will significantly reduce the computational effort.

Furthermore, Internet of Things (IoT) wearable solutions can be used for monitoring in real-time the EEG and transmit the data to cloud computing platforms [11].

3 Database

The records, grouped in 23 cases, were taken from 22 subjects: 5 males, ages 3 to 22, and 17 females aged 1.5 to 19 years. It is worth mentioning that one of the cases contains records from the same person, but at 1.5 years difference. Each case contains between 9 and 42 files in.edf format. Hardware limitations have caused delays of about 10 s or fewer between certain files, during which no signals have been recorded. To protect the identity of the subjects, all their health information has been replaced, keeping only the temporal relation between the individual files belonging to the same case. In most cases, the.edf file contains a digitally captured signal for one hour, although signals lasting between two and four hours may also appear.

All signals were taken at a rate of 256 samples/second at a resolution of 16 bits.

The data comes from the CHB-MIT database, which is available free of charge on the PhysioNet.org website [12].

The recording was made according to the international standard, which involves the installation of 21 sensors on the surface of the scalp. There is thus a precise positioning of reference points located one at the eye level (nasion) and the other at the base of the skull (inion). Starting from these points, the skull was divided into median and transverse planes, the location of the electrodes being determined by segments at intervals of 10 or 20%. Three electrodes are placed on one side and the other equidistantly to the adjacent ones [13].

In addition to the isolation of the 18 bipolar channels available, no other method has been applied to mitigate any errors that may arise, for example, due to involuntary muscular movements.

The LSTM model allows the evaluation of each characteristic before the classification, especially since there is no other module before it, which should separately analyze each characteristic. Space is internally assessed for each patient by the model that suits the most relevant information to provide a prediction as accurate as possible. Therefore, instead of classifying each individual segment, the network receives more input data representing segments and fits into a class the entire sequence.

4 Development of the System

4.1 The Architecture of a LSTM System

The basic principle consists in taking the initial signal, dividing it into non-overlapping segments and having a duration of 5 s. Each segment is categorized according to the stage of the patient: pre-crisis, during the ictal and after postictal.

EEG segments are passed through a module that extracts the features, producing a 643×1 vector. This module includes units for analyzing signals in time and frequency. Finally, the signal reaches an LSTM network that classifies, based on the extracted features, the state of the patient. The LSTM model thus designed allows the evaluation of each characteristic before the classification, especially since there is no other module before it, which should separately analyze each characteristic separately.

Therefore, instead of classifying each individual segment, the network receives more input data representing segments and fits into a class the entire sequence.

The LSTM model thus designed allows the evaluation of each characteristic before the classification, especially since there is no other module before it, which should separately analyze each characteristic. Space is internally assessed for each patient by the model that suits the most relevant information to provide a prediction as accurate as possible. Therefore, instead of classifying each individual segment, the network receives more input data representing segments and fits into a class the entire sequence.

The structure of the system can be seen in Fig. 1. Write gate takes the input. The output is calculated using the read gate. In the end, only the relevant information is kept by using the forget gate.

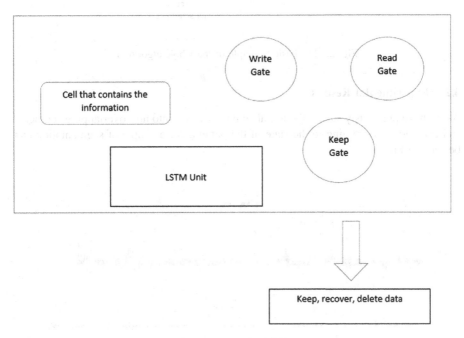

Fig. 1. The structure of a LSTM system

The basic principles of the entire architecture can be seen in Fig. 2.

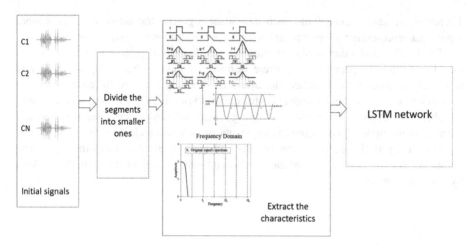

Fig. 2. The basic principle of the whole algorithm

4.2   Experimental Results

As we have previously stated, the initial signal was split into non-overlapping segments and categorized according to the state of the patient. An example of segmentation can be seen in Fig. 3.

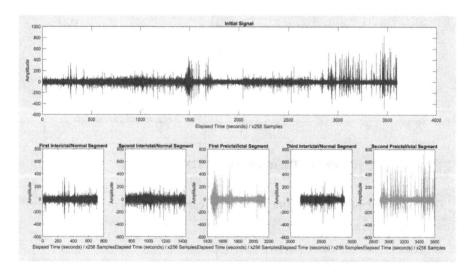

Fig. 3. An example of a divided signal

A single feature was used which shows how the signal behaves in time. Therefore, on the first layer, there will be a single neuron. The response of the system, Y, will have only two values that correspond to possible states of the signal: preictal and interictal.

Since the process of training such a big network that contains this high amount of long signals required computational power, there were chosen several signals to perform the training. The progress that was encountered in terms of accuracy and loss can be seen in Fig. 4.

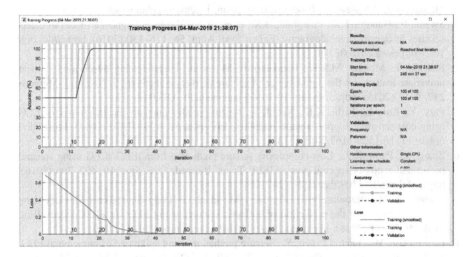

Fig. 4. Training progress of the network

5 Conclusion

The method using LSTM networks has not been used to date to predict epileptic seizures. However, they have found applicability in studies focusing on other areas of analysis of EEG signals. This paper attempts to demonstrate the potential for successful use of LSTM networks in predicting epilepsy seizures, proves that this method provides remarkable performance in terms of the classification of the various stages that occur in the disease, unlike other techniques based on deep learning algorithms used up to now.

Since EEG signals are complex and bring a large amount of color, it has been necessary to look for alternative solutions, and the LSTM-based network has proven to be effective.

In the future, this method can be tested in different clinics, using multiple sets of data this time from adults.

Acknowledgement. This paper has been supported in part by UEFISCDI Romania through projects ESTABLISH, PAPUD and WINS@HI, and funded in part by European Union's Horizon 2020 research and innovation program under grant agreement No. 777996 (SealedGRID project) and No. 787002 (SAFECARE project).

References

1. Li, S., Zhou, W., Yuan, Q., Liu, Y.: Seizure prediction using spike rate of intracranial EEG. IEEE Trans. Neural Syst. Rehabil. Eng. **21**, 880–886 (2013). https://doi.org/10.1109/tnsre.2013.2282153
2. Malmivuo, J., Plonsey, R.: Bioelectromagnetism. Electroencephalography
3. Swami, P., Gandhi, T.K., Panigrahi, B.K., et al.: A novel robust diagnostic model to detect seizures in electroencephalography. Expert Syst. Appl. **56**, 116–130 (2016). https://doi.org/10.1016/j.eswa.2016.02.040
4. Rasekhi, J., Mollaei, M.R.K., Bandarabadi, M., et al.: Preprocessing effects of 22 linear univariate features on the performance of seizure prediction methods. J. Neurosci. Methods **217**, 9–16 (2013). https://doi.org/10.1016/j.jneumeth.2013.03.019
5. Park, Y., Luo, L., Parhi, K.K., Netoff, T.: Seizure prediction with spectral power of EEG using cost-sensitive support vector machines. Epilepsia **52**, 1761–1770 (2011). https://doi.org/10.1111/j.1528-1167.2011.03138.x
6. Zhang, Z., Parhi, K.K.: Low-complexity seizure prediction from iEEG/sEEG using spectral power and ratios of spectral power. IEEE Trans. Biomed. Circ. Syst. **10**, 693–706 (2016). https://doi.org/10.1109/tbcas.2015.2477264
7. Tsiouris, K.M., Pezoulas, V.C., Zervakis, M., et al.: A Long Short-Term Memory deep learning network for the prediction of epileptic seizures using EEG signals. Comput. Biol. Med. **99**, 24–37 (2018). https://doi.org/10.1016/j.compbiomed.2018.05.019
8. Li, S., Zhou, W., Yuan, Q., Liu, Y.: Seizure prediction using spike rate of intracranial EEG. IEEE Trans. Neural Syst. Rehabil. Eng. **21**, 880–886 (2013). https://doi.org/10.1109/tnsre.2013.2282153
9. Swami, P., Gandhi, T.K., Panigrahi, B.K., et al.: A novel robust diagnostic model to detect seizures in electroencephalography. Expert Syst. Appl. **56**, 116–130 (2016). https://doi.org/10.1016/j.eswa.2016.02.040
10. Gonzalez, J., Yu, W.: Non-linear system modeling using LSTM neural networks. IFAC-PapersOnLine. **51**, 485–489 (2018)
11. Suciu, G., et al.: Big data, internet of things and cloud convergence–an architecture for secure e-health applications. J. Med. Syst. **39**(11), 141 (2015)
12. Ullah, I., Hussain, M., Qazi, E.-U.-H., Aboalsamh, H.: An automated system for epilepsy detection using EEG brain signals based on deep learning approach. Expert Syst. Appl. **107**, 61–71 (2018). https://doi.org/10.1016/j.eswa.2018.04.021
13. CHB-MIT Scalp EEG Database. https://www.physionet.org/pn6/chbmit/. Accessed 15 Jan 2019

A Novel Portable Tracking Device with Kalman Filter for Hand and Arm Rehabilitation Applications

Veselin Lalov and Agata Manolova[✉]

Faculty of Telecommunications, Technical University of Sofia,
blvd. Kliment Ohridski 8, 1796 Sofia, Bulgaria
veselinlalov@mail.bg, amanolova@tu-sofia.bg

Abstract. Utilising MEMS technology motion sensors and algorithms for motion data processing, a prototype device is proposed as a viable solution for movement diagnostics during sports or rehabilitation activities, based on the documented in the medical journals benefits of eccentric resistive training with full range of motion. The proposed device evaluates the quality of the movement by measuring the range of motion and both eccentric and concentric phases of the movement.

Keywords: Kalman filter · Tendopathy · Rehabilitation · Signal processing

1 Introduction

A lot of research from different fields experts is put into regaining or increasing the human body functionalities with the use of emerging technologies such as robotics, computer vision, virtual reality and braincomputer interfaces to enhance the user's independence or fitness level. These arising fields will make possible for a better living by allowing remote assistance from the medical personnel, which in turn may reduce the stress of a visit to the hospital [1] or the pain patients with mobility impairments experience [2]. The patients will benefit from the possibility of remote interaction with their doctors without going outside their comfort zone and also carry out the training from their home, under remote supervision, reducing the cost to the healthcare system. For doctors, these types of assistive rehabilitation mobile devices provide online remote monitoring of the rehabilitation process with possibility to record patient's history.

A connected wearable device with appropriately designed interface will enable therapists to engage with an increasing number of patients without the physical burden of providing the therapy in the hospital. Therapists would then be able to perform a more prescriptive role whilst the device takes care of the manual tasks. From the data gathered from research that has been made in the previous years in the physical medicine and rehabilitation branches of medicine, the

© ICST Institute for Computer Sciences, Social Informatics and Telecommunications Engineering 2019
Published by Springer Nature Switzerland AG 2019. All Rights Reserved
V. Poulkov (Ed.): FABULOUS 2019, LNICST 283, pp. 67–75, 2019.
https://doi.org/10.1007/978-3-030-23976-3_7

results for wearable devices have shown an emergence of a correlation with positive effects such as improved tendon healing and decreased rehabilitation time in patients suffering from tendinopathic conditions such as tendonitis and tendinosis when eccentric based exercises are used in the rehabilitation regimes of the patients [3–6].

Based on the numerous evidence in support of the eccentric training regimes in rehabilitation, it has led the authors of this study to the development of a device with a supportive purpose during rehabilitation or in aid of the research activities in the medical fields. This papers main objective is to provide a brief overview and description of the software and hardware parts of the developed device. Research and testing has been made on the algorithm for calculating the range of motion and angular velocity regarding it's accurate calculations and reliable use, during the intended operation of the device.

The main goal of this paper is to present a development of a prototype of a A novel portable tracking device with Kalman filter for hand and arm rehabilitation applications based on low-cost sensors with mobile interface.

The rest of the paper is organized as follows: the next section describes the device in details. Section III introduces the data analysis to evaluate the device's performance. The final section draws the conclusion and suggests the scope of future work.

2 Device Description

The device consists of an Arduino Micro-Pro as a processing unit, a three-axis accelerometer and gyroscope MPU-6050 and a HC-06 Bluetooth 2.0 module. The communications between the device and smartphone is established via Android application which shows in real time the range of motion in degrees and the corresponding phase of the movement (eccentric or concentric), measured by the angular speed with degrees per second. The prototypes modules are shown on the Fig. 1.

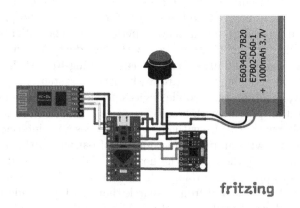

Fig. 1. Device overview.

The MPU-6050 measures raw data for the acceleration on the x, y and z axis (pitch, roll and yaw) and the angular velocity on the above described axes in the form of 16 bit words and transmits it to the Arduino Micro-Pro trough I2C interface. The orientation of the axes are shown on the figure below, provided in the data sheet of the manufacturer of the MPU-6050 (Fig. 2).

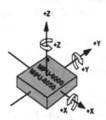

Fig. 2. Axis orientation of the MPU-6050 accelerometer and gyroscope

The processing unit calculates the acceleration and angular velocity trough the mathematical equations: Eq. 1 describes the Eulers angle on the y axis and Eq. 2 represents the rotation on the z axis with a constant provided by the data sheet of the manufacturer.

$$tan^{-1}\theta_y = \frac{-Acc_X}{\sqrt{(Acc_y)^2 + (Acc_z)^2}} \quad [deg] \tag{1}$$

$$Yaw_{rotation} = \frac{Gyro_Z}{32.8} \quad \left[\frac{deg}{s}\right] \tag{2}$$

Acc_x, Acc_y, Acc_z and $Gyro_Z$ represent the raw data readings from the MPU-6050.

After the raw data is converted to measurable units with Eqs. 1 and 2 the $Yaw_{rotation}$ angular velocity and the pitch angle are ran through a filtering algorithm.

The output data from the filter is then ran through an algorithm which describes the exercise done by the user. The algorithm in the processing unit is an if-else type state machine, which switches its conditional statements depending on the exercise selected by the user with the smartphone application. Each exercise is described with different conditional statements in order to ensure the correct execution of the movement by measuring the range of motion (ROM) and the quality of the movement as well by measuring the angular velocity (Yaw rotation). The pseudo code below illustrates an example algorithm flow of the exercise known as Bicep curl:

Algorithm 1. Range of motion and quality of movement

---

while ∞ **do**
  if $pitch > 45$ **then**
    $flagCon = 1$ {Concentric phase completed}
  end if
  if $pitch < -60$ and $flagCon = 1$ **then**
    $flagEcc = 1$ {Eccentric phase completed}
    $repetitions + +$ {One repetition of set is completed}
  end if
  if $GyroZ$ $<$ -650 or $sensorValue$ $<$ 0 and $GyroZ$ $>$ 650 and $flagCon = 1$ **then**
    $(bluetoothSendFailSet)${Exits Loop}
  end if
  if $repetitions = targetRepetitions$ **then**
    $(bluetoothSendSetCompleted)$ {Exits Loop}
  end if
end while

The algorithm detects if the user has reached the end of both phases of the movement by measuring the pitch angle, verifying if the exercise is executed with proper range of motion. There is a condition for ensuring the quality of the movement (e.g. the user is making the movement in a controlled manner) by measuring the angular velocity on the yaw axis. If the conditions are met then a counter, representing the number of repetitions is incremented until it is equal to the number of selected repetitions from the user, sending a Successful set. notification to the user. In case the user has not made the movement with the required range of motion conditions or if the movement is made in a fast manner, the device sends a Failed set. notification to the smartphone of the user.

The smartphone is used as a terminal between the user and the prototype device, with which the user can select the exercise, number of repetitions to perform and receive notifications from the device. Other functions of the application is to show the status of the connection and a test command to evaluate the connection between the device and the smartphone. The figure below shows the basic interface of the application.

Regarding the numerous research indicating correlation with faster healing of connective tissue, the constructed device could be used for sports and medical applications as a tool for doctors and medical personnel for diagnostic purposes [7] (Fig. 3).

Fig. 3. Smartphone application overview.

The next picture shows the developed prototype of the device (Fig. 4).

Fig. 4. Prototype of the device.

3 Data Analysis

In this chapter a comparison of the output data is made between the filtered and non-filtered data. The filtering algorithm is a Kalman filter [8], which filters the noise of the pitch angle data and corrects gyroscope data drift coming from the

MPU-6050. The point of this experiment is to show the key role of the application of a filtering algorithm to the device. Isometric contractions during an exercise performed by the user are a natural part of the movement when a muscle group is experiencing resistive load. These isometric contractions can lead the device being subjugated to vibrations (Fig. 5).

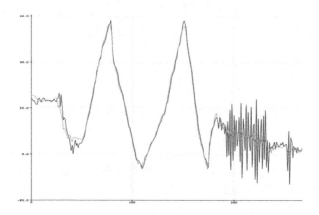

Fig. 5. Filtered data using Kalman filter versus no data filtration. (Color figure online)

On the graph above it is shown the output data from the accelerometer, illustrating the pitch angle. The red line represents the output data from the Kalman filter and the blue line, the data when there is no filtration applied. In the end of the graph the non-filtered data shows a large swing of the amplitude when there is vibration applied to the device. The red line representing the Kalman filtered data shows little variance of the pitch angle when there is vibration applied to the device. Thus, the implementation of a Kalman filter is crucial for achieving more accurate data for the pitch angle and preventing faulty notifications to the user, which can be a result of the inaccurate readings from the accelerometer when there is vibration applied to the device.

The next graph shows the second role of the Kalman filter, implemented in the device. Gyroscope data drift is a common problem of the MEMS technology based gyroscope devices. It is represented by linear increase or decrease of the angular velocity even though the device is not in motion. With the red line, the Kalman filter output data of the angular velocity is shown and with the blue line when there is no filtrating algorithm applied (Fig. 6).

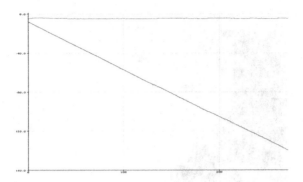

Fig. 6. Gyroscope data correction using Kalman filter. (Color figure online)

On the graph above it is shown that the corrected data is static and does not show any significant variance. When there is no filtration applied, it is shown linear change of the angular velocity. This would make the algorithm for quality of movement detection unusable, due to the inaccurate data for the eccentric and concentric phase of the movement, based on the angular velocity provided by the gyroscope. The next following pictures demonstrate the basic principle of operation of the device. On the left we see the subject reaching the end of both phases of the movements of the exercise. On the right it is shown the displayed information on the application in the smartphone of the corresponding phases of the movement.

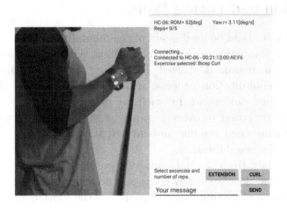

Fig. 7. Concentric phase reached.

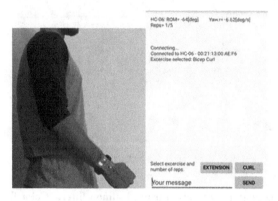

Fig. 8. Eccentric phase reached.

On the right side of the figures, we can see on the terminal application the current angle of the arm, which measures the range of motion of the user, denoted as "Range of motion" (Figs. 7 and 8) and the angular velocity, which measures the quality of the movement by how well the movement is executed in a controlled manner. The angular velocity is denoted as "Yaw rotation" on the display of the smartphone. Negative values of the angular velocity correspond to the eccentric phase of the movement, hence the eccentric phase representing the negative portion of the movement (Fig. 8) and suchlike interpretations can be made for the concentric, positive phase of the movement (Fig. 7).

4   Conclusion and Future Work

The proposed device could be used in aid of the rehabilitation process of patients, suffering from tendinopathy or similar conditions, when eccentric or concentric based rehabilitation regime is utilized, by helping the patient maintain proper form during the rehabilitation process, which is crucial for the effective treatment. The developed device can be used for further research about the effectiveness on eccentric based recovery regimes or similar as an useful tool in aid of researchers during their studies and investigations regarding the mentioned above techniques for rehabilitation.

The observed data from the data analysis provides evidence in the utility of the algorithm in the developed device as a practical and functional method of calculating the range of motion and the quality of the movement during exercise in a reliable and accurate way.

Future endeavours would include a better graphic user interface, graphing the movement as an useful insight of the history of the achieved range of motion for each executed repetition of the set. Statistical database showing the improvements of the range of motion of the patient over time. Improved hardware with an aim to decrease the dimensions of the device. Further software improvements would include faster algorithm calculations and the previously mentioned GUI improvements.

Acknowledgements. This work was supported by European Regional Development Fund and the Operational Program "Science and Education for Smart Growth" under contract UNITe- BG05M2OP001-1.001-0004-01 (2018–2023). The authors of this study would like to thank Michel Aflak and Kristian Lauszus. The base application "Bluetooth-Terminal", developed by Michel and the Kalman filter algorithm and blog post about the algorithm, developed and written by Kristian, proved to be of great use throughout the development of the device. The authors of this study would like also to thank the associate professors of the faculty of Telecommunications at Technical University of Sofia, Bulgaria for their recommendations, review and feedback, during the writing of this research paper.

References

1. Cranen, K., Drossaert, C.H., Brinkman, E.S., Braakman-Jansen, A.L., IJzerman, M.J., Vollenbroek-Hutten, M.M.: An exploration of chronic pain patients perceptions of home telerehabilitation services. Health Expect. **15**(4), 339–350 (2012)
2. Golomb, M.R., et al.: In-home virtual reality videogame telerehabilitation in adolescents with hemiplegic cerebral palsy. Arch. Phys. Med. Rehabil. **91**(1), 1–8 (2010)
3. Murtaugh, B., Ihm, J.M.: Eccentric training for the treatment of tendinopathies. Curr. Sport. Med. Rep. **12**(3), 175–182 (2013)
4. Jonsson, P., Alfredson, H., Sunding, K., Fahlström, M., Cook, J.: New regimen for eccentric calf-muscle training in patients with chronic insertional Achilles tendinopathy: results of a pilot study. Br. J. Sport. Med. **42**(9), 746–749 (2008)
5. Finestone, H.M., Rabinovitch, D.L.: Tennis elbow no more: practical eccentric and concentric exercises to heal the pain. Can. Fam. Physician **54**(8), 1115–1116 (2008)
6. Bernhardsson, S., Klintberg, I.H., Wendt, G.K.: Evaluation of an exercise concept focusing on eccentric strength training of the rotator cuff for patients with subacromial impingement syndrome. Clin. Rehabil. **25**(1), 69–78 (2011)
7. Aflak, O.: https://github.com/OmarAflak/Bluetooth-Terminal
8. Lauszus, K.: A practical approach to Kalman filter and how to implement it. Kalman Filter libraries and algorithm information blog. http://blog.tkjelectronics.dk/2012/09/a-practical-approach-to-kalman-filter-and-how-to-implement-it/

IoT and Sensor Networks

Data Analytics for Home Air Quality Monitoring

Petya Mihaylova[2], Agata Manolova[3(✉)], and Petia Georgieva[1]

[1] Department of Electronics, Telecommunications and Informatics,
University of Aveiro, Avero, Portugal
[2] English Language Faculty of Engineering,
Technical University of Sofia, Sofia, Bulgaria
[3] Faculty of Telecommunications, Technical University of Sofia, Sofia, Bulgaria
amanolova@tu-sofia.bg

Abstract. Modern air quality monitoring systems are characterised by high complexity and costs. The expensive embedded units such as sensor arrays, processors, power blocks, displays and communication units make them less appropriate for small indoor spaces.

In this paper we demonstrate that two widely available, in private houses, sensors (for Humidity and Temperature) are promising alternative, to the expensive indoor air quality solutions, provided with intelligent data processing tools. Our findings suggest that neural network based data analytics system can learn to discriminate unusual indoor gases from normal home air components based only on temperature and humidity measurements.

Keywords: Indoor air quality · Data analytics · Neural network ·
Deep Autoencoder Neural Network

1 Introduction

Nowadays, people spend much time in closed spaces, therefore monitoring of indoor air quality attracted much attention in recent years. Standards, guidelines and requirements, defined by international agencies, are used to evaluate the acceptable quality of air in indoor as well as outdoor environments. Research is carried out to bring dust free, noxious free and smell free environment at home, hospitals, schools, cars, etc. Several air quality monitoring systems have been recently proposed.

A grey model to indoor air quality management in rooms based on real-time sensing of nano and micro particles and volatile organic compounds is proposed in [1]. Pollution sources are analysed and a management model is defined to minimize the time during which the pollutant concentration falls below threshold value. An embedded system model for air quality monitoring is proposed in [2] using low cost gas sensors and Arduino microcontroller. The system is tailored to study the long-term impacts of bad air quality on health particularly with respect to allergic patients. An enhancement of the gas sensitivity and selectivity of a piezoelectric micro-cantilever by using chemically-modified carbon nanotubes as a sorbing layer and a gas sensitive film is studied in [3]. Two measurement modes are compared, the frequency mode that

© ICST Institute for Computer Sciences, Social Informatics and Telecommunications Engineering 2019
Published by Springer Nature Switzerland AG 2019. All Rights Reserved
V. Poulkov (Ed.): FABULOUS 2019, LNICST 283, pp. 79–88, 2019.
https://doi.org/10.1007/978-3-030-23976-3_8

requires a significant amount of nanotubes to coat the cantilever and trap target molecules and the resistance mode that needs a small amount of nanotubes for the film not to be too conductive. An improved sensor based on resistance mode is demonstrated to achieve good sensitivity to gases.

Smart home system with embedded gas sensors arrays to control not only the indoor air quality but also to discriminate room occupancy and human activities in presented in [4]. A portable chemical-based monitoring system built of 32 gas sensors array has been tested in NASA space craft cabin simulator. The compact autonomous system (3.6 L volume, 3.4 kg weight) is composed of polymer-carbon composite elements and is suitable for a long term continuous operation. The system detects the number of individuals present in the room and the number of people exercising. To correct for sensor drift and improve the precision, during periods of lack of activity in the room, the sensors' baselines can be adjusted. Due to air circulation, odours travel from one room to another and thus the sensing range of chemical sensors appear to be wider than video camera-based systems. Interestingly, the system is able to detect human behaviours that caused higher concentration levels of ethanol. Gas sensor arrays are usually used for discrimination of gas mixtures composed of air and single chemical such as hexane, ethanol, acetone, ethyl acetate and toluene. Method for gas mixtures discrimination based on sensor array, temporal response and data driven approach is proposed in [5]. Furthermore in [6], gas recognition by activated thin-film sensors array is studied. Principle Component Analysis (PCA) is applied to cluster target gases. Gas discrimination using nano-electronic nose has been applied in [7]. The integration of nanowire and carbon nanotube sensors, precise control of the sensor temperature, and the use of PCA for data processing resulted in effective discrimination between a wide variety of gases, including explosive ones and nerve agents. The response of these sensors to hydrogen, ethanol, and NO2 were measured at different concentrations and both at room temperature and at 200 °C.

A method for online de-correlation of chemical sensor signals from the effects of environmental humidity and temperature variations is proposed in [8]. The accuracy of electronic nose measurements for continuous monitoring is improved taking into account the simultaneous readings of environmental humidity and temperature. The electronic nose setup, built for this study, consists of eight metal-oxide (MOX) gas sensors, temperature and humidity sensors with a wireless communication link to external computer. The wireless electronic nose was used to monitor the air for two years in one residence and collected data continuously during 537 days with a sampling rate of 1 sample per second. To test the benefits of de-correlating humidity and temperature measurements from the MOX sensors' responses, a scenario with three gas stimuli has been designed – banana, wine and baseline responses. Multiclass inhibitory support vector machine (ISVM) method [9] is used to discriminate between the presence of banana, presence of wine, and baseline activity. To compare the performance of the classifier with and without decorrelation of humidity–temperature, four subsets of data were created by combining raw sensor responses, filtered sensor data, and temperature and humidity. Experimental results show that including the filtered data in the classification model improves significantly the discrimination capability of the model. In summary, it has been shown that simultaneous humidity and temperature recordings are promising to extract relevant chemical signatures.

The reviewed air quality monitoring systems are complex and costly. They integrate expensive components such as sensor networks, processors, power blocks, displays and communication units. Such technology is more appropriate for public building and less suitable for private houses. Moreover, the large number of sensors requires significant computational resources and processing time for data analytics.

In this paper we propose data analytics models for air quality monitoring adequate for small indoor spaces such as private houses. The models are based on machine learning approach (deep neural networks) and are demonstrated with real data provided by the authors of [8] in UCI Machine Learning Repository (Gas sensors for home activity monitoring Data Set). The task is to detect gas changes due to different home activities based on measurements of ten sensors (eight MOX gas sensors, temperature and humidity sensors). The proposed data analytics models differ in terms of number of sensors as inputs and temporal length of the sensor readings. The goal is to build reliable gas discrimination model based only on short time measurements of temperature and humidity sensors.

The rest of the paper is organized as follow. In Sect. 2 deep neural networks are introduced as the proposed data analytics model. In Sect. 3 the sensor array of data is described. The implementation aspects and obtained results are discussed in Sect. 4. Conclusions are drawn in Sect. 5.

2 Deep Neural Networks

Over the last decade, deep learning techniques have become very popular in various application domains such as computer vision, automatic speech recognition, natural language processing, and bioinformatics where they achieved excellent results on various tasks. For example, neural networks with multiple hidden layers (deep neural networks) are very successful in solving classification problems for high dimensional data. Each layer learns to represent the data at a different level of abstraction. The idea of having one algorithm that first maps data into a representative feature space and then solve recognition tasks gained the great success of deep neural networks (DNNs). DNN models have been applied within a wide range of applications including images, videos, speech, text, [10–12], and recently also in neuro-imaging domain [13, 14]. The DNN success is due to their ability to extract representations that are robust to partial translation and deformation of input patterns.

In the present study we explore the advantages of Deep Autoencoder Neural Network (DANN) in the context of sensor array data modelling and compare it with a shallow neural network (NN) model. The following training procedure for DANN was implemented:

(a) Training the first hidden layer of the auto-encoder without providing the labels. An auto-encoder is a neural network which attempts to replicate its input at its output. Thus, the input and the output have is the same size. The auto-encoder is comprised of an encoder followed by a decoder. The encoder maps an input to a hidden representation and the decoder attempts to reverse this mapping to reconstruct the original input.

(b) The next hidden layers (auto-encoders) are trained in a similar way. The main difference is that the features that are generated from the previous auto-encoder are the training data for the next auto-encoder. The size of each subsequent encoder is decreasing, so that it learns compressed input data representation.

(c) Unlike the auto encoders, the final (output) layer is trained in a supervised fashion using training data labels. Softmax function was used as a processing unit in this layer.

(d) Final retraining of the whole DANN is performed in a supervised mode applying error-backpropagation. This step is referred as fine DNN tuning.

3   Data and Experimental Scenario Description

The complete data set [15] consists of recordings of ten sensors (8 MOX gas sensors, temperature and humidity sensors). The sensors were exposed to two specific stimuli (wine or banana smells) and background home smells. The responses to banana and wine stimuli were recorded by placing the stimulus close to the sensors. The duration of each stimulation varied from 7 min to 2 h, with an average duration of 42 min. The dataset contains a set of time series from three different conditions: wine, banana and background activity. There are 35 inductions with wine, 33 with banana and 31 recordings of background activity, corresponding to measurements along 99 days. The dataset is composed of 99 snippets of time series, each being a single induction or background activity. In total, there are 919438 samples. For each induction, the time when the stimulus was presented is set to zero.

The system requirement is to detect on-line early change of indoor air composition and give an alarm. Therefore, the sensor response to a stimulus at the beginning of each experiment (the first few minutes) is of major importance. Sensor records over the first 160 s. of the experiment taken each 5 s were extracted from the original dataset. Figure 1 shows samples from all sensors taken from one experiment with banana stimulus. Samples for negative values of time correspond to sensor responses before the stimulus presentation.

Data structure (Table 1) consists of 99 examples (99 days of experiments with different stimulus) and time series of 32 readings per sensor for a total of ten sensors. Three hypotheses are studied: detection of air quality variation based on (i) all sensors; (ii) MOX sensors, and (iii) Temperature and Humidity sensors.

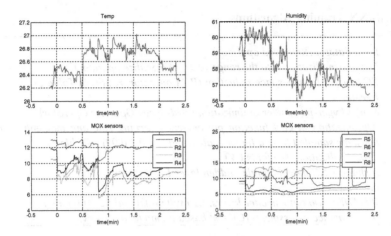

Fig. 1. Data visualisation (MOX, Temperature and Humidity sensor samples)

Table 1. Data structure

Exper.	T (temp.)	H (humidity)	MOX sensor R1	.....	MOX sensor R8
day1	Tt1, Tt2..... Tt32	Ht1, Ht2..... Ht32	R1t1, R1t2..... R1t32	.....	R8t1, R8t2..... R8t32
....	Tt1, Tt2..... Tt32	Ht1, Ht2..... Ht32	R1t1, R1t2..... R1t32	.....	R8t1, R8t2..... R8t32
day99	Tt1, Tt2..... Tt32	Ht1, Ht2..... Ht32	R1t1, R1t2..... R1t32	.....	R8t1, R8t2..... R8t32

4   Gas Discrimination – Implementation and Experimental Results

Two data analytics models for indoor gas discrimination were built- Deep Autoencoder Neural Network (DANN) and a shallow Neural Network (NN). The models were implemented in RapidMiner - open-source software environment. Training and hyper-parameter optimisation steps for both models are outlined in DANN/NN Training Algorithms. The PCA reduction of the feature space (Table 2) is a helpful step to speed up the analysis in online implementation.

Table 2. Original and PCA (95% accumulated variance) reduced feature space

Feature set	Feature space (# of features)	PCA reduced feature space (#)
Hum & Tem	64	5
MOX Sensors	256	17
H & T & MOX	320	19

DANN/NN Training Algorithms

1. *Load dataset (Retrieved operator)*
2. *Data normalization into the range (0,1] (Normalize operator)*
3. *PCA-based feature space reduction (PCA operator, results in Table 2)*
   Iterate
4. *Model hyper-parameter optimization (grid-based Optimize Operator)*
   Optimization of cost function parameters (learning rate and momentum) in ten steps sampled from a linear scale range of [0.1 0.99] , (Table 3).
5. *Cross Validation (10 folds CV)*
   If shallow NN model: single hidden layer L1 (9 units)
   or
   If DANN: two autoencoder layers, L1 (300 units) and L2 (100 units)
6. *Performance assessment (CV test based on model accuracy)*

Table 3. Model optimal hyper-parameters

Feature sets	Optimisation parameters	NN hyper-parameters
Hum & Tem	learning rate = 0.278, momentum = 0.1	rho = 0.9693, eps = 0.1
MOX Sensors	learning rate = 0.1, momentum = 0.634	rho = 0.2789, eps = 0.42
H & T & MOX	learning rate = 0.723, momentum = 0.189	rho = 0.18, eps = 0.74

4.1 DANN Model

The implemented training sequence for the DANN model is schematically outlined in Fig. 2. The module structure represents the complete data analysis process, starting from data normalization, feature space reduction (PCA), model hyper-parameter optimization, training, validation and finally model performance assessment on test data. The computationally most demanding step is the hyper parameter optimization. This procedure is repeated for the following data sets:

(i) All sensors (MOX, Temperature, Humidity sensors) – data structure of 99 examples with 320 features (10 sensors × 32 readings).

(ii) MOX sensors – data structure of 99 examples with 256 features (8 sensors × 32 readings).

(iii) Temperature and Humidity sensors – data structure of 99 examples with 64 features (2 sensors × 32 readings).

4.2 Shallow NN Model

The DANN hypothesis is compared with a shallow NN model. The NN process workflow is schematically represented in Fig. 3. The procedure is similar to the DANN model, however the Neural Net module undergoes different parameter optimization technique.

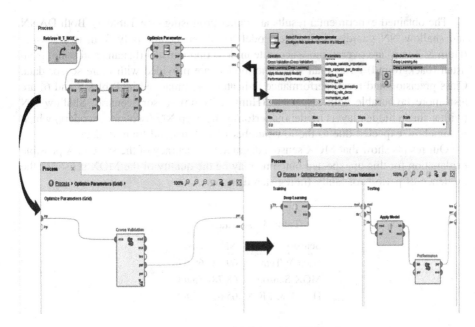

Fig. 2. DANN model fitting (RapidMiner)

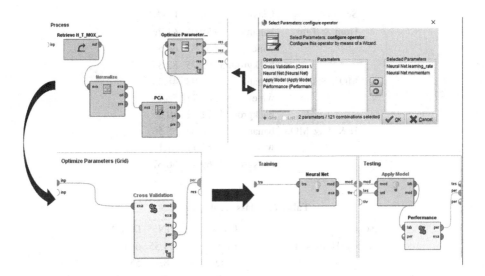

Fig. 3. Shallow NN model fitting (RapidMiner)

4.3 Experimental Results

The motivation behind the present study is to assess if the humidity and temperature sensors are sensitive to variations in the air composition and may account for changes in the air quality.

The obtained experimental results are rather promising (see Table 4). Both DANN and shallow NN gas discriminative model based on records only from two sensors (Hum & Temp) are overall more accurate in detecting unusual (banana and wine) from usual (background) gases than when the models are provided with more sensor data. Class precision and recall performance indicators (summarized in Tables 5 and 6) are also more favourable with respect to (Hum & Temp) sensor scenario. Shallow NN (with a single hidden layer) model outperforms the deep NN (two autoencoders) which is somehow expected due to the low number of features and training data.

Our results show that MOX sensors degrade the accuracy of the system. A possible explanation for this unexpected outcome may be the quality of the MOX sensor or the existence of periods of faulty (unregistered) states.

Table 4. Accuracy (%)

Sensors	NN	DANN
Hum & Tem	69.78	69.67
MOX Sensors	68.78	55.44
H & T & MOX	65.67	55.89

Table 5. Class precision (%)

Sensors	Class	NN	DANN
Hum & Tem	banana	58.06	61.76
	wine	58.33	64.52
	background	93.75	82.35
MOX Sens.	banana	68.98	48.39
	wine	65.71	58.45
	background	71.43	59.36
H & T & MOX	banana	66.67	55.56
	wine	61.11	51.11
	background	69.7	66.67

Table 6. Class recall (%)

Sensors	Class	NN	DANN
2 sensors (Hum & Tem)	banana	54.55	63.64
	wine	58.33	55.56
	background	100	93.33
8 MOX Sensors	banana	60.61	45.45
	wine	63.89	66.67
	background	71.43	53.33
10 sensors (H & T & 8 MOX)	banana	60.61	60.61
	wine	61.11	63.89
	background	76.67	40.00

5 Conclusion

Proper values of hydro-thermal parameters and good air quality are known to have a great influence on human health and comfort. Major efforts in the area of indoor air quality are focused into making our homes smart so that the healthy level of indoor air is automatically controlled.

In this paper we demonstrate that two widely available, in private houses, sensors are feasible to discriminate unusual gases from the usual house air composition. Humidity and Temperature sensors are a promising alternative to the expensive indoor air quality solutions provided with intelligent data analytics tools. Variations of the air composition due to new stimuli are encoded in trivial Hum & Temp readings and can be discriminated by a ML model trained to recognise the background home air composition.

We are aware that "wine" and "banana" are not widely accepted as typical stimuli to produce "unusual gases", however in the experimental scenario they have been selected as the new stimuli and the sensor recordings during their presence are labelled as anomaly.

For now, the proposed data analytics system is confident in binary discrimination between what has been learned as normal and abnormal home air composition. This research can be extended focusing on better recognition of various abnormal air states. Further to that considering more relevant unusual gas cases particularly those that may cause health risks is a research direction with high social impact.

Acknowledgements. This study has been done during the traineeship program of PhD student Petya Mihaylova in University of Aveiro funded by ERASMUS+EU programme for education, training, youth and sport, supported by technical University of Sofia, Bulgaria.

References

1. Mikuckas, A., et al.: A grey model approach to indoor air quality management in rooms based on real-time sensing of particles and volatile organic compounds. Appl. Math. Model. **42**, 290–299 (2017)
2. Jangid, S., Sharma, S.: An embedded system model for air quality monitoring. In: International Conference on Computing for Sustainable Global Development (INDIACom), pp. 303–308 (2016)
3. Clémenta, P., et al.: Gas discrimination using screen-printed piezoelectric cantilevers coated with carbon nanotubes. Sens. Actuators, B **237**, 1056–1065 (2016)
4. Fonollosaa, J., et al.: Human activity monitoring using gas sensor arrays. Sens. Actuators, B **199**, 398–402 (2014)
5. Szczurek, M.M., Flisowska-Wiercik, B.: Method of gas mixtures discrimination based on sensor array, temporal response and data driven approach. Talanta **83**, 916–923 (2011)
6. Penza, M., Gassano, G., Tortorella, F.: Gas recognition by activated WO_3 thin-film sensors array. Sens. Actuators, B **81**, 115–121 (2001)
7. Chen, P.-C., Ishikawa, F.N., Chang, H.-K., Ryu, K., Zhou, Ch.: A nanoelectronic nose: a hybrid nanowire/carbon nanotube sensor array with integrated micro-machined hotplates for sensitive gas discrimination. Nanotechnology **20**(12), 125503 (2009)

8. Huertaa, R., Mosqueiroa, T., Fonollosab, J., Rulkova, N.F., Rodriguez-Lujand, I.: Online decorrelation of humidity and temperature in chemical sensors for continuous monitoring. Chemo-metrics Intell. Lab. Syst. **157**, 169–176 (2016)
9. Huerta, R., Vembu, S., Amigó, J.M., Nowotny, T., Elkan, C.: Inhibition in multiclass classification. Neural Comput. **24**(9), 2473–2507 (2012)
10. Karpathy, A., Toderici, G., Shetty, S., Leung, T., Sukthankar, R., Fei-Fei, L.: Large-scale video classification with convolutional neural networks. In: Computer Vision and Pattern Recognition (2014)
11. Krizhevsky, A., Sutskever, I.G., Hinton, E.: Imagenet classification with deep convolutional neural networks. In: Advances in Neural Information Processing Systems (2012)
12. Hinton, G., Osindero, S., The, Y.-W.: A fast learning algorithm for deep belief nets. Neural Comput. **18**, 1527–1554 (2006)
13. Bozhkov, L., Koprinkova-Hristova, P., Georgieva, P.: Learning to decode human emotions with Echo State Networks. Neural Networks **78**, 112–119 (2016)
14. Bozhkov, L., Koprinkova-Hristova, P., Georgieva, P.: Reservoir computing for emotion valence discrimination from EEG signals. Neurocomputing **231**, 28–40 (2017)
15. UCI Machine Learning Repository: Data Sets. https://archive.ics.uci.edu/ml/datasets.html

Video Signal Recovery from the Smartphones Touchscreen LCD Display

Bogdan Trip[1(✉)], Vlad Butnariu[1], Alexandru Boitan[1],
and Simona Halunga[2]

[1] The Special Telecommunications Service Bucharest, Bucharest, Romania
bogdan.tripc@gmail.com
[2] Telecommunications Department, University Politehnica of Bucharest,
Bucharest, Romania

Abstract. In this paper we present several examples of video signal recovery from electromagnetic emissions generated by smartphones touchscreens as well as a number of measurements results performed in a specialized laboratory. We aimed the identification of the video signal parameters by using video images that were especially selected to facilitate this process. The measurements were performed by comparing two smartphones that have different display resolutions. In the final part we will also present a method to identify the emission frequencies for these compromising emanations.

Keywords: Smartphones · Touchscreen · Video signal · Recovery ·
TEMPEST · Compromising · Emanations

1 Introduction

The technological advances of recent years are reflected, among other things, in the exponential evolution of technologies used in the mobile phone industry. From the 90's, mobile communication systems evolved through several standards, from 2G - GSM to 3G - UMTS, 4G - LTE and now the 5G standard is under development. The size and complexity of the applications that can be run from a mobile terminal evolved too. While the first models of mobile phones had a 1.5 in. screen with a resolution of 84×48 pixels or even lower, today they have a size of 6.2 in. and a Full HD resolution of 2960×1440 pixels. Also, if at the beginnings the mobile phones were used only for voice and small rate data applications, today one can use such terminals for high-resolution images or high definition video (HD) transfer, but also for high security demanding applications like bank transactions or fulfilling various complex tasks imposed by the companies we work for. At this point we have come to handle a lot of information through our mobile devices and some of this information can be sensitive and important to us or to our companies. For this reason we have to discuss the issue of ensuring the confidentiality of the manipulated information that belongs to us or the employing companies.

Like any other electronic equipment, smartphones generate electromagnetic radiation. Before entering the market, they are generally tested for Electromagnetic Compatibility (EMC) compliance. In addition, they are also tested for Specific

© ICST Institute for Computer Sciences, Social Informatics and Telecommunications Engineering 2019
Published by Springer Nature Switzerland AG 2019. All Rights Reserved
V. Poulkov (Ed.): FABULOUS 2019, LNICST 283, pp. 89–95, 2019.
https://doi.org/10.1007/978-3-030-23976-3_9

Absorption Rate (SAR) levels for health reasons, and efforts have been made to reduce this parameter significantly during the last few years. The EMC rules and regulations [1] require that all electronic equipment should be checked so that the radiation emitted by the tested equipment should not interfere with the proper functionality of the electronic equipment in its vicinity. However, commercial electronic equipment is not tested also in terms of confidentiality of processed information and identifying the risk level of compromising information and, therefore, this task is analyzed in the TEMPEST domain. The TEMPEST regulations [2] study that part of electromagnetic emissions from which the information transmitted or processed by electronic equipment can be extracted. These electromagnetic radiations are called Compromising Emanations (CE), as they can compromise the information in question. The TEMPEST protection procedures have been presented in detail in [3, 4].

One of the most dangerous CE, is the one radiated by video display units and was first reported by van Eck [5]. Markus Kuhn has treated for a long time the risk of cathode ray tube (CRT) [6] and liquid crystal display (LCD) units [7] while in [8] the authors presented the possibility of measuring the CE from power conductors in the 100–1000 MHz range. Recent research has analyzed CE from the High Definition Multimedia Interface (HDMI) [9] by using simple display signals such as two black-and-white vertical stripes evenly spaced on the monitor screen while in [10] the CE level is analyzed by using a TEMPEST FSET22 receiver and presents the comparative results between the Video Graphics Array (VGA) interface and Digital Visual Interface (DVI). In [11] are presented for the first time examples of video signal recovery from small displays such as the 4.3 (in.) LCD display of a laser printer.

This paper is structured in six sections, as follows. Section 2 presents the measuring equipment, the test-bed as well as the devices under test (DUT). In Sect. 3, a method of detecting CE emission frequencies is exemplified while in Sect. 4 is presented the results of time domain measurements for the analyzed video signal. Section 5 illustrates some examples of video signal recovery and Sect. 6 contains the several interesting conclusions based on the results obtained.

2   Measurement Test-Bed

In our research we used a TEMPEST FSET22 receiver, an active AM524 antenna system and a Tektronix MSO5204B oscilloscope. The tested devices were two smart phones produced by two well-known companies, LG K4 (model 2016) and Samsung J5 (model 2015). All the tests were carried out in a TEMPEST specialized laboratory that is equipped with a semi-anechoic chamber.

The tested devices were placed, one by one, at a distance of 1 m from the receiving antenna, inside the testing room, according to MIL STD 461F military EMC standard. The rest of the measuring chain was placed outside the testing chamber to avoid possible influences that could interfere with the results.

3 CE Detection

In the first phase of the experimental part, we considered it useful to perform several frequency sweeps in order to be able to discover the frequency ranges in which the compromising signal is present. Thus, we chose as test message, an image consisting in three thin horizontal bars of equal size followed by a thick one.

The image was displayed on the screen of the two DUT's, resulting in two waveforms. In order to get a reference to compare them with, we choose to shut down the screens of the two phones and make a new set of sweeps, which are, further, considered as references. In the beginning of CE detection, we performed several tests in the whole frequency range, from 2 MHz to 1 GHz and we decided to focus our attention on the 30 ÷ 200 MHz subrange using a Resolution Bandwidth (RBW) of 2 MHz, respectively a Sweep Time (ST) of 35 milliseconds (ms). The receiver performs the frequency sweeps by dragging the capture filter (RBW) from the starting frequency to the end of the sweep range and the ST parameter signifies how long it stays in place at each slide. As the tested DUT has a declared refresh rate of 60 Hz, it results that the video signal has a period of 16.6 ms = 1/(60 Hz). The ST parameter was chosen to be longer than the video signal period to ensure that the CE will be detected. In Fig. 1 are shown the sweep results obtained using the LG K4 smartphone as testing device and in Fig. 2 are the ones obtained with the Samsung J5 device.

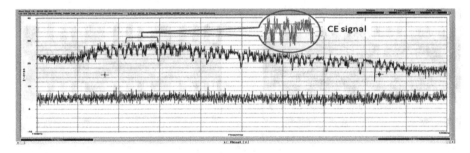

Fig. 1. CE detection for LG K4 smartphone, 110 ÷ 120 MHz

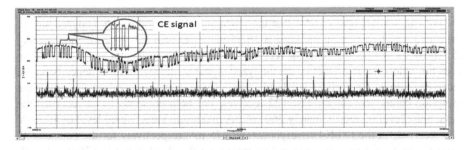

Fig. 2. CE detection for Samsung J5 smartphone, 30 ÷ 50 MHz

Thus, the upper waveform in the figures above represents the compromising signal and the lower one is the reference. For the LG K4 smartphone we chose to illustrate the 110 ÷ 120 MHz sub-range as the difference between the CE signal and the reference is the most significant, while for the Samsung J5 smartphone this is true for the 30 ÷ 50 MHz sub-range.

Also, we can notice that in Fig. 1 the CE signal is not received across the entire frequency range, such as 110–111 MHz and 119–120 MHz, and thus illustrates the result of the CE signal detection process.

4   Time Domain Measurements

The properties of video display signal were detailed in [11], as well as the difficulties encountered in detecting and visualizing the CE signal in order to assess the level classification according to the limits specified in [2], which is considered as classified information ("NATO Confidential").

Regarding this, measurements have been made to reveal the time parameters of video display signal for the smartphones that have been tested. We used the same test signal described in Sect. 3, and, as receiver, an oscilloscope that takes the analog signal after the 21.4 MHz intermediate frequency output of the FSET22 receiver. In Figs. 3 and 4 are presented the received signals for the two devices under test.

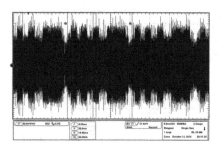

Fig. 3. Video frame period of 16.65 ms - LG K4 (3 thin bars and 1 thick bar)

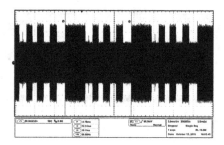

Fig. 4. Video frame period of 16.7 ms - Samsung J5 (3 thin bars and 1 thick bar)

We can see in Figs. 3 and 4 that the video signal's period of the analyzed signal, measured with two vertical markers, is 16.65 ms for LG K4 and 16.7 ms for Samsung J5. The oscilloscope is used as the receiver's time domain projection and in conclusion does not reflect the real level of the analyzed signal as the signal level depends on the receiver settings. Capturing signals via oscilloscope was done without changing the reception parameters for the FSET22 receiver. For both equipments we recorded the same noise level of approximately 360 mV. A maximum video signal level of 450 mV was received for the LG K4 smartphone and 675 mV respectively for the Samsung J5 smartphone. So we recorded a signal to noise ratio (SNR) of 20lg (450/360) = 1.9 dB for the LG K4 phone and 20lg (675/360) = 5.4 dB for Samsung J4 model.

5   Video Signal Recovery

In this section we tried to recover the image displayed on the two smartphones only based on the radiated CE. In Fig. 5 we obtained an intelligible image reconstructed from the CE radiation of the LG K4 smartphone. We observe that the image is still intelligible, even though is affected by noise. The "TEMPEST" message, written with a font size of 24, has the last letter "T" almost completely covered by noise. With further signal processing of the received signal, a much clear signal might have been obtained. In Fig. 6 we have another situation, this time a very clear image recovered from the CE radiation of Samsung J5. In this figure we can see the "TEMPEST" message, written with a font size of 48, 24, 16, 8 and also 4.

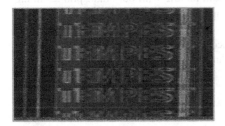

Fig. 5. Test message recovery for LG K4, on the 113 MHz reception frequency

Fig. 6. Test message recovery for Samsung J5, on the 31 MHz reception frequency

The video signal recovery examples, illustrated in Figs. 5 and 6, were performed under the same reception conditions, as described in Sect. 2. The differences in the images quality are given by the radiation differences of the CE signal existing between the two DUT's.

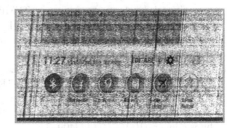

Fig. 7. LG K4 screensaver, 113 (MHz)

Fig. 8. Samsung J5 setting menu, 31 (MHz)

We have also performed some video signal recovery with no informational content such as the LG K4 screensaver on the 113 MHz frequency as shown in Fig. 7 and the Samsung J5 smartphone menu on 31 MHz. In Fig. 8 we can also observe that the "Bluetooth" and "airplane" modes are active during the image recovery process.

6   Conclusions

We can conclude that it is possible to recover video display signal from the reception of CE radiation generated by smartphone touchscreens that are today on the free market. From the measurements results we can see that the Samsung J5 smartphone is more vulnerable to interception than the LG K4 smartphone since, in all the cases, the signal can be recovered by an unwanted intruder easier and with better accuracy.

This unexplored vulnerability imposed by the use of modern mobile phones, often replacing personal computers, should be taken as a warning signal.

Our research should be continued to estimate the propagation distances for this CE radiation or identifying possible countermeasures. We recommend minimizing our sensitive and important information that we should handle with our smart phones in an open space area or without electromagnetic propagation obstacles.

Acknowledgment. This work was supported by contract no. 5Sol/2017 within PNCDI III, Integrated Software Platform for Mobile Malware Analysis (ToR-SIM).

References

1. The Electromagnetic Compatibility Regulations 2016. http://www.legislation.gov.uk/uksi/2016/1091/pdfs/uksi_20161091_en.pdf. Accessed 15 June 2018
2. NATO Standard, SDIP-27/1: NATO TEMPEST Requirements and Evaluation Procedures (NATO CONFIDENTIAL), NATO Military Committee Communication and Information Systems Security and Evaluation Agency (SECAN) (2009)
3. Bîndar, V., Popescu, M., Crăciunescu, R.: Aspects of electromagnetic compatibility as a support for communication security based on TEMPEST evaluation. In: 10th International Conference on Communications - COMM 2014, Politehnica University of Bucharest, Military Technical Academy, Bucharest, pp. 529–532 (2014)
4. Popescu, M., Bărtuşică, R., Boitan, A., Marcu, I., Halunga, S.: Considerations on estimating the minimal level of attenuation in TEMPEST filtering for IT equipments. In: Third International Conference, FABULOUS 2017, Bucharest, Romania, pp. 9–15 (2018)
5. van Eck, W.: Electromagnetic radiation from video display units: an eavesdropping risk? Comput. Secur. 4(4), 269–286 (1985)
6. Kuhn, M.G.: Compromising emanations: Eavesdropping risks of computer displays. https://www.cl.cam.ac.uk/techreports/UCAM-CL-TR-577.pdf. Accessed 20 June 2018
7. Kuhn, M.G.: Electromagnetic eavesdropping risks of flat-panel displays. In: Martin, D., Serjantov, A. (eds.) PET 2004. LNCS, vol. 3424, pp. 88–107. Springer, Heidelberg (2005). https://doi.org/10.1007/11423409_7
8. Sekiguchi, H., Seto, S.: Measurement of computer RGB signals in conducted emission on power leads. Prog. Electromagn. Res. C 7, 51–64 (2009)
9. Przesmycki, R.: High definition multimedia interface in the process of electromagnetic infiltration. In: PIERS Proceedings 2015/The 36th Progress in Electromagnetics Research Symposium, pp. 1173–1177 (2015)

10. Przesmycki, R., Nowosielski, L.: Compromising emanations from VGA and DVI interface. In: The 37th Progress in Electromagnetics Research Symposium (PIERS), pp. 1024–1028 (2016)
11. Boitan, A., Bărtuşică, R., Halunga, S., Bîndar, V.: Video signal recovery from the laser printer LCD display. The paper had been presented at ATOM-N 2018, The 9th edition of the International Conference on Advanced Topics in Optoelectronics, Microelectronics and NanotechnologiesConstanta, Romania, 23–26 August 2018 (proceeding still under publishing)

Low Power Wide Area Networks Operating in the ISM Band- Overview and Unresolved Challenges

Viktor Stoynov[✉], Vladimir Poulkov, and Zlatka Valkova-Jarvis

Technical University of Sofia, 8 Kl. Ohridski Street, Sofia, Bulgaria
{vstoynov, vkp, zvv}@tu-sofia.bg

Abstract. Today the Internet of Things connects millions of devices around the world, offering access to new services and technology development capabilities. The use of multiple small-sized sensors makes it possible to control and manage different processes in a new, intelligent and flexible way. In this paper a survey of Low Power Wide Area Networks operating in the ISM band is conducted, examining future development trends, major challenges and applications. Using this type of network it becomes possible to transmit information over very long distances, minimize the energy used and deploy huge quantities of sensors over large geographical areas. This paper also presents an overview of RF Data Analytics as a modern technique to enhance the network performance of LPWANs. This can be achieved by examining raw RF data in order to predict the trends that characterise it and subsequently to implement a range of methods and algorithms for interference management and intelligent spectrum utilisation.

Keywords: IoT · LPWAN · WSN

1 Introduction

Thanks to advances in wireless communications, sensors and machine intelligence, the Internet of Things (IoT) is rapidly becoming a reality. In IoT, physical objects can be managed remotely so that they act as access points for various Internet services. However there is still no wireless technology appropriate for all possible scenarios and applications of IoT. Until a comprehensive solution emerges, the industry is focussing on creating solutions that meet the needs of specific market segments. Currently, many hands-on systems use existing cellular technologies. Due to the power requirements of cellular modems and the fact that when operating in continuous mode they consume large amounts of energy, they do not have sufficient long-term battery power to provide the necessary capability for large intelligent sensor networks to process data from measuring devices. Therefore, new wireless technologies, some of them nearing implementation, are being developed.

LPWANs are used for delay-tolerant cases, when high data rates are not required but low power consumption and low cost of infrastructure are of great importance. In this area, the LPWAN technologies meet the needs of many applications for smart cities, smart metering, home automation, wearable electronics, logistics, environmental

V. Poulkov (Ed.): FABULOUS 2019, LNICST 283, pp. 96–109, 2019.
https://doi.org/10.1007/978-3-030-23976-3_10

monitoring, etc. In these cases an exchange of small amounts of data is needed and the data rates necessary for reliable communication are very low, which is the main reason why LPWAN technologies have attracted serious interest in the past few years.

The interference and the significant attenuation of the signals are two classic problems in the ISM range used by LPWANs. Along with the interference caused by heterogeneous and homogeneous devices, ISMs also suffer from interference due to coexistence and proximity to other networks. This interference, together with many other problems related to ISM's dynamic nature, can dramatically reduce the quality of service (QoS). Many of the studies have analysed the impact of interference but there is still a need for more in-depth research to study the peculiarities of transmitting signals, channel features and parameters. Interference largely depends on how different technologies coexist. A real challenge is the analysis of different IEEE 802.11 Wireless Local Area Network (WLAN) implementation scenarios operating in one frequency range with non-orthogonal carrier frequencies. In this case, interference management and spectrum utilisation may be accomplished by the development of a cloud architecture for a spectrum monitoring network where the collection, preservation and processing of RF signals or I/Q data in the baseband, as well as the processing of signals and protocols from the higher levels, are carried out entirely in the cloud.

In this paper, an overview of the most important LPWAN technologies is presented with a focus on their basic characteristics, major applications and susceptibility to interference. In addition, a review of RF Data Analytics is also conducted. The latter is an excellent starting point for the development of new resourceful algorithms for spectrum utilisation analysis and hence for more efficient use of the available spectrum, better interference management and transmission quality management.

2   Low Power Wide Area Networks Operating in the ISM Band

LPWAN is gaining increased popularity in industrial and research communities because of its low power, low-cost communication characteristics and long-range communication capabilities: around 10–40 km in rural zones and 1–5 km in urban zones [1]. In addition, these networks are highly energy efficient (up to 10 or more years of battery lifetime) and low-cost, at around the cost of a radio chipset [2]. These promising aspects of LPWANs have encouraged recent experimental studies on their performance in outdoor and indoor environments. LPWANs are highly suitable for IoT applications that need to transmit only small amounts of data but over long distances. Until recently, until 2013, the term "LPWAN" did not even exist. At present, many LPWAN technologies have sprung up in both the licensed and unlicensed frequency ranges. Among them are today's leading LPWAN technologies such as: SigFox, LoRa, and NB-IoT which, apart from individual innovations, also include many technical differences.

The LPWAN technologies being standardised by 3GPP possess several characteristics that make them especially attractive for market devices and applications requiring low mobility and low levels of data transfer:

- *Low power consumption* (to the range of nanoamps) that are required to operate without battery replacement;
- *Optimised data transfer* (supporting small, intermittent blocks of data);
- *Low device unit cost* - the simplicity of LPWAN end-devices makes these networks economically viable;
- *Simplified network topology and deployment* – LPWANs use: (a) narrowband to support a massive number of devices to efficiently utilize the limited spectrum; (b) multiple antenna systems to enable the base stations (BS) to support large numbers of nodes; (c) massively parallel communications in both directions using single antenna systems, thus providing opportunities to scale.
- *Improved outdoor and indoor penetration coverage* compared to existing wide area technologies;
- *Secured connectivity and strong authentication*;

Unlike traditional Wireless Sensor Networks (WSNs) that usually employ mesh topology, the state-of-the-art LPWAN technologies require the setting up of gateways, referred to as concentrators or BSs, to serve end-devices, i.e. end-devices communicate directly to one or more gateways. Depending on the technology, the coverage area of a single gateway may range from hundreds of meters to tens of kilometres and may include thousands or even millions of end-devices. Over the last few years, LPWAN technologies have drawn a lot of attention due to large investment from the private sector.

2.1   LPWANs - Overview and Comparison

LoRaWAN - LoRa Wide Area Networks are a low power specification for IoT devices operating in regional, national or global networks. It is frequency-agnostic and can use the 433, 868 or 915 MHz bands in the ISM (industrial, scientific and medical) range, depending on the region in which it is located. LoRa is the physical layer or wireless modulation that is used to implement a long distance communication link. Data transmission speeds vary from 0.3 kbps to 50 kbps, depending on whether channel aggregation is used. The standard LoRa operates in the 868 MHz (EU)/915 MHz (US) frequency range, at a distance of 2–5 km (urban environment) and up to 15 km (suburban), with a transmission speed not higher than 50 kbps. The advantage of the technology is the ability to achieve long distance connections, with a single base station having the capability to cover hundreds of square kilometres. The size of the covered range is highly dependent on the environment and the presence of obstacles, but LoRa and LoRaWAN have the best power supply organisation when compared to any other standardized communication technology [3].

SigFox - SigFox is a low power wireless communication technology for a diverse range of low-energy objects, such as sensors and M2M applications that send relatively little data. SigFox allows the realization of sensor networks that can run on batteries for several years. It resembles the cellular networks used by mobile operators, but instead of offering services for customers who need a high bandwidth, low jitter and high rate, SigFox provides services to devices. Therefore, the advantages of cellular networks are combined with lower energy consumption and lower cost. A SigFox network consists of cells, each with a gateway that communicates with sensors. It enables the transfer of small amounts of data at distances up to 50 km. Presently there increasing interest in such low power networks that work longer, as they are especially suited for battery-powered devices. SigFox works at the 868 MHz frequency bands in Europe and 915 MHz in the USA, with ranges from 3–10 km (urban), up to 50 km (rural) and provides transmission rates up to 100 bps. SigFox uses the Binary Phase Shift Keying (BPSK) modulation in an ultra-narrow (100 Hz) SUB-GHZ ISM band carrier. Nowadays SigFox works as a bidirectional technology, although with significant link asymmetry [4]. The downlink communication must be accomplished before the uplink communication, then the end-device must wait for a response from the BS. The number and size of the messages over the uplink are limited to 140 12-byte messages per day. Radio access link is asymmetric, allowing transmission of only 48-byte messages per day over the downlink from the BSs to the end-devices. This means that acknowledging every uplink message is not supported. The reliability of the uplink communication can be improved by using time and frequency diversity as well as redundant transmissions. In addition, intelligent support for acknowledgements must be implemented in order to increase the overall network performance.

Weightless - Weightless is a wireless technology introduced by the Weightless Special Interest Group (SIP) [5]. The latter proposed three open LPWAN standards known as Weightless-W, Weightless-N, and Weightless-P. Weightless is based on cognitive radio (Weightless-N, and Weightless-P) and TV white-spaces (Weightless-W) which enable devices to utilize these bands as opportunistic users. Thus a mitigation of inter- and intra-network interference is achieved to the primary user devices, which are defined as licensed owners. Weightless-N is an ultra-narrow band (UNB) standard providing only one-way communication from end-devices to the BS. Thus a significant energy efficiency is achieved, especially when compared to the other Weightless standards. However, Weighless-N has a very limited range of use cases. It uses differential binary phase-shift keying (DBPSK) modulation scheme in Sub-GHz bands. Weightless-P is based on two-way communication with two non-proprietary physical layers. It is based on the widely-used Gaussian minimum shift keying (GMSK) and Quadrature Phase Shift Keying (QPSK) and thus the end-devices do not require a proprietary chipset. Each single 12.5 kHz narrow channel in the SUB-GHZ ISM band offers a data rate in the range of 0.2 kbps to 100 kbps. Weightless-P eliminates the drawback of SigFox and offers full support for acknowledgments and bidirectional communication capabilities, enabling over-the-air upgrades of firmware. Similarly to LoRaWAN, the three Weightless standards employ symmetric key cryptography for the authentication of end-devices and integrity of application data.

DASH7 - the DASH7 Alliance Protocol is a new form of wireless transmission, like Wi-Fi, Bluetooth or ZigBee. DASH7 is the name of the technology promoted by the non-profit consortium named the DASH7 Alliance. Unlike most radio-frequency identification (RFID) technologies, DASH7 offers Tag-to-Tag communication which, combined with a long range and the benefits of 433 MHz signal propagation, makes it an easy substitute for most wireless sensors. DASH7 also supports midrange connectivity for low power sensors [6]. DASH7 communication is based on a narrow band modulation scheme using two-level Gaussian frequency-shift keying (GFSK) in Sub-GHz bands. Compared to other LPWAN technologies, DASH7 has a number of distinguishing differences: the usage of a tree topology by default with an option to also choose star layout; the end-devices are connected to duty-cycling sub-controllers, which then communicate to the BSs, which are always in active mode. The duty-cycling mechanism brings more complexity to the design of the upper layers. Also, the DASH7 media access control (MAC) protocol forces the end-devices to periodically check the channel for possible downlink transmissions, thus adding significant complexity. This results in lower latency for downlink communication compared to other LPWAN technologies but at the expense of higher energy consumption. Moreover, DASH7 defines a complete network stack, enabling applications and end-devices to communicate with each other without having to deal with the intricacies of the underlying physical or MAC layers. DASH7 supports forward error correction and symmetric key cryptography.

Ingenu RPMA - formerly known as On-Ramp Wireless, Ingenu RPMA is a proprietary LPWAN technology which utilizes the 2.4 GHz ISM band (as used by Wi-Fi and Bluetooth), unlike LoRa and SigFox which exploit the 915 MHz ISM band. Thus Ingenu RPMA leverages more relaxed regulations on spectrum use across different regions [7]. For example, the regulations in the USA and Europe do not impose a maximum limit on the duty-cycle for the 2.4 GHz band, enabling higher throughput and more capacity than other technologies operating in the Sub-GHz band. Ingenu RPMA uses star network topology with access nodes (BSs) that act as endpoint coordinators. The end-devices communicate with nodes using a patented Random Phase Multiple Access (RPMA) Direct Sequence Spread Spectrum (DSSS), which is distinguishes them from their competitors. RPMA is only used for transmitting data in the uplink - from the sensor to the BS - whereas a conventional code-division multiple access (CDMA) algorithm is used for the downlink. RPMA provides a better signal-to-noise ratio (SINR) than CDMA, but is also vulnerable in terms of security. RPMA enables multiple transmitters to share a single time slot. However, RPMA first increases the time slot duration of traditional CDMA and then scatters the channel access within this slot by adding a random offset delay for each transmitter. By not granting channel access to the transmitters exactly at once (i.e., at the beginning of a slot), RPMA reduces overlapping between transmitted signals and thus increases SINR for each individual link. On the receiving side, demodulators are used by the BSs in order to decode signals arriving at different times within a slot. Ingenu RPMA is based on bidirectional communication, although with a slight link asymmetry. For downlink communication, BSs spread the signals for individual end-devices and then broadcast them using CDMA. RPMA is reported to achieve up to -142 dBm receiver sensitivity and 168 dB link budget. It is possible to mitigate the interference to nearby devices by adjusting the transmit power of the end-devices. RPMA technology is compliant with the IEEE 802.15.4 k specifications.

Telensa – The Telensa protocol can provide fully bidirectional communication for LPWAN applications incorporating fully designed vertical network stacks with support for integration with third party software [8]. Telensa aims to standardize its technology using ETSI Low Throughput Networks (LTN) specifications for easy integration within applications. Telensa uses the UNB modulation technique, which operates in the licence-free Sub-GHz ISM band at low data rates. A Telensa BS can connect to up to 5000 nodes, and cover 2 km in urban and 4 km in rural areas. The Telensa nodes can continue their functioning even if the connection to their BS is lost, and have an estimated lifetime of 20 years. Telensa currently focuses on a few smart city applications such as intelligent lighting, smart parking, etc. Moreover, it supports integration with third-party applications by providing smart city application programming interfaces (API). Telensa have already deployed millions of nodes over 50 smart city networks globally, mostly in the United Kingdom but also in other cities around the world such as Shanghai, Moscow and Sao Paolo. The Telensa technology does not support indoor communications, which is its significant drawback.

2.2 LPWANs Major Applications

LPWANs can be found in almost all areas of the Business and Industrial sectors, as well as in other sectors such as Communal Living, Service, Science and Education, and others. The foremost application of LPWANs is in the Smart City, one example of such an application being Waste Management and another Smart Lighting, which not only substantially lowers street-lighting costs by varying the intensity of the lighting in accordance with the needs of the environment but also, through fault monitoring, reduces maintenance costs. Connected Vehicles are another example of a specific application; most newer vehicles have networking capability and come equipped with processors and sensors. IoT is able to use these to provide an improved driving experience through such factors as improved road sharing, accident reporting, parking detection etc. Transportation and Logistics applications need the support of factors such as long-range communications, low power, low cost and mobility. The Healthcare area is yet another major market for LPWAN applications; remote health monitoring being one example, etc. At present, the Healthcare sector has seen the widespread adoption of short range wireless technologies such as ZigBee, WiFi, 6LowPAN, together with cellular technologies such as LTE. However, these technologies will not scale due to the increase in the number of sensors giving rise to interference. Attention has therefore now focussed on LPWANs as an alternative communication solution for Healthcare applications due to the high cost of cellular technologies and the limitations of short-range wireless ones.

2.3 LPWANs Unresolved Challenges

Being in the stage of intensive development, LPWANs have a number of problems to solve. Some of them already have solutions but these are not efficient enough, while the solutions of others are still under development and yet other problems have still not been addressed.

Furthermore, there are major challenges of LPWANs which are not as yet satisfactorily resolved, in brief:

Penetration - some applications necessitate the location of the end node inside a building or underground, while the access point may be in another room or outside and above ground. In these applications network range can be considerably reduced by the absorption of walls, soil, etc. Such absorption is frequency-dependent, with lower frequencies generally offering better penetration than higher ones.

Short message handling - some IoT applications need to send substantial amounts of data frequently, while for others it is enough to send only brief messages, often infrequently. The ability of a wireless network to handle short messages efficiently can have a beneficial effect on the network's scalability and the end node's energy consumption. Such handling includes any overhead for the connection setup, interrogation, acknowledgement, and the like.

Bidirectional communications - some end nodes only report data and do not receive commands, so a unidirectional link is adequate for such applications. A bidirectional link, however, provides additional service attributes such as: handshaking with the access point to improve the reliability of data transfers, authentication exchanges for greater security, and sufficient bandwidth for remote software updates and the management of end nodes.

Secure communications - sensitive data needs a secure communications link between end node and access point but, even if the data is not sensitive, security may still be a concern. Without a secure link, an IoT application is more vulnerable to attacks such as spoofing, where a fraudulent end node injects false data into the network or a fraudulent access point hijacks end node data.

Higher level services - a wide-area IoT networking alternative can define any number of levels in the OSI model, from physical and data link layers through to application layers. In some cases the network itself is operated and managed by a service provider that leases users the time to run their network protocols and provides users with cloud services. Other alternatives define the lower layers only and have their access points connected to the Internet or to a private network, leaving the higher OSI layers to the user's choice.

Inter-technology communication - with the rapid growth of LPWAN technologies, the amount of coexisting LPWANs in the same geographical area increases and inter-network coordination becomes an important issue. A big challenge can arise when LPWANs from different vendors need to communicate with each other. Recently, cross-technology-communication (CTC) without additional hardware assistance has been studied for communication across WiFi, ZigBee, and Bluetooth devices. Future research is needed to enable CTC in LPWANs [9].

Increasing Density of LPWAN networks - coexistence challenges arise due to the increase in LPWAN technologies and the expanding deployment of gateways in urban areas. As a result of the random nature of access to the unlicensed bands and of its utilisation, co-existing gateways and a limited number of available channels raise questions about the performance achievable in isolated networks. The devising of coordination mechanisms between gateways from the same or different operators is indispensable if interference and collisions are to be eliminated. The necessary co-existence mechanisms must incorporate coordination and reconfiguration protocols for both gateways and end-devices.

Support for mobility - existing LPWAN technologies are not designed to support mobility, unlike cellular-based technologies, since they rely on wired infrastructure to handle mobility. However, wired infrastructure does not exist in rural environments, especially in remote areas (e.g. farms, oil fields, etc.) where cellular coverage is often weak or absent. The high cost of cellular service is also hindering the adoption of cellular technologies. Generally, support for mobility is quite a challenge for LPWANs and is not well-addressed as yet. Their performance is susceptible to even minor human mobility [10]. Technology-specific features of each LPWAN also make mobility issues such as base station discovery, handoff, and seamless communication quite difficult.

Support for high data rates - the typical data rate supported by LPWAN technologies ranges from 1–100 kbps. Narrowband communication offers long transmission range at the cost of low data rates. In the future, many IoT applications will evolve to include several use cases, such as video streaming, requiring very high data rates [11]. Different approaches to support high data rates in LPWANs should be investigated. Future research directions to enable high data rates include: support of different modulation techniques, borrowing different approaches used in technologies like WiFi, and designing new hardware to support multiple physical layers offering different data rates.

Adaptive power control - future LPWAN optimisation includes the investigation of the use of adaptive power control as a scalability feature. Adaptive power control is used to dynamically adapt the range of the transmissions, based on the distance between sender and receiver. This helps to significantly reduce the interference between stations, especially in densely deployed areas where a short transmission range is sufficient to reach the next hop.

Scheduling mechanisms - more research is needed to investigate the performance of intelligent and automated scheduling mechanisms in the context of long-range IoT networks with only one to a few hops and a variety of traffic patterns. Currently, many existing LPWAN MAC scheduling protocols are based on Carrier-Sense Multiple Access with Collision Avoidance (CSMA-CA) which requires very limited coordination between the access points and stations, and is very bandwidth efficient. However, as the number of the stations attempting to access the channel increases, so does the chance of collisions. This in turn increases the backoff timers and waiting times, causing highly degraded performance. In contrast, Time-Division Multiple Access (TDMA) -based MAC protocols avoid contention altogether. However, as the number of transmitting stations in the network grows, sending slot opportunities decrease, causing ever-growing latency.

Resource sharing and inter-LPWAN coordination - a next set of scalability improvements can be expected through resource sharing and inter-LPWAN coordination. The LPWANs all operate in unlicensed bands, allowing anyone to activate their own LoRaWAN or 802.15.4 network, for example. Considering a single LPWAN technology, this will result in a multitude of co-located networks without any coordination and consequently reduction in scalability due to interference. To share the resources, multiple networks need to cooperate, requiring cross-coordination to reduce interference between co-located single-technology LPWANs. So far, virtualization of wireless networks is focussed on 3GPP LTE and IEEE 802.11 [12]. Additional research is needed to design virtualization solutions and management techniques for LPWAN technology and to investigate the improvement in scalability that can be achieved by applying appropriate coordination mechanisms.

Technology co-existence and interference -as a great many separate networks are deployed in close proximity, mutual interference has to be controlled in order to maintain their operational status. At present, LPWANs are not geared up to handle this impending challenge, which will result in spectrum overcrowding. Existing studies of

LoRa, SigFox, and IQRF demonstrate that coexistence leads to severe performance degradation. The coexistence of four LoRa networks results in the throughput of each reducing to almost one. Current co-existence management for WiFi, existing WSN, Bluetooth does not transfer well to LPWANs as LPWAN devices, due to their large coverage domains, can be subject to an unparalleled number of hidden terminals. Great challenges arise when it comes to enabling the co-existent of different technologies on the same spectrum, due to entities owning so many varying examples. One avenue of research is the detection and identification of other technologies by the use of spectrum information, which can be achieved through the use of an efficient spectrum sensing method or dedicated hardware combined with machine learning techniques to identify those technologies which may be interfering [13].

Interference can be categorised as Inter-network Interference (IrnI) or Intra-network Interference (IanI) when the presence of different networks is being considered. The transmissions in the first category are generated by sensors from two or more different LPWANs. Spectrum sensing, radio environment maps or a spectrum occupancy database are all possible approaches to IrnI mitigation. Interference generated between sensors belonging to the same LPWAN is called IanI, or self-interference. Mitigation of this type of interference can be achieved through collision-recovery and collision-avoidance schemes. There are two known types of IrnI: homogeneous (HoI) and heterogeneous (HeI), the former occurring when two or more networks are utilising the same radio technology and the latter when, for example, different modulation schemes are used [14].

Some approaches to spectrum utilisation monitoring and interference identification used to decrease the negative impact of technology co-existence in LPWANs are discussed in the following section: RF Data Analytics.

An important element for efficient spectrum sharing, resource management and interference management is spectrum monitoring. It is generally agreed that spectrum monitoring should be long-term, ideally permanent; it should also be deployed in major markets and locations, and primarily be focused lower than 3 GHz. The amount of data produced is also agreed to be one of the challenges of spectrum monitoring. In general terms, the measurement and control of technical parameters of radio emissions, collecting spectrum occupancy information, and identification and location of sources of harmful interferences are the problems facing radio frequency (RF) spectrum monitoring. In order to achieve effective dynamic resource allocation, proper approaches to spectrum management are required. These in turn need information about past and present spectrum occupancy, together with information about future spectrum occupancy. An ability to predict variations in spectrum availability is likewise very desirable. Long-term continuous spectrum monitoring provides valuable historical information about spectrum usage, which provides a basis upon which to train an algorithm to predict the future profile of the spectrum. In addition, spectrum holes can be identified and operating frequency bands dynamically assigning to secondary users based on the results of the statistical processing of spectrum availability data.

An infrastructure that can support scalable spectrum data collection, transfer and storage is the first requirement for a spectrum monitoring framework. The end-devices will be required to perform distributive spectrum sensing in order to obtain a detailed overview of the spectrum use over a wide frequency range and to cover the area of interest. The predictive models can be pushed to the end-devices themselves so as to limit the data overhead caused by the vast quantities of I and Q samples generated by the monitoring devices. Electrosense, an initiative using low-cost sensors for large-scale spectrum monitoring in different regions of the world, offering the processed spectrum data as open data was recently proposed [15]. Having access to large datasets is crucial to the evaluation of research advances and to allow wireless communication researchers interested in the field to both acquire a deeper knowledge of spectrum usage and obtain valuable information that can be used to design improved wireless communication systems.

The diversity of technologies operating in different radio bands necessitates the continuous monitoring of multiple frequency bands, causing the volume and velocity of radio spectrum data to be several orders of magnitude higher than the typical data in other wireless communication systems such as WSNs (temperature, humidity reports, etc.). The handling of such a large volume of data, and the extraction of meaningful information across the entire spectrum, requires the design and implementation of a scalable platform to process, analyse and learn from big spectrum. There is therefore a need for efficient data processing and storage systems and algorithms for massive spectrum data analytics in order to extract valuable information from such data and incorporate it in real-time into the spectrum decision and policy process [16].

Inter-cell and cross-technology interference will be among the main communication challenges for 5G. In order to support spectrum decisions and policies in a system of such complexity, 5G networks require to support an architecture capable of flexible spectrum management. Radio-level softwarization will be one of the key enablers for flexible spectrum management, allowing as it does the automation of spectrum data collection, and the flexible control and reconfiguration of cognitive radio elements and parameters. Currently, there has been a growth in interest from academic and Industry circles in the application of Software Defined Networking (SDN) and Network Function Virtualization (NFV) to wireless networks [17]. Such initiatives as SoftAir, Cloud RAN, OpenRadio et al. are however only at the concept or prototype stage. In order to bring flexible spectrum management strategies into being there is still a lot of standardization work to be done. In addition, the spectrum will be monitored by a variety of different types of radio, such as WSNs, RFIDs and cellular phones and for these reasons, privacy must be assured at the spectrum data collection level.

2.4   RF Data Analytics

Thanks to both its expansion of the range of available data sources and its adoption of an approach based not only on quality of experience (QoE) but also on user-centricity, to the optimisation of end-to-end network performance, Data Analytics (DA) brings additional value to optimisation. One result of the widening of the data sources range is that analytics requires more work than standard optimisation, but its compensations include a unified, convergent platform for a multiplicity of optimisation targets. As well as providing traffic steering, network data analytics (NWDA), introduced by 3GPP (3rd Generation Partnership Project) automatically separates 3GPP and non-3GPP access analytics. An industry specification group, Experimental Network Intelligence (ENI), has been created by the European Telecommunications Standards Institute (ETSI) to define a cognitive network management architecture based on artificial intelligence (AI) techniques and context-aware policies. The ENI model assists MNOs to automate the process of network configuration and monitoring.

At present, RF data is regarded as being either time-domain baseband in-phase and quadrature (IQ), or frequency-domain (spectrum). RF data is produced using radio receivers that are able to cover a wide band but which operate in one narrowband at a time. The very high sampling rate requirement of IQ means that is usually appropriate for signals of short duration, this requirement having made the datafication of RF impractical for a long time. Nonetheless this has been something seen as extremely desirable and numerous platforms of generally-increasing capability to produce the so-called "digital IQ" have emerged. As regards spectrum data, the data rate is much lower and normally just an absolute value, obtained via long-term averaging, is retained.

Initially, regarding RF data as just "digital IQ" or spectrum data may appear to be sufficient. But, due to the absence of any information, such as location and centre frequency, about the RF signal this definition is inadequate, especially for RF data analytics. RF data is better defined as time-domain IQ data coupled with all of the metadata such as RF centre frequency, bandwidth, location etc. In this context additional signalling and service traffic must be considered as a major challenge. Likewise, spectrum values paired with metadata may be defined as RF spectrum data. It should be noted that "digital IQ" is not the same as the raw RF signal and thus correct interpretation cannot be achieved without knowledge of parameters such as the RF centre frequency and bandwidth. Such parameters are present, albeit implicitly, in a private cloud, thus leading to them being ignored in the past. When multiple data streams, generated by different types of devices, are present, such metadata cannot continue to be left implied and therefore must be both explicitly defined and paired through association with spectrum data or an IQ stream. Metadata can encompass a large variety of other parameters as well as bandwidth and RF centre frequency. These include antenna beamwidth, polarisation, location, time-stamp, noise, SNR, sampling frequency et al.

DA is made up of three types of data analysis [18]. The first, Descriptive Analysis (DesA), is a combination of Regression, Visualisation and Data Modelling. The purpose of these three steps is to ready the data for the ensuing analysis. Following data collection, a meaningful data representation is prepared, with the final step being the detection of a simple data trend. Spectrum monitoring for operation estimation is one illustration of such a descriptive RF DA service and application. In this instance the object of the monitoring is to commence from information about the systems known to be operational, then to supply spectrum management feedback, that is to say to close the loop by either providing confirmation that devices are operating in accordance with their authorise or showing evidence that they aren't. The architecture and platform under discussion here is able to realise this monitoring service in a more highly efficient way than currently deployed systems are capable of. For quite some time, spectrum usage was constant in terms of time, meaning that one-time measurement campaigns were essentially sufficient. However, the ever-increasing pressure for higher data rates and additional spectrum has resulted in increased complexity of the spectrum environment, meaning that in the future RF devices will be required to share spectrum. There is an increasing need for information on the efficiency of spectrum use, which clearly shows that one-time measurement of spectrum occupancy is no longer adequate. The technology of spectrum monitoring has progressed from one-time through long-term and on to a continuous capability which is no longer conducted using spectrum analysers but instead by specialised platforms.

Following completion of the DesA stage, a Predictive Analysis (PA), comprising Data Mining (DM) and Predictive Modelling (PM), is required. DM, the initial stage, extracts differing patterns from the totality of the collected data. The next step, PM, is aimed at trend recognition and the realization of different prediction techniques. Following completion of the PA the last step of DA is Prescriptive Analysis (PrA), the main objective of which is to use the preceding analysis for decision making and to optimize the entire process.

Two good examples of RF predictive and prescriptive analytics are interference identification and spectrum occupancy forecasting. PA aims to predict the future by developing models based on past data, using Machine Learning (ML) tools. [19] Introduces some of the emergent ML approaches employed as fundamental components of DA, together with an overview of a number of the issues in this field, while [20] presents an illustration of spectrum occupancy forecasting employing ML algorithms on RF data. This particular data was came from long-term spectrum monitoring at a Bulgarian airport traffic control station. It can be seen that the application of proper ML-based DA to the data obtained from long-term spectrum monitoring results in satisfactory forecasts more than 50% of the time.

Yet a further example of PA and PrA can be seen in the measurement results of [21], where the authors demonstrate an approach to the recognition of interference via the large-scale analysis of long term spectrum monitoring data. Unsupervised clustering-based ML analysis is used on long-term spectrum monitoring data to recognise and identify sources of electromagnetic (EM) emissions which adversely impact the performance of a mobile BS. The use of an appropriate RF DA approach is shown to be capable of detecting and identifying a specific type of interference caused by the so-called "ducting" effect in the uplink (UL) channel of a mobile BS.

The major requirements for RF DA is the long-term spectrum monitoring and the implementation of intelligent statistical techniques and ML algorithms. Moreover the RF DA platform must be characterized by high level of control and the ability of intelligent reconfiguration of radio parameters.

3   Conclusion

In this paper, the major applications and unresolved challenges of the most important LPWAN technologies operating in ISM band are presented. In order to enhance the network performance and susceptibility to interference of LPWANs a review of RF Data Analytics is also considered. We conclude that the implementation of the latter is obviously an excellent way to develop new intelligent algorithms for spectrum utilisation analysis and hence for more efficient use of the available spectrum, better interference management and transmission quality management.

In future work, development of models that can accurately describe the different spectrum utilization capabilities in the frequency and time domains aiming to create an energy efficient design of LPWANs is foreseen. Furthermore a research of the actual spectrum utilization in the ISM band across different scenarios and exploring approaches to the possible realization and implementation of mechanisms to provide more effective access to these resources will be considered.

Acknowledgement. This work was supported by Research Project D-054-2018 funded by the R&D&I Consortium of Sofia Tech Park, Bulgaria.

References

1. Centenaro, M., Vangelista, L., Zanella, A., Zorzi, M.: Long-range communications in unlicensed bands: the rising stars in the IoT and smart city scenarios. IEEE J. Wirel. Commun. **23**(5), 60–67 (2016)
2. Patel, D., Won, M.: Experimental study on low power wide area networks for mobile internet of things, In: Proceedings of VTC, pp. 1–5. Sydney, Australia (2017)
3. Cellular networks for massive IoT: Enabling low power wide area applications, Ericsson, Technical Report, January 2016, Ericsson White Paper. [Online]. https://www.ericsson.com/res/docs/whitepapers/wpiot.pdf
4. John Burns, P. M., Kirtay, S.: Future use of licence exempt radio spectrum. In: Plum Consulting, Technical Report 2015. http://www.plumconsulting.co.uk/pdfs/Plum July 2015 Future use of Licence Exempt Radio Spectrum.pdf
5. Weightless. http://www.weightless.org/
6. Weyn, M., Ergeerts, G., Berkvens, R., Wojciechowski, B., Tabakov, Y.: Dash7 alliance protocol 1.0: Low-power, mid-range sensor and actuator communication. In: 2015 IEEE Conference Standards for Communications and Networking (CSCN), pp. 54–59 (2015)
7. Rpma technology for the internet of things, Ingenu, Technical Report 2016. http://theinternetofthings.report/Resources/Whitepapers/4cbc5e5e-6ef8-4455-b8cd-f6e3888624cbRPMA%20Technology.pdf
8. Telensa (2017). https://www.telensa.com
9. Min Kim, S., He, T.: Freebee: cross-technology communication via free side-channel. In: MobiCom, ACM (2015)
10. Patel, D., Won, M.: Experimental study on low power wide area networks (LPWAN) for mobile internet of things. In: 2017 IEEE 85th Vehicular Technology Conference (VTC 2017 Spring) (2017)
11. Vasisht, D., Kapetanovic, Z., et al.: FarmBeats: an IoT platform for data-driven agriculture. In: 14th USENIX Symposium on Networked Systems Design and Implementation (NSDI 17), pp. 515–529 (2017)
12. Petajajarvi, J., Mikhaylov, K., Roivainen, A., Hanninen, T., Pettissalo, M.: On the coverage of LPWANs: Range evaluation and channel attenuation model for LoRa technology. In: Proceedings of the 14th International Conference on ITS Telecommunications (ITST), pp. 55–59, Denmark (2015)
13. Georgiou, O., Raza U.: Low power wide area network analysis: can lora scale? In: IEEE Wireless Communications Letters pp. 99, 1-1 (2017). ISSN: 2162-2337. https://doi.org/10.1109/lwc.2016.2647247
14. Stabellini, L.: Design of reliable communication solutions for wireless sensor networks. Licentiate Thesis in Radio Communication Systems Stockholm, Sweden (2009)
15. Liu, W., et al.: Heterogeneous spectrum sensing: challenges and methodologies. EURASIP J. Wireless Commun. Netw. **2015**, 70 (2015)

16. Zaslavsky, A., Perera, C., Georgakopoulos, D.: Sensing as a service and big data (2013). https://arxiv.org/abs/1301.0159

17. Kazaz, T., Van Praet, C., Kulin, M., Willemen, P., Moerman, I.: Hardware accelerated SDR platform for adaptive air interfaces. In: Proceedings Work- Shop Future Radio Technology (ETSI) Air Interfaces, pp. 1–26 (2016)

18. Khan, A., Rehmani, M., Rachedi, A.: Cognitive-radio-based Internet of Things: applications, architectures, spectrum related functionalities, and future research directions'. IEEE Wireless Commun. **24**(3), 17–25 (2017)

19. L' Heureux, A., Grolinger, K., Elyamany, H.F., Capretz, M.A.M.: Machine learning with big data: challenges and approaches. IEEE Access **5**, 7776–7797 (2017)

20. Baltiiski, P., Iliev, I., Kehaiov, B., Poulkov, V., Cooklev, T.: Longterm spectrum monitoring with big data analysis and machine learning for cloud-based radio access networks. Wirel. Personal Commun. **87**(3), 815–835 (2016)

21. Iliev, I., Bonev, B., Angelov, K., Petkov, P., Poulkov, V.: Interference identification based on long term spectrum monitoring and cluster analysis. In: Proceedings of the 2016 IEEE International Black Sea Conference on Communications and Networking, Varna, Bulgaria (2016)

Continuous Remote Ammonia Monitoring by Air Quality Measurement and Communication System

Rosen Miletiev[1(✉)], Ilia Iliev[1], Emil Iontchev[2], and Rumen Yordanov[3]

[1] Faculty of Telecommunication, Technical University of Sofia, Sofia, Bulgaria
miletiev@tu-sofia.bg
[2] High School of Transportation, Sofia, Bulgaria
[3] Faculty of Electronics, Technical University of Sofia, Sofia, Bulgaria

Abstract. The current paper represents the portable system for monitoring of air quality by detecting the concentrations of an ammonia gas based on compact MOS sensor. The presence of the ammonia gas in the outdoor or indoor air is very important for the human health and safety because it may be dangerous in high concentrations. The continuous monitoring of the This portable system is designed to meet the requirements of the health protection not only in the indoor environments but also in the urban, industrial and rural locations by continuous measurement and transmission of the data to the remote server for real-time analysis of the working space air. The paper discusses the calibration and test of the metal-oxide sensors due to the very wide range of the initial sensitive layer resistance and calculation of the ammonia gas concentration in the air.

Keywords: Ammonia measurement · Air quality measurement system

1 Introduction

Atmospheric ammonia (NH_3) has long been recognized as the key important air pollutant contributing to the human health [1]. It originates from both natural and anthropogenic sources, with the main source being agriculture, e.g. manures, slurries and fertilizer application. Also Ammonia (NH3) is a colorless gas with a characteristic pungent odor, which is a common precursor to fine particulate matter (PM2.5), making it an important consideration for PM-related health effects [2]. Primarily wet tissue (i.e. eyes, nose, and throat) irritation and damage are recognized as corneal and skin burns/blistering, intraocular pressure (glaucoma), coughing, pulmonary and laryngeal edema, chest pains, pinky/frothy sputum, etc. and it can be dangerous because there is no antidote for ammonia poisoning. Therefore the continuous ammonia monitoring also is important for security reasons and human health risks. OSHA has set an 8-h exposure limit of 25 ppm (25,000 ppb) and a 15 min exposure limit of 35 ppm (35,000 ppb) for ammonia in the workplace. The research arm of OSHA has recommended the ammonia level in a work room be no more than 50 ppm (50,000 ppb) per 5 min of exposure [3].

© ICST Institute for Computer Sciences, Social Informatics and Telecommunications Engineering 2019
Published by Springer Nature Switzerland AG 2019. All Rights Reserved
V. Poulkov (Ed.): FABULOUS 2019, LNICST 283, pp. 110–117, 2019.
https://doi.org/10.1007/978-3-030-23976-3_11

The mobile measurement of the air quality and gas concentrations is a very actual problem due to the great human mobility, pollution motion and the absence of measurement stations in most places especially for the closed spaces. The measurement data are sent via GSM/GPRS modem to the remote server but also may be transmitted to the located nearby devices via Bluetooth connection. The metal-oxide (MOX) sensors are widely used to measure the concentrations of the air pollutant gases. Their main advantages are recognized as low cost (around 10–15€ per sensor), long lifetime (>5 years), good sensitivity from mg/m^3 to $\mu g/m^3$, but also have some drawbacks - results are affected by temperature and humidity variations, long response time (5–50 min), output depends as well on history of past inputs and instability can be observed. Also in order to increase sensitivity the sensing layer needs to be heated to temperatures of at least 250 °C. Due to their small form factor, metal-oxide sensors are integrated in Internet of Things (IoT) devices and mobile platforms, but these sensors suffer from low selectivity and poor long-term stability. For example MICS-4514 sensor tests [4] shows good coefficient of determination values (0.76–0.78) with respect to reference measurements but the same models performed poorly during the 4.5 months validation phase with coefficient of determination values being less than 0.1.

The current paper discusses the short-term tests and calibration of the similar MOX sensors due to the very wide range of the initial sensitive layer resistance and calculation of the ammonia air concentrations.

2   System Description

Ambient air quality monitoring equipment includes gas detectors and portable and personal instruments that monitor ambient air in the workplace to help detect the presence of toxic vapors and gases. It is based on compact MOS sensor MiCS-6814 [5], which combines three independent sensing elements for ammonia, carbon oxide and nitrogen oxides on one package. Each sensor includes a heating circuit and sensing element (Fig. 1). The detecting layer changes its resistance according to the pollutant concentration. The sensing resistance in air varies from 10 to 1500 $k\Omega$ for the NH_3 sensor, therefore the sensor requires a calibration to measure the real concentrations.

The measurement and the communication device is described in our previous work [6] and consists of GPS receiver, GSM/GPRS modem and Bluetooth transceiver, power supply unit and user indication LEDs. The system microcontroller is based on PIC16F family (PIC16F1825) and has built-in I^2C interface as a part of Master synchronous serial port (MSSP) module and EUSART with an autobaud interface, which is connected to the GSM/GPRS modem with RTS/CTS hardware flow control. To meet the portable device requirements the measurement and the communication part may be powered by external power source via micro USB connector or by built-in Li-Ion battery with 900 or 1800 mAh capacity. As the external power source is connected the battery is charged by default. The charging current is set via an external resistor and its maximum value is equal to 500 mA. The power management chip employ a constant-current/constant-voltage charge algorithm and charge termination. Also the GPS receiver LDO chip has an enable input which is controlled via AT command by GSM/GPRS modem to switch off the GPS receiver to save power if GPS module is not needed or the device is stationary.

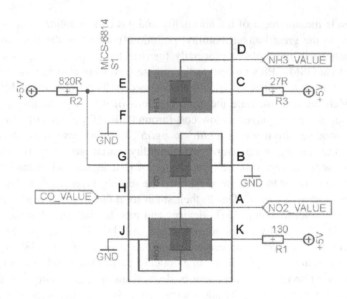

Fig. 1. Gas sensor [4]

3 System Calibration

Before the ammonia monitoring we have to calibrate the sensor data due to the high range fluctuation of the sensor resistance in air. The calibration is made in the environment of a pure nitrogen at normal temperature by measuring the sensing resistance R_0. When the sensor is exposed to the air the resistance is change to Rs value which corresponded to the gas concentration according to the Rs/R_0 to Concentration graphics (Fig. 2) [5].

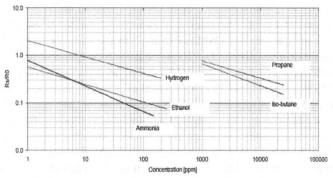

NH3 sensor, continuous power ON, 25°C, 50% RH

Fig. 2. Ratio Rs/R_0 as a function of concentration [5]

The sensing resistance Rs is converted to voltage using resistor divider and then the built-in in the microcontroller 10-bit ADC converts this voltage to a digital word (Fig. 3). The second resistor in the divider is chosen to be equal to $R_1 = R_0$ to guarantee the maximum amplitude response of the ammonia gas to the sensing element. The sensing resistance may be affected by the temperature, humidity and time [6], so the temperature also have to be measured and the calibration procedure have to be accomplished if an optimum accuracy is required.

According to the manufacturer curves [7], the gas concentration is calculated by the equation $lgY = a*lgX + b$, where X and Y denote the gas concentration in ppm and Rs/R_0 value respectively and a and b are constants. If we denote adc as the ADC digital word (resolution $N = 10$ bit) and $Uref$ as the ADC reference voltage, than the concentration Y_1 may be obtained from the data from the other concentration Y_0 which may be the calibration concentration according to the following calculations:

1/Calculate divider voltage $Uadc$ from the power supply voltage VCC and resistance of the sensing element and the second divider resistance R1 (Fig. 3) according to the manufacturer recommendations:

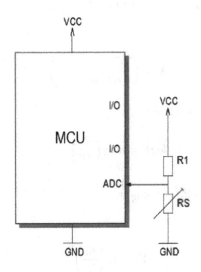

Fig. 3. MiCS-6814 sensor measurement circuit

$$Uadc = VCC.\frac{Rs}{Rs+R1} \tag{1}$$

$$Uadc = Uref.\frac{adc}{2^N} \tag{2}$$

Therefore:

$$\frac{Rs + R1}{Rs} = \frac{VCC}{Uref} \cdot \frac{2^N}{adc} \tag{3}$$

$$\frac{R1}{R0} = \left(\frac{Rs}{R0}\right) \cdot \left(\frac{VCC}{Uref} \cdot \frac{2^N}{adc} - 1\right) = const \tag{4}$$

2/According to Eq. (4) at two different concentrations Y_0 and Y_1:

$$\left(\frac{Rs}{R0}\right)_0 \cdot \left(\frac{VCC}{Uref} \cdot \frac{2^N}{adc_0} - 1\right) = \left(\frac{Rs}{R0}\right)_1 \cdot \left(\frac{VCC}{Uref} \cdot \frac{2^N}{adc_1} - 1\right) \tag{5}$$

Therefore:

$$\frac{\left(\frac{Rs}{R0}\right)_1}{\left(\frac{Rs}{R0}\right)_0} = \frac{K_0}{K_1} \tag{6}$$

where

$$K = \left(\frac{VCC}{Uref} \cdot \frac{2^N}{adc} - 1\right) \tag{7}$$

3/From the calibration equation

$$logY = alog\left(\frac{Rs}{R0}\right) + b$$

follows that $log\frac{Y_1}{Y_0} = alog\frac{\left(\frac{Rs}{R0}\right)_1}{\left(\frac{Rs}{R0}\right)_0} = alog\frac{K_0}{K_1}$

Respectively

$$Y_1 = Y_0\left(\frac{K_0}{K_1}\right)^a \tag{8}$$

We establish the following constants for the dependence of the Rs/R_0 value towards the concentration of NH_3: $a = -0{,}50084$; $b = -0{,}1728$.

4 Results

The measurements are accomplished in the indoor situation such as office room. Two ammonia sensors are situated at the different places in the room and the test duration is over 36 h. The data are sent to the remote server every 30 s and are written in the MySQL database via Bluetooth or GPRS connection. Furthermore the data are extracted in the CSV file and analyzed. The ammonia concentration and the room temperature are shown at Figs. 4 and 5 respectively. The results show very good data correlations especially after the initial start-up period. The stable data are obtained after the 20 min power-up period. The measurement data also may be more accurate if the sensor outputs are buffered due to the sensitive layer resistance which varies from 10 to 1500 kΩ while the PIC ADC input recommendations requires maximum sensor output resistance of 1 kΩ.

The experimental results show that the ammonia concentration in the indoor environment sometimes may be continuously measured and analyzed to minimize the human health risks due to the ammonia exposure. The both sensors shown similar ammonia concentrations which are much below the dangerous levels but may reach the levels of 3–4 ppm for a time period of 1 h or more.

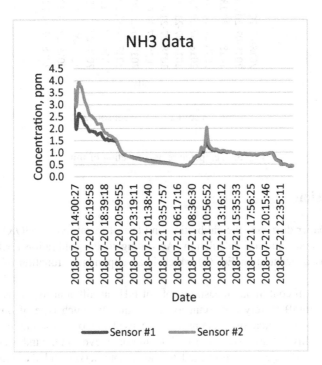

Fig. 4. Ammonia concentration as a function of time

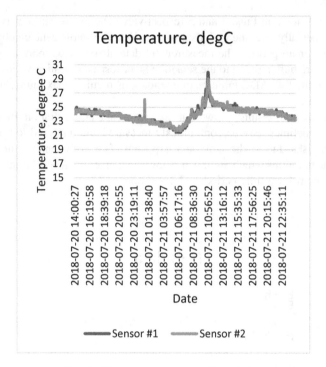

Fig. 5. Temperature as a function of time

5   Conclusion

The current paper discusses the calibration and test of metal-oxide (MOX) sensors for ammonia gas concentration calculation. According to the calibration coefficients we obtain the gas concentration Eq. (8) which is an exponential function of the system parameters.

The long-term continuous measurements of NH_3 at different locations (i.e. urban, industrial and rural) is very important to the air quality. Such type of portable measurement and communication systems may be used not only for monitoring of the working air quality but also to alarm for high ammonia levels in the industry, transport, etc. The measured data are transmitted to the remote server and the ammonia concentration geolocation may be very useful for the people which may have not such device but may be alarmed for the hazard levels of the ammonia gas by the installed application in the smartphones. This application may read the GPS position of the human and check in the server data the current ammonia level to prevent health risks.

Acknowledgement. This work was supported by European Regional Development Fund and the Operational Program "Science and Education for Smart Growth" under contract UNITe № BG05M2OP001-1.001-0004 -C01 (2018-2023).

References

1. Heber, Al., Jones, D., Sutton, A.: Controlling Ammonia Gas In Swine Buildings, February 2004 (2002)
2. Wang, Shanshan, et al.: Atmospheric ammonia and its impacts on regional air quality over the megacity of Shanghai, China. Sci. Rep. **5**, 15842 (2015)
3. Occupational Safety and Health Administration - Permissible Exposure Limits/ OSHA Annotated Table Z-1 (2008). https://www.osha.gov/dsg/annotated-pels/tablez-1.html
4. Spinelle, L., Gerboles, M., Villani, M.G., Aleixandre, M., Bonavitacola, F.: Field calibration of a cluster of low-cost commercially available sensors for air quality monitoring. Part B: NO, CO and CO_2. Sens. Actuators B: Chemical **238**, 706–715 (2017)
5. SGX Sensortech – MiCS-6814 datasheet 14143 rev 8
6. Miletiev, R., Iontchev, E., Yordanov, R.: Mobile system for monitoring of air quality and gas pollution. In: International Scientific Conference on Information, Communication and Energy Systems and Technologies ICEST 2018, 28–30 June, Sozopol (2018)
7. SGX Sensortech - SGX Metal Oxide Gas Sensors, AN-0172, Issue 1, 14-Jul-2014

IoT Open Architecture Ground Control System by Adaptive Fusion Intelligent Interfaces for Robot Vectors Applied to 5G Network Densification Era

Luige Vladareanu[✉], Victor Vladareanu[✉], Ionel-Alexandru Gal,
Daniel-Octavian Melinte, Vlad Grosu, and Mihai Radulescu

Computer Science Editorial, Springer-Verlag,
Tiergartenstr. 17, 69121 Heidelberg, Germany
luigiv2007@yahoo.com.sg,
{luige.vladareanu, victor.vladareanu}@vipro.edu.ro

Abstract. The paper present IoT Open Architecture Ground Control System by adaptive fusion intelligent interfaces to the robot vectors communications applied to network densification in 5G Era. Intelligent interfaces for optimization and decision-making using neural networks, neutrosophic logic and deep learning convolutional are analyzed. The proposed solution providing efficient information management and decision grounding at a tactical and operative level in a wide array of applications.

Keywords: IoT · 5G access networks · Autonomous navigation ·
Software defined networking · Intelligent control interfaces · Robots vectors ·
Ground Control System · Aerial robots navigation systems ·
Wireless sensor networks

1 Introduction

The approach of the IoT Ground Control System (GCS) versus 5G densification network is of great importance and actuality in the current global context, in which unmanned aerial and terrestrial robotic systems [1–3] and the types of missions available to them have registered a significant evolution and growing interest [4–6]. The ever-increasing performance and miniaturization of available components places the field on the cusp of significant breakthroughs in theoretical research and practical applications alike [7–10].

IoT Open Architecture Ground Control System [3, 6, 9] by adaptive fusion intelligent interfaces for robot vectors communications presented in paper is intended for robot vectors with real-time control that involves, through the data volume of communications and quick response between system agents, the need for 5G network Densification Era communications. The system is made up of 3D (three-dimensional) - aerial, terrestrial and aquatic intelligence robot vectors, fulfilling the role of smart agents, the command and control center (CTC2), the Mission Management Center

© ICST Institute for Computer Sciences, Social Informatics and Telecommunications Engineering 2019
Published by Springer Nature Switzerland AG 2019. All Rights Reserved
V. Poulkov (Ed.): FABULOUS 2019, LNICST 283, pp. 118–123, 2019.
https://doi.org/10.1007/978-3-030-23976-3_12

(CMM) and the SRA radio communication system. The GCS system has implemented artificial intelligence algorithms for optimization and decision-making.

2   3D VERO VIPRO Versatile, Intelligent, Portable Platform for Special Control Mission by 3D Robot Vectors

The VERO 3D platform integrated in the VIPRO platform has the role of the Mission Management Center CMM providing, by the way in which the VIPRO platform was designed, the ability to design, test and validate optimization and decision-making interfaces for the 3D robot vectors control - aerial, terrestrial, aquatic. In addition, the platform provides the e-learning and e-courses components for the dissemination of research results in the academic environment. Hardware configuration of the architecture 3D VERO VIPRO platform's architecture for special control mission by 3D robot vectors is presented in Fig. 1.

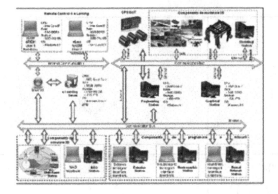

Fig. 1. Architecture 3D VERO VIPRO platform for special control mission by 3D robot vectors

The proposed 3D VERO VIPRO platform has a multi-agent real-time control system for robot vectors VRs, respectively aerial, terrestrial, aquatic robots, performance capabilities beyond the current state of the art and an open architecture design that allows greater flexibility further development and better customization of applications, with communication which require the 5G densification network in terms of speed and volume of data.

Aspects related to user needs and requirements as well as human-robot interaction have been considered to ensure the solutions' acceptance and usefulness.

3 Intelligent Optimization and Decision-Making Interfaces

By implementing a number of optimization and decision-making intelligent interfaces, the UAV command and control system (C2UAV) ensures high performances of the robot vectors VRs, and optimal decision-making support by sending in real time the coordinates of critical situations, determining the impact of decisions and designed actions, providing explanations for operations triggered.

C2UAV has the necessary features and capabilities to implement artificial intelligence algorithms that allow decentralized use of learning functions as tools for planning recognition operations and event mapping.

3.1 The VRs Optimization and Control Intelligent Interface in the Recognition/Monitoring Missions

The VRs optimization and control intelligent interface in mission performs optimization and control the position of the robot vector engaged in the recognition/monitoring missions. The optimization problem considers the existence of obstacles in the search space. The number of points modeled between two consecutive positions of the robot vectors VRs depends on the speed required by operator or the motion trajectory tracking algorithm.

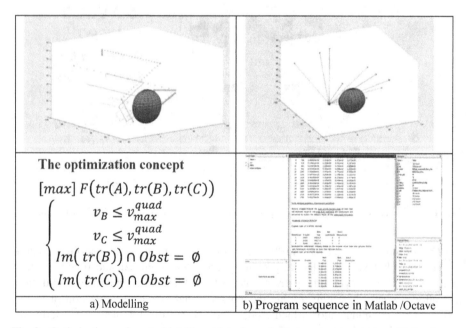

The optimization concept	b) Program sequence in Matlab /Octave
$[max]\ F\big(tr(A), tr(B), tr(C)\big)$ $\begin{cases} v_B \leq v_{max}^{quad} \\ v_C \leq v_{max}^{quad} \\ Im\big(tr(B)\big) \cap Obst = \emptyset \\ Im\big(tr(C)\big) \cap Obst = \emptyset \end{cases}$	
a) Modelling	b) Program sequence in Matlab /Octave

Fig. 2. Optimization and control intelligent interface of robot vectors in missions (Color figure online)

Running the optimization function script in Fig. 2 is presented sequentially following all the steps of the optimization problem [11, 12]. The intermediate results of each step are shown in the blue border. The optimization algorithm is written in the Maltab/Octave code, called by Python's main VRs control program.

3.2 Optimization and Decision-Making Intelligent Interfaces Using the Neutrosophic Logic

The intelligent interfaces for optimization and decision-making was developed using the neutrosophic logic algorithm, by applying the Desert-Smarandache DSmT theory. The robotic neutrosophic control (RNC) systems is known as the Vladareanu-Smarandache method. The proposed decision-making method developed by Gal and Vladareanu [9, 10] presented in Fig. 3 for real-time control of the 3D aerial, terrestrial and aquatic vector robots can be successfully applied.

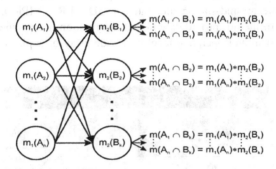

Fig. 3. Optimization and decision-making intelligent interfaces for robot vectors neutrosophic control (RNC) systems

3.3 Intelligent Deep Learning with Convolution NNs Interface

The intelligent interface performs image processing optimization by Deep Learning with Convolutional Neural Networks (NNs). In order to recognize the objects in images, the results obtained by using deep learning with convolutional NNs algorithms were investigated. These networks function like the human brain [11].

a) Drone recognition trust factor   b) Boat recognition trust factor.

Fig. 4. Image processing intelligent interface through deep learning with convolutional NNs

OpenCV is an open-source image processing library and can be used along with other libraries and software platforms to develop deep learning and machine learning algorithms. For experiments performed in this work the OpenCV 3.4.3 library along with the NumPy library were used, the algorithm was developed in Python 3.7 and run on a Windows 10 operating system.

The experimental results and the trust factor in the recognition of the drones and the Naval Vehicles after modelling by the image processing intelligent interface using Deep Learning are shown in Fig. 4.

4 Results and Conclusions

The IoT Open Architecture Ground Control System using multi-agent systems is based on a network of modular aerial and terrestrial vectors of various concepts and architectures, equipped with an array of sensors, cooperative operation and control capabilities and portable ground-station integrated in 3D VERO VIPRO, which are not found in the state of the art, providing efficient information management and decision grounding at a tactical and operative level in a wide array of applications.

Fig. 5. 3D VERO VIPRO implementation and running on the VIPRO MULTIMOND platform

The proposed solution could have implications towards societal safety, security and privacy. Therefore, 3D VERO VIPRO implemented on the VIPRO MULTIMOND platform (Fig. 5) has an established risk management process to identify and assess risks towards an acceptable risk criterion, propose and develop mitigations, and to monitor the risk by analyzing the data from the IoT Open Architecture Ground Control System using 5G densification network.

The obtained results lead to missions of the robot vectors on surveillance in areas of interest in reducing environmental pollution and for rescue missions in areas where people's lives are at risk, such as natural disasters, terrorist acts or fires.

Acknowledgments. This work was supported by a grant of the Romanian Ministry of Research and Innovation, CCCDI-UEFISCDI, MULTIMOND2 project number PN-III-P1-1.2-PCCDI 2017-0637/33PCCDI/01.03.2018, within PNCDI III, and by the European Commission Marie Skłodowska-Curie SMOOTH project, Smart Robots for Fire-Fighting, H2020-MSCA-RISE-2016-734875. The authors gratefully acknowledge the financial support of Department of Technical Sciences of the Romanian Academy.

References

1. Wendel, J., Metzger, J., Moenikie, R., Maier, A., Trommer, G.F.: A performance comparison of tightly coupled GPS/INS navigation systems based on extended and sigma point kalman filters. NAVIGATION J. Inst. Navig. **53**(1), 21–31 (2014)
2. Prisacariu, V., Boscoianu, M., Circiu, I.: Morphing wing concept for small UAV, optimization of the intelligent systems and their applications in aerospace. Appl. Mech. Mat. **332**, 44–49 (2014). WOS:000345269700007
3. Vladareanu, V., Moga, R., Schiopu, P., Vladareanu, L.: Multi-sensors systems using semi-active control for monitoring and diagnoses of the power systems. IFAC Proc. Vol. (IFAC-PapersOnline) **2**(PART 1), 78–83 (2013)
4. Şandru, O.I., Vlădareanu, L., Şchiopu, P., Vlădareanu, V., Şandru, A.: Multidimensional extenics theory. UPB Sci. Bull. Ser. A: Appl. Math. Phys. **75**(1), 3–12 (2013)
5. Vladareanu, V., Schiopu, P., Vladareanu, L.: Theory and application of extension hybrid force-position control in robotic. UPB Sci. Bull. Ser. A Appl. Math. Phys. **76**(3), 43–54 (2014)
6. Hoffmann, G.M., et al.: Stanford Test Bed of Autonomous Rotorcraft for Multi-Agent Control, St. Louis, MO, USA, 10–15 October 2009
7. Deif, T.N., Kassem, A.H., El-Baioumi, G.M.: Attitude stabilization of indoor quad rotor using classic control. Int. Rev. Aerosp. Eng. (I.RE.AS.E) **7**(2) (2014)
8. Boscoianu, M., Cioaca, C., Vladareanu, V., Boscoianu, C.E.: An active support instrument for innovation in deep uncertainty - the strategic management ingredients in robotics and mechatronics. Procedia Comput. Sci. **65**, 210–217 (2015). WOS: 000373831000024. ISSN: 1877-05094
9. Vladareanu, V., Munteanu, R.I., Mumtaz, A., Smarandache, F., Vladareanu, L.: The optimization of intelligent control interfaces using Versatile Intelligent Portable Robot Platform. Procedia Comput. Sci. **65**, 225–232 (2015). WOS: 000373831000026. ISSN: 1877-0509
10. Gal, A., Vladareanu, L.: DSmT decision-making algorithms for finding grasping configurations of robot dexterous hands. Symmetry **10**(6), 198–214 (2018)
11. Vladareanu, L., IMSAR coordinator, Vladareanu, V., Gal, A., Melinte, O., et al.: MULTIMOND2 project PN-III-P1-1.2-PCCDI2017-0637/33PCCDI/01.03.2018
12. Vladareanu, V., IMSAR coordinator, Vladareanu, L., Gal, A., Melinte, O., et al.: MASIM project PN II, MEN-UEFISCDI, PN-II-PT-PCCA-2013-4-1349

Overview of IoT Basic Platforms
for Precision Agriculture

Ioana Marcu[1(✉)], Carmen Voicu[1], Ana Maria Claudia Drăgulinescu[1],
Octavian Fratu[1], George Suciu[2], Cristina Balaceanu[2],
and Maria Madalina Andronache[1]

[1] University Polytechnic of Bucharest,
Splaiul Independentei no. 313, Bucharest, Romania
{imarcu, carmen.voicu, maria.andronache}@radio.pub.ro,
ana.dragulinescu@upb.ro, ofratu@elcom.pub.ro
[2] Beia Consult International, 16 Peroni Road, Bucharest, Romania
{george, cristina.balaceanu}@beia.ro

Abstract. Nowadays, more than ever, agriculture area has to face difficult challenges due to numerous technological transformations used for increasing productivity and products quality. Due to the extended growth in agricultural product use, farmers and big companies operating in the "Big Data" area invest in precision agriculture by using sensor networks, drones, satellites and GPS tracking systems. Agricultural plants are extremely sensitive to climate change such as higher temperatures and changes in the precipitation area increase the chance of disease occurrence, leading to crop damage and even irreversible destruction of plants. Current advances in Internet of things (IoT) and Cloud Computing have led to the development of new applications based on highly innovative and scalable service platforms. IoT solutions have great potential in assuring the quality and safety of agricultural products. The design and operation of a telemonitoring system for precision farming is mainly based on the use of IoT platforms and therefore, this paper briefly presents the main IoT platforms used in precision agriculture, highlighting at the same time their main advantages and disadvantages. This overview can be used as a basic tool for choosing an IoT platform solution for future telemonitoring systems.

Keywords: IoT platforms · Precision agriculture · Cloud computing · Efficiency

1 Introduction

In the Cluster of European Research Projects (CERP) report, the Internet of Things (IoT) is defined as an integrated part of the future Internet, which ensures that 'things' with identities can communicate with each other. IoT will be applied in different areas, e.g. smart cities, agriculture, energy, environment protection, health, home automation, etc. [1]. The applications of IoT-based smart farming not only target conventional, large farming operations, but could also be new levers to uplift other growing or common trends in agricultural like organic farming, family farming (complex or small

V. Poulkov (Ed.): FABULOUS 2019, LNICST 283, pp. 124–137, 2019.
https://doi.org/10.1007/978-3-030-23976-3_13

spaces, particular cattle and/or cultures, preservation of particular or high-quality varieties etc.), and enhance highly transparent farming.

In precision agriculture a key component is the use of IoT and various items like sensors, control systems, robotics, autonomous vehicles, automated hardware, variable rate technology, etc. [2]. Possible applications for wireless sensors networks include precision agriculture [3], agricultural production process management [4], greenhouses monitoring [5, 6], optimization of plant growth [7], farmland monitoring, crop protection to divert animal intrusions [8, 9].

More recently, the advent of aerial imagery systems, such as drones, has enabled farmers to get richer sensor data from the farms. Drones can help farmers map their fields, monitor crop canopy remotely and check for anomalies. Over time, all this data can indicate useful practices in farms and make suggestions based on previous crop cycles; resulting in higher yields, lower inputs and less environmental impact [10].

Considering the limitations of Wireless Sensor Networks (WSN) and drone use in precision agriculture [11], the design and operation of a telemonitoring system for precision farming is mainly based on the use of IoT platforms.

The rest of the paper is structured as follows: Sect. 2 presents state of the art for IoT platforms, Sect. 3 describe platform for precision agriculture and lastly, Sect. 5 concludes the paper.

2   State-of-the-Art: IoT Platforms

Cadavid et al. [12] proposes an extension of Thingsboard, a scalable platform for device management and for collecting, processing and visualizing telemetry data [13]. The authors intend to develop a MaaS (Monitoring as a Service) Smart Farming platform that is Cloud-based and that involves sensing devices, decision support system and remotely controlled actuators and devices as drones. As extensions, the work contributes to the default data model by adding concepts as Farm, Land Lot, Crop. It also integrates complementary database engines as MongoDB, GridFS and REDIS. Moreover, an API is provided for allowing the interaction with third-party platforms. The proposed architecture was tested by means of a simulation of a scenario that implies the detection of a potato pest determined by Phytophthora infestans fungus. Smith Period prediction model was used and 25 sensors in 5 different crops were simulated.

In [14] SmartFarmNet platform is emphasized and evaluated. The platform is aimed to support a plethora of IoT devices and enables do-it-yourself real-time statistical analysis, being able to handle high velocity data streams. Also, it uses semantic web technologies to allow the exchange of data with other IoT services and to tailor the platform to new domains.

In [10], the authors propose a low-cost IoT platform for agriculture which supports high bandwidth sensors via TVWS (low-cost, long range technology). Within the FarmBeats platform, data from low-cost sensors in soil and drones work together with machine learning algorithms and farmers' knowledge in order to gather and analyse data about specific farms (information regarding when, where and what to plant in order to obtain cost reductions and higher yields). FarmBeats system has the following components: sensors and drones, IoT Base Station which is weather aware solar powered, IoT Gateway that ensures availability of both Cloud and offline services, and the Cloud component. The advantages of the FarmBeats system are that the gateway implements a web service while providing offline operating capability. Also, having access to data gathered from multiple types of sensors enables unique summarization technologies for the sensor data and drone videos.

An IoT-enabled private platform dedicated to smart agriculture was designed in [15]. The proposed solution should comprise telemetry, intelligent systems, wireless communications and cloud computing. The platform should offer the possibility to add, remove, identify or modify sensor nodes. Also, it should allow the collection and calibration of raw data. Data collection and import are possible through communication protocols and API.

In [16], the authors propose a flexible platform in order to cope with soilless culture needs in greenhouses. Within the system architecture, Cyber-Physical Systems interact with crop devices in order to gather data and perform real-time actions.

3   IoT Basic Proprietary Platforms for Precision Agriculture

For data collection related to environmental monitoring, air quality and testing of monitoring parameters of interest parameters, existing IoT platforms such as uRADMonitor, Libelium, Vaisala, Kaa, etc. are considered. Their main features, advantages and disadvantages, as well as several use cases are detailed below.

3.1   Libelium – Waspmote

Waspmote Plug & Sense [17] line allows simple implementation of IoT networks in facile and scalable manner with low management costs. The platform consists of a waterproof carcass with a dedicated external socket to connect the sensors, the solar panel, the antenna and even the USB cable to reprogram the node. The main features of Libelium-Waspmote platform include [18]:

- External solar panel option;
- Radio technologies: 802.15.4/868 MHz/900 MHz/WiFi/4G/Sigfox/LoRaWAN;
- programming multiple nodes simultaneously (via WiFi or 4G interfaces);
- Graphical and intuitive interface Cloud Service Programming;
- External reset without contact with magnet;
- External battery module optional;

Libelium-Waspmote platform is used mainly in applications such as [19]: precision agriculture (lead moisture, fruit diameter), irrigation systems, greenhouses: (solar radiation, humidity, temperature), weather stations.

3.2   A3-uRADMonitor

uRADMonitor A3 is an advanced air quality monitoring station, enclosed in an aluminium body (robust design), it has gamma, formaldehyde, CO_2, VOC, air quality + air temperature, barometric pressure, air humidity and sensor laser dispersion for

PM2.5 particles. A3 also comes in 4 forms, with the same sensors but with different connection options: Ethernet, Wi-Fi, GSM (with a SIM card) and LoraWAN. Most pollutants measured by the A3 model can have a negative impact on people's health and can cause mild illnesses (simple allergies) to serious illnesses (such as various types of cancer) [20]. The uRADMonitor A3 (Fig. 1) uses the Bosch BME680 to measure air temperature, barometric pressure, humidity and volatile organic compounds or VOC. A high-quality laser scattering sensor is used to detect the PM2.5 particle concentration in the air. There exists also a non-dispersive infrared sensor for measuring the CO2 concentration in air, and a Geiger SI29BG tube to detect gamma ionizing radiation and X radiation. An inbuilt fan provides an active air flow through the elements to detect.

Fig. 1. A3-uRADMonitor model [18]

The uRADMonitor A3 can be mounted both indoors and outdoors, but not directly exposed to the sun, to avoid overheating in warmer areas. uRADMonitor connects to the power supply using a DC adapter with voltage between 6 V and 28 V and the Internet router using the Ethernet cable. The Internet Router must have DHCP enabled. When powered, uRADMonitor automatically obtains an IP address through DHCP, and will appear on the map. It uses very little energy to function.

3.3 Observant

Observant™ is a world leader in providing Cloud-based hardware applications for accurately managing water used in agriculture. Use cases include: *water level monitoring* (with the possibility of updating every 30 min; graphical representation of data acquired during a day, week or month to better visualize water use trends; the ability to adapt to different heights of water tanks (from about 46 cm to 127 cm) and alarms sent by SMS or email if the water level is too low or if the upper threshold is exceeded [21], etc.); *soil moisture monitoring* (increase the efficiency of irrigation and to better manage the use of certain nutrients [22]: irrigation management; nutrient management; process programming on crops; water infiltration/leakage management [23]); *irrigation programming* (Fig. 2); *pressure monitoring*, *climate monitoring* (useful for irrigation management, prediction of harvesting, frost prediction, pest management [24]); *pumps management* (capabilities of the Observant system: monitoring the pump's operating state, monitoring the pump's alarms (made by text messages alerting the farmer instantly so that he or she can know whether or not to take urgent action); *pump input/output monitoring* (pressure and flow switches are observed, pump inputs/outputs to ensure proper operation); turning on/off the pump remotely (commands that can be given on your computer, tablet, or smartphone)).

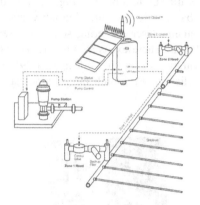

Fig. 2. Observant™ irrigation system [23]

Among the disadvantages of Observant™ solution there can be noticed: the need to use of certain proprietary devices, the relatively small number of electromagnetic locking valves that can be used in the irrigation system, the necessity of a qualified electrician (in this case an electrician) qualified to connect the electric pump to the C3 telemetry platform or to another telemetry platform and also the number of telemetry platform outputs causes other limitations [25].

3.4   Arable Mark (Pulsepod)

The Arable Mark (or Pulsepod) is a solar powered device [26] to monitor weather conditions and crops [27]. It provides real-time information. The Pulsepod Arable Device [28] (Fig. 3) has three types of sensors: *acoustic disdrometer* (it measures rainfall, observing the size and number of drops falling on the surface of the device); *the differential radiometer* (it helps determine the amount of sunlight the plants around the device receive by measuring short wave radiation (coming directly from the sun) and long wave radiation (sunlight that was reflected back by plants)); *the spectrometer* (it is used to monitor how much plants grow, the amount of plant chlorophyll and the use of water by plants). The Pulsepod sends data to a Cloud platform via WiFi, cellular or Bluetooth connectivity. An embedded GPS device allows data to be mapped to weather and ground images. Farmers can access data and reports created by Arable, allowing them to make decisions about irrigation and soil fertilization. Pulsepod measures over 40 parameters including rain, hail, leaf surface, crop water, environmental stress, and even air pollution.

Fig. 3. Surface of arable mark device [25]

3.5 Pycno Sensors and Platform for Agriculture

The Pycno Platform is designed to continuously monitor data and control the farming system. Pycno develops and integrates wireless sensors and a software platform that provides farmers with weather information and real-time soil information [29]. General characteristics and measurement areas include [30]: 2 W high power monocrystalline solar panel; internal battery; solar irradiation, between 300–1100 nm, and the accuracy is 16 bits; Air temperature between −40 and 125 °, with an accuracy of ±0.3 °C; air humidity, between 0–100% RH, with an accuracy of ± 2%; soil temperature, between −10 and 85 °C, with an accuracy of ±0.4 °C; soil moisture has a precision of 28bit.

3.6 Agri M2M [29]

According to GSMA Intelligence, cellular M2M connections (across all sectors) reached 146 million in Q4 2014, growing at a CAGR of 35% from 73 million in Q4 2010. M2M in agriculture has the potential to increase efficiencies in the following areas: improve availability of information about the condition of crops and livestock; through real-time monitoring and alert services; maximize efficiency and longevity of agricultural equipment through real-time remote control and monitoring; reduce losses during transportation of produce through distributors and retailers to the end users by monitoring the logistics. M2M can be used to send and receive data about temperature, weight, location and any number of other agricultural factors, as well as requests to each other and to central management systems, autonomously. The stakeholders in the M2M value chain include module vendors, connectivity providers, M2M platform and application providers, device platform providers, mobile operators, aggregators and mobile virtual network operators (MVNOs) (Fig. 4). The information is collected through M2M modules mounted on the assets and transmitted via connectivity providers (mobile operators in this case). This information is then received by system integrators and solution providers which gather and process the data, to be finally displayed via mobile or web applications to the end users.

The end users for M2M applications include crop and livestock farmers, cooperatives and agri-businesses. The individual or small-hold farmers typically use Agri M2M solutions for equipment and fleet monitoring in their farms.

However, given the high cost of M2M implementation (arguably the biggest barrier to the adoption of this technology), agribusinesses and cooperatives are better placed to make full use of the potential of M2M in agriculture.

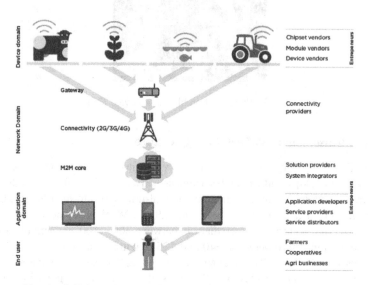

Fig. 4. Cellular M2M in agriculture (Agri M2M) – value chain [30]

Table 1 reveals the most important agriculture use cases and the suitability of each proprietary platform to these use cases.

Table 1. Comparison between precision agriculture platforms

Agriculture use case	A3-uRADMonitor	Libelium	Observant	Arable Mark	Pycno	Agri M2M
Weather monitoring	Yes	Yes*	Yes	Yes	Yes	Yes
Rainfall	No	Yes*	Yes	Yes	No	–
Crop monitoring	No	Yes*	No?	Yes	No	Yes
Irrigation	No	Yes*	Yes	No	No	Yes
Air quality/Pollution	Yes	Yes*	No	Yes	No	Yes
Pump management	No	Yes*	Yes	No	No	–
Soil information	No	Yes*	Yes	No	Yes	–
Equipment monitoring	No	No	Yes	No	No	Yes

The asterisk in the case of Libelium platform means that the platform is not able to respond to the use case in Table 1 by default, as it does not embed any sensor. The sensors must be purchased separately from the platform.

The communication protocols for platforms presented above are showed in the Table 2.

Table 2. Communication protocols

IoT platforms	Communication protocol
Libelium – Waspmote	4G
A3-uRADMonitor	Wi-Fi, GSM, LoraWAN
Observant	Wi-Fi
Arable Mark (Pulsepod)	WI-FI
Pycno sensors	4G
Agri M2M	4G

4 Research and Development Precision Agriculture Platforms

Other precision agriculture initiatives may be found in literature. The proposed platforms implement the intelligent control in agriculture, data reliable transmission and intelligent processing of data, leading to an increase in crop production and reducing the impact of the agriculture activities towards the environment [31].

In [31], Zhang et al. intend to develop a system that monitors the citrus soil humidity and nutrients. Another goal of the proposed solution would be the reduction of pollution caused by chemical fertilizers and the reduction of the costs associated to the physical labour. A decision support system will guide the farmers to adapt the fertigation system.

The IoT Platform (Fig. 5) is structured on 4 layers: (1) Perception layer, (2) Network layer, (3) Middleware layer and (4) Application layer.

Perception layer is composed of sensing and data acquisition devices as soil and humidity sensors, portable soil nutrients detector.

A wireless sensor network based on ZigBee protocol represents the shortrange component of the transmission of the Network layer. The core of the wireless sensor network is the Internet of Things Gateway which assures the connection with the public network and the protocol conversion.

Middleware layer is responsible for service management, data storing and decision making, whereas Application layer comprises a sensor network management system, a monitoring data analysis and querying system based on WEB-GIS and a fertigation decision support system.

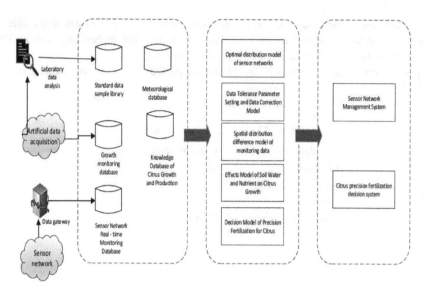

Fig. 5. IoT architecture for soil humidity and nutrients monitoring [31]

In [32], the authors describe an IoT architecture dedicated to prediction of a disease specific to a Korean strawberry variety, Seolhyang.

They proposed an integrated Cloud-based system following a new paradigm, *Farming as a Service* (FaaS). The system allows data collection, analysis and the prediction of the information concerning agriculture practices.

This initiative is based on other paradigm, called PaaS (Platform as a Service). In Fig. 6, the IoT system's four-layer architecture was represented. The available sensors are greenhouse environmental sensors, growth monitoring sensors and nutrient solution sensors.

The system is able to predict the infection with Botrytis cinerea bacteria based on an algorithm that uses images and environmental data collected from the greenhouse.

Another model was presented in [33]. The platform is based on a 5-layer architecture depicted in Fig. 7 and is aimed to irrigation control. Among these 5 layers, Thing, Edge and Fog layers will be described.

The Thing layer comprises the monitoring and environmental conditions control devices specific to a greenhouse: soil temperature, humidity electrical conductivity and pH sensors, water temperature, electrical conductivity and pH sensors, air temperature, relative humidity and light sensors for greenhouse environment monitoring, temperature, humidity and wind sensors for outdoor monitoring. In addition, the system includes water valves and pumps.

Edge layer may be responsible for data filtering, predictive data computing for climate conditions, classification services.

Fog layer, as extension of Cloud, facilitates real-time application, reducing system latency and triggering the actuators without being necessary that the information arrives firstly in Cloud.

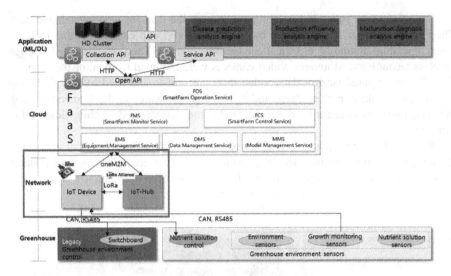

Fig. 6. R&D Precision agriculture platform for strawberry crop monitoring [32]

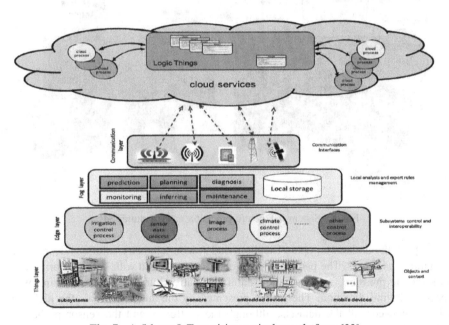

Fig. 7. A 5-layer IoT precision agriculture platform [33]

In [34], the authors have proposed a system that monitors a crop, providing a method to enhance the decision making process by analysing the crop statistics and by correlating them with the information regarding the monitored crop.

The system (Fig. 8) includes three main components: crop monitoring subsystem, statistic prediction subsystem and text-mining analysis block.

The monitoring subsystem is aimed to acquire the data for creating reliable data. The Perception layer is represented by an IoT sensor Group component that includes soil temperature, humidity, electrical conductivity and pH. They are connected through wireless technology. Moreover, video cameras were mounted to monitor the crop.

All data acquired (sensor data, video flux) are sent to and used by the prediction server that is able to process them and to transmit afterwards to the farmers, through Internet, forecasts concerning domestic production, harvest and seeding time, delivering time.

The architecture proposed in [34] has as main advantage the possibility to enhance the quality of agriculture products by providing to the farmers significant and valuable information about the entire cycle seeding-delivery. Moreover, such a system can analyze present conditions and forecast future crops.

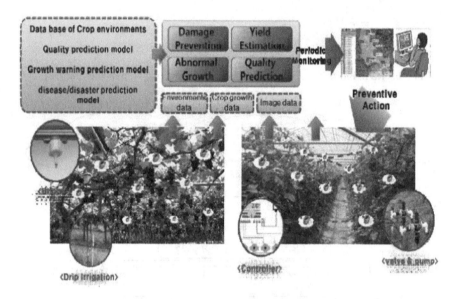

Fig. 8. Sistem IoT pentru producția în agricultură [34]

In [35], the authors compare Libelium and Adcon telemetry solutions deployed in agriculture use cases. The parameters that could be measured with both platforms were atmospheric pressure, solar radiation, rainfall, relative humidity, soil moisture, wind speed and wind direction. The results presented by the authors reveals the high correlation between all the datasets, although the platforms and the sensor probes are different from the point of view of the structure.

To conclude Sects. 4 and 5, one can observe that an end-to-end precision agriculture platform is very necessary, as many efforts were focused in this direction. This platform should include several important components and concepts as: soil, weather and, in general, environmental parameters monitoring, yield forecasting, product quality monitoring, disease prediction, environment preservation methods, agriculture asset management.

5 Conclusions

The introduction of the IoT platform helped people to analyse all the information from the different type of fields. Integration of IoT in agriculture field brings benefits regarding monitoring of crops, weather conditions, and pollution of the environment and finally the right decision can be taken in order to increase yield and agricultural production. Considering the climate change context, the introduction of IoT in the agriculture brings a dramatic progress. Using precision agricultural platforms, the farmers can reduce the production costs and increase the sales because they can fight diseases by applying the suitable type and amount of treatment at the right time, reducing in this way the use of pesticide or other toxic treatments, which leads to healthy crops. Also the usage of IoT platforms will reduce the water consumption by watering the crops only when is needed and with the adequate amount of water. So, in function of the Internet connection, place of implementation, the type of crops etc. the farmers can choose from a large diversity of platforms, which will improve their work. The scope of the paper was to achieve a comparative study between the most common agriculture platforms, highlighting various aspects like knowledge base, monitoring modules, efficiency etc. We can say that the role of these platforms is to bring together the users (farmers) and professional suppliers. Using the smart agriculture, the farmers will receive guidance at the right time and at the end of the season will have an improved harvest.

Acknowledgment. This work has been supported in part by Minister of Research and Innovation Romania through project SmartAgro (contract no. 8592/2018), UEFISCDI, project number 33PCCDI/2018 within PNCDI III and through contract no. 5Sol/2017, PNCDI III, Integrated Software Platform for Mobile Malware Analysis (ToR-SIM).

References

1. Ganchev, I., Ji, Z., O'Droma, M.: A generic IoT architecture for smart cities. In 25th IET Irish Signals & Systems Conference 2014 and 2014 China-Ireland International Conference on Information and Communications Technologies (ISSC 2014/CIICT 2014), Electronic ISBN: 978-1-84919-924-7, Ireland, 2013
2. IoT Applications in Agriculture 2018. https://www.iotforall.com/iot-applications-in-agriculture/
3. Deepika, G., Rajapirian, P.: Wireless sensor network in precision agriculture: a survey. In: 2016 International Conference on Emerging Trends in Engineering, Technology and Science (ICETETS), ISBN: 978-1-4673-6725-7, India, 2016
4. Khairnar, P., et al: Wireless sensor network application in agriculture for monitoring agriculture production process. In: International Journal of Advanced Research in Computer Engineering & Technology (IJARCET), ISSN: 2278–1323, vol. 5, Issue 5, May 2016
5. Ahonen, T., Virrankoski, R., Elmusrati, M.: In: Greenhouse monitoring with wireless sensor network. In: IEEE/ASME International Conference on Mechatronic and Embedded Systems and Applications (2008)

6. Gupta, G., Quan, V., In: Multi-sensor integrated system for wireless monitoring of greenhouse environment. In: 2018 IEEE Sensors Applications Symposium (SAS), ISBN: 978-1-5386-2092-2, South Korea (2018)
7. Kameoka, S., et al.: In: A Wireless Sensor Network for Growth Environment Measurement and Multi-Band Optical Sensing to Diagnose Tree Vigor, Sensors (Basel) (2017). https://doi.org/10.3390/s17050966
8. Bapat, V., et al.: WSN application for crop protection to divert animal intrusions in the agricultural land. In: Computers and Electronics in Agriculture, vol. 133, pp 88–96, Elsevier (2017)
9. Ojha, T.: Wireless sensor networks for agriculture: the state-of-the-art in practice and future challenges. In: Elsevier Computers and Electronics in Agriculture 118, 66–84 (2015)
10. Vasisht, D., et al.: FarmBeats: an IoT platform for data-driven agriculture. In: 14th USENIX Symposium on Networked Systems Design and Implementation (NSDI 2017), ISBN 978-1-931971-37-9, USA (2017)
11. Sharma, V.: Limitation associated with wireless sensor network, In: IJCST, vol. 5, Issue 1, ISSN: 0976-8491 (Online), Jan–March 2014
12. Cadavid, H.F., Garzón, W., Pérez, A., López, G., Mendivelso, C., Ramirez, C.: Towards a smart farming platform: from IoT-based crop sensing to data analytics. In: Proceedings 13th Colombian Conference, CCC 2018, Cartagena, Colombia, 26–28 September 2018
13. ThingsBoard Open-source IoT Platform. https://thingsboard.io/
14. Jayaraman, P.P., Yavari, A., Georgakopoulos, D., Morshed, A., Zaslavsky, A.: Internet of Things platform for smart farming: experiences and lessons learnt. Sensors 2016, 16 (1884)
15. Popovic, T., Latinovic, N., Pesic, A., Zecevic, Z., Krstajic, B., Djukanovic, S.: Architecting an IoT-enabled platform for precision agriculture and ecological monitoring: a case study. Comput. Electron. Agric. 140, 255–265 (2017)
16. Miguel, A., Antonio, F.: Skarmeta, smart farming IoT platform based on edge and cloud computing. Biosyst. Eng. 177, 4–17 (2019)
17. Libelium Waspmote. http://www.libelium.com/products/waspmote/sensors/
18. Libelium Plug & Sense. http://www.libelium.com/products/plug-sense/technical-overview/
19. uRAD Monitor. https://www.uradmonitor.com/uradmonitor-model-a3/
20. Observant™, Observant™ water level monitoring brochure. https://observant.net/
21. Observant™, Observant™ Soil Moisture Monitoring brochure. https://observant.net/
22. Observant™, Observant™ solution datasheet - Soil Moisture Monitoring. https://observant.net/
23. Observant™, Observant™ Weather and Environmental Monitoring brochure. https://observant.net/
24. Observant™, Observant™ solution datasheet – Irrigation Scheduling. https://observant.net/
25. Takahashi, D.: https://venturebeat.com/2016/06/07/arable-labs-introduces-pulsepod-solar-powered-farm-sensor/
26. Arable: Decision Agriculture. www.arable.com
27. A complete water-budgeting solution. www.arable.com/solutions_irrigation
28. Turn raw data from your field into actionable analytics. www.pycno.co/sensors
29. Quick start guide. www.pycno.co/quick-start
30. GSMA, Agricultural machine-to-machine (Agri M2M): a platform for expansion. www.gsmaintellgence.com/research/?file=9186f77efc0a47fe7f127d79d789c64c&download
31. Zhang, X., Zhang, J., Li, L., Zhang, Y., Yang, G.: Monitoring citrus soil moisture and nutrients using an iot based system. Sens. J. 17(3), 447 (2017)
32. Kim, S., Lee, M., Shin, C.: IoT-Based Strawberry Disease Prediction System for Smart Farming. Sens. J. 18(11), 4051 (2018)

33. Ferrández-Pastor, F.J., García-Chamizo, J.M., Nieto-Hidalgo, M., Mora-Martínez, J.: Precision agriculture design method using a distributed computing architecture on internet of things context. Sens. J. **18**(6), 1731 (2018)
34. Lee, M., Hwang, J., Yoe, H.: Agricultural production system based on IoT. In: 2013 IEEE 16th International Conference on Computational Science and Engineering, pp. 833–837. Sydney, NSW (2013)
35. Suciu, V., et al.: Analysis of Agriculture Sensors Based on IoT. In: 2018 International Conference on Communications (COMM), pp. 423–427 (2018)

Improved Remote Control System for Analog Audio Mixers Featuring Internet of Things Elements

Florina-Violeta Anghel[✉], Alina-Elena Marcu,
Robert-Alexandru Dobre, and Ana Maria Claudia Drăgulinescu

Politehnica University of Bucharest, Bucharest, Romania
anghelvioleta. f@gmail.com

Abstract. Music is often found in people's lives, as a form of relaxation and inspiration. Small or medium concert venues use analog audio mixers to process the audio signals produced by each instrument and by the singer to deliver a pleasant sound to the audience. The problem is that the position of the mixer is, in most cases, on the stage or in a corner of the hall. This way the sound that the sound engineer hears will not be the same as what the audience hears. His place should be in public for a qualitative assessment of sound. Analog mixers cannot be controlled remotely, and the current alternative involves the replacement with a new and expensive digital audio mixer. The paper presents a cost-effective system that can be attached to any analog audio mixer, allowing to remote control main parameters like the attenuation of each signal. The remote control is a smartphone application, allowing easy further development and connectivity. The system was implemented, tested and the results and performances are presented in the paper, along with the details about the developed custom remote-to-mixer synchronous communication.

Keywords: Audio signal · Analog mixer · Synchronous communication · IoT

1 Introduction

At any musical events, the optimum place of the team adjusting the sound should be in front of the stage. This place is also called Front of House (FOH). Unfortunately, installing the mixer and the other audio equipment in front of the stage in small or medium venues is avoided because the equipment will take most of the place and the people would not be able to enjoy the artistic performance properly. Consequently, the sound engineer is usually placed in a corner of the hall or even on stage. The placement of the sound engineer will not allow him to correctly hear the sound that will be delivered to the audience. An improvement would be if the mixer and the other audio equipment could be placed where is convenient in the venue and the audio engineer could control the mixer from various places using his smartphone or tablet while making the necessary adjustment and monitoring the results from the audience perspective. In most of the small or medium venues an analog audio equipment is available.

V. Poulkov (Ed.): FABULOUS 2019, LNICST 283, pp. 138–145, 2019.
https://doi.org/10.1007/978-3-030-23976-3_14

In the recent years, as the music technology began to evolve, the digital audio mixers began to feature more advanced capabilities than the analog audio mixers [1]. One important capability of the digital audio mixer is the remote control [2]. Comparing the costs between the analog and the digital version, the latter is much more expensive. Unfortunately, investing in a digital audio mixer is not always considered by venue owners because of the supplementary cost and the fact that they already own an analog one with can still organize concerts even if it cannot be remotely controlled and the audition quality will not be the best.

The system proposed in this paper uses the dedicated "Insert" connector available on most analog audio mixers to allow to remote control the levels of the audio signals using and Android application which can be installed on a smartphone or on a tablet [3]. Therefore, the sound engineer now has the possibility to set the important parameters from the desired position within the venue. The proposed equipment has several advantages: it is compatible with most analog audio mixers because total cost is affordable, allowing the sound engineer (and not the venue owner) to own it and use it in any location that he works in.

Several weighted audio mixing algorithms were proposed, some of which being able to increase the voice quality of the mixer output. But the voice quality cannot be maintained by these algorithms if the background has high noise levels, therefore leading to lower mean opinion scores. A new weighted audio mixing algorithm [4] was introduced, including enhancement algorithms such as noise reduction, automatic level control and voice activity detection. The weighted factor is calculated by the proposed algorithm based on the root mean square values of the input streams of the participants of the conference. Thus, the algorithm is able to adaptively smoothen the input streams and provide a scaled mixer output which is better in perceived speech quality. Perceptual Evaluation of Speech Quality (PESQ) and Perceived Audio Level (PLL) measures are used to compare the results of this new algorithm with earlier work in different background noise levels. Better and consistent speech quality was demonstrated by this new algorithm in all background noise levels.

Another research group [5] developed a standalone audio mixer either for wireless microphones or for working cooperatively with audio consoles. The universal serial bus (USB)-based Software Defined Radio hardware component employs an SDR to perform personal computer (PC)-based computations, and the free open-source software (OSS) GNU radio companion (GRC) is chosen to build the block-diagram of the SDR application. Using Software Defined Radio to perform computations, GNU radio companion to build block-diagram of the SDR and Open Source Software as Jitsi for the XMPP client in a PC, Empathy for a client in a laptop and Openfire for the XMPP server, the authors tested these three technologies and the hardware and software components in several scenarios and demonstrated the efficiency of the proposed solution.

In a previous paper written by our research group [6], a system was designed that allows the remote control to perform an attenuation of the audio signals entering an analog mixer using an Android application which can run on a phone or tablet. This system allows a critical upgrade to analog audio mixers having much lower costs than an upgrade to a digital mixer.

The paper is organized as follows: Sect. 2 comprises the system architecture, whereas Sect. 3 describes the mobile application designed for controlling the mixer. Section 4 was dedicated to the presentation of the technical characteristics of the system. In Sect. 5, the analog audio mixer connections and signals processing are described. Finally, the conclusions are drawn in Sect. 6.

2   System Architecture

The proposed system (Fig. 1) consists of two subsystems. The first subsystem is called the effects processor and contains a power block, an attenuation block, a command and communication control block, and the communication radio interface. The second subsystem is a remote controller implemented as a smartphone application allowing multiple communication means like Bluetooth or Wi-Fi [7].

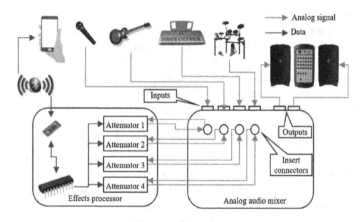

Fig. 1. The functional diagram of the proposed system

3   Mobile Application for Controlling the Mixer

The developed mobile application (Fig. 2) is described onwards. The sound engineer pairs his smartphone running the developed application with the effects processor by pressing the "Connect" button, selecting the Bluetooth transceiver of the effects processor from the list and entering the password. Each effects processor has a unique password, so other users cannot connect to it. In this way, the security of the system is increased.

Next, the channel to be controlled can be selected by pressing on the button illustrating the channel's number (from 1 to 4 in this implementation). After this, the user can drag the displayed fader like it would use a real fader on the analog mixer, to set the desired attenuation on the selected channel. At each movement of the slider, the selected channel and the current attenuation is sent to the Bluetooth transceiver which is part of the effects processor.

Fig. 2. The developed smartphone application.

The Bluetooth communication can be considered a serial communication tunnel, sending ASCII characters. This communication contains synchronization symbols, very important because it allows correct interpreting of the code word even if some characters are lost, allowing robust resynchronization with the data flow. The structure of the code word is "*CCAAA#" where "*" and "#" are the start and end of code word markers, "CC" is a two-digit number representing the selected channel (e.g., 00 would mean the first channel, 01 the second, 02 the third etc.), and "AAA" is the set value of the attenuation, expressed in dB. When a channel is selected, the last set value for the attenuation on that channel is automatically set on the slider, so no accidentally changes in the attenuation will occur. Figure 1 shows the interface of the developed application and Fig. 2 illustrates the functional diagram of the proposed system in the context of a live performance situation.

4   Technical Characteristics of the Control System

The system was designed keeping portability as a priority. The primary power supply is a 5 V battery power bank, having great capacities nowadays and being compact.

The attenuators need a larger supply voltage to accommodate the whole dynamic range that is typical for signals passing through an analog audio mixer. To obtain the needed 9 V, a step-up miniature switching power supply is used-not described in detail as it is not the main subject of this paper. Also, the microcontroller and the Bluetooth transceiver require a 3.3 V supply voltage, obtained using a LM317 regulator [8].

The voltage obtained using the switching power supply should be thoroughly filtered since it powers the attenuators which process the audio signal, and noise contamination should be avoided. It can be observed in Fig. 3 that each LM1971 attenuator [9] and the operational amplifiers [10] which participate in the audio signal processing are accompanied by a pair of power supply filtering capacitors.

Fig. 3. The developed remote-controlled effects processor featuring four audio channels.

Since the analog audio signal processing blocks in the developed effects processor are powered by a single supply source, and not using a symmetrical split power supply that could deliver positive and negative supply voltage, DC coupling capacitors must be used because audio signals have no DC components.

The capacitance was chosen to be 1μF. In this way, the lower cutoff frequency of the system is smaller than 20 Hz, outside the audio bandwidth. For correctly biasing the input and output, the attenuator circuit needs a voltage reference that is provided using a resistive divider made by R1 and R2 resistors, as shown in Fig. 3. The reference voltage is filtered using the capacitor labeled with C4 and furthermore the equivalent reference voltage source made using R1, R2, and C1 is improved by using an operational amplifier-based buffer, to decrease its output impedance.

A buffer is also used at the output of the attenuators to assure a large load impedance for the attenuator, no matter the load connected at the output of the system.

The data connection between the microcontroller and the attenuators is similar to the standard SPI communication and uses 3 lines: LOAD, DATA and CLOCK. The LOAD line of the destination chip is kept low during the communication. The DATA line will contain the desired value of the attenuation (in dB) delivered bit by bit, one bit in each clock period. The clock signal is delivered on the CLOCK line [9].

The commands to be sent to the attenuators are received by the microcontroller from the Bluetooth transceiver through serial communication. The decoding process of a code word is started when the "*" character is received. Then five more characters are received, and then it is tested that the next character is "#". If it is, then the selected channel and the value of the attenuation are extracted from the code and sent to the corresponding attenuator as it was described above. It must be observed that the attenuation value is received as a decimal number and must be sent to the attenuators as a binary value, so a decimal to binary conversion was implemented in the software code running on the microcontroller.

The whole code word can be treated like an integer number, processed as described further. Because C programming language was used, the channel can be identified by dividing the number by 1000 and the attenuation value would be the remainder after division. The initialization of the attenuators should be done when the system is powered up by setting the attenuation value to 0 dB (no attenuation).

The proposed system involves the use of a smartphone and this represents an open door to accessing many Internet of Things features and advantages [11]. For example, the smartphone is equipped with multiple communications means, like Wi-Fi, Bluetooth, and communications over a mobile network (in the form of data or voice) and, in this application, could be considered an IoT node. With these features, the system could be easily controlled from the Internet, simplifying the work of the sound engineer.

The proposed effects processor was implemented and tested. It is illustrated in Fig. 3. The developed hardware module can process four audio channels and it is a fully working prototype. The design could be improved by making the solution scalable with easy adding or removing audio channel modules and by redesigning the layout to occupy less space. The use of SMD components could also bring space and cost improvements.

5   Analog Audio Mixer Connections and Signals Processing

The musical instruments and the microphones are connected to the analog audio mixer, each on a separate channel, as shown in Fig. 2. Each channel on almost any analog audio mixer is featured with a connector named "Insert". This connector allows the connection of external audio signal processors. The connections are made so the external processors are cascaded in a way that allows the audio signal from a channel to be sent to the external effects processors and received back after it was processed using a single TRS (Tip-Ring-Sleeve) jack connector which is very convenient. Thanks to this connectivity type, the developed system is compatible with any analog audio mixer, but also with any other audio processor designed to work in this configuration.

After being processed using the external audio processors, the signals are summed and then sent to the main output of the mixer which is connected to the speakers, delivering the sound to the audience. A very important element of this proposes system is that the command terminal is a smartphone. This allows the commands to be sent not only from operating the developed smartphone application, but also using SMS or the data connection, behaving like an IoT node, greatly increasing the flexibility of the system. The circuit diagram of the proposed remote-controlled signal processor is shown in Fig. 4.

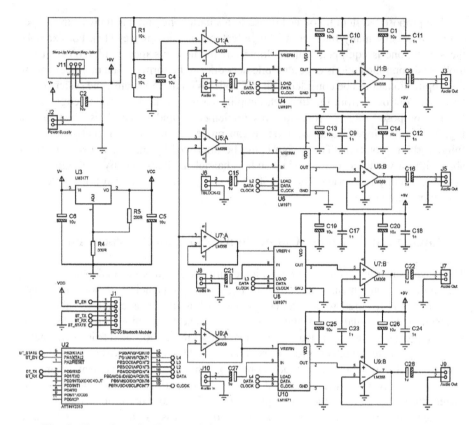

Fig. 4. The schematic diagram of the proposed remote-controlled signal processor.

6   Conclusion

The paper has proposed a system that allows the remote control of the level of the signals in an analogue audio mixer. The system consists of two subsystems: a remote controller implemented as a smartphone application which transmits selected channel and current desired value for the attenuation, and an effects processor that receives this information, decodes it and sends the attenuation information to the correct attenuator. The system allows communication via Bluetooth or Wi-Fi.

In this implementation, a Bluetooth communication between the smartphone and the effects processor was chosen. This is a serial communication tunnel. The transmitted code contains synchronization symbols, which are useful for correctly interpreting code words, even if some characters are lost during the transmission.

The proposed system has several advantages: it is secured with passwords to prevent access by other unknown users, it is compatible with most analog audio mixers because it can be inserted in the signal's path using the "Insert" connector that is available on the majority of the analog audio mixers, it is cost effective (especially compared to digital audio mixers which have this feature), and it is flexible due highlighted IoT capabilities.

The system was tested on a Soundcraft Spirit Rac Pac analog audio mixer and its correct functioning was confirmed. The range of the Bluetooth communication of around 10 m is enough for the targeted application, given the dimensions of small and medium concert venues. The system could be further improved by considering a scalable solution, because the audio channels on an analog audio mixer varies greatly from model to model, improving also the economical aspect of the solution.

Acknowledgments. This work was supported by a grant of the Ministry of Innovation and Research, UEFISCDI, project number 33PCCDI/01.03.2018 within PNCDI III, Platform of multi-agent intelligent systems for water quality monitoring on Romanian sector of Danube and Danube Delta (MultiMonD2).

References

1. Copîndean, R., Holonec, R., Drăgan, F.: Audio Mixer Ordered Microcontroller, vol. 56. Acta Electrotehnica, Cluj-Napoca (2015)
2. Bermúdez-Ortega, J., Besada-Portas, E.A., López-Orozco, J., de la Cruz, J.M.: A new open-source and smart-device accessible remote-control laboratory. In: 4th Experiment@International Conference (exp.at'17), Faro, pp. 143–144 (2017)
3. Chueh, T.F., Fanjiang, Y.Y.: Universal remote control on smartphone. In: 2012 International Symposium on Computer, Consumer and Control, Taichung, pp. 658–661 (2012)
4. Sethi, S., Kaur, P., Ahuja, S.: A new weighted audio mixing algorithm for a multipoint processor in a VoIP conferencing system. In: 2014 International Conference on Advances in Computing, Communications and Informatics (ICACCI), pp. 295–300 (2014)
5. Jaloudi, S.: Software-defined radio for modular audio mixers: making use of market-available audio consoles and software-defined radio to build multiparty audio-mixing systems. IEEE Consumer Electron. Mag. **6**(4), 97–104 (2017)
6. Marcu, A.E., Vlădescu, M., Dobre, R.A.: Cost effective remote control system for analog audio mixers. In: 2018 IEEE 24th International Symposium for Design and Technology in Electronic Packaging (SIITME), pp. 280–283 (2018)
7. Drumea, A.: Low power aspects of a microcontroller-based module with wireless communication. In: Proceedings of 23rd IEEE International Symposium for Design and Technology in Electronic Packaging (SIITME 2017), Constanța, pp. 134–137 (2017)
8. Texas Instruments datasheet. LM317 3-Terminal Adjustable Regulator, Revision X (2015)
9. Texas Instruments datasheet: LM1971 Overture™ Audio Attenuator Series Digitally Controlled 62 dB Audio Attenuator with/Mute, Revision B (2013)
10. Texas Instruments datasheet: LMx58-N Low-Power, Dual-Operational Amplifiers, Revision I (2013)
11. Lo, S.C., Yu, T.H., Tseng, C.C.: A remote control and media-sharing system using smart devices. J. Syst. Archit. **60**, 671–683 (2014)

Low-Power Intelligent Displaying System with Indoor Mobile Location Capability

Marius Vochin[1(✉)], Alexandru Vulpe[1], Ioana Marcu[1],
and George Suciu[2]

[1] University POLITEHNICA of Bucharest, Sector 6, Bucharest, Romania
marius.vochin@upb.ro
[2] Beia Consult International, Bucharest, Romania

Abstract. Modern buildings require different IT facilities, therefore integrated communication services have become a must. Although there are already commercial products on the market, most of them need well trained operators, while others require manual and time-consuming operations. The present paper introduces an intelligent displaying and alerting system (SICIAD), implemented over a communication infrastructure with support for wireless ePaper and iBeacon technologies to enhance displaying static and dynamic information, as well as to ease the indoor orientation of guests using smartphones. An Android mobile application is developed which enables indoor user location and guidance. Possible beneficiaries of such systems are educational and research institutions due to remote authentication support in research facilities through Eduroam technology. The paper gives functional validation and performance evaluation aspects are presented for the indoor positioning component of the proposed system.

Keywords: ePaper · iBeacon · Alerting system · Indoor positioning ·
Low power display

1 Introduction

Nowadays, the need for an intelligent, integrated, sustainable and easily managed system for digital and up-to-date room signage for offices, meeting rooms and conferences has an increase importance for modern public and office buildings. The emergence of Internet of Things (IoT) and digital interactions using electronic paper (ePaper) [1, 2] technology has marked a new phase of technological innovation in this direction. Important advantages are also brought by iBeacon [3] technology, which relies on the Bluetooth Low Energy (BLE) standard to create stationary constellations of low-power beacons which can be used to determine the indoor position of mobile terminals or signaling points of interest.

This work is part of the SICIAD [4, 5, 6] research project which proposes an intelligent displaying and alerting system that relies on wireless ePaper and iBeacon technologies from LANCOM to create custom displays for both static and dynamic information, as well as to ease the indoor orientation of guests.

V. Poulkov (Ed.): FABULOUS 2019, LNICST 283, pp. 146–153, 2019.
https://doi.org/10.1007/978-3-030-23976-3_15

In this paper, the iBeacon capabilities of the SICIAD system are investigated in respect to indoor advertising, guidance and location.

The paper is organized as follows: in Sect. 2 we present the mobile device positioning system, Sect. 3 contains detailed experimental validation scenarios, while Sect. 4 outlines the conclusions.

2 Mobile Positioning System

A mobile application was developed for Android system which enables the user to detect its location based on the availability of Wi-Fi and iBeacon (BLE based radio packets) signal presence. The main functionalities of this software module are to capture BLE packets, to extract location relevant information and to process them in order to display notification or alerts related to current status and user position. The application functional validation was performed on a commodity hardware such as LG K8 mobile phone with BLE 4.2 support and Android 6.0 operating system.

The application tests if the device is Bluetooth enabled, whether the adapter is turned on, if multiple Bluetooth notifications are allowed, and whether access to the current location of the phone is allowed. As the instructions are parsed, a checkup is made to see if the permissions have been granted, and the user is asked to allow access. If all the conditions are met, the necessary processes are created, and the application continues to function. If something is missing, a corresponding error message will be displayed, and the application will stop.

The list of retrieved devices is presented with details (name, address, time since the last occurrence, current and average Received Signal Strength Indicator (RSSI) level, relative distance estimation, RSSI mediated levels, and details display button). Only details about the rooms where LANCOM devices with iBeacon capabilities are located are shown; other received BLEs beacons are displayed by the app, but as no details are known about their location or configuration, only a general message will be displayed if the user selects them. These unknown devices can be filtered before adding them to the list, resulting in faster application performance (no need to process their data).

Different measurements were conducted on the access points in the University Politehnica of Bucharest (UPB) campus, which is a reinforced concrete building, with 30 cm thick walls. The location chosen to test the positioning solution is on the 3rd floor of Building A from Faculty of Electronics, Telecommunications and Information Technology, Bucharest, which is an area with offices and laboratories, as shown in Fig. 1. Commodity hardware has been used at the BLE receiver part, such as SM-G361F, G930FD smartphones, and also a HP ENVY x360 laptop. Three Lancom access points with integrated iBeacon transmitters were installed, one LN-830 E [7] model and two L-151E [8]. They were scheduled to periodically emit BLE advertising beacons to be visible to mobile devices, and a maximum power lever was choosen from three available levels.

Lancom iBeacon has been factory calibrated to provide three power levels at a distance of 1 m: high (−52 dBm), medium (−58 dBm), and low (−75 dBm) of the broadcasted beacon message, which allows an approximation of the distance between the access point and BLE receiver. For beacon broadcasting dedicated frequencies can

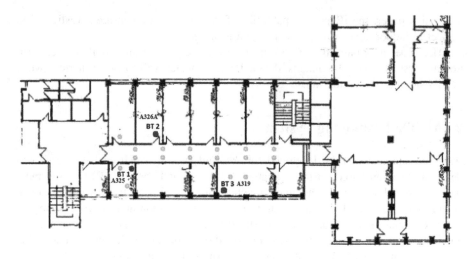

Fig. 1. Testbed location plan

be used: 2402 MHz, 2426 MHz, and 2480 MHz. With our off-the-shelf smartphone, the measurements at reception indicate −40, −46, −62 dBm, at a distance of several cm of the antenna.

3 Experimental Evaluation

It has been concluded from the measurements that a −10dBm attenuation is induced by a campus wall placed between the sender and receiver BLE device. Therefore, by setting the access point emission power at the lowest level and having one beacon in each room we would accurately provide room signage capability.

Each router used a unique MAC physical address, and different major and minor beacon values were set allowing the packets to be differentiated according to their source.

In the lobby, the points of measurement are aligned along two straight lines parallel to the hall walls. These two straight lines are 0.5 m from the nearest hallway, and within a distance of one meter. Along each straight line there were six measuring points, which represent a total of twelve locations. To calculate the distance between the router and the mobile terminal at each of these points, a simple Pythagoras' theorem for rectangular triangles was used.

The corresponding colors in Fig. 2 are: green for "x" - the measured average values of the RSSI, red for the maximum values obtained and blue for the minimum values corresponding to the respective distance between the terminal and each of the three access points. Thus, there can be observed the variation and distribution of values for each location. There can be noticed quite large variations, although the transmitter and the receiver were fixed during the measurements. These variations occur because the radio signal reaches the receiver on several paths that have different lengths and are attenuated due to passing through various objects or by the reflection of radio waves.

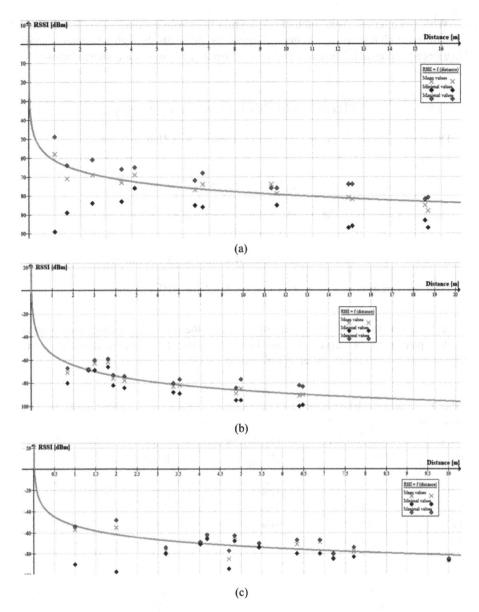

Fig. 2. Variation of RSSI with distance increasing for (a) AP1, (b) AP2 and (c) AP3 (Color figure online)

With green, curves were plotted considering the average values of the RSSI. They have different characteristics, being influenced by the walls through which the signals have been propagated. Their descriptive mathematical formulas are shown below:

$$F1(x) = -8.04738496 * \ln(x) - 61.27611836$$

Distance variation of the reception power level for AP1 transmitter.

$$F2(x) = -13.73284621 * \ln(x) - 54.99489558$$

Distance variation of the reception power level for AP2 transmitter.

$$F3(x) = -12.23482004 * \ln(x) - 53.26174039$$

Distance variation of the reception power level for AP3 transmitter.

It can be noted that each function is different from the other. In addition, they depend on the placement of objects in the building. Table 1 illustrates how good the approximations were with the actual measured values.

Table 1. Comparison between estimated and measured values for access point (a) AP1, (b) AP2 and (c) AP3

Distance [m]	Computed RSSI [dBm]	Measured RSSI [dBm]	Error [dBm]	Mean error [dBm]
(a)				
1	−61.28	−58	3.28	2.45
1.48	−64.43	−71	6.57	
2.47	−68.55	−69	0.45	
3.6	−71.58	−73	1.42	
4.11	−72.65	−69	3.65	
6.46	−76.29	−77	0.71	
6.76	−76.65	−74	2.65	
9.41	−79.32	−74	5.32	
9.62	−79.49	−79	0.49	
12.39	−81.53	−81	0.53	
12.54	−81.63	−82	0.37	
15.37	−83.26	−85	1.74	
15.49	−83.33	−88	4.67	

(continued)

Table 1. (*continued*)

Distance [m]	Computed RSSI [dBm]	Measured RSSI [dBm]	Error [dBm]	Mean error [dBm]
(b)				
1.72	−62.44	−71	8.56	3.31
2.7	−68.64	−68	0.64	
3	−70.08	−63	7.08	
3.64	−72.74	−62	10.74	
3.87	−73.58	−76	2.42	
4.39	−75.31	−78	2.69	
6.71	−81.14	−83	1.86	
7.02	−81.76	−82	0.24	
9.64	−86.11	−89	2.89	
9.86	−86.42	−85	1.42	
12.61	−89.8	−91	1.2	
12.78	−89.98	−90	0.02	
(c)				
1	−53.26	−57	3.74	5.47
2	−61.74	−55	6.74	
3.19	−67.45	−77	9.55	
4.02	−70.28	−70	0.28	
4.18	−70.76	−63	7.76	
4.71	−72.22	−85	12.78	
4.84	−72.56	−64	8.56	
5.43	−73.96	−72	1.96	
6.34	−75.86	−71	4.86	
6.89	−76.88	−69	7.88	
7.22	−77.45	−82	4.55	
7.71	−78.25	−78	0.25	
10.01	−81.45	−86	4.55	
10.37	−81.88	−85	3.12	

4 Conclusions

The system presented in this work implements an integrated communication infrastructure which offers dynamic display capabilities using the ePaper technology, as well as enables indoor location-based services such as visitor guidance and alerting using iBeacon-compatible mobile devices.

Being based on the BLE standard, iBeacon technology can potentially operate with almost all off the shelf smart mobile terminals, providing a cost-effective solution for an indoor positioning system. In combination with a smartphone application and a wireless communication system, BLE can enable advertising and distribution of location-based content.

In order to maintain real-life relevance of achieved data, commodity hardware was chosen to be used in test scenarios. A professional mobile BLE receiver was considered in order to improve indoor location awareness precision, but this would question relevance of data obtained in the context of commercial and industrial applicability.

While the iBeacon emitters integrated in the used Wireless access points can enable location-based services, accurately determining each users' location may require additional, battery-powered BLE beacons. Such a network (or constellation) of beacons could provide a more performant indoor guidance system, due to its effectiveness at a range of several meters (compared to several centimeters for NFC tags). Moreover, although the investment in Beacon devices may be significant, the already widespread use of compatible smart devices may reduce the necessity of other hand-held devices.

ACKNOWLEDGMENT. This work has been funded by UEFISCDI Romania under grant no. 60BG/2016 "Intelligent communications system based on integrated infrastructure, with dynamic display and alerting - SICIAD", and partially funded by grants no. 270CI / 2018 Intelligent Hive Colony Monitoring System- SIMCA, project number 33PCCDI/2018 within PNCDI III, SmartAgro (contract no. 8592/2018), and contract no. 5Sol/2017, PNCDI III, Integrated Software Platform for Mobile Malware Analysis (ToR-SIM).

Engineer CALIN Mihai-Catalin contributed to this work, during the preparation of his master thesis.

References

1. The technology behind LANCOM Wireless ePaper Displays. https://www.lancomsystems.com/fileadmin/download/reference_story/PDF/Wireless_ePaper_Solution_at_a_private_college,_Germany_EN.pdf. Accessed on 14 Aug 2018
2. Lancom Wireless ePaper Displays Specification sheet. https://www.lancomsystems.com/fileadmin/produkte/lc_wireless_epaper_displays/LANCOM-Wireless-ePaperDisplays-EN.pdf. Accessed on 14 Aug 2018
3. Sykes, S. Pentland, S., Nardi, S.: Context-aware mobile apps using iBeacons: towards smarter interactions. In: Proceedings of the 25th Annual International Conference on Computer Science and Software Engineering, 2015, pp. 120–129 (2015)
4. Vulpe, A., Vochin, M., Boicescu, L., Suciu, G.: Intelligent low-power displaying and alerting infrastructure for secure institutional networks. In: Fratu, O., Militaru, N., Halunga, S. (eds) Future Access Enablers for Ubiquitous and Intelligent Infrastructures. FABULOUS 2017. Lecture Notes of the Institute for Computer Sciences, Social Informatics and Telecommunications Engineering, vol 241. Springer, Cham. https://doi.org/10.1007/978-3-319-92213-3_21
5. Vochin, M., Vulpe, A., Suciu, G., Boicescu, L.: Intelligent displaying and alerting system based on an integrated communications infrastructure and low-power technology. In: WorldCist 2017 - 5th World Conference on Information Systems and Technologies, 2017, pp. 135–141 (2017)
6. Boicescu, L., Vochin, M., Vulpe, A., Suciu, G.: Intelligent Low-Power Displaying and Alerting Infrastructure for Smart Buildings. In: Rocha, Á., Adeli, H., Reis, L.P., Costanzo, S. (eds.) WorldCIST'18 2018. AISC, vol. 747, pp. 136–145. Springer, Cham (2018). https://doi.org/10.1007/978-3-319-77700-9_14

7. https://www.lancom-systems.com/products/wireless-lan/wireless-epaper-ibeacon/lancom-ln-830e-fi/. Accessed on 16 Aug 2018
8. https://www.lancom-systems.com/products/wireless-lan/lancom-l-151e-wireless/.   Accessed on 18 Aug 2018

IoT Security in the Digital Transformation Era

On How Instantaneous Path Loss Modeling Is a Need of Internet of Drones Based Intelligent Aerial Infrastructure

Purnima Lala Mehta[1] and Ambuj Kumar[2(✉)]

[1] IILM College of Engineering and Technology, Greater Noida, India
purnima.mehta@iilmcet.ac.in
[2] Aarhus University, Herning, Denmark
ambuj@btech.au.dk

Abstract. Drone technologies have become integral component to a lot of civilian and military applications. Talking of wireless communication, Aerial Base Stations are being proposed to act as relay and/or to provide cellular communications to the ground users. Most of the work has been concentrated to enhance the coverage and capacity of the network by finding the optimal parameters like aerial BS height, power etc. using definite or statistical path loss models. However, no work has been done to analyze the path loss performance of aerial BS ad-hoc network in serving moving ground users aka Place Time Capacity (PTC). A concept of hovering base stations (HANET) has been proposed previously to serve the PTC problem and in this paper, we put forward the need for instantaneous path loss modeling for network situations where both user and BS are itinerant.

Keywords: Drones · Cellular communications · Path loss modeling

1 Introduction

The need for design and development of wireless infrastructure to serve the massive capacity with high data rates as high as 1 Tbps for the state-of-the-art 5G networks and beyond explains an upgradation of the existing wireline infrastructure. A key challenge for telecom operators has always been serving hotspot areas that are densely packed by potential subscribers. Large subscriber base trying to access the radio resources at the same time is a major cause of network congestion leading to connection failures. Nonetheless, when such subscribers move in a group attempting to use mobile internet concurrently at events like festivals, carnivals, etc., they tend to create capacity demand at every position they traverse. Ambuj et al. have termed this condition of moving hotspot, even more precisely capacity-in-motion with respect to time as Place Time Capacity (PTC) [1, 2].

As reviewed in [3] and [4], adding low power Pico nodes have been proposed to be a promising proposal in enhancing network coverage and capacity to meet the high user traffic and data rate demand. However, under PTC situations, deploying small pico base stations does not seem to be an appropriate solution as capacity in demand is erratic and

© ICST Institute for Computer Sciences, Social Informatics and Telecommunications Engineering 2019
Published by Springer Nature Switzerland AG 2019. All Rights Reserved
V. Poulkov (Ed.): FABULOUS 2019, LNICST 283, pp. 157–166, 2019.
https://doi.org/10.1007/978-3-030-23976-3_16

tend to cease with time. Moreover, the number of handovers might increase posing a burden to the pico base stations. PTC congestion does not occur all-round the year and adding permanent base stations will be under-utilized at all other times.

Internet of Drones or IoD, which is a term dedicated for the integration and synergy of two independent technologies, which are Internet of Things, or IoT, and Unmanned Aerial Vehicles, aka Drones has been suggested into variety of applications [5]. One of the application of Aerial base stations are being considered in providing effective network coverage to ground users during emergency and disaster recovery situations and to serve the traffic hotspots. Recent trends in UAV based applications indicate in employing autonomous small aerial based radio nodes as a solution to assist the existing fixed infrastructure to provide cellular services to the ground users [6, 7]. Exploiting the current advances in compact physical structures, mountable small radio equipment along with small antenna array and accurate sensors are making it feasible for the aerial cells to communicate reliably with the ground nodes. We believe that deploying such multi-UAV radio devices working in teams can greatly solve PTC congestion in countries with potentially dense subscribers, e.g. India.

To service the moving subscriber groups aka Place Time Capacity (PTC) [1] a solution has been suggested in [8] had put forward the need for self-itinerant intelligent radios as a team of swarm intelligence based hovering base stations that were coined in as Hovering Ad-Hoc Network (HANET) that will be elaborated in the next sub-section.

When utilizing the low-altitude aerial vehicles, a consideration must be given to the signals travelling in multipaths due to the obstacles that can appear between the transmitter in the air and the receiver on the ground [9]. In this paper we attempt to explain the need for the analysis on the multipath propagation of Air to Ground (A2G) signal transmission.

1.1 The HANET Architecture

A Hovering Ad-hoc Network (HANET) is a network of aerial radio nodes that collaborate and coordinate to serve accumulated PTC situations at the AoE [10]. To understand the working of HANET, Fig. 1 depicts a conventional network architecture with an AoE served by two conventional base stations (following a PTC congestion and overloading), BS1 and BS2. The modified architecture will comprise additional elements that are:

(1) HANET Members
(2) HANET Gateway Base Station (HGBS)

The flying HANET members that include HANET Serving Members (HSM) and/or HANET Relay Members (HRM) is defined under HANET Base Station Subsystem (HBS) and is a separate network subsystem other than conventional Base Station Subsystem (BSS) involving the overloaded Base Stations BS1 & BS2. A team of HRM that are connected to a HGBS form a HANET Relay Subsystem (HRS). The role of HSM is to provide service to the mobile users underneath and the HRM are used to relay user data from HSM to HGBS. Each HANET member is capable of being a part of either HSM or HRM or both.

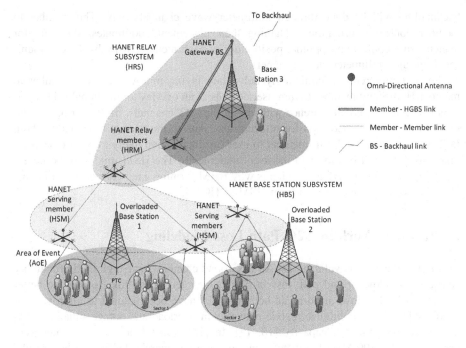

Fig. 1. The HANET architecture

Each HANET member will service the subscribers using four sectors comprising of directional antennas. As we can see from Fig. 1, the four sectors are mainly taking advantage of the proposed HANET design with a quadcopter base with four arms. Covering these arms with aerodynamic carbon-based casing will provide sufficient room for sticking metallic wafers to form a directional antenna and therefore, we can have four directional antennas for each of the technology (IMT and MM). Further, having more sectors per 360-degree span will provide better control on the dynamic subscriber movements in the HANET member's vicinity. Also, the higher number of sectors will provide the opportunity to increase the antenna gain by narrowing the beamwidth without losing coverage at the sector boundaries. Depending on many propagation related factors, more sectors will likely also give us better confinement of interference in the system.

In dense urban, urban and suburban scenarios, it is inevitable to face severe propagation loss due to shadowing, diffraction, reflection, etc. Therefore, direct backhaul from HSM may lead to loss of communication. In this case, the HRM can relay the user data to the nearby base station (HGBS). The communication in the HBS requires member to user communication that will be provided through IMT channels and possible future millimeter wave cellular channels by the HSM. User data will be relayed by the HRM to service the moving crowd continuously. By making HANET follow the moving subscribers, the number of handovers that could have possibly occurred in the network otherwise would eventually reduce thereby potentially relieving the bulk handover issues within the overloaded network. Further, the backhauling will be done through millimeter wave channels only. The member to member control information containing their placement coordinates, IDs, etc. for maneuvering control and optimal positioning of each member will also be communicated through millimeter wave channels.

For our research, we particularly delve into laying mm-waves for a member to member/HGBS and member to mm-user devices as an overlay to traditional IMT layer. This is because (i) no interference with any of the IMT channels, (ii) higher bandwidth to serve mm-user devices and for relaying user data to the nearest base station (both IMT and mm data), and, (iii) member to user communication likely to be in LOS at all times as HSM will be closer to the users underneath. The HSM might not be necessarily in LOS with the HGBS, which is why HRM forming a network chain will come into play to relay the user data from HSM to HGBS.

2 Previous Work in A2G Path Loss Modeling

In [11–13], the authors validate that Air to Ground channels have high LOS probability and lesser shadowing and path loss in NLOS over terrestrial links to provide better coverage with By now, airborne ad-hoc networks have been studied to improve connectivity [12, 14], to optimize mobile networks in overload and outage situations [15] and to enhance the cell capacity [16, 17]. In [18], some field measurements were conducted LTE 800 MHz frequency band, using a commercial UAV and their results show that path loss exponent decreases as the UAV moves up, away from the ground.

It is essential to model the Air to Ground propagation channel by accommodating the path loss effects and shadowing due to ground obstacles. Statistical path loss models for urban environments were defined in [11] and as a part of ABSOLUTE project in [19], where the path loss and shadowing were evaluated as a function of elevation angle. The ABSOLUTE project also investigated on the optimal altitude of Low Altitude aerial Platforms (LAPs) to provide maximum radio coverage [14]. Their study showed that optimal altitude is a function of maximum allowed path-loss and statistical parameters of urban environment by considering a fixed value of 10 dB for maximum allowable path-loss for their analysis.

Optimal altitude of drone small cells [20] was examined based on path loss analysis performed in [16]. Cognitive relay nodes to improve the coverage of airborne LTE emergency network were also proposed [21] considering the path loss models defined in [7] and [19]. Authors in [21] considered standard models like Okumara-Hata, COST-Hata and COST- WI propagation models for evaluating the coverage of UAV wireless networks to provide cellular services. Further the authors in [22] have extended the Rice channel model to account for multipath effects introduced by the flight altitude of UAVs using the IEEE 802.11 communication link. In [23], authors have proposed a method to apply approximately the multipath channel models of terrestrial broadcasting in UAV based broadcasting.

The work aforementioned used an invariable path loss model and/or definite value of mean path loss for their analysis. In this paper, we direct our investigations to the instantaneous path loss modeling wherein the UAV mobility plays a significant role in transmitting signals to the ground receivers.

3   Instantaneous Path Loss Modeling in HANET

Any existing Path Loss Model (PLM), which is primarily static in nature, can be perceived as the instantaneous path loss model (iPLM) if the system dynamics are taken into account and the eventual value of the iPL is time dependent and time variant. Such PLMs are inevitable for non-conventional approach of the network deployment and network architectures.

3.1   Need for IPL Estimation

As the HANET comprises of hovering base stations to follow and serve PTC groups, because of their movements, different physical morphologies and RF signal characteristics might be encountered. Each member hovering to different positions with time across the Area of Event (AoE) will observe variation in land morphology like buildings, open spaces, trees, water bodies, etc., on the ground that constitute the AoE along with the PTC subscribers.

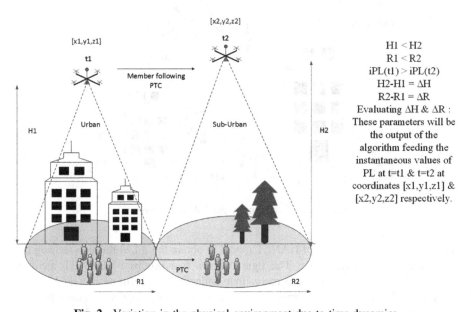

Fig. 2. Variation in the physical environment due to time dynamics

As depicted in Fig. 2, to follow a PTC group, the HANET member needs to displace itself from coordinate [x1, y1, z1] at time t1 to coordinate [x2, y2, z2] at time t2. At t1, the physical terrain observed by the member was urban and is it hovered, the environment observed by the member at time t2 was sub-urban. It is evident that with change in physical environment, the maximum allowable path loss will also differ. This change in path loss due to physical land morphology computed at different time instants is called as the *instantaneous path loss (iPL)*. Computing with the new iPL value the member will move to a new position and transit its altitude from H1 to a new altitude H2 to deliver the required performance. With the change in altitude eventually the coverage radius will also vary. The increase or decrease in height from the previous position will be governed by the ground physical morphology encountered.

3.2 Estimation of IPL by HANET

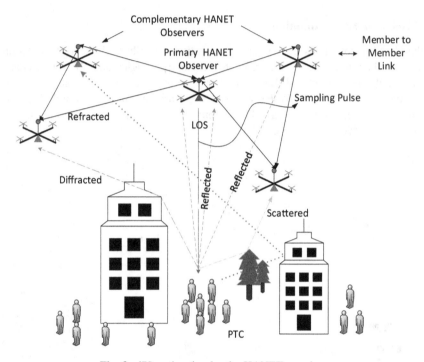

Fig. 3. iPL estimation by the HANET members

Figure 3 depicts the concept of HANET model to obtain the iPLM through sensing the land morphology in real time. The figure shows two groups of HANET member observers, primary and complementary, that collectively determine the iPLM for a given network situation. The primary observer sends a pulse that will bounce back to antenna arrays fitted in the chassis of the member and is responsible for the majority of sensing. However, it can be assisted by complementary observers with the role of sensing the reflected, refracted and diffracted signal spread of the sampling pulse that could be used to determine the signal fading of the AoE. The HANET members are low altitude serving BSs with inter-member distance approximately >300 m, the presence of such complementary members nearby is quite likely. Hence, neighboring members, whose primary job is to serve the user clusters beneath, might help the primary observer to estimate the losses in the area beneath it. Eventually, these members can help each other by swapping the responsibilities and to estimate the iPL for a significant land area where the user clusters may traverse. Needless to say, more are the neighbors, more efficient is the path loss estimation. Since, the very concept of this HANET model is to work cooperatively as a team, this kind of real time estimation of the path loss can help in enhancing the coverage and capacity of the system.

3.3   Challenges in Formulating IPL by HANET

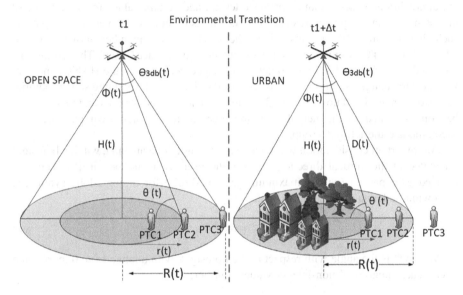

Fig. 4. Dynamics due to environmental transition

The innovative architecture, discussed in this paper, composed of hovering base stations is what we define as A Self-Itinerant Intelligent Aerial Radio Architecture (SIIARA). This SIIRA model, consisting of multiple HANET members will be efficient when all the participating members are well coordinated and placed as per demand. It is proposed that members use a separate channel to communicate with each other to itinerate and configure according the environment beneath each of them. It is also expected from this architecture to proactively predict and follow the user cluster thereby, creating a jittery signal reception for users below the transiting member due to variant morphology across the path that each cluster follow. Figure 4 describes such situation by exemplifying a single member that is in transit. We can see in this figure that from any arbitrary time t1 to a next time instant t1 + Δt, there can be significant variation in the morphology beneath a serving member as it itinerates (here from an open space such as park to an urban type house cluster). Such jitters, when occur unexpectedly, may cause severe disruptions in the member-member relations and configurations time to time. Hence, the parameters that relate coverage radius (R), member height are likely to vary with time. Although, each parameter here are variables themselves and can accommodate the changing values, however, when morphological variations below a member are function of time, then incorporating them in modeling the relations will provide more convenience in configuring a SIIARA network.

The A2G radio access channel between a HANET member and a subscriber group beneath will accommodate variable physical characteristics at any given time. In Fig. 4, we present a case where PTC groups move from one place to another from a given initial condition at time 't1'. Here we represent the PTC groups as single users. The initial conditions observed an open space terrain and certain values for the altitude of the member, transmit power, distance between transmitter and receiver, throughput etc. such that all three PTC groups fall in the service of the member above them. At 't1 + Δt', the PTC groups traversed the member also displaced itself. The terrain now observed was urban and in order to deliver the same performance the HANET member will have to change its altitude and come closer to the ground. By doing so the footprint has also decreased and now the PTC3 group is outside its service area and this needs to be communicated to the neighboring members to adjust their own parameters to accommodate the left-out group.

An important consideration will be in using a single-lobe antenna, with its boresight orientated in the vertical direction towards the users as mentioned in [8]. The normalized gain pattern (with a maximum gain of 0 dBi) for a single-lobe symmetric beamwidth antenna can be approximated as,

$$G_r = \cos^m \Phi \tag{1}$$

Where Φ is the angle with respect to the boresight, with a range from 0 to $\pi/2$; and m can take integer and non-integer values. Further,

$$\cos^m \left(\frac{\theta_{3db}}{2} \right) = 0.5 \tag{2}$$

Θ_{3dB} is the half-power beamwidth (HPBW);

The users within the half power beamwidth shall receive the maximum power with decrease in power when moving away from it. While user group is moving the member following it must ensure to accommodate majority if the users within the half power beamwidth. The top to bottom approach of illuminating the challenge area is more feasible than any other probable methods, as this leads to line-of-sight convenience between user and the serving base station.

In case of iPLM, the beam width estimation must include the system dynamics and the augmented equations shall not be as simple as Eqs. (1) and (2). With every iterative move that the users groups on the ground take, there an entire new PLM scenario that the HANET members have to take to cater of new situations. This also includes changes in the propagation environment, user densities, deployment feasibility and many more. Hence, proactive knowledge of the iPL is inevitable for the drones for network coverage solutions.

4 Conclusions

This paper is an attempt to put forward the need for modeling the path loss between an aerial vehicle serving as base station in the air and the ground receivers which are the cellular users. Because the serving base stations are in mobility at all times and target to serve the moving user groups on the ground, we suggest that the path loss should be taken into account depending on the physical and land morphology that might change in mobility-driven scenario. We have coined this concept as *instantaneous path loss (iPL)*. We present the need for the same and discuss the challenges in formulating the instantaneous path loss modeling where Internet of Drones based intelligent aerial infrastructure is used to service the ground users.

Acknowledgements. This paper is supported by the "*Capacity building and ExchaNge towards attaining Technological Research and modernizing Academic Learning*," or CENTRAL Project, which is the Erasmus+ *Capacity Building in Higher Education* (CBHE) initiative under the *Education, Audiovisual and Culture Executive Agency* (EACEA) of the European Commission.

References

1. Kumar, A., Mehta, P.L., Prasad, R.: Place time capacity- a novel concept for defining challenges in 5G networks and beyond in India. In: 2014 IEEE Global Conference on Wireless Computing Networking (GCWCN), pp. 278–282 (2014)
2. Kumar, A.: Active Probing Feedback based Self Configurable Intelligent Distributed Antenna System: For Relative and Intuitive Coverage and Capacity Predictions for Proactive Spectrum Sensing and Management. Aalborg Universitetsforlag (2016)
3. Heterogeneous networks - Ericsson: Ericsson.com, February 2012. https://www.ericsson.com/en/white-papers/machine-intelligence
4. Stanze, O., Weber, A.: Heterogeneous networks with LTE-advanced technologies. Bell Labs Tech. J. **18**(1), 41–58 (2013)
5. On How the Internet of Drones is going to Revolutionize the Technology Applications in Business Paradigms - Research - Aarhus University. https://pure.au.dk/portal/en/publications/on-how-the-internet-of-drones-is-going-to-revolutionize-the-technology-applications-in-business-paradigms(a1a6526c-7966-4c78-b59a-f0426db9fa31).html. Accessed 17 Mar 2019
6. Goddemeier, N., Rohde, S., Wietfeld, C.: Experimental performance evaluation of role-based connectivity management for cooperating UAVs. In: 2014 IEEE 79th Vehicular Technology Conference (VTC Spring), pp. 1–5 (2014)
7. Rohde, S., Wietfeld, C.: Interference aware positioning of aerial relays for cell overload and outage compensation. In: 2012 IEEE Vehicular Technology Conference (VTC Fall), pp. 1–5 (2012)
8. Mehta, P.L.: A Self-Itinerant Intelligent Aerial Radio Architecture (SIIARA), Ph.D. thesis, Aarhus University, Herning, Denmark (2018)
9. Bae, J., Kim, Y., Hur, N., Kim, H.M.: Study on air-to-ground multipath channel and mobility influences in UAV based broadcasting. In: 2018 International Conference on Information and Communication Technology Convergence (ICTC), pp. 1534–1538 (2018)

10. Mehta, P.L., Prasad, R.: Aerial-heterogeneous network: a case study analysis on the network performance under heavy user accumulations. Wirel. Pers. Commun. **96**(3), 3765–3784 (2017)
11. McGeehan, J., Tameh, E.K., Nix, A.R.: Path loss models for air-to-ground radio channels in urban environments. In: 2006 IEEE 63rd Vehicular Technology Conference, vol. 6, pp. 2901–2905 (2006)
12. Feng, Q., McGeehan, J., Nix, A.R.: Enhancing coverage and reducing power consumption in peer-to-peer networks through airborne relaying. In: 2007 IEEE 65th Vehicular Technology Conference - VTC2007-Spring, pp. 954–958 (2007)
13. Košmerl, J., Vilhar, A.: Base stations placement optimization in wireless networks for emergency communications. In: 2014 IEEE International Conference on Communications Workshops (ICC), pp. 200–205 (2014)
14. Al-Hourani, A., Kandeepan, S., Lardner, S.: Optimal LAP altitude for maximum coverage. IEEE Wirel. Commun. Lett. **3**(6), 569–572 (2014)
15. Al-Hourani, A., Kandeepan, S.: Cognitive relay nodes for airborne LTE emergency networks. In: 2013, 7th International Conference on Signal Processing and Communication Systems (ICSPCS), pp. 1–9 (2013)
16. Gomez, K., Hourani, A., Goratti, L., Riggio, R., Kandeepan, S., Bucaille, I.: Capacity evaluation of aerial LTE base-stations for public safety communications. In: 2015 European Conference on Networks and Communications (EuCNC), pp. 133–138 (2015)
17. Guo, W., Devine, C., Wang, S.: Performance analysis of micro unmanned airborne communication relays for cellular networks. In: 2014 9th International Symposium on Communication Systems, Networks Digital Sign (CSNDSP), pp. 658–663 (2014)
18. Wang, K., et al.: Path loss measurement and modeling for low-altitude UAV access channels. In: 2017 IEEE 86th Vehicular Technology Conference (VTC-Fall), pp. 1–5 (2017)
19. Al-Hourani, A., Kandeepan, S., Jamalipour, A.: Modeling air-to-ground path loss for low altitude platforms in urban environments. In: 2014 IEEE Global Communications Conference, pp. 2898–2904 (2014)
20. Mozaffari, M., Saad, W., Bennis, M., Debbah, M.: Drone small cells in the clouds: design, deployment and performance analysis. In: 2015 IEEE Global Communications Conference (GLOBECOM), pp. 1–6 (2015)
21. Goddemeier, N., Daniel, K., Wietfeld, C.: Coverage evaluation of wireless networks for unmanned aerial systems. In: 2010 IEEE Globecom Workshops, pp. 1760–1765 (2010)
22. Goddemeier, N., Wietfeld, C.: Investigation of air-to-air channel characteristics and a UAV specific extension to the rice model. In: 2015 IEEE Globecom Workshops (GC Wkshps), pp. 1–5 (2015)
23. Amorim, R., Nguyen, H., Mogensen, P., Kovács, I.Z., Wigard, J., Sørensen, T.B.: Radio channel modeling for UAV communication over cellular networks. IEEE Wirel. Commun. Lett. **6**(4), 514–517 (2017)

Facial Analysis Method for Pain Detection

Oana Subea[1,2(✉)] and George Suciu[2]

[1] Faculty of Electronics, Telecommunications and Information Technology,
University Politehnica of Bucharest, Bucharest, Romania
oana.subea@beia.ro
[2] R&D Department BEIA Consult International, Bucharest, Romania
{oana.subea,george}@beia.ro

Abstract. Facial expression recognition has been an active research topic for many years. In this paper a method for automatically recognizing pain intensity in images with facial expressions will be implemented. The method presented will contain a first step in which the face and the important points on the face will be located using the DLIB library. The second step consists of the calculation of HOG-type traits in order to describe the face found. The traits will be used to train a Random Forest (RF) regressor that will estimate the intensity of the pain. Training and testing will be done on the public UNBC-McMaster shoulder Pain Expression Archive database, using Python programming.

Keywords: Image processing · Facial recognition ·
HOG(Histogram of oriented Gradients) · Random Forest · DLIB

1 Introduction

Charles Darwin's book in 1872, entitled "Expression of Emotion in Man and Animals", has had a great impact on nowadays facial expression recognition technology. This area has been later studied by other scientists who have demonstrated that emotions are communicated in different facial and vocal ways, and this is available for every culture and species. Researchers in this filed, such as Keltner, Ekman, Gonzaga, & Beer, reviewed the literature regarding how emotion can be expressed in facial features. Scherer, Johnstone, & Klasmeyer wrote about the expression of emotion by voice, the theme of language as a way in which people can express their emotions was approached by Reilly & Seibert, and Snowdon studied different displays amongst various nonhuman species.

It is a fact that one of the stronger and most immediate means of communication for individuals is the facial expression. Sometimes, human beings can show involuntarily their intentions or emotions through facial features and they can do that faster than they would using words [1].

20 years ago the situation of research and literature in terms of emotional expression was largely based on facial expression [2]. Keltner, Ekman, Gonzaga, and Beer showed that each emotion is characterized by a distinct facial expression. Also, the types of emotions on which these studies were based were limited [4].

Published by Springer Nature Switzerland AG 2019. All Rights Reserved
V. Poulkov (Ed.): FABULOUS 2019, LNICST 283, pp. 167–180, 2019.
https://doi.org/10.1007/978-3-030-23976-3_17

The community of scientists became more interested in emotions and facial expression recognition in the last 10 years, the number of surveys on this topic increasing every year. Paul Ekman is the one who laid the foundation for the detection of facial expression by formulating in 1970 the "theory of basic emotions". The basic emotions are the following: surprise, joy, fear, sadness, anger and disgust. This theory has subsequently led at the appearance of the Facial Action Coding System (FACS) which is based on 44 Action Units (AUs). These Action Units are labeled according facial muscles movements and more Action Units form a facial expression [3]. The Facial Action Coding System is presented in Fig. 1 [9]. In Fig. 2 are presented Upper Face Action units and some combinations.

Upper Face Action Units					
AU 1	AU 2	AU 4	AU 5	AU 6	AU 7
Inner Brow Raiser	Outer Brow Raiser	Brow Lowerer	Upper Lid Raiser	Cheek Raiser	Lid Tightener
*AU 41	*AU 42	*AU 43	AU 44	AU 45	AU 46
Lid Droop	Slit	Eyes Closed	Squint	Blink	Wink
Lower Face Action Units					
AU 9	AU 10	AU 11	AU 12	AU 13	AU 14
Nose Wrinkler	Upper Lip Raiser	Nasolabial Deepener	Lip Corner Puller	Cheek Puffer	Dimpler
AU 15	AU 16	AU 17	AU 18	AU 20	AU 22
Lip Corner Depressor	Lower Lip Depressor	Chin Raiser	Lip Puckerer	Lip Stretcher	Lip Funneler
AU 23	AU 24	*AU 25	*AU 26	*AU 27	AU 28
Lip Tightener	Lip Pressor	Lips Part	Jaw Drop	Mouth Stretch	Lip Suck

Fig. 1. FACS action units (AU). AUs with "*" indicate that the criteria have changed for this AU, that is, AU 25, 26, and 27 are now coded according to criteria of intensity (25A-E), and AU 41, 42, and 43 are now coded according to criteria of intensity

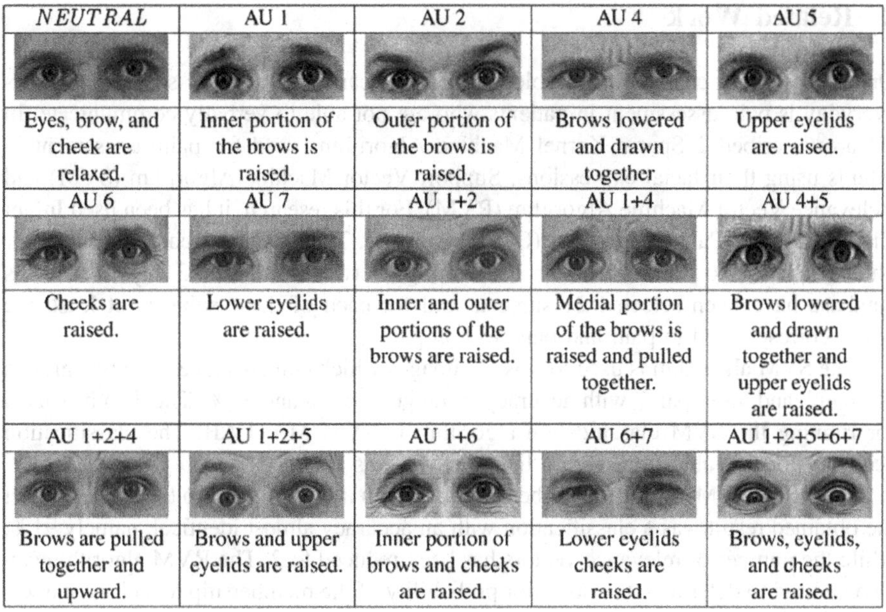

NEUTRAL	AU 1	AU 2	AU 4	AU 5
Eyes, brow, and cheek are relaxed.	Inner portion of the brows is raised.	Outer portion of the brows is raised.	Brows lowered and drawn together	Upper eyelids are raised.
AU 6	AU 7	AU 1+2	AU 1+4	AU 4+5
Cheeks are raised.	Lower eyelids are raised.	Inner and outer portions of the brows are raised.	Medial portion of the brows is raised and pulled together.	Brows lowered and drawn together and upper eyelids are raised.
AU 1+2+4	AU 1+2+5	AU 1+6	AU 6+7	AU 1+2+5+6+7
Brows are pulled together and upward.	Brows and upper eyelids are raised.	Inner portion of brows and cheeks are raised.	Lower eyelids cheeks are raised.	Brows, eyelids, and cheeks are raised.

Fig. 2. Upper face action units and some combinations

The method for estimation of pain intensity will be implemented using a database which contains facial images annotated with pain-specific expressions and action units. Part of this database will be used for the training of the classifier and the rest will help us to test the classifier.

Having an input image, we will be able to detect the face and its important facial points, in this way, in the area of the facial points of interest, we will calculate features using HOG (Histogram of Oriented Gradients) descriptor. The resulting traits will be used to train a classifier, such as Random Forest (RF). After the training, the method will be tested to see the result to different types of training (we will use random images).

As an application of this method, we will take real-time images from a webcam and we will display next to the detected face the corresponding action unit represented by an emoticon.

The rest of the paper is organized as follows: Sect. 2 describes related work in this area, like pain assessment in patients who aren't unable to verbally communicate with medical staff or face analysis for security and surveillance applications. Section 3 presents the principle of HOG (Histogram of Oriented Gradients) descriptor. Section 4 represents the description of the process, and Sect. 6 is the conclusion and future work of this project.

2 Related Work

One of the most challenging problem in patient care that medical staff experiences everyday is pain assessment in patients who are not able to verbally communicate. In [5] are described 2 Sparse Kernel Machine Algorithms used for pain assessment in infants using their facial expressions: Support Vector Machine Algorithm (SVM) and Relevance Vector Machine Algorithm (RVM). For this research, it has been used Infant Classification of Pain Expressions (COPE) database. Theis database contains 204 color photographs of 26 Caucasian neonates with age between 18 h and 3 days. From this database have been selected 21 subjects and for each of these subjects at least one photo corresponded to pain and oane to non-pain.

The SVM algorithm is used to classify images which contains faces into two groups of "pain" and "non-pain" with accuracy in range of 82% and 88%. The Toolbox used for running the SVM classification algorithm is SVM MATLAB. The classification accuracy for this algorithm with a linear kernel was 90%.

When the RVM algorithm has been applied with a linear kernel to the same data set the obtained result was a classification with an accuracy almost identical, namely 91%, while the number of relevance vectors has been reduced to 2. The RVM algorithm can also be used to determine the posterior probability of the membership to a class of a test image.

Further, the results obtained using the RVM method were compared to human assessment. For measuring the agreement in the main intensity assessment between the human examiners and the RVM algorithm the weighted kappa coefficient has been used. This coefficient has a value of 0.48 for human experts and 0.52 for non-experts as compared with the RVM. This result shows that the agreement is moderate, and the classification is almost identical for binary classification [5].

Besides the importance that Face Analysis has in the medical field, it can be also very useful in other areas, such as security and surveillance, human-computer interaction, biomechanical applications, customized applications, etc.

In [6] it's presented a system framework of facial expression recognition for video surveillance purpose. The system is composed of four modules:

1. Face processing
2. Domain transformation
3. Feature extraction

Expression recognition
The first module, Face Processing, consists 3 steps. The first one is face detection which is performed by adopting the Viola-Jones face detection system. This face detector is used to select the desired face area. Next step is face cropping in order to obtain the required facial part of the image. The third and final process is scale normalization which is made in order to reduce the feature extraction area and to improve the execution time. This stage supposes the normalization of the cropped facial part to a window of size 128 × 128 pixels. For the scaling of the image, the method of the nearest neighbor is used.

Domain transformation involves applying the Discrete Wavelet Transform (DWT) in order to obtain local information by decomposing image into low and high frequency subbands. These subbands can be further combined with descriptors like HOG. The orientation information of the image is obtained by following combinations of scaling functions $\phi(x)$ and wavelet functions $\psi(x)$.

- $\phi_{LL}(x, y) = \phi(x)\phi(y)$ (1.1)

- $\psi_{LH}(x, y) = \phi(x)\psi(y)$ (1.2)

- $\psi_{HL}(x, y) = \psi(x)\phi(y)$ (1.3)

- $\psi_{HH}(x, y) = \psi(x)\psi(y)$ (1.4)

The feature extraction process is based on the use of a histogram of oriented gradients (HOG) feature. It counts the number of occurrences of gradient orientation in the local patch of an image. The gradient information changes meaningfully near edges and corners. At every pixel, the gradient has a magnitude G and a direction θ which is determined using LL subband (ϕ_{LL}) of DWT.

$$G = \theta\sqrt{\phi_{LL}^2(x) + \phi_{LL}^2(y)} = \tan^{-1}\frac{\phi_{LL}(y)}{\phi_{LL}(x)} \qquad (1.5)$$

where:

- $\phi_{LL}(x)$ – is x – direction derivative of LL subband

- $\phi_{LL}(y)$ – is y – direction derivative of LL subband

The most important step is expression recognition module. The expressions are classified using a Support Vector Machine (SVM) classifier with OVA architecture. After feature computation, SVM classifier is trained and tested. For the recognition of expressions in the testing videos sequences, the training labels have been used. Experiments were performed in Matlab 8.3 environment. The results show that the proposed approach is effective towards recognition of angry, disgust, fear, happy, sad and surprised expression [6].

3 HOG Descriptor

A features descriptor is a representation of an image, or of a portion of an image, which simplifies the given image by extracting the useful information and by eliminating the unnecessary information. Usually, this kind of features descriptor converts an image with width $\times$ length $\times$ 3 dimensions, where 3 represents the 3 color channels, into a dimension vector. This vector can be further used for image recognition or objects detection in images.

Such a descriptor is also HOG (Histogram of Oriented Gradients). It can be used for images of any size, the only condition being that the images or the region of the image have a fixed aspect ratio. For example, for 1:2 report, the used image has to be 100×200, 128×256, 1000×2000 dimension. For this kind of descriptor, the input image has commonly $64 \times 128 \times 3$ dimension. In this case, the vector will have the length: n = 3780 [7].

3.1 The Principle of the Gradient Method

The principle of this method consists of defining contour points. These points represent the image's pixels whose gray levels present big changes. Therefore, we will use derivative gradient operators. If the input image has continuous space support, the derivative will have the maximum value in the direction of an edge. The linear combination of partial derivatives in horizontal and vertical directions represents the derivative of an image in the r direction, which forms θ with the horizontal direction.

$$\frac{\partial f}{\partial r} = \frac{\partial f}{\partial x}\frac{\partial x}{\partial r} + \frac{\partial f}{\partial y}\frac{\partial y}{\partial r} = \frac{\partial f}{\partial x}\cos\theta + \frac{\partial f}{\partial y}\sin\theta \tag{1.6}$$

$$\frac{\partial f}{\partial r} = f_x \cos\theta + f_y \sin\theta \tag{1.7}$$

The maximum value of this derivative is given by the equation below:

$$\frac{\partial}{\partial\theta}\left(\frac{\partial f}{\partial r}\right) = -f_x \sin\theta + f_y \cos\theta = 0 \tag{1.8}$$

The solution to the equation is:

$$\theta_0 = \tan^{-1}\left(\frac{f_y}{f_x}\right) \tag{1.9}$$

In the direction of the θ angle the gradient module is:

$$\left(\frac{\partial f}{\partial r}\right)_{max} = \sqrt{f_x^2 + f_y^2} \tag{2.1}$$

Practically, the implementation of this method involves the calculation of partial derivatives f_x and f_y, the calculation of the maximum gradient module and its direction, for each point of the image. The maximum value of the gradient that we have obtained will be compared to a fixed threshold. If the gradient is greater than the threshold the pixel for which we have calculated the gradient will be a contour pixel.

To calculate the partial derivatives f_x and f_y, we need first to make their translation in discrete time as follows.

$$f_x = \frac{\partial f}{\partial x} = \frac{\Delta f(m,n)}{\Delta m} \qquad (2.2)$$

$$f_y = \frac{\partial f}{\partial y} = \frac{\Delta f(m,n)}{\Delta n} \qquad (2.3)$$

These derivatives can be implemented in many ways using linear combinations of pixels in the image that are positioned in the vicinity of the current pixel with the coordinates (m,n). All these operations can be achieved by linear filtering using special masks. These masks are presented in Eqs. (2.5), (2.7), (2.9).

1. $\begin{cases} f_x = f(m,n) - f(m+1,n) \\ f_y = f(m,n) - f(m,n+1) \end{cases}$ \qquad (2.4)

The mask used : $\begin{cases} W_x = (-1 \quad \boxed{1}) \\ W_y = \begin{pmatrix} \boxed{1} \\ -1 \end{pmatrix} \end{cases}$ \qquad (2.5)

2. $\begin{cases} f_x = f(m-1,n) - f(m,n) \\ f_y = f(m,n-1) - f(m,n) \end{cases}$ \qquad (2.6)

The mask used : $\begin{cases} W_x = (1 \quad \boxed{-1}) \\ W_y = \begin{pmatrix} 1 \\ \boxed{-1} \end{pmatrix} \end{cases}$ \qquad (2.7)

3. $\begin{cases} f_x = f(m-1,n) - f(m+1,n) \\ f_y = f(m,n-1) - f(m,n+1) \end{cases}$ \qquad (2.8)

The mask used : $\begin{cases} W_x = (1 \quad \boxed{0} \quad -1) \\ W_y = \begin{pmatrix} 1 \\ \boxed{0} \\ -1 \end{pmatrix} \end{cases}$ \qquad (2.9)

Because of the small size of the derivation masks, Wx, Wy, the results can be very easily affected by noise. In this case, it is necessary to combine the derivation filtering with smoothing filtering so that the noise effects will be reduced. If we consider that the noise is Gaussian and additive type, when we will apply the smoothing filter we will obtain a lower value of the contrast (the blurry effect). To minimize these effects, the mediation operation for smoothing filtering has to be in a perpendicular direction to that of the contours, more exactly, for vertical derivation, we will use a horizontal mask for the smoothing operation, and for horizontal derivation, we will use a vertical mask.

Another alternative, used in most cases, is the use of a weighted mediation for the smoothing process. This one allows us to give greater importance to the currently processed pixel. It is preferably to use the (2.9) type derivative operators. In this way, we obtain the following horizontal and vertical masks for the derivative operators.

$$W_x = \begin{pmatrix} 1 & 0 & -1 \\ c & \boxed{0} & -c \\ 1 & 0 & -1 \end{pmatrix} \qquad (3.1)$$

$$W_y = \begin{pmatrix} 1 & c & -1 \\ 0 & \boxed{0} & 0 \\ -1 & -c & -1 \end{pmatrix} \qquad (3.2)$$

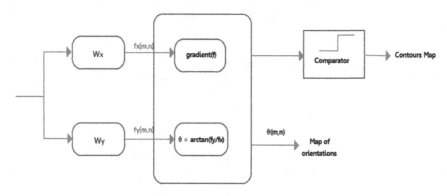

Fig. 3. Contour extractor based on the gradient method

Where: c = weight constant

Depending on the value of the weight constant we have several types of contour extraction operators: Prewitt (c = 1), Izotrop (C = $\sqrt{2}$), Sobel (c = 2).

In Fig. 3 is presented the diagram of the principle of contour extractor based on the gradient method.

3.2   The Orientations Map

An important part of this process it's the orientations map. It represents an image which contains, for each pixel, the orientation of the gradient with the maximum value of the module. It can be useful for further processing contours.

Contours map it's a binary image where the marked points correspond with the position of contour points (the points which have a gradient with a high value of the module) [8]. An example of a contours map using the HOG method is presented in Fig. 4 [11].

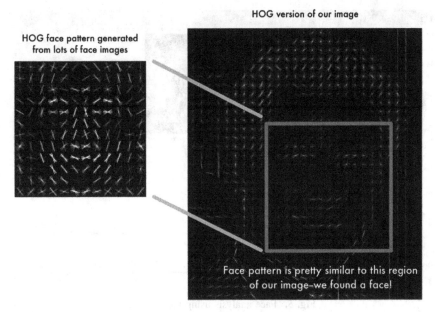

HOG version of our image

HOG face pattern generated
from lots of face images

Face pattern is pretty similar to this region
of our image–we found a face!

Fig. 4. The result of the HOG method

4 Experiments with FaceReader Software

FaceReader is a program for facial analysis. It can detect emotional expressions in the face. It can identify six basic expressions: happy, sad, angry, surprised, scared, disgusted, a neutral state. The program works with many independent variables: age and gender, ethnicity and facial hair. These variables can be automatically estimated from a video, camera input or an image.

The facial expression detection is made in three steps:

- Face finding – in this step is found the position of the face
- Face modeling – in this step the artificial face model is synchronized and used to describe the location of 500 key points and the texture of the face. The results are combined with those of the Deep Face algorithm for a higher classification accuracy.
- Face classification – in this step are presented the six basic expressions and a neutral state [13].

The results obtained by using FaceReader on different participants are presented in Figs. 5 and 6. In both situations the feeling with the highest weight that has been detected is happiness. Furthermore, heart rate detection can be performed using facial analysis [14].

Fig. 5. Face analysis using FaceReader

Fig. 6. Face analysis using FaceReader

The process of detecting emotions can become more complex by adding a stimulus. This stimulus can be a video, an image or a stimulus given by an external program. In this way, the emotion analysis can be done while the subject is watching this stimulus. For this experiment we used as stimulus three images, for which we set up a duration of 10 s. The results obtained using these stimuli are presented in Fig. 7.

Fig. 7. Face analysis using FaceReader software after three stimulus have been applied

As is shown in Fig. 7, the emotions that have been detected on the face of the subject, after that we have applied three stimulus, are intuitively presented in a separate box under the images taken from the webcam. In most of the time the subject was neutral.

5 Evaluation of the Facial Analysis Process

This method involves the existence of a database which contains facial images anno-tated with facial expressions specific to pain, and with action units. We will use part of this database to train the Random Forest classifier and the other part to test this classifier. The operating principle of the Random Forest classifier is presented in the Fig. 8 [10].

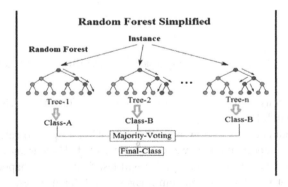

Fig. 8. The operating principle of random forest classifier

Firstly, we have to detect the facial points in the image. For facial landmarks detection, DLIB library will be used. The detection of facial landmarks represents a big challenge for shapes prediction process. Having an input image (and of course a Region Of Interest – ROI – which is specific for the object of interest) a shape predictor tries to detect the points of interest of the shape.

The detection of facial landmarks has 2 steps:

– Locate the face inside the image
– Detect the key facial-structures on the face from the region of interest (ROI)

The most important regions of the face are:

– The mouth
– Eyebrows
– The eyes
– The nose
– Maxillary

The facial landmarks detector is presented in Fig. 9 [12].

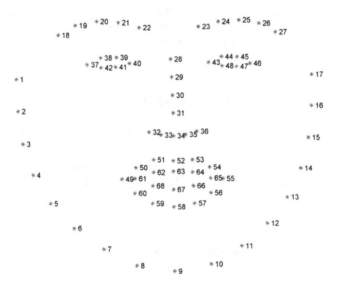

Fig. 9. 68 facial landmark coordinates from the iBUG 300-W dataset

These annotations are part of the set of 68 points iBUG 300-W. This set has been used to train the dlib Predictor.

After the facial points detection, we will use HOG descriptor to calculate the traits in the areas of the important points we have just detected. These traits will be used for the Random Forest classifier's training. We will test further what happens and which are the results that we obtain for random images and different faces.

The results obtained with our program can be further compared with the results obtained using FaceReader software. In this way we can obtain the accuracy of this implementation.

The application will be implemented using the Python programming language. It involves taking real-time images from a webcam, and display on the screen, near the detected face, the correspondent action-unit and, eventually, an emoticon to illustrate the pain emotion. This method would be more intuitive for those who are not specialist in this domain. We can also use a video from the database where we can detect the faces, instead of using live images from the webcam. In Fig. 6 is shown the facial landmarks obtained using the DLIB library in a Python code. In Fig. 10 is presented the results obtained after applying facial landmarks detection on the picture.

Fig. 10. Facial landmarks detection

6 Conclusion and Future Work

Facial expression recognition and the intensity of emotions have been an active research topic for many years. It is one of the most powerful and immediate means for human beings to communicate their emotions and intentions. The face can express emotion sooner than people verbalize or even realize their feelings. In this paper is presented a method for facial analysis and the estimation of pain intensity based on HOG descriptor, the Random Forest classifier and the UNBC-McMaster shoulder Pain Expression Archive database. Future research will focus on analyzing the influence of ambient light on the accuracy of the method.

Acknowledgment. This work has been supported in part by UEFISCDI Romania and MCI through projects VIRTUOSE, EmoSpaces and PAPUD, funded in part by European Union's Horizon 2020 research and innovation program under grant agreement No. 777996 (Sealed-GRID) and No. 787002 (SAFECARE).

References

1. Tian, Y.-L., Kanade, T., Cohn, J.F.: Recognizing action units for facial expression analysis. IEEE Trans. Pattern Anal. Mach. Intell. **23**(2), 97–115 (2001)
2. Zhang, D., et al. (Eds.) Advanced Data Mining and Applications. In: Proceedings 8th International Conference, ADMA 2012, Nanjing, China, 15–18 December 2012 (2012)
3. Tornincasa, S., et al.: Department of management and production engineering, politecnico di torino. In: 3D Facial Action Units and Expression Recognition using a Crisp Logic (2019)
4. Davidson, Rj., Scherer, K.R., Goldsmith, H.H. (eds.): Introduction: Expression of Emotion, Handbook of Affective Sciences. Oxford University Press, New York (2003)
5. Gholami, B., Haddad, W.M., Tannenbaum, A.R.: Agitation and pain assessment using digital imaging. In: 31st Annual International Conference of the IEEE EMBS Minneapolis, Minnesota, USA, 2–6 September (2009)
6. Nigam, S., Singh, R., Misra, A.K.: Efficient facial expression recognition using histogram of oriented gradients in wavelet domain, Springer Science + Business Media, LLC, part of Springer Nature, pp. 5–10 (2018)
7. Histogram of Oriented Gradients. https://www.learnopencv.com/histogram-of-oriented-gradients/. Accessed 01 Feb 2019
8. Vertan, C., Ciuc, M., Zamfir, M.: Analiza Imaginilor: Îndrumar de laborator, pp. 32–35 (2001)
9. what-when-how, In Depth Tutorials and Information. http://what-when-how.com/face-recognition/facial-expression-recognition-face-recognition-techniques-part-1/. Accessed 21 Feb 2019
10. Medium. https://medium.com/@williamkoehrsen/random-forest-simple-explanation-377895a60d2d. Accessed 21 Feb 2019
11. StackExchange. https://datascience.stackexchange.com/questions/21926/application-of-histogram-of-oriented-gradients-in-colored-image. Accessed 21 Feb 2019
12. pyimagesearch. https://www.pyimagesearch.com/2017/04/03/facial-landmarks-dlib-opencv-python/. Accessed 26 Feb 2019
13. Nodulus. https://www.noldus.com/facereader/facial-expression-analysis. Accessed 26 Feb 2019
14. Carmen, N., Poenaru, V., Suciu, G.: Heart rate measurement using face detection in video. In: 2018 International Conference on Communications (COMM), pp. 131–134. IEEE (2018)

Real Time Analysis of Weather Parameters and Smart Agriculture Using IoT

George Suciu Jr.[1,2(✉)], Hussain Ijaz[2], Ionel Zatreanu[2],
and Ana-Maria Drăgulinescu[1]

[1] University Politehnica of Bucharest, Bucharest, Romania
george@beia.ro, ana.dragulinescu@upb.ro
[2] Beia Consult International, Bucharest, Romania
{george,ijaz,ionel.zatreanu}@beia.ro

Abstract. Modern day agriculture and civilization demand for increased production of food to feed fast increasing global population. New technologies and solutions are being adopted in agricultural sector to provide an optimal alternative to gather and process information while enhancing net productivity. At the same time, the alarming climate changes, increasing water crisis and natural disasters demand for an agricultural modernization with state-of-the-art technologies available in the market and improved methodologies for modern era agricultural and farming domains. Internet of things (IoT) has been broadly applied to every sector of agriculture and has become the most effective means & tools for booming agricultural productivity and for making use of full agricultural resources. The advent of Internet of Things (IoT) has shown a new way of innovative research in agricultural sector. The introduction of cloud computing and Internet of Things (IoT) into agricultural modernization will perhaps solve many issues. Based on significant characteristics of key techniques of IoT, visualization, Libelium and Adcon can build up data regarding agricultural production. It can accelerate fast development of agricultural modernization, integrate smart farming and efficiently solve the issues regarding agriculture. Our motive is to perform the research that would bring new solutions for the farmers to determine the most effective ways to manage and monitor the agricultural fields constantly.

Keywords: Libelium · Adcon · Sensors · Smart agriculture ·
Environmental sensors · Precision farming · Crop monitoring

1 Introduction

Smart technology sets out for modern farms cutting edge together with the area of precision agriculture. Public administration and farmers are getting access to several multimedia browsers and auto-guidance systems supported by agro-machinery manufactures. There exist additional sensors and tools which could add new and useful features to the agro-system if they could only be integrated with it. The Internet of Things (IoT) can assist us to join all these elements. Our motivation to perform research comes up because farmers require new methods and technologies to determine the agricultural fields, such as for fertilization talks, watering, pesticides, etc. From a

© ICST Institute for Computer Sciences, Social Informatics and Telecommunications Engineering 2019
Published by Springer Nature Switzerland AG 2019. All Rights Reserved
V. Poulkov (Ed.): FABULOUS 2019, LNICST 283, pp. 181–194, 2019.
https://doi.org/10.1007/978-3-030-23976-3_18

decade, information and communication technologies have been introduced in agriculture, improving overall turn over from the fields and crop production. The IoT (Internet of Things) based agricultural convergence technology is a technology that produces a higher result such as improvement of production efficiency, quality increase in agricultural products in the entire procedure of agricultural production [1–3]. The IOT technologies include radio frequency identification (RFID) technology, sensor technology, sensor network technology and internetwork communication, all of them have been involved in a link of IOT industrial chain, named as identification, sensing, processing and information delivery [4]. It is used in pattern identification fields like measurement and computing and computer and communication fields like sensing, communication, information collection and processing and proving results [5–8].

The important factors in agriculture are considered: measuring soil moisture, soil temperature, environmental weather and humidity to help farmers manage their irrigation systems efficiently. The farmers can use less water to grow a crop, but they are able to increase yields and the quality of the crop by better management of soil moisture, temperature during critical plant growth stages. Monitoring is an important phase of agriculture, knowing the condition of the crop, soil and climate is essential for farmers as their decisions to irrigate the crop, spray pesticide, apply fertilizer, etc. are dependent on their states. Physical monitoring for wide agriculture land does not bring up with good results as it is almost impossible to perform 24/7 monitoring and to keep on checking for multiple variants at a time. Sensor network technology is strongly in use to get the local microclimate measurement as well as to measure soil attributes and the plant state. The connection of technologies is also providing the gain in having a mix of various local and global specialties to take appropriate decision [9–11]. An Embedded system for automatic monitoring of an agriculture field offers a potential solution to support site-specific irrigation management that allows farmers to maximize their productivity. Current technological advances in low power integrated circuits and wireless communications have provided an efficient, inexpensive, and low power device that can be utilized in remotely sensing applications to collect the data and to analyze it on home computer system. The combination of these factors has improved the viability of using a sensor network containing many intelligent sensors, making them able to collect, process, analysis, and disseminate valuable data [12].

This paper presents an efficient agricultural environment monitoring and 24/7 weather and agricultural fields monitoring system, with the purpose of improving the productivity and managing agricultural issues regarding appropriate water and crop production. In Sect. 2, the related work is presented, then Sect. 3 describes technology and devices used in agrarian field management. In Sect. 4, the experimental part illustrates telemetry solution for weather monitoring and agricultural fields, by considering environmental parameters and condition and, finally, Sect. 5 concludes the results.

2   Related Work

The concept of smart agriculture has been in practice from more than a decade now on small level agriculture. The purpose of the paper is making agriculture smart using automation and IoT based devices and technologies. This paper gives information about field activities, irrigation issues and storage for smart irrigation system [13], monitoring the crop-field using soil moisture sensors, temperature and humidity sensors, light sensors [14]. Geocledian platform [15] is used to monitor the crop fields on large scale with efficient results.

Internet of Things (IoT) is used with IoT frameworks to have an easily view, handle and interact with data and information. Within the system, users can register their sensors, create streams of data and process them and compare data from different time periods. In addition to this, the system has searching capabilities, helping the user with a full-text query language and phrase suggestions, allowing a user to use APIs to perform operations based on data points, streams and triggers. It is also applicable in various agricultural areas. Few areas are:

• Water quality monitoring
• Monitor soil constituent
• Soil humidity
• Water irrigation
• Scientific disease and pest monitoring

To develop cost-efficient and affordable system by avoiding the necessity of maintenance, free from geographic constraints and able to access reachable services, extended "as-a-Service" framework in cloud computing can be integrated with IoT to deliver financially economical IT resources [16].

Internet of things (IoT) is an intelligent technology which includes identification, sensing and intelligence. Life and even intelligence of life itself can also be regarded as part of IoT technology. It is used in pattern identification fields like measurement and computing as well as computer and communication fields like sensing, communication, information collection and processing. The definition of IoT changes as the time of cloud computing evolves. Now, IoT is defined by cloud computing plus ubiquitous network along with intelligent sensing network. Cloud computing management platform is the "backbone" of storing and processing IoT data. It involves management of accession of cloud computing customization application by users of these IoT, computing and processing that is involved in customization service; organizing and coordinating service nodes in the data center. Ubiquitous network includes LTE, GSM, WLAN, WPAN, WiMAX, RFID, Zigbee, NFC etc. are used to gather the data and can provide restful based web services for communicating between IoT cloud and sensors in terms of ecological sustainability [17].

The research in agricultural field is enhanced in various aspects to improve the quality and quantity of productivity of agriculture. Researchers have worked on various projects on soil attributes, different weather conditions as well as scouting crops. Work has been done on plant nursery availing Wireless Sensor Technology [18]. Wireless Sensor Network based polyhouse monitoring system is illustrated in [19] which makes use of environment temperature, humidity, CO2 level and enough light detection modules. This polyhouse control technology deliver automatic adjustment of polyhouse. The development of WSN for the above mentioned parameters can be applied for agriculture using ZigBee protocol and GPS technology [20]. In some projects, rice production was enhanced through the implementation of a system that monitors the crop [21]. Leaf wetness sensors get the data until a certain point such as a gateway or fog/edge computing node [22–24]. IoT provides platform to research to maintain real time data and send notifications immediately to farmers. IoT implementation provides easy access to information that is gathered from sensor nodes. IoT is also utilized for product supply chain business process. Cloud architecture provides additional support to IoT in maintaining Big data of agriculture information visualization history information, soil properties, fertilizers distribution, image cultivation via camera and information gathered through sensors, recording information etc. Collected data is analyzed to find correlation between environment, work and yield for standard work model construction, monitoring for adverse signs and fault detection. It has been discussed in [25] the application of data mining using WEKA tool and analysis model through machine learning algorithms. In [26] authors have concentrated on crop monitoring; information of temperature and rainfall is collected as initial spatial data and analyzed to decrease the crop losses and to enhance the crop production. An optimization method is used to show progressive refinement for spatial association analysis.

3   Technical Description

We provide a description of the technology and devices being used in achieving the target of monitoring weather parameters and agriculture fields and explaining the features of a specific device, like scientific instruments or computer programs. This technology and devices help the formers to keep the track of previous weather reports and plan the strategies accordingly.

3.1   Smart Agriculture

The control architecture of smart agriculture based on cloud computing and IoT [27] consists in control platform and database, and the platform further consists in subsystems as agroecological environment control, agricultural resource control, production process control, farm produce, agricultural equipment and facility. It includes computer system and other facilities. Also, it comprises redundant data communication links and environment control facility.

The agroecological environment control subsystem includes:

- Water quality monitoring.
- Accurate fertilization saves fertilizer
- Monitor soil constituent, soil humidity, light, wind, air, etc.

The agricultural resource control subsystem includes:

- Intelligent greenhouse that allows automatic adjustment of temperature.
- Water irrigation that can automatically control flow and save water
- Scientific disease and pest monitoring

The production process control subsystem includes:

- Identification of individual animals allows healthy cultivation
- Monitoring of animal and plant growth
- Product sorting guarantees quality

Farm produce and food safety subsystem includes:

- Get informed of the entire logistics process
- Rationally arrange storage in warehouse
- Traceability system of farm produce supply chain

Agricultural equipment and facility system include:

- Diagnosis of farm machinery breakdown
- Remote control of farm machinery
- Operation monitoring of farm machinery

3.2 Adcon

Adcon Telemetry equipment is being successfully functional in agriculture, hydrometrics, irrigation control systems, meteorology, water and air quality measurements, water management systems, measurement of renewable energy potential, plant disease management etc. ADCON supported sensors are temperature and relative humidity, solar radiation, barometric pressure and soil temperature. The remote transmissions unit is responsible for transmitting the data via radio waves from the site back to the master station at the gateway [28, 29].

3.3 Libelium

Libelium analyses the level of pollution - air pollution, agricultural, noise, water, meteorology, water management systems, measurement of renewable energy potential, plant disease management etc. Libelium supported sensors are temperature and relative humidity, solar radiation, barometric pressure and soil temperature. The data from these sensors are stored in a gateway called Meshlium [30, 31].

3.4 Geocledian Platform

Geocledian platform [15] helps in farm management systems. Up-to-date satellite information is monitored, the vegetation development or seasons and fields are analyzed. Crop health problems due to pests, diseases or missing nutrients are being detected in time so that actions can be planned. In different types of information systems, satellite images can be used for production monitoring to get an overview about agricultural activities in a region or originate statistical information.

Also, the data can be utilized in estimation of harvest, harvest loss or the area of active farmland. In agricultural advisory systems, the management practices on farms can be analyzed and improvements can be planned and monitored.

Vitality and variations products are based on the Normalized Difference Vegetation Index (NDVI). It is based on measurements of visible and near-infrared light and ranges from +1 to −1. Vegetative areas show always positive values, whereas bare soil and rocks approach 0. The NDVI is a measure of plant vitality. It correlates with biomass, leaf area, chlorophyll content and plant health. The data for parcels will immediately be updated as soon as new measurements are available.

Analysis functions available are:

- NDVI & other vegetation index time series statistics per parcel
- Phenology statistics on a variety of specialized parameters
- Notification messages
- Crop type verification
- Parcel comparisons & benchmarking
- Others on request

The basic Monitoring package provides a REST API supporting typically GET, PUT and DELETE commands keys. For accessing the API, one needs a user key and the base URL. This stack is updated as soon as a new sensor measurement is available. It makes the most sense to register parcels with one single crop. Parcels with mixed crops can be used, too, but some API functions may not deliver the precise required results. Parcel is being registered as follows:

- Geometry of the parcel.
- Crop types.
- Planting date.
- Harvesting date.

4   Experiments

To have a proper view of the comparative measurements of the Adcon and Libelium telemetry stations, those were installed in the same analytical perimeter. The communication protocol and data transmission modalities for Adcon and Libelium telemetry station are presented in Table 1.

Table 1. Data transmission and communication protocols

Telemetry station	Data transmission	Communication protocol
Adcon	addUPI	GPRS
Libelium	HTTP	4G

A fixed period for environmental parameter analysis has been chosen. The data acquired from the sensors was centralized into a database and was used to highlight the sensor events, based on timestamps and sensor types. Figure 1 explains the whole phenomena that occur from collecting data to transmission, integration and visualization. The presented architecture is inspired from [32].

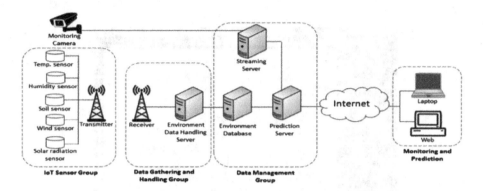

Fig. 1. IoT service architecture based on [32]

Smart Agriculture is characterized as "a method to recognize the basic requirements as well as the changes in the current environment due to external factors built on the information and utilization of compiled data to optimize sensors' operation or influence the operations of actuators to change the current environment.

Using above mentioned technologies, we performed experiments and collected the data in their respective platforms. Adcon station installed provides 24/7 weather related data as seen in Fig. 2.

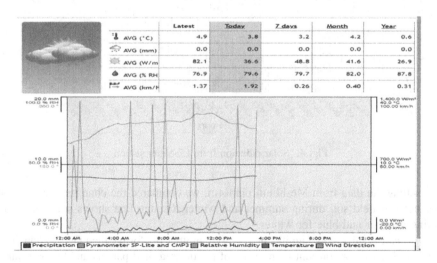

Fig. 2. Adcon telemetry station readings at BEIA office

Libelium devices has been installed in fields nearby Bucharest, Romania, setting up the data transmission time, sleep time and channel through programming codes. After running the codes, we get the readings of the installed sensors in Meshlium platform, it can be seen in the picture below (Fig. 3).

Fig. 3. Meshlium dashboard

The variation of the values for the measured parameters (temperature, solar radiation) are presented in Figs. 4 and 5.

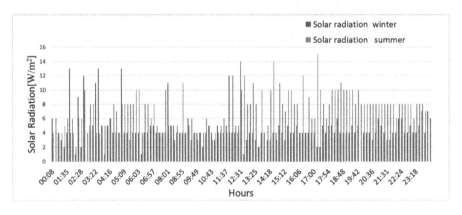

Fig. 4. Solar radiation from Libelium station

Getting the data from Meshlium platform, we compared the changes occurring in weather and field soil during summer and winter. Orange line shows solar radiation during summer and blue for winter.

To make results more significant, we used another platform called Geocledian. The platform is used for constant monitoring of the desired field parcels and helps in farm management systems using up-to-date satellite information. Also, the vegetation development, seasons and fields are analyzed. As mentioned before, using Geocledian platform, crop health problems due to pests, diseases or missing nutrients are being

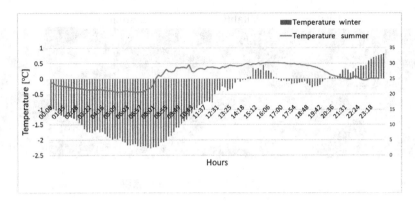

Fig. 5. Temperature variation measured by Libelium station

detected on time so that actions can be planned. The experiments have been performed on 5 different parcels chosen near to Bucharest, Romania, in 2018. Two of them can be seen in Fig. 6. One can observe the variations in vegetation index, visibility, vitality and variation with respect to time.

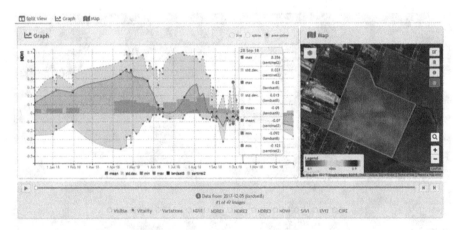

Fig. 6. Complex cultivation patterns and graphical representation

Uneven irrigation patterns: comparing the Vitality image (MIDDLE) of this irrigated field near Bucharest Romania, data from 2018-07-15 (sentinel2) to the Visible (LEFT) and Variations image (RIGHT) indicates that certain features are only visible in the Vitality or Variations, such as in Fig. 7. With the help of visibility, vitality and variation one can easily analyze what area needs to be watered and what area areas required more attention for better yield.

Visually comparing the Vitality images for a parcel. A Vitality time series during growth and ripening should look like the series of pictures shown in Fig. 8. As in the start of the experiment, when we started getting the pictures with the satellite and

Visible   Vitality   Variation

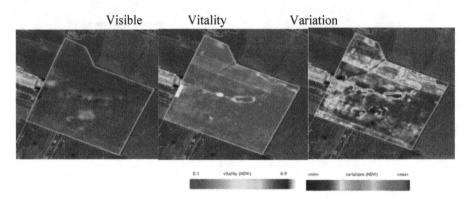

Fig. 7. Uneven pivot irrigation patterns

visualized in the platform, the land is clear, first top left picture indicating the results. As the crop starts growing, the picture changes in time, the green regions show the growth of the crop. After a period of months, it gets to the point when the wheat crop starts ripping, that is, the regions in the picture become yellowish, a fact that indicates the harvesting season.

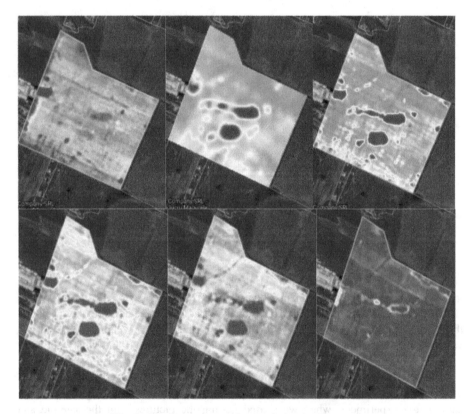

Fig. 8. Seeding to harvesting evolution in the parcel

If a crop develops normally the NDVI should follow a crop-specific development curve as in the figure above. The NDVI will steadily increase during the growth period (maybe interrupted by winter for winter cereals or bloom as with rapeseed) and reaches the maximum just before the start of ripening. The NDVI starts to decrease when ripening sets in and reaches its minimum at harvest. Normally, all pixels in a field should follow a similar NDVI curve with possibly different absolute values due to varying soil, nutrition or water conditions or management practices.

The Vitality image in Fig. 9 is from a field in Bucharest, August 14, 2018. Here, the plant biomass is different due to different crop development stages and shows how the soil is during the period of experimentation. This picture helps in monitoring the area where expected crop can be less or where it can be satisfying. Wherever the crop is weak, multiple steps can be taken to make it better. For example, that area must be fertilized or watered for better yield.

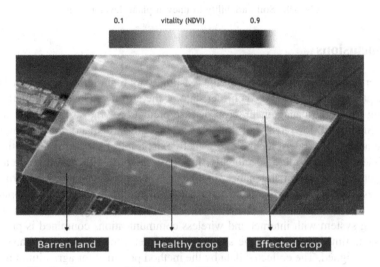

Fig. 9. Biomass variability due to different crop development stages

Uneven plant development due to soil variability. The Vitality image in Fig. 10 is from a field near Bucharest, Romania, August 14, 2018. Here, the plant development is uneven due to soil variability, also found in Fig. 9. It indicates weakness of some areas of the parcel, which requires attention to treat the area for equal results of the whole parcel.

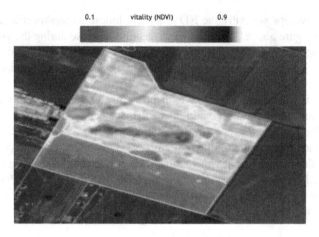

Fig. 10. Soil variability in uneven plant development

5 Conclusions

The paper first performed a survey of the existing work regarding real time analysis of weather parameters and analyzed current state-of-the-art offers Goecledian platform for analyzing irrigation management, crop disease prediction, vineyard precision farming mostly. Simplified, low cost, and scalable systems are in demand. At the same time, with the advent of modern technologies, there exist a lot of scope for innovating new and efficient systems, more specifically, low cost solution with features like autonomous operation and low maintenance. In this paper, we present a connected farm based on IoT systems for monitoring fields and smart farming, the IoT technology application in agriculture and selected wireless communication technology to obtain a remote monitoring system with internet and wireless communications combined is presented. At the same time, considering the system management, the information management system is designed. The collected data by the method provided for agricultural research and management facilities. Research shows the field monitoring system based on IoT technology can have precision in monitoring and controlling the state of agricultural fields. According to the need of surrounding monitoring, this system has realized the automatic monitoring of the environmental temperature, humidity, soil moisture, soil temperature. Thus, field condition is monitored continuously throughout seeding to harvesting. The system has offered an excellent growth condition; it is easy to operate, the interface is friendly, offering real-time environmental factors in the fields. It can revise environmental control parameters; this system realizes the operation online and, also, has the following characteristics: it runs reliably, and it is high performant. As future work, we envision investigating fruit ripening analysis using the platform presented in this paper.

Acknowledgement. The work presented in this paper has been funded by SWAM and the SmartAgro project subsidiary contract no. 8592/08.05.2018, from the NETIO project ID: P_40_270, MySmis Code: 105976 and was supported by UEFISCDI through contract no. 33PCCDI/01.03.2018 within PNCDI III, Platform of multi-agent intelligent systems for water quality monitoring on Romanian sector of Danube and Danube Delta (MultiMonD2).

References

1. Moummadi, K., Abidar, R., Medromi, H.: Generic model based on constraint programming and multi-agent system for M2M services and agricultural decision support. In: 2011 International Conference on Multimedia Computing and Systems (ICMCS), pp. 1–6 (2011)
2. Doss, R., Gang, L.: Exploiting Affinity propagation for energy-efficient information discovery in sensor networks. In: Global Telecommunications Conference (IEEE GLOBECOM 2008), pp. 1–6 (2008)
3. Duan, R., Chen, X., Xing, T.: A QoS architecture for IOT. In: 2011 International Conference on Internet of Things and 4th International Conference on Cyber, Physical and Social Computing (iThings/CPSCom), pp. 717–720 (2011)
4. Hong, L.: IOT and cloud computing: advance strategic new industry. In: Beijing, Posts & Telecom Press, China (2011)
5. Qi-Bo, S., Jie, L., Shan, L., Chun-Xiao, F., Juan-Juan, S.: Internet of things: summarize on concepts, architecture and key technology problem. Beijing Youdian Daxue Xuebao/J. Beijing Univ. Posts Telecommun. **33**(3), 1–9 (2010)
6. Guang, Y., Guining, G., Jing, D., Zhaohui, L., He, H.: Security threats and measures for the Internet of Things. Qinghua Daxue Xuebao/J. Tsinghua Univ. **51**(10), 1335–1340 (2011)
7. Gao, K., Wang, Q., Xi, L.: Controlling moving object in the Internet of Things. IJACT: Int. J. Adv. Comput. Technol. **4**(5), 83–90 (2012)
8. Ren, X., Chen, L., Wan, H.: Homomorphic encryption and its security application. JDCTA Int. J. Dig. Content Technol. Appl. **6**(7), 305–311 (2012)
9. Holman, I.P., Brown, C., Janes, V., Sandars, D.: Can we be certain about future land use change in Europe? A multi-scenario integrated-assessment analysis. Agric. Syst. **151**, 126–135 (2017)
10. Chhetri, A.K., Aggarwal, P.K., Joshi, P.K., Vyas, S.: Farmers' prioritization of climate-smart agriculture (CSA) technologies. Agric. Syst. **151**, 184–191 (2017)
11. Kissoon, D., Deerpaul, H., Mungur, A.: A smart irrigation and monitoring system. Int. J. Comput. Appl. (0975 – 8887) **163**(8) (2017)
12. Akyildiz, I.F., Su, W., Sankarasubramaniam, Y., Cayirci, E.: Wireless sensor networks: a survey. Comput. Netw. **38**, 393–422 (2002)
13. Gondchawar, N., Kawitkar, R.S.: IoT based smart agriculture. Int. J. Adv. Res. Comput. Commun. Eng. **5**(6) (2016). ISSN (Online) 2278-1021 ISSN (Print) 2319 5940, June 2016 (2016)
14. Rajalakshmi, P., Mahalakshmi, S.D.: IOT based crop-field monitoring and irrigation automation. In: 10th International Conference on Intelligent systems and control (ISCO) (2016)
15. https://www.geocledian.com. Accessed 07 Mar 2019
16. Sharma, S., Tim, U.S., Gadia, S., Wong, J.: Growing Cloud Density and as-a-Service Modality and OTH-Cloud Classification in IOT Era (2015). www.public.iastate.edu/sugamsha/articles/OTH-Cloud/in/IoT.pdf

17. Benzi, F., Anglani, N., Bassi, E., Frosini, L.: Electricity smart meters interfacing the households. IEEE Trans. Industr. Electron. **58**(10), 4487–4494 (2011)
18. Zubairi, J.A.: Application of Modern High Performance Networks, pp. 120–129. Bentham Science Publishers Ltd. (2009)
19. Song, Y., Ma, J., Zhang, X., Feng, Y.: Design of wireless sensor network-based greenhouse environment monitoring and automatic control system. J. Netw. **7**(5) (2012)
20. Satyanarayana, G.V., Mazaruddin, S.D.: Wireless sensor based remote monitoring system for agriculture using ZigBee and GPS. In: Conference on Advances in Communication and Control Systems (2013)
21. Sakthipriya, N.: An effective method for crop monitoring using wireless sensor network. MiddleEast J. Sci. Res. **20**(9), 1127–1132 (2014)
22. Kaloxylos, A.: Farm management systems and the Future Internet era. Comput. Electron. Agric. **89**, 130–144 (2012)
23. Wang, X., Liu, N.: The application of Internet of Things in agricultural means of production supply chain management. J. Chem. Pharm. Res. **6**(7), 2304–2310 (2014)
24. Minbo, L., Zhu, Z., Guangyu, C.: Information service system of agriculture IoT. Automatica **54**(4), 415–426 (2013)
25. Cunningham, S.J., Holmes, G.: Developing innovative applications in agriculture using data mining. In: SEARCC 1999 Conference Proceedings (1999)
26. Rajesh, D.: Application of spatial data mining for agriculture. Int. J. Comput. Appl. **15**(2), 7–9 (2011)
27. Qingbo, W., Xing, J., Le, H., Yang, Z., Zhile, Z., Yuhui, W., et al.: Virtualization and Cloud Computing. Publishing House of Electronics Industry, Beijing (2009)
28. Suciu, G., Vulpe, A., Martian, A., Halunga, S., Vizireanu, D.N.: Big data processing for renewable energy telemetry using a decentralized cloud M2M system. Wireless Pers. Commun. **87**(3), 1113–1128 (2016)
29. Application Information for Adcon Telemetry Systems, Adcon Telemetry, Klosterneuburg, Austria. http://www.adcon.at. Accessed 28 Feb 2019
30. Gangwar, D.S., Tyagi, S.: Challenges and opportunities for sensor and actuator networks in indian agriculture. In: 8th International Conference on Computational Intelligence and Communication Networks, pp. 38–42 (2016)
31. Libelium IoT. http://www.libelium.com/. Accessed 28 Feb 2019
32. Lee, M., Hwang, J., Yoe, H.: Agricultural production system based on IoT. In: 16th IEEE International Conference on Computational Science and Engineering, Sydney, NSW, pp. 833–837 (2013)

Wireless Communications and Networks

Spatial Multiplexing MIMO 5G-SDR Open Testbed Implementation

Ciprian Zamfirescu[✉], Alexandru Vulpe, Simona Halunga,
and Octavian Fratu

Faculty of Electronics, Telecommunications and Information Technology,
University Politehnica of Bucharest, Bucharest, Romania
ciprian.zamfirescu@yahoo.com

Abstract. Future 5G networks will demand high increases in capacity which are not acquirable by existing 4G implementations. The objective of this paper is to propose an open testbed solution in order to perform applied studies for 5G New Radio, using SDR, optimal parameter configuration, vendor equipment benchmarking, real life consistent tests for radio equipment behavior and create the possibility to extend the current platform to be able to accommodate future technical needs. GNU Radio, provides the opportunity to create software-defined radios based on virtual signal processing blocks using low-cost external RF hardware or simulation-like environment. This offers the opportunity to telecom mobile operators to set up the networks at the highest capabilities and also to have a clear vision before making strong investments in new equipment.

Keywords: 5G · SDR · MIMO · Massive-MIMO · Testbed · New Radio · Embedded · GNU Radio · Case studies · Benchmarking · IoT · RF

1 Introduction

Applications of multiple input, multiple output (MIMO) technology such as massive MIMO can provide enormous gains in capacity and spectral efficiency by using large numbers of antennas. Software-defined radio (SDR) is a radio communication system where physical hardware modules and components implemented in hardware (e.g. mixers, filters, amplifiers, modulators/demodulators, detectors, etc.) are instead developed as software blocks on computers or embedded systems. Flexible yet affordable SDRs are able to turn a standard PC into a next-generation wireless tool. The future telecom networks are not only characterized by faster data throughputs and higher capacity, but the seamless, real-time interaction between end-users and billions of smart devices. 5G wireless technology promises a high-reliability and all-connected world. New bands and wider bandwidths will be used, new beamforming technology and use cases can be approached and 5G New Radio (NR) equipment require adequate design, reliable prototypes and tough tests challenges to be ready for large-scale deployments.

This paper is proposing a testbed solution to analyze and test technologies and equipment, addressable to universities, vendors and also to telecom mobile operators. The testbed offers the possibility to run a number of customized tests, set and try different parameters in order to understand better the equipment capabilities or to set a

© ICST Institute for Computer Sciences, Social Informatics and Telecommunications Engineering 2019
Published by Springer Nature Switzerland AG 2019. All Rights Reserved
V. Poulkov (Ed.): FABULOUS 2019, LNICST 283, pp. 197–213, 2019.
https://doi.org/10.1007/978-3-030-23976-3_19

mobile networks at their truly potential in 5G New Radio context. Mobile operators are targeting massive 5G deployments in the near future, to keep up with the competition. Before making investments, mobile operators have to test equipment in laboratory and also in real life field scenarios. Also, some mobile operators are requiring custom made equipment with certain parameters and it is absolutely necessary to have access to a benchmarking framework to be able to choose the right vendor.

The proposed test framework was built taking in consideration many theoretical concepts presented in Sect. 2, like MIMO channel models, channel capacity and signal detection at the reception. Section 3 is dedicated to the testbed setup approach and it describes how the system was implemented, the technical objectives and what kind of hardware equipment and software packages were used. The experimental results and how the data was interpreted are presented in Sect. 4. The conclusions, future work and objectives are exposed in Sect. 5.

2   Theoretical Prerequisites for MIMO SDR Testbed Development

Theoretical characteristics are necessary to be understood in order to implement a MIMO testbed system. The radio channel, MIMO channel capacity, statistical models for the MIMO channel, the modulation techniques used for transmission, the detection algorithms used to separate the data streams that reach receiving antennas, the parameters and platform models together with the secondary modules specific to each desired function are some of the main prerequisites underlying the current work.

The second step is the deepening process of GNU Radio simulation environment on the Ubuntu Linux operating system and its available functions.

Some of the theoretical concepts and equations used in the software processing blocks development are described in the following subsections.

2.1   MIMO Statistical Channel Model

To characterize SISO systems (single input, single output), the spread delay and the Doppler effect have to be considered. The first may be interpreted as the difference between the arrival time of the earliest multicast component received and the time of arrival of the last significant multicast component, this notion being used to characterize the radio channels. Doppler displacement refers to the fact that when a user is in motion, his speed causes a frequency shift of the transmitted signal. Several signals crossing different paths and areas may have Doppler displacements that differ from each other, corresponding to different phase shifts [1].

The difference between Doppler displacements between different components of a signal leads to the occurrence of a fading channel known as Doppler spread. Multiple antennas for broadcast and reception are used in MIMO systems (multiple input, multiple output). The correlation between the broadcast antenna and the receiving antenna is a very important aspect of the MIMO channel. This depends on the angle of incidence of each multipath component [12].

2.2 MIMO Channel

The MIMO channel must be described for all antenna pairs, transmitter-receiver. For M broadcasting antennas and N receiving antennas, the MIMO transmission channel can be represented by an N × M size matrix shown in Eq. 1 [1].

This matrix is:

$$\mathbf{h}(t, \tau) = \begin{bmatrix} h_{11}(t, \tau) & \cdots & h_{1M}(t, \tau) \\ \vdots & \ddots & \vdots \\ h_{N1}(t, \tau) & \cdots & h_{NM}(t, \tau) \end{bmatrix} \tag{1}$$

$h_{NM}(t, \tau)$ is the variation in pulse response in time between the m input of the transmitting antenna and the n output of the receiving antenna. Each pulse response is the cascaded effect of the transmitting antenna, the propagation medium and the receiving antenna. The spatial and temporal correlation between the signals received at different antennas is reflected in the matrix elements.

MIMO channels can be physical or analytical. Physical models are based either on physical theory (geometry) or on physical measurements. They are specific to a type of environment or area (urban, suburban and rural) and are used in network planning. Analytical models are independent of the physical implementation area and are often used for system creation, comparisons, and tests.

Physical models can be subdivided into deterministic and stochastic. Deterministic models are specific to the external environment and are derived from the physical radio propagation processes: reflection, diffraction, shading, etc. Stochastic models are more generic than deterministic models. It is based on data used in the absence of a database of application environments, specific propagation parameters. Probabilistic models can be built for these parameters. These models are more computerized. The SCM model, the spatial channel model, is a stochastic model [1].

The MIMO channel matrix was used to create the MIMO channel model block in GNU Radio.

2.3 MIMO Channel Capacity

Multicast propagation has long been considered an impediment because of the fact that the signal is affected by fading. To eliminate this problem, diversity techniques have been introduced. The theory of information has shown that by multiple propagation, multiple antennas at both transmit and receive can produce multiple parallel channels that can operate simultaneously in the same frequency band with the same transmit power. Antenna correlation varies drastically depending on the obstacles encountered by the signal in its propagation path, depending on the distance between the transmitter and the receiver, depending on the configuration of the antennas and the Doppler displacement. Recent research has shown that multicast propagation actually contributes to the capacity.

The increase in spectral efficiency offered by MIMO systems is based on the use of spatial diversity in both emission and reception. The high spectral efficiency obtained with an MIMO system is due to the fact that in an obstacle-rich environment, the signal from each transmitter appears uncorrelated to the receiving antennas. When the signals go through uncorrelated channels, the signals from the transmitting antennas have different spatial characteristics. The receiver can use these differences between spatial characteristics to separate signals from different antennas simultaneously and at the same frequency.

The most important idea in MIMO is that different signals can be sent using the same frequency band and there is the possibility of correct decoding at the receiver. It is like creating a channel for each of the transmitters. It can linearly increase the capacity of MIMO channels by carefully adding a larger number of transmitting antennas. It is more beneficial to transmit data using several different power channels smaller than one high power one [3].

In practice, the capacity of a N × M MIMO system when the channel is known, is shown in Eq. 2 [3]:

$$C_{MIMO} = B \cdot \log_2 \left| \det \left[I_N + \frac{SNR}{M} HH^* \right] \right| \text{bps/Hz} \qquad (2)$$

2.4 Signal Detection for MIMO Systems with Spatial Multiplexing

There are different detection schemes for MIMO systems such as ML (maximum-likelihood), which require computational resources over the power of most practical systems. To reduce the complexity of MIMO detection techniques, equalization techniques such as zero-forcing (ZF) and minimum mean square error (MMSE) can be used.

MIMO systems are used to support very high data transfer rates, but the power balance and performance requirements are maintained for SISO systems. The MIMO channel at the reception is inverted to minimize total interference from other transmitted signals. The ZF filter output is the function of the data to be detected and the reception noise [4].

The best detector that minimizes the probability of error is the ML detector. This is hard to implement in practice due to the complexity of the algorithm. The paper results are based on ZF and MMSE algorithms. They need less computational power.

The reception of data that is transmitted serially through the dispersing media is a complex operation due to the emergence of ISI.

MIMO systems that use spatial multiplexing can transmit data at higher speeds than systems that use spatial diversity. However, spatial demultiplexing or signal detection at reception is a difficult task for MIMO systems that use spatial multiplexing (Fig. 1).

The MIMO system of N_R x N_T antennas is considered. The matrix H is defined as the channel matrix with the h_{ji} element representing the channel gain between the transmitting antenna "i" and the receiving antenna "j", $j = 1, 2, \ldots, N_R$ and $i = 1, 2, \ldots, N_T$. The data from a spatially multiplexed user are represented as $\mathbf{x} = [x_1, x_2, \ldots, x_{NT}]^T$, respectively the received data $\mathbf{y} = [y_1, y_2, \ldots, y_{NR}]^T$, x_i and y_j represent the signal transmitted from the antenna i, respectively the signal received at the

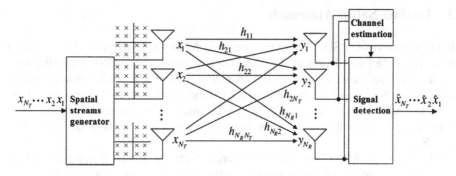

Fig. 1. Spatial multiplexing MIMO system [5]

antenna j. It is defined z_j as Gaussian white noise with the variant σ_z^2 at the receiver antenna j and $\mathbf{h}_i$ represents the second column vector of the H channel matrix [5].

$$\mathbf{y} = \mathbf{Hx} + \mathbf{z} = \mathbf{h}_1 x_1 + \mathbf{h}_2 x_2 + \ldots + \mathbf{h}_{NT} x_{NT} + \mathbf{z}, \mathbf{z} = [z_1, z_2, \ldots, z_{NR}]^T \quad (3)$$

Taking in consideration the two presented detection algorithms, a Matlab implementation was developed for this paper and a BER comparison for 2×2 MIMO system is shown in Fig. 2.

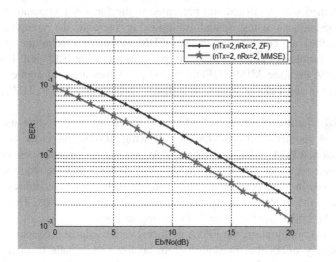

Fig. 2. BER for 2×2 MIMO system (BPSK and MMSE)

The graph shows that compared with Zero Forcing detection, at a 10^{-3} BER, MMSE detection has an improvement of 3 dB.

Also, for the real life tests, presented in the following sections, ZF and MMSE detection algorithms were implemented and used.

3   Testbed Setup Approach

In order to develop a SDR platform to integrate MIMO technology, a software and a hardware testbed was deployed. An open-source software, called GNU Radio [6], with a variety of applications, particularly SDRs, was used. Open-source software attracts contributors because of the cost advantage. At the same time, more compelling benefits, like enhanced security, quality, flexibility and customizability, exist. The hardware used for the testbed is made by National Instruments and the product is called USRP [7].

The term USRP comes from "Universal Software Radio Peripheral". USRP products are radio equipment managed by software running on computing units (PCs). These were designed, built and sold by the American company Ettus Research, which is part of National Instruments company. USRP boards can be connected to a computer via a high-speed USB or Gigabit Ethernet cable, through which the computer-programmed software is able to control the physical platform to transmit or receive data. The USRP family has been designed for accessibility, and most of the programs that are used to use physical platforms have free access and the ability to contribute to their development. To control these platforms, a UHD driver with a free license is used. Most of the time, USRP boards are used with the GNU Radio software suite, which allows the creation of complex radio system programs, but also with LabVIEW.

GNU Radio provides the possibility to design a series of signal graphs to model all the operations required for the processing of radio signals. Following these simulations, the data obtained were analyzed and presented in the form of comparative graphs.

MIMO techniques using spatial multiplexing increase the complexity of the receivers, so they are combined with the OFDM modulation technique to effectively eliminate the problems caused by the multipath channel. The IEEE 802.11n standard, issued in 2009, uses the MIMO-OFDM technique. Other areas of application of this technique are in the field of mobile telephony, through the 3GPP, HSPA and LTE standards.

The USRP family of products includes a variety of models that use a similar architecture. A motherboard provides the following subsystems: clock generator and synchronization, FPGA, ADC converters, DAC, external computer connection interface and power regulator. These are the basic components that are required for signal baseband processing. For other operations such as filtering or conversions, some boards are attached to the motherboard by two slots, called daughterboards. This modularity property of the USRP platform serves many applications.

In the basic configuration, the FPGA performs various signal processing operations, which ultimately offers the translation from analog real signals to complex digital signals in the baseband. In most cases, these complex samples are transferred from applications running on an external processor on the operating computer. The FPGA code is free of license and can be modified to allow for high speeds or slow processing operations [7] (Figs. 3 and 4).

The signal received from the radio frequency module is brought into the base band and then converted to digital format using an ADS62P44 ADC converter, which performs a signal sampling at a rate of 100 Mbps, with a 14-bit precision. Two signals

Fig. 3. Central panel of USRP N210 SDR platform [7]

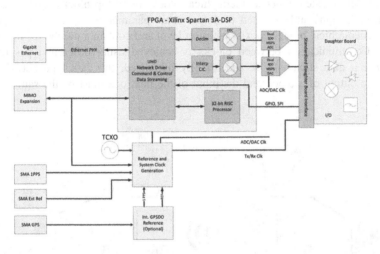

Fig. 4. USRP N210 block diagram [7]

are obtained, one in phase (I) and one in quadrature (Q). The IQ digital signal is further processed by the FPGA module. In this module, filtering and decimation take place. There are three cascaded filters, a CIC filter (cascaded integrator) and two HB filters. Decimation takes place at a rate of 2 for HB filters and at a rate between 1 and 128 for the CIC filter; with cascading, a rate of between 4 and 512 is achieved. For data transfer to be supported by the Ethernet interface that is limited to 1 Gbps, a decimation of at least 4 is required.

GNU Radio is a suite of free software licensed by Eric Blossom in 1998. This software coupled with hardware such as the USRP N210 allows the creation of a complete SDR platform. GNU Radio can also be used as a standalone simulation program. The operating system recommended for GNU Radio is Linux. It can also be installed on other operating systems such as Mac OS or Windows using the Cygwin application, but total functionality is not guaranteed. It is used for personal, academic or commercial use.

Most GNU Radio applications are written in Python, and C++ is used to implement signal processing blocks. Python commands are used to control all parameters of the USRP module, such as transmission power, gain, frequency, antenna used, etc., certain aspects being editable while the application is being executed. GNU Radio performs all signal processing. It can be used to write applications that receive or transmit data.

GNU Radio is built on two structural entities: signal processing blocks and signal graphs. The blocks are structured to have a number of input and output ports, consisting of small signal processing components. When the blocks connect to each other, a spreadsheet is formed. The GNU Radio blocks can be divided into several categories: sources, modulators, operators, filters, viewing tools, etc. Sources are blocks that contain only outputs and represent the starting point of a signal graph. Sinks or rescue or display blocks have only inputs [7].

Graphs are created either as hierarchical blocks or as top blocks. Top blocks are found in all graphs and are used to define some parameters and have no inputs or outputs. Hierarchical blocks coexist with top-level and contain a number of inputs and outputs. Communication between blocks is achieved using different types of data flows. For a data stream to be successfully initialized, the data type between two blocks, the output of a block and the input of the next one must be the same.

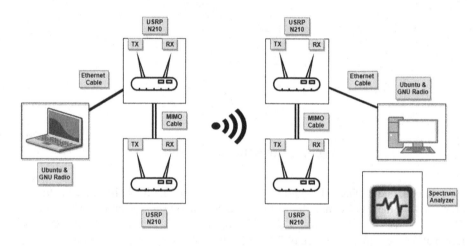

Fig. 5. Testbed block diagram

The purpose is to analyze in GNU Radio environment using the test platform built with USRP N210 and WBX/XCVR2450 submodules, the 2×2 MIMO system, shown in Fig. 5. The chosen development environment was GNU Radio Companion, in which transmission and reception, each running on a different computer, were implemented (Fig. 6) (Table 1).

In order to achieve the desired setup, two USRP N210 boards each having a WBX transceiver module were used. The chosen operating frequency was 2 GHz. Each WBX module has two antennas accordingly to the selected frequency band. It is very important that at least a USRP board has a Jackson GPS module installed, because even if the antenna is not connected to it, the program execution routine will check its existence. After all hardware connections have been completed on the USRP boards, they can be fed in DC at a voltage of 6 V.

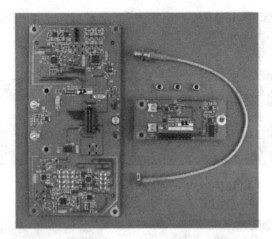

Fig. 6. WBX submodule

Table 1. PCs specifications

Name	Configuration
PC1 - laptop	Intel Quad Core i7 2.8 Ghz, 8 GB dual RAM
PC2 - desktop	Intel Core 2 Duo 2.4 Ghz, 4 GB dual RAM

In order for the two USRPs to be a MIMO system, it was necessary to connect a MIMO cable between the two boards, which allows the synchronization of the clock from the master board to the slave board. To link the computing unit to MIMO, it was necessary to connect a cable between the Ethernet interfaces of the computer and the USRP master board. Using this cable and using the IP protocol and the UHD driver installed on the computer, the signal graph implemented in GNU Radio Companion could be run successfully.

The next step was to enter the IP addresses for each Ethernet interface. USRP boards come from the factory with fixed IP 192.168.10.2 but can be easily changed. A wired connection must be enabled on the computer interface and an IP address on the same network as the USRP address, for example 192.168.10.1, must be entered.

Once all of these steps have been executed, you can verify that your computer sees the USRP as attached running the command: "uhd_find_devices".

Only one antenna on each board is able to transmit data. The second one is for receiving data, in order to create a duplex communication system (Figs. 7 and 8).

In order to transmit data from one board to another and to implement the complete testbed scenario, GNU Radio was used and different functions blocks were created and programmed. Some of the blocks were part of GNU Radio library of signal processing blocks written in C++. Those blocks include signal sources, data rescue blocks, and filters. Processing blocks are stuck together using Python.

In Fig. 9, the transmission part was designed, the blocks were created and the parameters were set according to the desired signal.

Fig. 7. Transmission and Reception 2 × 2 MIMO

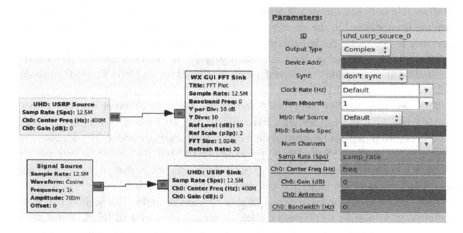

Fig. 8. OFDM live spectrum on spectral analyzer

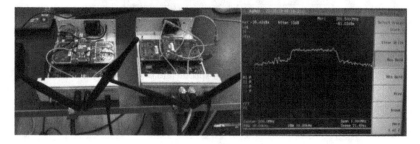

Fig. 9. Data transmission and reception – signal graph and characteristic parameters

By entering the property menu of a source USRP block, the following parameters can be selected: Block ID, type of output data (received), clock, number of motherboards, number of channels, sampling rate, carrier frequency, gain, name of the receiving antenna, bandwidth.

The UHD driver links the software that processes data to the GNU Radio environment and the USRP physical card. Parameters that can be selected are: Output data type, USRP board IP address, Number of motherboards, Synchronization type, Number of radio channels, Sampling frequency, Frequency of carrier to be transmitted, Name of antenna reception and earnings.

Figure 10 represents the setting of two receiving channels corresponding to the two antennas of the RF module, each USRP board was modeled by an individual block.

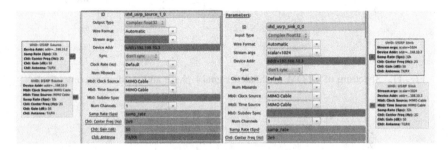

Fig. 10. Parameters of receiving and transmitting blocks using four USRP platforms

To create a 2 × 2 MIMO system with 4 USRP board, different IP addresses on the motherboards that are connected by the MIMO cable have to be set, the synchronization source for the second card as the MIMO cable has to be selected, and the same procedure is followed at the receiving side. This type of implementation requires two computing units (PCs).

4 Preliminary Experimental Results for MIMO 5G Ready SDR System in GNU Radio

To be able to observe the maximum capacity and the error rate of a MIMO channel that uses two transmitting antennas and two receiving antennas, two individual transmission paths were modeled in GNU Radio, using OFDM modulated random data sources transmitted through a Gaussian white, additive, virtual noise channel. After the demodulation, the received data was compared to the data emitted by an error rate calculation block. To find the error rate of the entire 2 × 2 MIMO channel, the arithmetic mean between the two parallel rates is made and the data is stored in a file.

In Fig. 11, OFDM modulated signal spectrum was captured. Next, the components in time domain, phase (I) and quadrature (Q) can be observed. Depending on the number of tones used, the spectrum of the OFDM signal may appear narrower or wider, shown is Fig. 12.

It is difficult to implement a MIMO 2 × 2 system in the GRC Companion simulation environment due to the lack of already implemented detection blocks. It is considered the signal graph in Fig. 13. The existence of four random data sources is explained by the need to emphasize how on each receiving antenna nR_x1 and nR_x2,

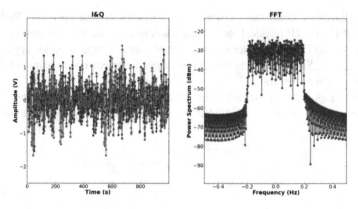

Fig. 11. Spectrum of OFDM modulated signal - phase and quadrature components

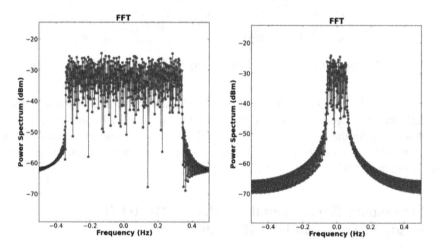

Fig. 12. OFDM spectrum, 350 tones vs. 50 tones

data from each of the two transmit antennas nT_x1 and nT_x2, arrives. Two data streams per each transmission antenna were generated. A transmission path was designed through a "channel model" block [8] that introduces propagation attenuation. The two data streams coming from the two antennas are affected by the same noise, so the three-input summation block was used in which the two paths and the total noise are accumulated. The same procedure was used for the second receiving antenna. Being in a simulation environment, the data is digital and the analog-to-digital converter is not necessary in this situation. Two additional blocks have been introduced for each receiving antenna: removing the OFDM specific cyclic prefix and applying the FFT transform. At this point, a Zero-Forcing or MMSE detection algorithm can be applied using either a Python script or Matlab.

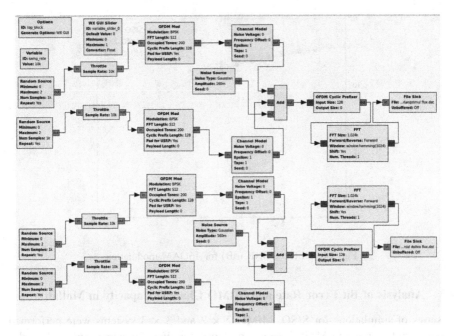

Fig. 13. Signal graph for analyzing 2 × 2 MIMO transmission

4.1 Data Detection and Error Rate Analysis Using Python

By installing the GNU Radio program using the script presented, users are provided with a number of libraries that allow to display the captured data and trace curves of interest. For the MIMO system a new library called gr-off was added, where the ZF detection algorithm is implemented in Python. Using this source and importing the obtained data as input to the another script, called berawgn.py, which was modified to display the bit error rate for a SISO, 2 × 2 and 3 × 3 MIMO systems, the graphs in Fig. 14 were obtained using 16QAM modulation.

The more complicated the modulation technique, the risk of error increases and the BER is higher for the same signal-to-noise ratio. The higher the SNR, the BER decreases. A value of 15 dB (SNR) was considered for this report. The BER increases with the number of antennas, but not much, which leads to the advantage of using a multi-antenna MIMO system, achieving a higher transfer rate with the disadvantage of increasing BER. For 16QAM modulation, considering a SNR of 14 dB, the BER value is higher in case of 3 × 3 MIMO compared to SISO, because the complexity of the system also increases.

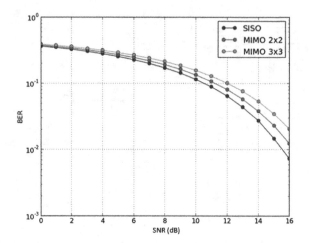

Fig. 14. BER vs. SNR (dB) for 16QAM modulation

4.2   Analysis of Bit Error Rate and MIMO Channel Capacity in Matlab

A series of simulations for SISO, MIMO 2 × 2 and 3 × 3 systems were performed using Zero-Forcing and MMSE detection algorithms. For this paper, 16QAM modulation was analyzed.

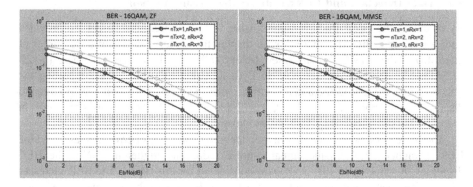

Fig. 15. BER vs. E_b/N_0 using 16QAM modulation, ZF detection and MMSE

Analyzing the graphs in Fig. 15, the following conclusions can be drawn:

- BER values based on E_b/N_0 are similar for the three transmission systems to those obtained running the Python script.
- The higher the number of transmit and receive antennas, the transmission rate increases, but the BER is negatively affected.
- Using the MMSE detection algorithm, the BER obtained for a multi-antenna system is very close to that obtained with a SISO system.

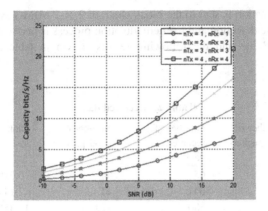

Fig. 16. MIMO Channel Capacity vs. SNR

The capacity obtained by analyzing the four systems starting with SISO and ending with MIMO 4 × 4 is higher as the number of antennas increases, shown in Fig. 16, but there is an empirical limit of the maximum number of antennas that can be used due to strong interference and high error rate. Massive-MIMO and beamforming will address this issue in 3GPP Release 15 and 16, 5G related.

4.3 Data Transmission Capabilities Test

In order to test the system data transmission capabilities, two separate source file blocks in ".txt" format, containing characters, modeled the sources. It is noticeable in Fig. 17 that the byte type (pink color) was chosen.

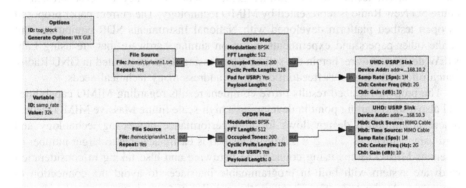

Fig. 17. Block selection for transmission signal graph (Color figure online)

The data stream must be subjected to an OFDM modulation process, which has a 128 prefix, a FFT window length of 512 samples, and the modulation of the symbols is BPSK. In order to transmit them with broadcasting antennas, USRP sink blocks are needed. The information is sent to the block chain of 2 × 2 MIMO system, previously presented. After the detection and the demodulation process is performed, the data was stored in "out.txt" file and the following results shown in table x were obtained (Table 2):

Table 2. Received data

Modulation	Number of sent packets	Number of received packets	Number of good packets	Packet loss rate	Errored packets rate
BPSK	655	653	644	0.31%	1.68%
QPSK	655	641	447	2.14%	31.75%
16QAM	655	580	379	11.45%	42.13%

The best modulation in terms of error resistance is BPSK, but it is the slowest, achieving a required transmission time of 8.371 s. QPSK is the following modulation, but it introduces large errors. The weakest modulation for laboratory conditions was 16QAM, with a transmission time of 2.647 s.

5   Conclusions and Future Work

Next generation wireless networks require significant capabilities to accommodate more users at higher data rates, offering better reliability with less power consumption. In order to prototype large-scale antenna systems that can be mass-produced and deployed in real-life telecom networks, experimental testbeds have to be built to enhance current technology for further achievements. One key use-case present in future 5G New Radio is represented by MIMO technology. The current paper proposed an open testbed platform developed with National Instruments SDR equipment, but unlike other papers and experiments based on similar hardware that are using Lab-VIEW design software, herein the software processing units are created in GNU Radio, which offers an enormous freedom degree to address many technical needs.

The proposed testbed results prove confident results regarding MIMO capabilities and also a solid starting point in developing a high-scale future Massive MIMO testbed based on simplified design flows for high-performance processing technology and hardware evaluations. The 2 × 2 MIMO testbed is easily scalable to larger number of antennas MIMO setups using connectable hardware and also taking in consideration hardware system with built-in programmable interfaces to avoid the connection to computers. At the same time it offers the possibility to prototype technologies and setups that can be used on large-scale deployments in 5G future networks.

The current work demonstrates that using SDR solutions and minimal RF physical equipment, vendors and mobile operators can perform tests for different scenarios and use cases. Different setups can be arranged according to mobile operators' requests.

This kind of approach using SDR capable equipment and customized software interfaces is the beginning of a future objective, the development of a complete air interface with higher order modulations schemes using Massive MIMO [9] for 5G New Radio [10] and it can add high value to 3GPP Release 16 [11] on aspects proposed in 3GPP Release 15 regarding 5G specifications.

Acknowledgments. This work was supported by UEFISCDI through contract no. 5Sol/2017, PNCDI III, Integrated Software Platform for Mobile Malware Analysis (ToR-SIM).

References

1. Darbari, F., Stewart, R.W., Glover, I.A.: MIMO Channel Modelling, University of Strathclyde, Glasgow, United Kingdom, pp. 7–12 (2010)
2. Dohler, M.: Virtual Antenna Arrays, University of London (2003)
3. Brown, T., Carvalho, E., Kyritsi, P.: Practical Guide to the MIMO Radio Channel. Wiley, Hoboken (2010)
4. Sankar, K.: MIMO with zero forcing equalizer (2008)
5. Linder, S., Eriksson, G., Wiklundh, K.: Evaluation of transmit diversity and spatial multiplexing for MIMO systems in an urban peer-to-peer scenario. Submitted to IEEE Transactions on Wireless Communications (2010)
6. GNU Radio. https://www.gnuradio.org/docs/. Accessed 10 Jan 2019
7. Ettus, M.: Universal software radio peripheral. http://www.ettus.com. Accessed 15 Jan 2019
8. Ferrari, P., Sisinni, E., Flammini, A., Depari, A.: Adding accurate timestamping capability to wireless networks for Smart Grids, University of Brescia, Italy (2014)
9. National Instruments. http://www.ni.com/white-paper/52382/en/. Accessed 15 Jan 2019
10. Ghosh, A.: http://www.5gsummit.org/hawaii/docs/slides/Amitava-Ghosh.pdf. Accessed 10 Dec 2018
11. 3GPP, Release 16. http://www.3gpp.org/release-16. Accessed 15 Jan 2019

Hybrid Noise-Resilient Deep Learning Architecture for Modulation Classification in Cognitive Radio Networks

Antoni Ivanov[1]([⊠]), Krasimir Tonchev[1], Vladimir Poulkov[1], Hussein Al-Shatri[2], and Anja Klein[2]

[1] Faculty of Telecommunications, Technical University of Sofia, 1000 Sofia, Bulgaria
{astivanov,k_tonchev,vkp}@tu-sofia.bg
[2] Department of Electrical Engineering and Information Technology,
Technical University Darmstadt, 64283 Darmstadt, Germany
{h.shatri,a.klein}@nt.tu-darmstadt.de

Abstract. The increasing maturity of the concepts which would allow for the operation of a practical Cognitive Radio (CR) Network require functionalities derived through different methodologies from other fields. One such approach is Deep Learning (DL) which can be applied to diverse problems in CR to enhance its effectiveness by increasing the utilization of the unused radio spectrum. Using DL, the CR device can identify whether the signal comes from the Primary User (PU) transmitter or from an interferer. The method proposed in this paper is a hybrid DL architecture which aims at achieving high recognition rate at low signal-to-noise ratio (SNR) and various channel impairments including fading because such are the relevant conditions of operation of the CR. It consists of an autoencoder and a neural network structure due to the good denoising qualities of the former and the recognition accuracy of the latter. The autoencoder aims to restore the original signal from the corrupted samples which would increase the accuracy of the classifier. Afterwards its output is fed into the NN which learns the characteristics of each modulation type and classifies the restored signal correctly with certain probability. To determine the optimal classification DL model, several types of NN structures are examined and compared for input comprised of the IQ samples of the reconstructed signal. The performance of the proposed DL architecture in comparison to similar models for the relevant parameters in different channel impairments scenarios is also analyzed.

Keywords: Cognitive Radio · Deep Learning ·
Modulation classification · Spectrum sensing

V. Poulkov (Ed.): FABULOUS 2019, LNICST 283, pp. 214–227, 2019.
https://doi.org/10.1007/978-3-030-23976-3_20

1   Introduction

The increasing effort to improve the applicability of modern telecommunications and introduce new generations of networks and services has significantly accelerated the maturity of all concepts and functionalities of CR systems. This tendency has also influenced the development of the spectrum sensing function which allows for dynamic access to the spectrum that is not by default allocated for the CR device but has incumbent (primary) users, the transmission of which must be protected from intolerable levels of interference. For this reason it is required for this function to be fast and accurate enough in order to determine whether the frequency band is available (the incumbent users' signals are not present in it) or not [10]. In addition, it is desirable to have the possibility to predict the amount of time during which the spectrum is expected to remain unused by the primary users (PU) to avoid hampering their transmission. In order to increase the utilization of the spectrum by the CR network it can be beneficial for the equipment not only to detect the signal present in the spectrum but also to identify its type. That is because the CR device is required to be able to detect very weak signals to ensure that the primary user is distinguished from the noise even at the edge of the PU network's coverage [25]. As a result, the cognitive equipment may confuse an interfering signal from the point of view of the PU for the actual PU signal. In this case, the CR device will miss the opportunity to utilize a portion of the spectrum in which the incumbent user (IU) is not in fact present. This is why studies on recognizing the type and source of the received signal, are necessary. Consequently there have been multiple works which attempted to achieve this [1,4,6,10,11,18,19,22,30]. Other applications of signal recognition include identifying illegal transmitters or malfunctioning equipment, TV white space access planning, improving the capabilities of Emergency and Public Safety services, mapping spectrum occupancy, electrosmog monitoring, location identification for military purposes, demodulation without overhead information, reconnaissance and satellite relay selection [22,28].

Extensive research in the field of signal interception has led to the introduction of modulation classification (MC) as the most commonly employed technique for recognition of the received signal's type [4]. There have been a large variety of proposed algorithms for achieving efficient signal recognition but they can in general be separated into two groups - likelihood [4,29] or feature [18,22] based MC. The advantages of the former group of methods is the possibility to recognize a large variety of signals with very little or none a priori data. Their implementation in realistic receivers, however, could be problematic considering that they might need intolerable amount of time to estimate the necessary parameters for signal classification [29]. The receiver devices themselves might not be designed with the computational power to handle these complex operations. In contrast the concept behind the feature-based methods is the possibility for near-instantaneous recognition of the modulation type of a received signal. These algorithms use a supervised learning procedure like Machine Learning (ML). Only in the recent years has the modern concept of Deep Learning (DL) been applied to the MC problem [1,2,9,13,16,18,19,21,22,30–33]. The characteristic trait of these algorithms is the utilization of large amounts of preprocessed data which is used for preliminary training a deep Neural Network (NN) that afterwards will be able to recognize newly-received signals with sufficient probability under specified conditions (most often the SNR level). At this point the emerging obstacles before using DL for signal recognition are seen as following. First of all, a sufficient volume of suitable data for the training of the NN needs to be recorded or generated. Subsequently, the design of the NN itself is not trivial as there are a few parameters which require careful and most often empirical determination. Finally the training process typically has a high computational cost on the host computer and can take a lot of time depending on the amount of data and the choice of parameters of the NN. These considerations will be explored in the subsequent sections of this paper. Section 2 presents the review of available literature for MC using DL algorithms. The parameters for dataset generation and the channel and noise models are described in Sect. 3. Section 4 details the proposed architecture and the relevant parameters. In Sect. 5 the results in terms of recognition accuracy are analyzed and the conclusions are discussed in Sect. 6.

2   State of the Art

The current works related to the field of DL-based MC can be summarized according to the following aspects: the kinds of input given to the NN, the amount of data vectors (or realizations of the signal) used for training and testing, the DL architectures utilized for the classification and the channel model which is used for generation of the testing data.

When it comes to the data used for the training of the NN, there are mostly two types of input in regard to signal recognition - the vector of signal samples [1,18,22,30], statistical features extracted from those samples [1,2,13,16,19,21, 28], or a combination of both [1]. Vast majority of the published works examine cyclostationary and other kinds of statistical features derived from the signals as inputs of the classifier. These are utilized for MC because they represent the signal components which are resilient to the effects of noise. For this reason they have gained popularity with likelihood-based algorithms and are consequently explored in the studies of MC based on DL. The most often utilized input is the high-order statistical features [1,13,19] which are easy to define mathematically and they are not very computationally intensive [17]. Other features used are the center points in the modulation constellation [1], more varied statistical features like kurtosis, peak to average power ratio, etc. [13] and the amplitude, frequency and phase of the signal which are estimated as part of the learning process of the NN [21]. When the signal itself is fed into the NN, it is most often represented as a matrix of 2 columns and N rows where N is the number of samples, the first column contains the in-phase while the second - the quadrature components of the input signal [18,22]. There is also a vast margin between the number of data vectors utilized for training and testing varying from a few thousand to several hundreds of thousand realizations. It is apparent, though, that whenever larger amounts of signal data vectors were used, they contained much less samples so in terms of overall volume of data, there is not a big difference. The largest database of 1.44 million signal realizations each composed of 1024 samples was studied in [19].

All of the main DL structures have so far been studied in the literature for application to the MC problem because they are all useful for recognition of data which consists of sequential samples (like the signal representation in time domain) [5]. These include Convolutional NN (CNN) [2,18,19,30], Recurrent NN (RNN) [22], autoencoder (AE) [1,30] and Restricted Boltzmann Machines (RBM) [16]. The most often utilized DL architecture is the CNN with different number of layers[1], normally consisting of from 2 to 4 [2,18,30] but can reach up to 7 [19]. CNNs employ convolution instead of multiplication in their layers and are especially interesting because they can learn the features of the input data without the need for them to be extracted separately [5]. Generally the number of nodes (filters) in each convolutional sub-layer is in the order of hundreds. As for the RNN, it normally consists of 2 long-short term memory (LSTM) [22] or gated recurrent unit (GRU) layers and a fully-connected (FC) layer. Their structure is based around cells which process the data through gates and are able to classify sequential data. The AE has also been popular in recent works [1,30] because of its property to learn and reproduce (encode and decode) the form of a given input signal to its output with sufficiently low error [5]. Structures composed of 2 hidden layers [1] or 3 to 4 convolutional AE layers [30] which combine the traditional encoder/decoder of the AE with layers which are typically used in CNNs. Similarly to the AE, the RBM models aim to reconstruct the input data into its output but each node is connected to all the nodes in the consecutive layer [5]. This model is used in [16] and it has 5 layers. The input data used is images representing the spectral correlation function (SCF) of the signals. Additionally, some papers examine more novel DL models like the hierarchical residual network [19] or Extensible NN [21].

Finally there comes the important question of what channel model should be chosen for the testing data as to determine the performance of the proposed solution in realistic environments. Some of the studies [30,33] include just additive white Gaussian noise (AWGN) in their considerations but there are those that introduce frequency and phase offset [1,19] as well as Rayleigh, Rician fading or both [13,19,21]. A few [2,18,19,22] have utilized real-world recorded signals produced using software-defined radio (SDR) transceivers and the GNU Radio [26] package which are publicly available.

As a result of the analysis done in this section, the contributions of this paper are the following: design of a multi-layered architecture which combines an AE (Denoising AE or DAE) for the purpose of recovering distorted signals

---

[1] The term "layer" in the context of CNNs throughout this paper, is understood in the sense described in [5], i.e. each "complex" convolutional layer is composed of sub-layers which can, because of the coherence of their functions, be denoted as a single unit.

and a NN classifier with improved optimization algorithms; comparison between the performance of a CNN and of an RNN classifier with the inclusion of three (CNN and RNN-based) DL models presented in the literature which have shown very good recognition accuracy in low SNR levels (<5 dB) [22,30]. In addition to testing the NN performance with signals in AWGN and Rayleigh fading channels, the effects of non-Gaussian noises and generalized fading on the precision are also explored. Some of the most often considered modulation types are used for input of the DL model.

3   Dataset Generation

This Section gives an outline of the way in which the input signals are generated and the channel models are simulated. This is done in MATLAB and the resulting signal data is saved in files to be later used as an input of the NNs.

There are 11 modulation types considered in this study - BPSK, QPSK, PSK8, 16QAM, 64QAM, PAM4, AM-DSB, AM-SSB, GFSK, OFDM-16 (OFDM symbols with 16QAM modulated bits) and OFDM-64 (with 64QAM). All of them are generated with the same parameters as follows. Each data vector consists of a matrix composed of two vectors, 2048 samples each, the first containing the real while the other - the imaginary component of the signal. The sampling frequency is 1 GHz, the carrier frequency is 100 MHz, each bit is represented by 8 samples, bandwidth is 25 MHz. The length of the cyclic prefix of the OFDM signals is 15% of the length of each symbol, the modulation depth for the amplitude modulations is 30% and the standard deviation for the Gaussian filter used to form the GFSK signals, is equal to 6. There are 4096 realizations of each modulation for training and 512 for testing. The test set contains the same 5632 realizations (512 per modulation type) for each SNR level in the range $[-20; 20]$ dB. There are 6 test sets which contain signals corrupted by different combinations of channel distortions.

As it was stated in Sect. 2, to the best of the authors' knowledge, signals corrupted in complex fading and non-Gaussian channels have not been studied in works examining MC based on DL. Therefore, some channel impairments studied in signal detection literature are described here.

3.1   Middleton Noise

The Middleton Class A is a narrowband impulse noise model which describes the "coherent" interference created by man-made sources (mostly unintended radiations by various appliances, antennas, etc.) [3,24]. This form of the noise has been used in some signal detection and reception performance studies to model impulsive distortions [3,24]. It can be presented analytically and it is thus convenient for simulations. The probability density function (PDF) of the Middleton A noise used to describe it and the relevant parameters are found in [24].

3.2   Cauchy Noise

The Cauchy noise has also been studied in signal detection literature [8,27] due to its attributes which make it viable for describing impulse distortions in the propagation environment. These are created by normal human activities, the mechanical operation of machines, natural phenomena and others [27]. The PDF of the Caucy noise is given in [8]. In order to define the SNR levels for both the Cauchy and Middleton noises, the generalized expression for the SNR defined in [27] is used.

3.3   Generalized Gamma Fading

The generalized Gamma (also known as Stacey or $\alpha - \mu$) distribution is a basis out of which several of the most commonly used fading models can be derived. It consists of a non-linear sum of the multipath components and represents the small-scale fluctuations of the received signal [7]. The distribution of this fading model as well as the applicable parameters to describe it are taken from [7].

4   Proposed Architecture

This Section describes the proposed DL algorithm's structure, the methodology of training and testing, and how the input which consists of signal vectors in time domain is processed. First, the DAE learns the shape of the training signal data vectors (they do not have any channel impairments added to them) and afterwards, reconstructs the signals from the corrupted testing set. For all DL models examined in this study the training dataset is randomly shuffled. The recovered test data vectors are then saved into files and the classifier NN is trained with the same training set as the DAE was. Finally the reproduced testing set is given to the classifier which gives the probability for correct recognition between all modulation types for each SNR level. All of the algorithms were run on a NVIDIA TITAN X (Pascal) graphical processor unit which was kindly donated by the NVIDIA Corporation. They were implemented using Tensorflow.

4.1   Denoising Autoencoder

As it was stated earlier, this study explores how the DAE's capability to reduce the effect of noise by recovering the signal's shape, influences the performance of the NN classifier. A representation of the DAE's structure is shown in Fig. 1. It is composed of two layers, the first having 64 nodes and the second - 32. Both of them operate by simple matrix multiplication (Eq. (1)) use the sigmoid activation function. Increasing the number of layers leads to degradation in the performance. Using only two layers is also established in other works which study the AE structure [1,33].

$$Y = xW + b, \tag{1}$$

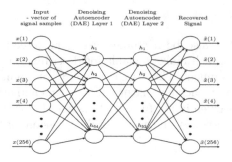

Fig. 1. Structure of the DAE

where the output Y is obtained by multiplying the input vector x by the matrix of weights W, and adding the biases b.

The Minimum mean square error (MMSE) method is used to reduce the cost function and the optimization is performed by the popular and effective Adam algorithm [12]. Empirically it was deduced that the autoencoder reconstructs shorter sequences with greater precision than long ones and therefore the input is divided into signals composed of 256 samples[2] (it is for this reason that the DAE has 256 input nodes). After the reconstruction is done the signals $\tilde{x}$ are reshaped again into series of 2048 samples. Another experimental observation is that the DAE provides the lowest error when the input signals are normalized in the $[0, 1]$ interval, whereas if the data is not normalized, the error becomes too high for viable reconstruction to be achieved. Faster convergence (in this case, obtaining the lowest cost function possible) is achieved by utilizing low learning rate (0.001) and batch size (11264 for the DAE, which means that the number of batches into which the training set will be divided is 64). Combining low values of both of these parameters is also commonly used in DL algorithms [5,18,20,22]. With this configuration, the training is performed in about 30 min.

4.2 Convolutional Neural Network

The first deep NN classifier the performance of which is analyzed in this paper, is the CNN. It learns from the training set and afterwards takes the reconstructed test sets which include the same signal data vectors for all SNR levels in the $[-20, 20]$ dB interval and all fading and noise scenarios as described in Sect. 3. Then, the CNN gives the classification accuracy for each SNR level and each scenario. The structure of the model is illustrated in Fig. 2

As it is seen in Fig. 2, the CNN contains four 2-dimensional convolutional layers, each one composed of convolution sub-layer, rectified linear unit (ReLU) and a 2-dimensional max-pooling sub-layer (using the terminology described in [5]), a ReLU layer and a class-prediction layer. Essentially, all convolution

---

[2] Consequently, the number of data vectors in both the training and test sets will be 8 times higher than it was originally.

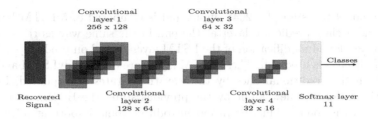

Fig. 2. Structure of the CNN

sub-layers and the prediction layer implement Eq. (1). The input of the CNN is 4 dimensional tensor with dimensions [Batch Size, 2, 2048, 1] because as explained in Sect. 3, each signal realization is composed of a [2 × 2048] matrix. As seen in Fig. 2, the first convolution sub-layer has a kernel with dimensions [256 × 128], the second with [128 × 64], third - [64 × 32] and fourth with [32 × 16]. All max-pooling sub-layers have kernel sizes of [2 × 2] and strides with dimensions of [2 × 2]. At the end of the CNN there is a softmax layer which is a widely-used activation function. Such depth of the NN structure is employed to increase the capability of the model to learn sophisticated functions such as signals corrupted by noise and fading. As it was the case for the DAE, the Adam optimizer is utilized but it is also enhanced with a weight-decay algorithm which adapts the weights with small gradients [15]. This modification allows for separation of the weight decay and the gradients' update in order for the regularization to be applied properly for the Adam optimizer. Recognition accuracy is computed using MMSE. The weight decay factor is 0.0001 [30], the exponential decay rates are $\beta_1 = 0.9, \beta_2 = 0.999$ and the stability constant ϵ is 10^{-8} [15]. As for the learning rate and batch size, they are usually chosen to both have small values (around 0.001 and 40 or more times smaller than the training set's size) but in this work, the recently proposed in the field of image classification, opposite direction is followed [23]. The authors in [23] conclude that using batch size around 10 times smaller than the training set and high learning rate can produce roughly the same results as in the alternative case but reach convergence much faster. For this reason, the values chosen for the learning rate and batch size are 0.1 and 4096 (number of batches is 11), respectively. Preliminary experiments showed that very similar results are achieved if small learning rates and batch sizes are used but, as expected, after much slower training. Increasing the depth of the model does not give any significant performance gains as well. The time needed for training of the CNN is discussed in Sect. 5.

4.3 Recurrent Neural Network

The performance of the deep CNN is compared to a mutli-layered RNN which is described here. It is trained with the same training set but it was shown that it cannot recognize any of the reconstructed test datasets even after rigorous training. Thus, this classifier uses the noisy test data that is provided to the DAE, i.e. no denoising is performed on it.

The model takes an $[2 \times 2048]$ input and is composed of 5 LSTM layers, a ReLU and a class prediction layer at the end in the same way as the CNN. A recently developed modification of the LSTM layers based on the Independently RNN (IndRNN) is used [14]. These LSTM layers are called IndyLSTM and they differ from the traditional ones by the way their states are updated. Instead of multiplication the new input by the previous state, the Hadamard product of these two is found. This alteration introduces some important advantages to the training of the RNN, namely, independence of the nodes in each layer, efficient training due to LSTMs being enhanced for robustness against gradient decay and ability to handle much longer series of data. Additionally, constructing multi-layered RNNs is also much more viable [14]. As it is recommended in the reference, the IndRNNs require low learning rate in order to converge, however large batch size can still be used for faster training. After preliminary experiments, optimal results were achieved for the following parameters. The learning rate is 0.001, batch size is 4096, the number of nodes in each layer is 128 and the forget bias of the IndyLSTMs is 1. Again, the Adam optimizer with weight decay is employed in this classifier with the same parameters. Training is performed in about an hour.

5   Results

This Section presents a thorough analysis of the results in terms of recognition accuracy for the two proposed DL classifiers in six channel scenarios:

Scenario 1: AWGN
Scenario 2: Additive white Gaussian, Middleton and Cauchy noises
Scenario 3: AWGN and generalized Gamma fading
Scenario 4: AWGN and Rayleigh fading
Scenario 5: Additive white Gaussian, Middleton and Cauchy noises, and generalized Gamma fading
Scenario 6: Additive white Gaussian, Middleton and Cauchy noises, and Rayleigh fading.

In addition, three NN classifiers from [22,30] are used for reference. They follow the structure described in the respective papers that proposed them and are indicated as "Reference RNN" [22], "Reference Convolutional AE" and "Reference CNN" [30]. For better clarity, the graphical representations of the results for every two scenarios in the case in which the input is the signal vectors in time domain, are shown in a common plot in Figs. 3, 4 and 5. The effective SNR range of $[-20; 20]$ dB which is relevant for CR applications, is considered in all experiments.

The most notable characteristics exposed in all graphics are those of the CNN classifiers (the proposed CNN, the reference convolutional AE and CNN). In Figs. 3, 4 and 5 it is seen that for reference CNN the recognition accuracy is constant for the whole SNR range. The convolutional AE and proposed CNN models show some insignificant variations in the results. This effect is related

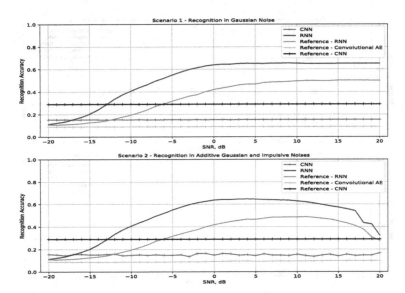

Fig. 3. Recognition accuracy in Scenarios 1 and 2 with signal input

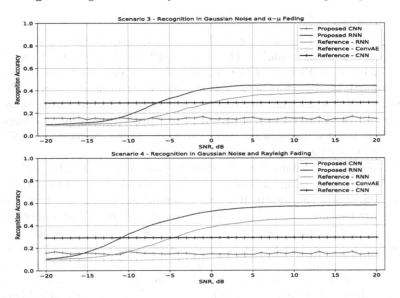

Fig. 4. Recognition accuracy in Scenarios 3 and 4 with signal input

to the training of the CNNs which showed that at every run, the NN gets to a certain accuracy for the noiseless test sets very quickly and at that point, it does not show any alternation in its learning process. Consequently, all test datasets have the same classification accuracy as the one obtained during training. For that reason, the results are collected in the following manner. Each CNN is

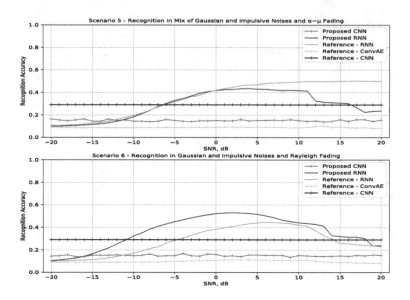

Fig. 5. Recognition accuracy in Scenarios 5 and 6 with signal input

trained 13 times and the average of the achieved accuracy values, is taken for all test sets and in all scenarios. Thus, the model is trained in about two hours which combines all 13 runs of the classifier. It is evident that the "Reference Convolutional AE" has more noticeable fluctuations than the proposed CNN and the reference CNN and they demonstrate a linearly-ascending trend. However, this model still shows the worst performance. In the results for the proposed CNN, there is some insignificant variation where as the "Reference CNN" has the best accuracy but it is yet poor.

The effects of the channel on the classification accuracy can be explored in much greater depth using the curves of the proposed and reference RNNs. In almost all channel scenarios, the RNN presented in this study shows much greater performance gains in comparison to its alternative. Figures 3 and 5 illustrate an interesting trend in that the accuracy experiences a significant decline in high SNR levels (>10 dB). This tendency is not present in the scenarios which exclude impulse noises so naturally, it can be attributed to them. The reason can be found in the distortions that these noise components introduce into the signal. Their impulsive nature reduces the classification efficiency of the RNN because it dramatically changes the shape of the signal. The deterioration in high SNR rates can be ascribed to the way that the SNR is calculated for the impulse noises (as explained in Sect. 3). As a consequence, the peaks added to the signal in high SNR, even though they are much smaller than the signal's amplitude, still have significant presence when it comes to recognition accuracy. In contrast, when the impulses are comparable to the signal's amplitude (around SNR = 0 dB), the classifier shows better performance. Thus, it is evident that the influence of the noise is much greater than that of the fading. However, as seen from Figs. 4 and 5, there is a considerable degradation in the classification effectiveness when the generalized Gamma fading model is adopted. The performance decline in high SNR levels is not observed in the scenario which combines impulsive noises and generalized Gamma fading for the reference RNN. This can be attributed to the model having less layers and thus, being able to process the particular test dataset more efficiently.

6   Conclusions and Future Work

This paper presents a study on the signal recognition capabilities of a hybrid DL framework composed of an AE and a NN classifier. The input data is composed of a large volume of signal vectors in time domain. The test datasets contain signals corrupted with complex generalized channel fading and non-Gaussian impulse noise models. The influence of these impairments on the classification performance is explored and the comparison between the proposed CNN and RNN classifiers and three other reference NNs. On the basis of the results obtained during the simulations there are a number of aspects which pertain to the type of input data and the DL architecture, that are important and may guide further steps in the development of algorithms for MC. When it comes to the input data, an important consideration is how the particular model performs depending on whether the data is normalized or not. A significant difference in recognition accuracy is not observed in the proposed CNN and RNN models but it is a crucial factor in the efficiency of the AE. As for the CNN and RNN classifiers it is shown that the RNN has better performance even though it is not tested on the denoised testset of signals. As for the parameters of each NN model, there are useful guidelines in the recent studies but the need for empirical adjustment during training and testing is ever-present. In view of this fact, the adaptation of the learning rate and batch size during training has real potential.

Acknowledgment. The paper is published with the support of the project No BG05M2OP001-2.009-0033 "Promotion of Contemporary Research Through Creation of Scientific and Innovative Environment to Encourage Young Researchers in Technical University - Sofia and The National Railway Infrastructure Company in The Field of Engineering Science and Technology Development" within the Intelligent Growth Science and Education Operational Programme co-funded by the European Structural and Investment Funds of the European Union.

References

1. Ali, A., Yangyu, F., Liu, S.: Automatic modulation classification of digital modulation signals with stacked autoencoders. Digit. Signal Process. **71**, 108–116 (2017)
2. Arumugam, K.S.K., Kadampot, I.A., Tahmasbi, M., Shah, S., Bloch, M., Pokutta, S.: Modulation recognition using side information and hybrid learning. In: 2017 IEEE International Symposium on Dynamic Spectrum Access Networks (DySPAN), pp. 1–2. IEEE (2017)

3. Bhatti, S.A., et al.: Impulsive noise modelling and prediction of its impact on the performance of WLAN receiver. In: 2009 17th European Signal Processing Conference, pp. 1680–1684. IEEE (2009)
4. Dobre, O.A., Abdi, A., Bar-Ness, Y., Su, W.: Blind modulation classification: a concept whose time has come. In: 2005 IEEE/Sarnoff Symposium on Advances in Wired and Wireless Communication, pp. 223–228. IEEE (2005)
5. Goodfellow, I., Bengio, Y., Courville, A.: Deep Learning. MIT Press, Cambridge (2016). http://www.deeplearningbook.org
6. Gouldieff, V., Palicot, J., Daumont, S.: Blind automatic modulation classification in multipath fading channels. In: 2017 22nd International Conference on Digital Signal Processing (DSP), pp. 1–5. IEEE (2017)
7. Gurugopinath, S.: Energy-based bayesian spectrum sensing over α-μ/stacy/generalized gamma fading channels. In: 2016 8th International Conference on Communication Systems and Networks (COMSNETS), pp. 1–6. IEEE (2016)
8. Gurugopinath, S., Muralishankar, R., Shankar, H.: Spectrum sensing in the presence of cauchy noise through differential entropy. In: Distributed Computing, VLSI, Electrical Circuits and Robotics (DISCOVER), pp. 201–204. IEEE (2016)
9. Hong, D., Zhang, Z., Xu, X.: Automatic modulation classification using recurrent neural networks. In: 2017 3rd IEEE International Conference on Computer and Communications (ICCC), pp. 695–700. IEEE (2017)
10. Ivanov, A., Mihovska, A., Tonchev, K., Poulkov, V.: Real-time adaptive spectrum sensing for cyclostationary and energy detectors. IEEE Aerosp. Electron. Syst. Mag. **33**(5–6), 20–33 (2018). https://doi.org/10.1109/MAES.2018.170098
11. Jang, W.M.: Blind cyclostationary spectrum sensing in cognitive radios. IEEE Commun. Lett. **18**(3), 393–396 (2014)
12. Kingma, D.P., Ba, J.: Adam: a method for stochastic optimization. arXiv preprint arXiv:1412.6980 (2014)
13. Lee, J.H., Kim, J., Kim, B., Yoon, D., Choi, J.W.: Robust automatic modulation classification technique for fading channels via deep neural network. Entropy **19**(9) (2017). https://doi.org/10.3390/e19090454, http://www.mdpi.com/1099-4300/19/9/454
14. Li, S., Li, W., Cook, C., Zhu, C., Gao, Y.: Independently recurrent neural network (IndRNN): building a longer and deeper RNN. In: Proceedings of the IEEE Conference on Computer Vision and Pattern Recognition, pp. 5457–5466 (2018)
15. Loshchilov, I., Hutter, F.: Fixing weight decay regularization in adam. arXiv preprint arXiv:1711.05101 (2017)
16. Mendis, G.J., Wei, J., Madanayake, A.: Deep learning-based automated modulation classification for cognitive radio. In: 2016 IEEE International Conference on Communication Systems (ICCS), pp. 1–6. IEEE (2016)
17. Orlic, V.D., Dukic, M.L.: Automatic modulation classification: sixth-order cumulant features as a solution for real-world challenges. In: 2012 20th Telecommunications Forum (TELFOR), pp. 392–399. IEEE (2012)
18. O'Shea, T.J., Corgan, J., Clancy, T.C.: Convolutional radio modulation recognition networks. In: Jayne, C., Iliadis, L. (eds.) EANN 2016. CCIS, vol. 629, pp. 213–226. Springer, Cham (2016). https://doi.org/10.1007/978-3-319-44188-7_16
19. O'Shea, T.J., Roy, T., Clancy, T.C.: Over-the-air deep learning based radio signal classification. IEEE J. Sel. Top. Signal Process. **12**(1), 168–179 (2018)
20. Peng, S., Jiang, H., Wang, H., Alwageed, H., Yao, Y.D.: Modulation classification using convolutional neural network based deep learning model. In: 2017 26th Wireless and Optical Communication Conference (WOCC), pp. 1–5. IEEE (2017)

21. Qing Yang, G.: Modulation classification based on extensible neural networks. Math. Probl. Eng. **2017** (2017)
22. Rajendran, S., Meert, W., Giustiniano, D., Lenders, V., Pollin, S.: Distributed deep learning models for wireless signal classification with low-cost spectrum sensors. arXiv preprint arXiv:1707.08908 (2017)
23. Smith, S.L., Kindermans, P.J., Le, Q.V.: Don't decay the learning rate, increase the batch size. arXiv preprint arXiv:1711.00489 (2017)
24. Spaulding, A., Middleton, D.: Optimum reception in an impulsive interference environment - Part I: coherent detection. IEEE Trans. Commun. **25**(9), 910–923 (1977). https://doi.org/10.1109/TCOM.1977.1093943
25. Stevenson, C.R., Chouinard, G., Lei, Z., Hu, W., Shellhammer, S.J., Caldwell, W.: IEEE 802.22: the first cognitive radio wireless regional area network standard. IEEE Commun. Mag. **47**(1), 130–138 (2009)
26. The GNU Radio Foundation: GNU Radio, the free and open software radio ecosystem, October 2018. https://www.gnuradio.org/
27. Tsakalides, P., Nikias, C.L.: Maximum likelihood localization of sources in noise modeled as a stable process. IEEE Trans. Signal Process. **43**(11), 2700–2713 (1995)
28. Xiong, X., Feng, J., Jiang, L.: Automatic digital modulation classification for ors satellite relay communication. In: 2015 International Conference on Wireless Communications & Signal Processing (WCSP), pp. 1–5. IEEE (2015)
29. Xu, J.L., Su, W., Zhou, M.: Likelihood-ratio approaches to automatic modulation classification. IEEE Trans. Syst. Man Cybern. Part C (Appl. Rev.) **41**(4), 455–469 (2011)
30. Xu, Y., Li, D., Wang, Z., Guo, Q., Xiang, W.: A deep learning method based on convolutional neural network for automatic modulation classification of wireless signals. Wireless Networks. Springer, New York (2017). https://doi.org/10.1007/s11276-018-1667-6
31. Zhang, D., et al.: Automatic modulation classification based on deep learning for unmanned aerial vehicles. Sensors **18**(3), 924 (2018)
32. Zhang, Z., Hua, Z., Liu, Y.: Modulation classification in multipath fading channels using sixth-order cumulants and stacked convolutional auto-encoders. Wirel. Netw. **11**(6), 910–915 (2017)
33. Zhu, X., Fujii, T.: A novel modulation classification method in cognitive radios using higher-order cumulants and denoising stacked sparse autoencoder. In: 2016 Asia-Pacific Signal and Information Processing Association Annual Summit and Conference (APSIPA), pp. 1–5, December 2016. https://doi.org/10.1109/APSIPA.2016.7820860

Evaluation of Channel Estimation Algorithms Using Practically Measured Channels in FDD Massive MIMO

Nikolay Dandanov$^{(\boxtimes)}$, Krasimir Tonchev, Vladimir Poulkov,
and Pavlina Koleva

Faculty of Telecommunications, Technical University of Sofia, Sofia, Bulgaria
{n_dandanov,k_tonchev,vkp,p_koleva}@tu-sofia.bg

Abstract. An important problem for massive multiple-input multiple-output (MIMO) systems operating with frequency-division duplexing (FDD) is to accurately estimate the channel response with low pilot signal overhead. Most existing algorithms for efficient channel estimation are based on compressive sensing (CS) and assume sparse structure of the channel vector. Relying on it, they try to minimize estimation error and reduce the number of required pilot signals. Utilizing real-world channel responses, we evaluate the performance of 11 state-of-the-art channel estimation algorithms for FDD massive MIMO systems. Results from simulation experiments with channel measurements for carrier frequency in the 2.4 GHz and 5 GHz bands for three environments and two levels of mobility are presented. Channel structures of theoretical and practically measured channels are compared and it is shown that the latter does not follow a specific sparse structure which leads to a significant increase in estimation errors according to our results. A comprehensive analysis of estimation quality and its dependence on signal-to-noise ratio (SNR) and number of pilot signals is provided. The results demonstrate that some algorithms perform well when applied to practical channels while others do not provide confident results. The effects of pilot matrix choice and angular domain channel representation are also studied and evaluated.

Keywords: Channel estimation · Massive Mimo · Practical channels · Frequency-division duplexing · Compressive sensing

1 Introduction

Up to the present moment, the amount of wireless communications has been growing at an exponential pace for many decades [2]. In order to satisfy the vast demands for mobile data rate and capacity, 5G techniques will be employed for future wireless networks. One potential technology to support this growth is the massive MIMO [9,16] which is a promising solution to handle several orders of magnitude increase in wireless data traffic than current technologies [2]. In order

© ICST Institute for Computer Sciences, Social Informatics and Telecommunications Engineering 2019
Published by Springer Nature Switzerland AG 2019. All Rights Reserved
V. Poulkov (Ed.): FABULOUS 2019, LNICST 283, pp. 228–242, 2019.
https://doi.org/10.1007/978-3-030-23976-3_21

to process the uplink (UL) and downlink (DL) signals and to fully exploit the potential benefits for efficient spectrum and energy utilization, accurate information about the channel responses is needed which presents one of the key challenges in practical application of massive MIMO [2]. The channel responses need to be estimated regularly and the current set of channel response realizations is called the channel state whereas the knowledge that the base station (BS) has of them is referred to as the channel state information (CSI) [2].

The main method for CSI acquisition is pilot signaling. To estimate the channel response from N transmitting antennas, N orthogonal pilot signals are required in order to ensure signal separation which introduces overhead and wastes resources [2]. In traditional systems, the BS sends pilots to user equipments (UEs) which feedback the DL channel estimation to the BS which does not scale well with the number of antennas at the BS [11]. In a system with K users utilizing time-division duplexing (TDD), the channels in the UL and DL are assumed to be reciprocal so the pilot overhead is proportional to K [2,17]. If FDD is used, the channels in the UL and DL are different [17] which leads to a pilot and feedback overhead of $N + K/2$ on average if the frequency resources are divided equally between UL and DL and the system operates in the preferable regime with $N/K \geq 4$ [2]. Such overhead is prohibitive for mobile scenarios, however designing and demonstrating an efficient FDD massive MIMO implementation is a great challenge which needs to be solved [2]. This is the reason why our work is focused on evaluating efficient channel estimation algorithms FDD systems.

1.1 Related Channel Estimation Techniques and Algorithms for FDD Massive MIMO Systems

One major approach to reduce the pilot and CSI feedback overheads in FDD massive MIMO systems is to exploit the hidden sparsity and low-rank properties of the massive MIMO channel via CS and sparse recovery methods [5,11,14]. According to CS, a signal which exhibits sparsity in some transformation domain can be recovered from far fewer samples than those required by the classical Shannon-Nyquist theorem [3]. Hence, channel estimation in massive MIMO systems can be realized by (i) transforming channel measurements into sparse matrices, (ii) compressing the sparse signals into signals with far lower dimensions than real channel estimates and (iii) recovering the original signals from the compressed signals. The goal is to estimate large-sized channels from small-sized measurements using few pilot signals by carefully designing the transformation matrix.

Examples for CS-based algorithms are the classical orthogonal matching pursuit (OMP) [6], least absolute shrinkage and selection operator (LASSO) [4,11], maximum likelihood (ML), expectation-maximization (EM), Turbo-CS [12] and others. The classical OMP algorithm [6] is a straightforward extension of the CS model to CSI estimation problems without assuming any common structure among channel responses of different users. The joint OMP (J-OMP) [14] exploits the hidden joint sparsity structure in the user channel matrices due to the shared local scatterers in the physical propagation environment. The select-discard simultaneous OMP (SD-SOMP) [10] is a universal robust recovery algorithm under different joint sparsity models. Compressive Sampling Matching Pursuit (CoSaMP) [6,13] is an iterative greedy algorithm which recovers the channels individually without taking into account any particular sparsity structure. The Distributed Sparsity Adaptive Matching Pursuit (DSAMP) [7] leverages the spatially common sparsity of massive MIMO channels to jointly estimate multiple channels associated with different subcarriers. The L1 LASSO [4,11] is a ℓ_1 minimization problem which aims to introduce a sparse structure in the recovered channel whereas the burst LASSO [11] assumes that the channel response has a burst sparse structure. Both LASSO algorithms recover the channel response individually while the joint burst LASSO algorithm [11] exploits the additional joint burst-sparse structure in MU massive MIMO channels. The EM Bernoulli-Gaussian (BG) approximate message passing (AMP), EM-BG-AMP [19], is a signal reconstruction algorithm which models the signal as i.i.d BG with unknown prior sparsity, mean and variance, while the noise is considered as zero-mean Gaussian with unknown variance. The signal is simultaneously reconstructed while learning the prior signal and noise parameters [19]. The Turbo-CS [12] algorithm is based on the turbo principle in iterative decoding. It consists of a minimum mean squared error (MSE)—MMSE, and a linear MMSE (LMMSE) estimators and assumes an i.i.d. prior distribution of the channel response. However, it cannot exploit the structured sparsity of massive MIMO channels and the structured Turbo-CS [5] algorithm was proposed to overcome this limitation by assuming a Markov prior. The conventional Least Squares (LS) method correlates the received signal with the known pilot sequence, but suffers from lack of orthogonality between desired and interfering pilots (pilot contamination). Hence, the estimation performance is limited by the signal-to-interference ratio at the BS [20]. The performance in terms of CSI recovery error of some of these CS methods is experimentally verified in this work and the results are presented in Sect. 4.

Other approaches to reduce the pilot and CSI feedback overheads in FDD massive MIMO systems are to use channel parametrizations [2], the opportunistic channel sounding policies [8] and methods exploiting machine learning and artificial neural networks.

1.2   Contributions

This work evaluates the practical performance of state-of-the-art channel estimation algorithms with real-world channel responses for application in FDD massive MIMO systems. Simulation experiments to demonstrate the dependence of CSI recovery error of the algorithms on SNR, number of pilot signals, pilot matrix choice and channel response representation have been carried out. The results are compared with a baseline for a realistic theoretical channel model. The channel structures of the theoretical model and practical channel responses are compared. To the best of the authors' knowledge, such study has not been considered in the literature before.

1.3 Structure of the Paper

The rest of the paper is organized as follows. The system model is presented in Sect. 2. A description of the measurement data and used methodology follow in Sect. 3. In Sect. 4, analysis and discussions of the simulation results are provided. Finally, Sect. 5 concludes the paper and highlights future research directions on the topic.

2 System Model

In the present work, we consider a flat block-fading MU massive MIMO system operating in FDD mode. There is one BS with N antennas serving K single-antenna user terminals. The BS transmits a sequence of M pilot signals $\mathbf{x}_t^H \in \mathbb{C}^{1 \times N}$, $t = 1, \ldots, M$ for estimating the downlink channel. User k receives the signal $\mathbf{y}_k \in \mathbb{C}^{M \times 1}$

$$\mathbf{y}_k = \mathbf{X}\mathbf{h}_k + \mathbf{n}_k, \tag{1}$$

where $\mathbf{X} = [\mathbf{x}_1, \ldots, \mathbf{x}_M]^H \in \mathbb{C}^{M \times N}$ is a pilot matrix which is known in both the BS and UE, $\mathbf{h}_k \in \mathbb{C}^{N \times 1}$ is the channel response of user k and $\mathbf{n}_k \sim \mathcal{CN}(\mathbf{0}, \sigma^2 \mathbf{I}) \in \mathbb{C}^{M \times 1}$ is the additive complex Gaussian noise at user k with each element having zero mean and variance σ^2.

In many related works (e.g., [11,14]), the pilot signals matrix $\mathbf{X}$ is selected to have independent and identically distributed (i.i.d.) Gaussian elements. Nevertheless, as elaborated upon in [12], a partial orthogonal sensing matrix achieves better performance under the Turbo-CS algorithm than an i.i.d. Gaussian sensing matrix which is experimentally confirmed for various other algorithms in [5]. Therefore, the present work utilizes a partial discrete Fourier transform (DFT) random permutation (PDFT-RP) pilot matrix modeled as presented in [5]. Nevertheless, experiments have also been carried out with an i.i.d. Gaussian sensing matrix to verify the performance gain.

Some works consider the channel transformed into the virtual angular domain $\mathbf{h}_k^\omega = \mathbf{F}\mathbf{h}_k$ where $\mathbf{F} \in \mathbb{C}^{N \times N}$ denotes the unitary matrices for the angular domain transformation at the BS [5,11,14]. Resulting from the limited scatterers at the BS, $\mathbf{h}_k^\omega$ usually exhibits individual burst sparsity due to local scattering at the BS and joint sparsity due to common scattering at the BS [11]. Assuming an angular domain transformation, the received signal 1 can be rewritten as

$$\mathbf{y}_k = \mathbf{X}\mathbf{F}^H \mathbf{h}_k^\omega + \mathbf{n}_k = \mathbf{A}\mathbf{h}_k^\omega + \mathbf{n}_k, \tag{2}$$

which is a standard CS model with sensing matrix $\mathbf{A}$ and sparse channel $\mathbf{h}_k^\omega$.

3 Description of the Measurement Data and Methodology

Since the massive MIMO concept started to gain research interest around 2010, a number of testbeds to demonstrate the feasibility of massive MIMO systems have been developed by academia and industry. Some of the first publications describing practical design, realization, and evaluation of such systems are with regard to the Argos prototype by Rice University [17, 18]. A detailed analysis of practically measured massive MIMO channels and their properties is presented in [16]. With the help of the Argos system, the authors have conducted a comprehensive many-antenna multi-user (MU) MIMO channel measurement campaign resulting in over 100 traces made publicly available for further research on [1]. The dataset spans 20 topologies providing over one billion channel measurements and approximately 1 terabyte of data covering measurements across the UHF (470–698 MHz), 2.4 GHz, and 5 GHz bands in diverse environments. At 2.4 GHz and 5 GHz, up to 104 BS antennas are deployed to serve 8 UEs.

Throughout the present work, this measurement dataset was utilized for evaluating various CS-based channel estimation methods. It was selected because it consists of a rich set of practically measured wireless channel responses in multiple environments with various levels of mobility and at three frequency bands. Moreover, this was the only publicly available massive MIMO measurement dataset at the time of writing this paper to the best of the authors' knowledge. Specifically, we use the "Asilomar2016" dataset described in [16].

Out of the dataset, 8 traces with carrier frequency in the 2.4 GHz and 5 GHz bands were selected for experimental analysis. They were conducted in three environments—indoor line of sight (LOS) and non-LOS (NLOS), as well as outdoor with two types of mobility—static and environmental [16]. The reason behind choosing only two types of marginal mobility is that our aim is to compare and evaluate the performance of various channel estimation algorithms and not to study the effects of mobility on channel correlation and aging. Nevertheless, aspects related to mobility can be further exploited for efficient channel estimation techniques, such as the opportunistic method outlined in [8]. From the selected 8 channel traces, only some subcarriers and frames were used in the experiments in order to reduce computation time amounting to a total of around 3840 simulated channel responses.

The authors of ArgosV2 provide a channel measurement and analysis software framework [1] which computes the actual frequency response of the wireless channel. Using this framework, the normalized magnitude of three wireless channels is depicted in Fig. 1—the theoretical 3rd Generation Partnership Project (3GPP) spatial channel model (SCM) [15] and two practically measured channels. The theoretical channel response (a) has a burst sparse nature and could also be jointly burst sparse among users depending on the multipath environment [11]. On the other hand, the practically measured channel responses (b) and (c) have many more significant elements and do not follow any certain sparsity structure, independent on the environment, scatterers located therein and carrier frequency.

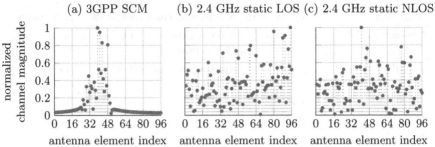

Fig. 1. Comparison of normalized channel magnitude of various channel responses—theoretical (3GPP SCM) and practically measured, for a BS antenna with 96 elements.

4   Simulation Results and Analysis

In this Section, the performance in terms of CSI recovery error of 11 CS-based channel estimation algorithms is evaluated and compared by utilizing practically measured channel responses as described in Sect. 3. Ranging from well-known estimators to algorithms tailored specifically to the massive MIMO channel response structure, the algorithms are listed with their specifics in Table 1. The algorithms were selected based on their applicability to FDD massive MIMO systems and reported low estimation error.

Table 2 presents an overview of the main simulation parameters. The Argos system operates in TDD and it is assumed that the UL and DL channel responses are perfectly reciprocal [2,16]. Hence, the channel response estimated by the Argos system can be used as the channel response to be estimated in the DL in Eqs. 1 and 2. The number of users K and of antenna elements in the BS array N match the Argos testbed measurements. The pilot signals M and SNR values are chosen in accordance with the widely used scenarios in recent works [5,11,14] and larger bounds for M are considered in order to highlight algorithm behavior in the borderline cases. The two selected carrier frequency bands are broadly used in modern wireless communications below 6 GHz. The environments and mobility levels selected for the simulation were outlined in Sect. 3. Although the practically measured channel response by the ArgosV2 testbed is mainly used, the CSI recovery error is compared with the results achieved with the theoretical 3GPP SCM channel model. Some of the experiments also consider the virtual angular domain channel representation $\mathbf{h}^\omega$ to illustrate how it affects estimation performance. Several experiments have also been carried out with an i.i.d. Gaussian pilot signals matrix to compare estimation quality with the PDFT-RP pilot signals matrix.

The normalized MSE (NMSE) of the estimated CSI was selected to serve as the performance metric as it is well-established in the literature for ranking algorithm performance [5,11,14,19,20]. The NMSE is defined as

Table 1. Simulated channel estimation algorithms and methods.

Algorithm	$\mathbf{h}_k$ recovery	Assumptions and comments	References
Classical OMP	*individual*	A naive extension of CS to CSI estimation	[6]
J-OMP	*joint*	Hidden joint sparsity is exploited	[14]
SD-SOMP	*joint*		[10]
CoSaMP	*individual*		[6,13]
DSAMP	*joint*		[7]
L1 LASSO	*individual*		[4,11]
Burst LASSO	*individual*	Burst sparsity in the structure of $\mathbf{h}_k$	[11]
EM-BG-AMP	*individual*	Apriori independent and Bernoulli-Gaussian distributed coefficients	[19]
Turbo-CS	*individual*	i.i.d. prior	[12]
Structured Turbo-CS	*individual*	Markov prior to model the structured sparsity of $\mathbf{h}_k$	[5]
Conventional LS	*individual*	$\hat{\mathbf{h}}_k = \mathbf{y}_k \mathbf{X}^\dagger$, $\mathbf{X}^\dagger$ – Moore-Penrose pseudoinverse	[14]

$$\mathrm{NMSE} = \frac{1}{K} \sum_{k=1}^{K} \frac{\|\mathbf{h}_k - \hat{\mathbf{h}}_k\|^2}{\|\mathbf{h}_k\|^2}, \tag{3}$$

where $\hat{\mathbf{h}}_k \in \mathbb{C}^{N \times 1}$ is the estimated channel response vector. For clear representation and better readability of the results, the NMSE in decibels defined as $\mathrm{NMSE(dB)} = 10 \log_{10} \mathrm{NMSE}$ is depicted. It is of high interest to draw the dependence of NMSE on M because the main goal of evaluated algorithms is to minimize M while maintaining a feasible error. On the other hand, noise can have detrimental effect on estimation errors, hence dependence of NMSE on SNR is also studied.

4.1 Average NMSE as a Function of SNR

Figure 2 compares the NMSE of the estimated CSI in decibels depending on the SNR of the received signal $\mathbf{y}_k$. The NMSE results have been averaged over all environments, frames, subcarriers and carrier frequency bands described in Sect. 3. An exception is made for the L1 and burst LASSO algorithms due to the high computational complexity of the burst LASSO, therefore simulations for only a single subcarrier and frame were carried out for these two algorithms.

The performance of analysed algorithms using the 3GPP SCM [15] is plotted with dotted lines to serve as a reference. Based on the difference between NMSE

Table 2. Simulation parameters.

Parameter	Notation	Modeling	Value	Dimension
Number of UEs	K	[16]	8	—
Number of BS antennas	N	[16]	96	—
Number of pilot signals	M	—	15–90	—
Carrier frequency bands	f	—	2.4; 5	GHz
SNR	SNR	—	0–40	dB
Channel response	**h**	[15,16]	3GPP SCM; ArgosV2 measured	—
Pilot matrix	**X**	[5,11,12]	PDFT-RP; i.i.d. CG	—
Noise	**n**	[5,11]	Additive complex Gaussian	—
Environment	—	[16]	Indoor (LOS, NLOS); outdoor	—
Mobility	—	[16]	Static; environmental	—

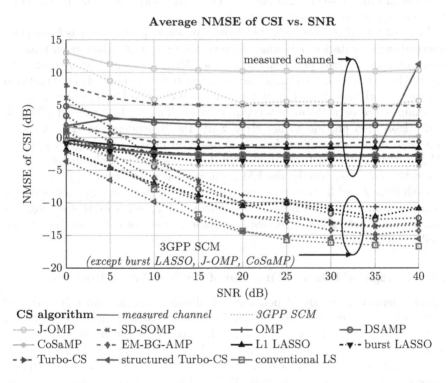

Fig. 2. Average NMSE of CSI in decibels versus SNR of analyzed algorithms for $M = 45$ pilot signals. Results achieved with the 3GPP SCM [15] are depicted as a reference.

for practically measured channel responses and for channels generated with the 3GPP SCM, it can be concluded that all algorithms perform better when using the burst sparse channel response provided by the 3GPP SCM. With this model, all CS-based methods apart from the J-OMP provide a negative NMSE of down to −16 dB at SNR > 10 dB . Lowest NMSE is achieved with the structured Turbo-CS algorithm for SNR < 20 dB, while conventional LS provides lowest NMSE for higher SNR. EM-BG-AMP, SD-SOMP and Turbo-CS also perform moderately well at high SNR. Notably, highest error under this channel model is achieved by the CoSaMP, burst LASSO and J-OMP algorithms. The J-OMP algorithm exploits the hidden joint sparsity among user channel vectors in order to recover CSI with a smaller error [14]. As demonstrated in Fig. 1, such joint sparsity is not present in the measured channel responses. This could explain the low performance of J-OMP which would perhaps be further improved by fine-tuning algorithm parameters. This assumption is valid for all algorithms—the achieved results depend on the particular settings of algorithm-specific parameters. It is important to note that the structured Turbo-CS algorithm does not perform well at the highest simulated SNR = 40 dB setting. Such errors can be observed in other results described further in the work and could be based on slow convergence or ill-conditioning.

Figure 3(left) illustrates only the algorithms whose performance is feasible for practical implementation, i.e., which achieve NMSE < 0 dB. The conventional LS algorithm achieves best performance with a NMSE of down to around −2.8 dB followed by the burst LASSO and Turbo-CS (both in its canonical and structured variants) algorithms. However, at low SNR ≈ 0 dB, the LS algorithm recovers the channel vector with an unacceptable error. The L1 LASSO and EM-BG-AMP algorithms provide higher error while the dependence of EM-BG-AMP on SNR is inconsistent. The algorithms based on message passing, such as the EM-BG-AMP and structured Turbo-CS, learn the required channel statistical parameters automatically by the EM framework as pointed out in [5].

Both Figs. 2 and 3 show that the achieved error does not drop significantly when increasing the SNR after 20 dB. This is the reason why this setting was chosen for estimating the dependence of algorithm performance on the number of pilot signals M.

4.2   Average NMSE as a Function of the Number of Pilot Signals M

Figure 4 demonstrates the dependence of algorithm performance in terms of NMSE of CSI in decibels on the number of pilot signals M. The averaging explained in Subsect. 4.1 was applied. Achieved NMSE when using the 3GPP SCM [15] is plotted with dotted lines with NMSE down to almost −20 dB for $M = 90$ and the LS algorithm with all other algorithms achieving similar performance except the CoSaMP, J-OMP and burst LASSO. However, J-OMP performs well after $M = 70$ pilot signals. All simulated methods confirm the negative exponential dependence of NMSE on the number of pilot signals which leads to lower error as M grows. As pointed out in the previous discussions, the structured Turbo-CS algorithm does not perform well at $M = 50$ and $M > 65$ settings while the conventional LS algorithm leads to high error at the highest simulated $M = 90$ setting.

Figure 3 (right) illustrates only feasible algorithms with NMSE < 0 dB. The conventional LS algorithm performs best at $M \leq 85$ followed by the burst

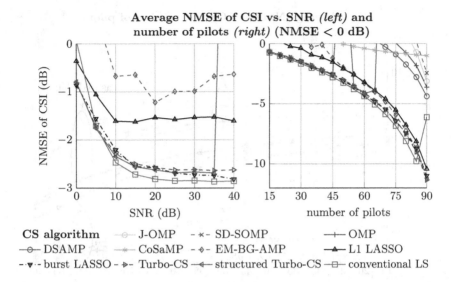

Fig. 3. Average NMSE of CSI in decibels versus SNR (left, $M = 45$ pilot signals) and number of pilot signals M (right, SNR $= 20$ dB). Only algorithms achieving NMSE < 0 dB are shown.

LASSO and Turbo-CS algorithms. The L1 LASSO and EM-BG-AMP algorithms also provide acceptable results for $M \geq 50$. It is noteworthy to mention that in order to reduce the pilot and feedback overhead, values of $M > 65$ do not make much sense in a practical FDD massive MIMO scenario due to the increased overhead.

4.3 Effect of Pilot Matrix Choice and Channel Representation on CSI Estimation Errors

As discussed in Sect. 2, a pilot matrix $\mathbf{X}$ comprised of PDFT-RP elements was reported to perform better than an i.i.d. Gaussian pilot matrix under various CS-based algorithms [5,12]. This was experimentally confirmed in our simulations and the results for indoor LOS environment at 2.4 GHz are presented in Fig. 5(top). Notably, the Turbo-CS algorithm, both in its canonical and structured version, performs much better with a PDFT-RP pilot matrix as the NMSE of both Turbo-CS algorithms with an i.i.d. Gaussian pilot matrix is around 40 dB. The performance difference for other algorithms is not so strongly expressed, however the EM-BG-AMP performs much better with an i.i.d. Gaussian pilot matrix which might be due to the i.i.d BG assumption on the signal model. This is in line with the described results in [5].

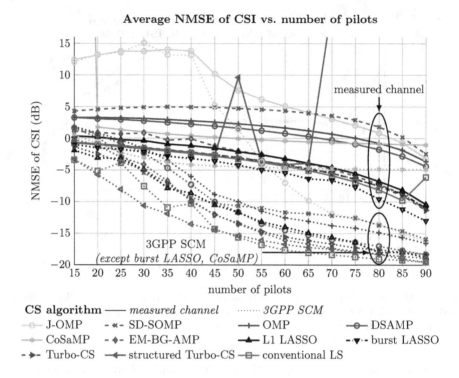

Fig. 4. Average NMSE of CSI in decibels versus number of pilot signals M of analyzed algorithms for SNR = 20 dB. Results achieved with the theoretical 3GPP SCM [15] are depicted as a reference.

All simulations described in the previous subsections suggest CSI estimation according to Eq. 1. However, considering Eq. 2, i.e. the transformed channel response into the virtual angular domain $\mathbf{h}_k^\omega$, might introduce additional sparsity in the channel vector as elaborated upon in Sect. 2. The usual definition of such transformation is $\mathbf{h}_k^\omega = \mathbf{F}\mathbf{h}_k$ where $\mathbf{F} \in \mathbb{C}^{N \times N}$ is a DFT matrix [5,11]. Simulation experiments with such transformation were carried out for indoor NLOS and static outdoor environments at 2.4 GHz and the results are depicted in Fig. 5 (bottom). For most algorithms except the J-OMP, the channel in angular domain leads to higher CSI recovery error, however the differences are minor.

Average NMSE of CSI vs. SNR *(left)* **and number of pilots** *(right)* **depending on pilot matrix choice** *(top)* **and channel representation** *(bottom)* **at 2.4 GHz and NMSE < 0 dB**

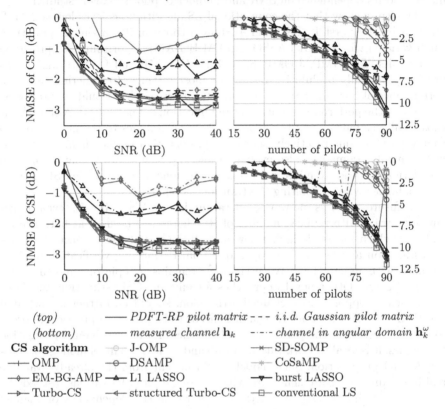

(top)	—— *PDFT-RP pilot matrix*	- - - *i.i.d. Gaussian pilot matrix*
(bottom)	—— *measured channel* $\mathbf{h}_k$	-·--· *channel in angular domain* $\mathbf{h}_k^\omega$

CS algorithm   ─⊖─ J-OMP   ─✳─ SD-SOMP
─┼─ OMP   ─⊖─ DSAMP   ─✳─ CoSaMP
─◇─ EM-BG-AMP   ─▲─ L1 LASSO   ─▼─ burst LASSO
─▶─ Turbo-CS   ─◀─ structured Turbo-CS   ─□─ conventional LS

Fig. 5. NMSE of CSI in decibels versus SNR (left, $M = 45$) and number of pilot signals M (right, SNR $= 20$ dB) of analyzed algorithms depending on pilot matrix (top, averaged for indoor LOS) and channel representation (bottom, averaged for indoor NLOS and static outdoor environments) at 2.4 GHz.

5   Conclusions and Future Work

In this work, we evaluate the performance of 11 CS-based channel estimation algorithms utilizing real-world channel responses in the context of FDD massive MIMO systems. Most of the analysed algorithms assume some sort of sparse structure in the channel response vector and rely on it to reduce the number of required pilot signals and minimize estimation error. We show that the examined practically measured channels do not follow such structure. For the simulation experiments, channel measurements for carrier frequency in the 2.4 GHz and 5 GHz bands for three environments with two levels of mobility were selected from the publicly available measurement dataset recorded by the ArgosV2 system. Performance with the theoretical 3GPP SCM is used as a baseline and it clearly shows a reduction in estimation error due to the burst-sparse channel response structure. NMSE of the estimated CSI is the chosen performance metric and its dependence on SNR and number of pilot signals is studied.

The results show that the conventional LS algorithm achieves lowest NMSE followed by the burst LASSO and Turbo-CS (both in its canonical and structured variant) with the L1 LASSO and EM-BG-AMP algorithms also providing good results. The OMP, J-OMP, SD-SOMP, CoSaMP and DSAMP algorithms provide practically prohibitive results for most settings. Considering the good performance of burst LASSO, as part of a future research it would be interesting to evaluate the performance of its joint modification defined in [11]. Although the chosen pilot signals matrix is a PDFT-RP, its advantages to the i.i.d. Gaussian counterpart are quantitatively shown. Representation of the channel response in the angular domain is also evaluated and the results prove that using such transformation leads to minor performance differences, however the CSI recovery error is higher when exploiting the transformed channel.

For future wireless networks operating in mmWave bands, even larger antenna arrays with reduced number of RF chains will be used at both the BS and UEs which makes designing new and efficient methods for accurate channel estimation and feedback an open question. Performing verification of these methods with practical mmWave channels remains a topic of importance for future research. Other novel approaches for efficient CSI estimation and feedback, such as opportunistic channel estimation, should be further investigated and their feasibility for realistic channels needs to be proven in practice. In order to precisely estimate the performance of existing and future channel estimation techniques, it is vital to work with accurate and realistic channel models for massive MIMO propagation. Such models could benefit from the already available real-life channel measurement data which were gathered by various testbeds. It would be also interesting to practically determine the dependence of channel estimation quality on the number of BS and UE antennas, and particularly the effects of reducing the number of BS antennas. For this purpose, the dataset utilized in this work could be further examined.

Acknowledgement. This paper is published with the support of project No BG05M2OP001-2.009-0033 "Promotion of Contemporary Research Through Creation of Scientific and Innovative Environment to Encourage Young Researchers in Technical University - Sofia and The National Railway Infrastructure Company in The Field of Engineering Science and Technology Development" within the Intelligent Growth Science and Education Operational Programme co-funded by the European Structural and Investment Funds of the European Union.

References

1. Argos—Practical Many-Antenna MU-MIMO. http://projectargos.org/. Accessed 20 Mar 2019
2. Björnson, E., Hoydis, J., Sanguinetti, L.: Massive MIMO networks: spectral, energy, and hardware efficiency. Found. Trends® Signal Process. **11**(3–4), 154–655 (2017). https://doi.org/10.1561/2000000093

3. Busari, S.A., Huq, K.M.S., Mumtaz, S., Dai, L., Rodriguez, J.: Millimeter-wave massive MIMO communication for future wireless systems: a survey. IEEE Commun. Surv. Tutor. **20**(2), 836–869 (2018). https://doi.org/10.1109/COMST.2017. 2787460

4. Candes, E.J., Wakin, M.B.: An introduction to compressive sampling. IEEE Signal Process. Mag. **25**(2), 21–30 (2008). https://doi.org/10.1109/MSP.2007.914731

5. Chen, L., Liu, A., Yuan, X.: Structured turbo compressed sensing for massive MIMO channel estimation using a Markov prior. IEEE Trans. Veh. Technol. **67**(5), 4635–4639 (2018). https://doi.org/10.1109/TVT.2017.2787708

6. Duarte, M.F., Eldar, Y.C.: Structured compressed sensing: from theory to applications. IEEE Trans. Signal Process. **59**(9), 4053–4085 (2011). https://doi.org/10. 1109/TSP.2011.2161982

7. Gao, Z., Dai, L., Wang, Z., Chen, S.: Spatially common sparsity based adaptive channel estimation and feedback for FDD massive MIMO. IEEE Trans. Signal Process. **63**(23), 6169–6183 (2015). https://doi.org/10.1109/TSP.2015.2463260

8. Guerra, R.E., Anand, N., Shepard, C., Knightly, E.W.: Opportunistic Channel Estimation for Implicit 802.11af MU-MIMO. pp. 60–68. IEEE (2016). https://doi. org/10.1109/ITC-28.2016.117

9. Larsson, E.G., Edfors, O., Tufvesson, F., Marzetta, T.L.: Massive MIMO for next generation wireless systems. IEEE Commun. Mag. **52**(2), 186–195 (2014). https:// doi.org/10.1109/MCOM.2014.6736761

10. Liang, J., Liu, Y., Zhang, W., Xu, Y., Gan, X., Wang, X.: Joint compressive sensing in wideband cognitive networks. In: 2010 IEEE Wireless Communication and Networking Conference, pp. 1–5, April 2010. https://doi.org/10.1109/WCNC. 2010.5506392

11. Liu, A., Lau, V., Dai, W.: Joint burst LASSO for sparse channel estimation in multi-user massive MIMO. In: 2016 IEEE International Conference on Communications (ICC), pp. 1–6, May 2016. https://doi.org/10.1109/ICC.2016.7511075

12. Ma, J., Yuan, X., Ping, L.: Turbo compressed sensing with partial DFT sensing matrix. IEEE Signal Process. Lett. **22**(2), 158–161 (2015). https://doi.org/10. 1109/LSP.2014.2351822

13. Needell, D., Tropp, J.A.: CoSaMP: iterative signal recovery from incomplete and inaccurate samples. Appl. Comput. Harmon. Anal. **26**(3), 301–321 (2009). https:// doi.org/10.1016/j.acha.2008.07.002

14. Rao, X., Lau, V.K.N.: Distributed compressive CSIT estimation and feedback for FDD multi-user massive MIMO systems. IEEE Trans. Signal Process. **62**(12), 3261–3271 (2014). https://doi.org/10.1109/TSP.2014.2324991

15. Salo, J., et al.: MATLAB implementation of the 3GPP Spatial Channel Model (3GPP TR 25.996), January 2005. http://www.tkk.fi/Units/Radio/scm/

16. Shepard, C., Ding, J., Guerra, R.E., Zhong, L.: Understanding real many-antenna MU-MIMO channels, pp. 461–467. IEEE, November 2016. https://doi.org/10. 1109/ACSSC.2016.7869082

17. Shepard, C., et al.: Argos: Practical Many-antenna Base Stations. p. 53. ACM Press (2012). https://doi.org/10.1145/2348543.2348553

18. Shepard, C., Yu, H., Zhong, L.: ArgosV2: A Flexible Many-antenna Research Platform. p. 163. ACM Press (2013). https://doi.org/10.1145/2500423.2505302

19. Vila, J., Schniter, P.: Expectation-maximization Bernoulli-Gaussian approximate message passing. In: 2011 Conference Record of the Forty Fifth Asilomar Conference on Signals, Systems and Computers (ASILOMAR), pp. 799–803, November 2011. https://doi.org/10.1109/ACSSC.2011.6190117

20. Yin, H., Gesbert, D., Filippou, M., Liu, Y.: A coordinated approach to channel estimation in large-scale multiple-antenna systems. IEEE J. Sel. Areas Commun. **31**(2), 264–273 (2013). https://doi.org/10.1109/JSAC.2013.130214

A Queue in Overall Telecommunication System with Quality of Service Guarantees

Velin Andonov[1(✉)], Stoyan Poryazov[1], Anna Otsetova[2], and Emiliya Saranova[1]

[1] Institute of Mathematics and Informatics, Bulgarian Academy of Sciences,
Acad. G. Bonchev Str., Block 8, 1113 Sofia, Bulgaria
{velin_andonov,stoyan}@math.bas.bg, emiliya@cc.bas.bg
[2] University of Telecommunications and Post, 1 Acad. S. Mladenov Str.,
1700 Sofia, Bulgaria
aotsetova@abv.bg

Abstract. For the first time a queue, related to the shortage of network resources, is included in a model of overall telecommunication system with finite number of users and facilities which makes the model closer to the real system. The service in the queue depends on feedbacks of call attempts and of the state and duration of services in the overall system. The server of the queuing system has more than one exits. The results presented are a base for future development of tools for management, design, dimensioning and redimensioning of the system.

Keywords: Overall telecommunication system · Conceptual model · Queuing system with feedbacks · Quality of Service

1 Introduction

The classical conceptual model of overall telecommunication system is described in [4] and developed in more details in [5]. We briefly mention the most important features of the model and some basic notation.

The classical conceptual model considers user's behaviour, finite number of homogenous users and terminals, losses due to abandoned and interrupted dialing, blocked and interrupted switching, unavailable intent terminal, blocked and abandoned ringing and abandoned communication. The traffic of the calling (denoted by A) and the called (denoted by B) terminals and user's traffic are considered separately but in their interrelation. Two types of virtual devices are included in the model: base and comprising base devices.

At the bottom of the structural model presentation, we consider basic virtual devices that do not contain any other virtual devices. A basic virtual device has a general graphical representation as shown in Fig. 1.

The parameters of the basic virtual device x are the following (see [2] for terms definition):

V. Poulkov (Ed.): FABULOUS 2019, LNICST 283, pp. 243–262, 2019.
https://doi.org/10.1007/978-3-030-23976-3_22

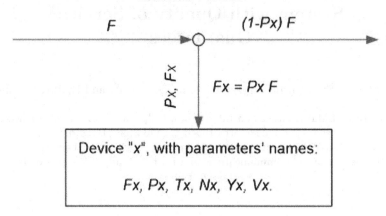

Fig. 1. A graphical representation of a basic virtual device x.

- Fx - intensity or incoming rate (frequency) of the flow of requests (i.e. the number of requests per time unit) to device x;
- Px - probability of directing the requests towards device x;
- Tx - service time (duration of servicing of a request) in device x;
- Yx - traffic intensity [Erlang];
- Vx - traffic volume [Erlang - time unit];
- Nx - number of lines (service resources, positions, capacity) of device x.

The graphic representations of the base virtual devices together with their names and types are shown in Fig. 2 (see [4]). The type of each of the basic virtual devices is also shown in Fig. 2. Each basic virtual device belongs to one of the following types: Generator, Terminator, Modifier, Server, Enter Switch, Switch and Graphic connector. With the exception of the Switch, which has one or two entrances and one or two exits, every other virtual device has one entrance and/or one exit.

The names of the virtual devices are concatenations of the first letters of the branch exit, branch and stage in that order (see Fig. 2). For example **ad** stands for the virtual device "abandoned dialling" while **rad** – for "repeated abandoned dialling".

For the better understanding of the model and for a more convenient description of the intensity of the flow, a special notation including qualifiers (see [2]) is used. For example $dem.F$ for demand flow; $inc.Y$ stands for incoming traffic; $ofr.Y$ for offered traffic; $rep.Y$ for repeated traffic.

The following comprising virtual devices denoted by **a, b, s** (see Fig. 2) and **ab** (not shown in Fig. 2) are considered in the model.

- **a** comprises all calling terminals (A-terminals) in the system. It is shown with continuous line box in Fig. 2;

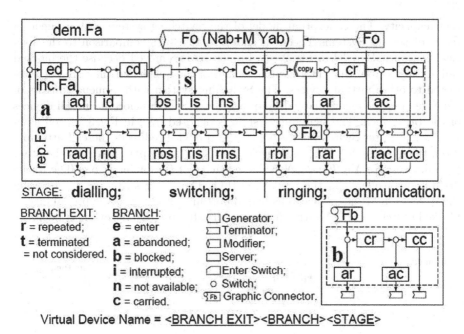

Fig. 2. Classical conceptual model of an overall telecommunication system (see [4]).

- **b** comprises all called terminals (B-terminals) in the system. It is shown in box with dashed line in the down right corner in Fig. 2;
- **ab** comprises all the terminals (calling and called) in the system. It is not shown in Fig. 2;
- **s** virtual device corresponding to the switching system. It is shown with dashed line box into the a-device in Fig. 2.

2 Representation of the Queuing System Within the Switching Stage of an Overall Telecommunication System

In this section, we propose a representation of a Queuing system in the Switching system of an overall telecommunication system. In the classical conceptual model (see [4]), once the Switching system reaches its capacity, the incoming call attempts are blocked and they are redirected to the "blocked switch" branch which begins at the virtual device denoted by bs on Fig. 2.

With the inclusion of queue in the Switching stage of the model when the Switching system has reached its capacity the incoming call attempts wait in a buffer until a service line in the Switching system becomes available. We consider the buffer size of the queuing system to be of finite length and the number of servers (service lines) also to be finite. In such queuing system, the call attempts will be blocked only when both the Switching system and the buffer have reached their capacity. The conceptual model of the Switching system with a queue in terms of Service Systems Theory is shown in Fig. 3. In comparison to the classical conceptual model in Fig. 2, the branch **bs** is removed because the blocked call attempts from the Enter Switch remain in the queue and they are not redirected to other virtual devices. The Switching system with a queue consists of a device of type Queue denoted by **q**, the Enter Switch before it and all devices of the **bq** branch. The switching system is denoted by **s** in Fig. 3 as well as in Fig. 2. The Enter Switch device before the **q** device redirects the call attempts when the queue is full. The base device **q** has the same parameters as the other base devices: Fq, Yq, Tq, Pq, Nq. The capacity of the buffer is Nq. The queue discipline considered in the model is FIFO. The Enter switch device between the **q** device and the **s** device has one important parameter – the probability of blocked switching (Pbs) with which the call attempts remain in the **q** device.

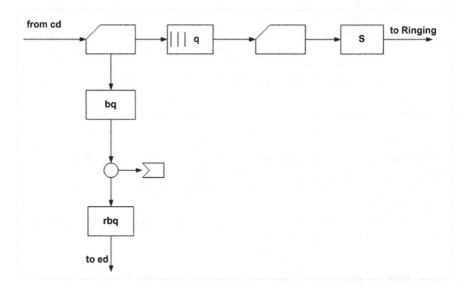

Fig. 3. Conceptual model of a part of the Switching stage of an overall telecommunication system with a queue. **cd** stands for "carried dialing", **q** for the Queue device, **s** for "Switching system", **bq** for "blocked queuing", **rbq** for "repeated blocked queuing", **ed** for "enter dialing".

In [6] four conceptual models of a queuing system are compared. One of the models (see Fig. 4) illustrates the important concept of "zero queuing". The internal structure of the queue is presented, including two virtual devices: "carried queue" (cq) and "zero queuing" (zq). Requests pass the Queue without delay, with probability $Pzq = 1 - Pbs$, in case there are free places available in the Server, in the moment of their arrival. The duration of the zero queuing (Tzq) may be zero, or close to it. The total queuing time (Tq) is given by

$$Tq = Pbs(1 - Pbq)Tcq + (1 - Pbs)Tzq. \tag{1}$$

This approach is a detailization of the classical approach (Fig. 3). It represents explicitly the important concept of zero queuing and the probability of blocked server (*Pbs*). It is more complex, but allows more clear and full presentation of the processes in the queuing system.

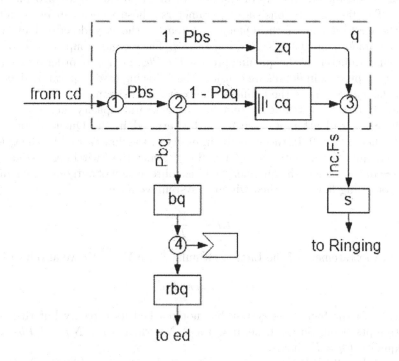

Fig. 4. More detailed representation of a queuing system.

The parameters of the queuing system in the case of service of the call attempts without waiting can be obtained using Eqs. (42) and (43) from Sect. 4.

In order to compactly describe single queuing stations in an unambiguous way, the so called Kendall notation is often used (see [1]). A queuing system is described by 6 identifiers separated by vertical bars in the following way:

$$Arrivals \,|\, Services \,|\, Servers \,|\, Buffersize \,|\, Population \,|\, Scheduling$$

where "Arrivals" characterises the arrival process (arrival distribution), "Service" characterizes the service process (service distribution), "Servers" – the number of servers, "Buffersize" – the total capacity, which includes the customers possibly in the server (infinite if not specified), "Population" – the size of the customer population (infinite if not specified), and finally, "Scheduling" – the employed service discipline.

In our model, the queuing system in the Switching stage of the telecommunication network in Kendall notation is represented as $M|M|Ns|Ns + Nq|Nab|$

$FIFO$, where M stands for exponential distribution, Ns is the capacity of the Switching system (number of equivalent internal switching lines) and Nab is the total number of active terminals which can be calling and called. This is related to the derivation of the analytical model of the system.

The important parameters of the devices in Fig. 3 can be divided into two groups. The first group consists of parameters whose values can be obtained from the environment of the Queuing system in the way described in [4,5]. These parameters are $Ts, Ns, Pbs, Ys, ofr.Fq$. The second group consists of the unknown parameters of the queuing process Fq, Pbq, Tq, Yq. In order to describe the queuing process in details we consider the following cases separately depending on the value of Ys – the traffic of the Switching system.

Case 1. If the Switching system has reached its capacity, i.e. $Ys = Ns$, and there are call attempts waiting to be serviced in the Queue device, i.e. $Yq > 0$, then $Pbs > 0$. In this case the intensity of the flow carried by the Queue device is equal to the intensity of the flow leaving the Switching system, i.e. $crr.Fq = out.Fs$ where the qualifier "out" is abbreviation of outgoing. Generally, for the outgoing flow from the Switching system we have

$$out.Fs = \frac{Ys}{Ts} \tag{2}$$

which is a restatement of the Little's formula. Since $Ys = Ns$ we also have

$$out.Fs = crr.Fq. \tag{3}$$

Case 2. If the Switching system has not reached its capacity but there are call attempts being serviced, i.e. $0 < Ys < Ns$, then $Yq < Nq$ and $Pbs < 1$. The equality $Fq = Fs$ holds.

Case 3. Finally, if there are no call attempts being serviced by the Switching system, i.e. $Ys = 0$, then $Fq = Fs = 0$ and $Yq = 0$.

3   Conceptual Model of Overall Telecommunication System with Queue in the Switching Stage

By combining the representation of the queue in terms of Service System Theory shown in the previous section and the classical model from [4] we obtain conceptual model of the overall telecommunication system with queue in the Switching stage. Its graphical representation is shown in Fig. 5.

In the conceptual model in Fig. 5 there are at least 37 important virtual devices. Of them 33 are basic virtual devices and 4 (**a, b, s, ab**) are comprising. They are of interest because the values of their parameters characterize the state of the overall telecommunication system. Every device has five parameters: P, F, T, Y and N. Therefore the total number of parameters is 185.

The meaning of two of the parameters – Fo and M' – should be explained separately. Fo is the intent intensity of calls of one idle terminal. M' is a constant, characterizing the Bernoulli-Poisson-Pascal (BPP) flow of demand calls

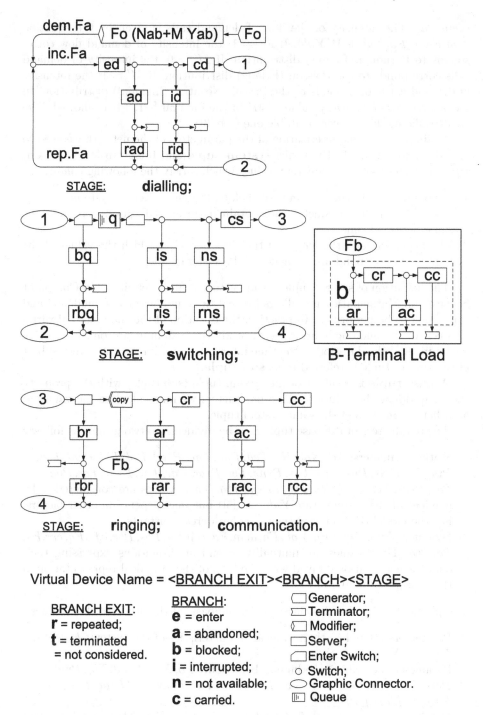

Fig. 5. Conceptual model of an overall telecommunication system with a queue in the Switching stage.

($dem.Fa$). The intensity of the flow of demand calls is given by the equation $dem.Fa = Fo(Nab + M'Yab)$. If $M' = 1$, the intensity of demand flow corresponds to Bernoulli (Engset) distribution. If $M' = 0$, the intensity of demand calls corresponds to the Poisson (Erlang) distribution. If $M' = 1$, the intensity of demand calls corresponds to the Pascal (Negative Binomial) distribution. In our analytical model every value of M' in the interval $[-1, +1]$ is allowed. The BPP-traffic model is a very suitable one (see [3]).

To simplify the characterization of the parameters of the network we need to introduce, following [4], the terms **system tuple** and **base tuple**. A **system tuple** is a finite set of parameters' values which satisfy the following conditions:

1. All parameters in the system tuple belong to one particular system;
2. All values of the parameters are obtained (measured) during one and the same period of time;
3. The beginning and the length of the time period to which the values of the paramers correspond are elements of the system tuple.

The definition of system tuple is similar to the tuple definitions in Computer Science and Mathematics and allows for real time measurements, modeling and simulation to be performed. In practice, the duration of the time interval varies between 15 min and one hour. Since we study the system in stationary state the beginning and the duration of the time interval are not important. Every subset of the system tuple is referred to as **sub-tuple**.

A **base tuple** is a subset of the system tuple (sub-tuple) with the property that if we know the values of these parameters we may calculate the values of all other parameters of the same system tuple.

The parameters of the base tuple may be divided into two groups as follows:

– Static parameters: $M', Nab, Ns, Ted, Pad, Tad, Prad, Pid, Tid, Prid, Ted,$ $Pis, Tis, Pris, Pns, Tns, Tes, Prns, Tbr, Prbr, Par, Tar, Prar, Tcr, Pac,$ $Tac, Prac, Tcc, Prcc, Nq, Tbq, Trbq, Prbq$. Their values are considered independent of the system state Yab (see [5]) but may depend on other factors. For the model time interval they are considered constants.
– Dynamic parameters: $Fo, Yab, Fa, dem.Fa, rep.Fa, Pbs, Pbr, ofr.Fq, crr.Fs,$ Tq, Pbq. Their values are mutually dependent. Equations expressing their dependencies can be derived with the help of the graphical representation of the conceptual model in Fig. 5.

The parameters can be also classified on the basis of the origin of their values.

– Parameters related to the technical characteristics of the system: $Pid, Pis,$ Tcs, Ns, Nq;
– Parameters describing the human behaviour: $Fo, Nab, Prad, Tid, Prid,$ $Pris, Tis, Pns, Tns, Prns, Tbr, Prbr, Par, Tar, Prar, Tcr, Prac, Tcc,$ $Prcc, Tbq, Trbq, Prbq$;
– Mix factors' parameters: $Ted, Pad, Tad, Tcd, Pac, Tac$. They are dependent on the first two groups;

- Parameters whose value is determined by the modellers: M'. It characterizes a Bernoulli-Poisson-Pascal (BPP) flow;
- Parameters derived from the previous groups: $Yab, Fa, dem.Fa, rep.Fa,$ $Pbs, Pbr, ofr.Fq, crr.Fs, Tq, Pbq.$

The parameters characterizing the Quality of Service (QoS) are Pbr, Pbs, Tq.

This classification of the parameters allows for different types of teletrafic tasks to be formulated and solved. These tasks are divided into two groups: Stationary teletraffic tasks and Dynamic teletraffic tasks. There are three main Stationary teletraffic tasks.

- **QoS prediction task** is the task of finding values of the parameters determining the QoS (Pbs, Pbr, Pbq) if the parameters related to the technical characteristics and the human behavior are known. This allows for the values of the indicators for QoS to be obtained (see [7]);
- **Technical characteristics task** is the task of finding the values of those parameters related to the technical characteristics (the first group) which guarantee a given QoS if the values of the parameters describing the human behavior and the desired QoS are known. The rest of the base parameters in the same base tuple are known. The important Network Dimensioning and Redimensioning tasks belong to this type.
- **Human behavior task** is the task of finding the values of a set of parameters characterizing the behavior of the users who would generate call attempts serviced with the desired QoS if the parameters related to the technical characteristics and the QoS are given. The users' behavior can be influenced through changes in the tariff policies and the technical limitations. For instance, the allowed duration of listening to busy and dialing tone.

In the Dynamic teletraffic tasks the system's dynamic is represented as a series of tuples. There are long and short term dynamics. In the long term dynamics, all parameters of the system may have variable values while in short analysis, some of the parameters are assumed to have constant values. In the present paper systems in stationary state for a short time interval are considered.

4   Main Assupmtions and Derivation of Some Analytical Expressions for Parameters of the Queuing System

We consider the conceptual model of overall telecommunication system with queue shown in Fig. 5 and described in the previous section. Parameters with known values are all probabilites for directing the call to a device (the P–parameters), the holding time parameters of the base virtual devices (T – parameters) and the values of the intensity of the incoming calls flow – F_a. The unknown parameters are the parameters of the comprising virtual devices except Fa and Nab. We want to express analytically the unknown parameters' values of the Queue: Tq, Pbq, Yq.

4.1 Main Assumptions

To obtain simple analytical models of the system in the process of solving different teletraffic tasks, as in [4], we need to state the following assumptions.

1. The telecommunication system considered is represented graphically and functionally in Fig. 5 and it is closed.
2. All base virtual devices except the Queue device have unlimited capacity. The Queue has capacity Nq which is the buffer size. The comprising virtual devices have limited capacity: the **ab** device contains all active terminals $Nab \in [2, \infty)$. The switching system (**s**) has capacity Ns. One internal switching line can carry only one call for both incoming and outgoing calls.
3. Every call from the incoming flow to the system ($inc.Fa$) occupies only a free terminal which becomes a busy A-terminal.
4. The system is in a stationary state and the Little's theorem can be applied for every device.
5. Every call occupies one place in a base virtual device independently from the other devices.
6. Any calls in the telecommunication network's environment (outside the **a** and **b** devices) do not occupy any of the telecommunication system's devices.
7. The probabilities of directing the calls to the base virtual devices and the holding time in the devices are independent from each other and from the intensity of the incoming flow $inc.Fa$. Their values are determined by the users' behavior and the technical characteristics of the telecommunication system. Exception to this assumption are the devices of type Enter Switch corresponding to Pbq and Pbs, and Pbr (see Fig. 5).
8. For the base virtual devices **ar, cr, ac** and **cc** the probabilities of directing the calls to them and the duration of occupation of the device are the same for the A and B calls.
9. The variables in the model are random with fixed distributions. The Little's theorem allows us to use their mean values.
10. Every call occupies simultaneously all base virtual devices through which it has passed, including the device where it is at the current moment of observation. When a call leaves the comprising devices **a** or **b** the occupied places by it in all base virtual devices are released.

4.2 Expressing Analytically the Parameters of the Queue

In most publications on Queuing Theory and its applications in Telecommunication Systems the queuing systems studied have either one service line (server) or infinite servers and the buffer size of the queue is also infinite. In the few sources where queuing systems of type M|M|n|m|FIFO are studied such as [8,9], analytical expressions for their parameters such as mean duration of service, queue length, probability of blocking due to full buffer, probability of waiting in the queue etc, are only partially found. Here we start, following [8], with the simplest queuing systems to determine the queue parameters. Then, using the same approach, we determine the parameters of the queuing system M|M|Ns|Ns + Nq|FIFO, where as usual, M stands for exponential distribution, Ns is the number of switching lines in Switching system (finite), Nq is the length of the buffer (also finite) and FIFO stands for First In First Out discipline of service.

Finding the Parameters of the Queuing System M|M|1|FIFO. The density functions of the arrival and service times are respectively

$$a(t) = \lambda e^{-\lambda t}, \tag{4}$$

$$b(t) = \mu e^{-\mu t}, \tag{5}$$

where $1/\lambda$ is the mean value of time between two arrivals (interrarival time) and $1/\mu$ is the mean time of service. For our model $\lambda = ofr.Fq$ and $\mu = (crr.Fs + Fis + Fns + Fbr + Far + Fac)/Ys = crr.Fs + Fis + Fns + Fbr + Far + Fac$ because in this case there is only one service line in the Switching system. They are assumed to be statistically independent which results in a birth-death process. Let us denote with p_n the probability that the queuing system is in state n that is

$$p_n = Pr\{\text{there are n call attempts in the queuing system}\}.$$

There are different ways to solve the birth-death equations. The solution is well-known and can be found for example in [8]:

$$p_n = p_0(\lambda/\mu)^n, \ (n \geq 1) \tag{6}$$

$$p_0 = \frac{1}{\sum\limits_{n=0}^{\infty} (\frac{\lambda}{\mu})^n}. \tag{7}$$

Since the fraction λ/μ is found often below, in order to simplify the expressions we introduce the notation $\rho = \lambda/\mu$. Then the expression for p_0 for $\rho < 1$ becomes

$$p_0 = \frac{1}{\sum\limits_{n=0}^{\infty} \rho^n} = 1 - \rho. \tag{8}$$

Let X_{s+q} be the random variable "number of call attempts in the queuing system" and Y_{s+q} be its expected value. Then we obtain

$$Y_{s+q} = E[X_{s+q}] = \sum_{n=0}^{\infty} n p_n = (1-\rho) \sum_{n=0}^{\infty} n\rho^n. \tag{9}$$

The last sum can be written as

$$\sum_{n=0}^{\infty} n\rho^n = \rho + 2\rho^2 + 3\rho^3 + \ldots = \rho \sum_{n=1}^{\infty} n\rho^{n-1} = \rho \frac{d[1/(1-\rho)]}{d\rho} = \frac{\rho}{(1-\rho)^2}. \tag{10}$$

Therefore

$$Y_{s+q} = \frac{(1-\rho)\rho}{(1-\rho)^2} = \frac{\lambda}{\mu - \lambda}. \tag{11}$$

Let Yq be the expected number of call attempts in the buffer. Then

$$Yq = \sum_{n=1}^{\infty}(n-1)p_n = \sum_{n=1}^{\infty}np_n - \sum_{n=1}^{\infty}p_n = Y_{s+q} - (1-p_0) = \frac{\rho}{1-\rho} - \rho$$

$$= \frac{\rho^2}{1-\rho} = \frac{\lambda^2}{\mu(\mu - \lambda)}. \tag{12}$$

Now, using Little's theorem we can find the mean waiting time of a call attempt in the queue (T_q) and the mean time spent in the queuing system of a call attempt (T_{s+q}):

$$T_{s+q} = \frac{Y_{s+q}}{\lambda} = \frac{\rho}{\lambda(1-\rho)} = \frac{1}{\mu - \lambda}, \tag{13}$$

$$Tq = \frac{Yq}{\lambda} = \frac{\rho^2}{\lambda(1-\rho)} = \frac{\rho}{\mu - \lambda}. \tag{14}$$

After reverse substitution of λ, μ and ρ in (11), (12), (13) and (14) we obtain

$$Y_{s+q} = \frac{ofr.Fq}{crr.Fs + Fis + Fns + Fbr + Far + Fac - ofr.Fq}. \tag{15}$$

$$Yq = \frac{(ofr.Fq)^2}{crr.Fs + Fis + Fns + Fbr + Far + Fac}$$
$$\cdot \frac{1}{crr.Fs + Fis + Fns + Fbr + Far + Fac - ofr.Fq}. \tag{16}$$

$$T_{s+q} = \frac{1}{crr.Fs + Fis + Fns + Fbr + Far + Fac - ofr.Fq}. \tag{17}$$

$$Tq = \frac{ofr.Fq}{crr.Fs + Fis + Fns + Fbr + Far + Fac}$$
$$\cdot \frac{1}{crr.Fs + Fis + Fns + Fbr + Far + Fac - ofr.Fq}. \tag{18}$$

Finding Parameters of the Queuing System M|M|Ns|FIFO. In this queuing system, there are Ns serving lines in the Switching system and the buffer has infinite length. The serving lines are assumed to have independent and identically exponentially distributed service times and the arrival process is Poisson. Again, we have a birth-death process and $\lambda_n = \lambda$ for all n. If there are more than Ns call attempts in the Queuing system, i.e. $Ys+Yq > Ns$, all Ns lines in the Switching system are occupied and each of them is serving the call attempts with mean rate $\mu = (crr.Fs + Fis + Fns + Fbr + Far + Fac)/Ys$ and the output rate is $Ns\,\mu$. If there are n call attempts in the queuing system and $n < Ns$, only n of the Switching lines are occupied and the system output rate is μ_n where

$$\mu_n = \begin{cases} n\mu & \text{for } 1 \leq n < Ns. \\ Ns\,\mu & \text{for } n \geq Ns. \end{cases} \tag{19}$$

Through the same procedure as in the case with one line in the Switching system we obtain the probability of the system to be in state n:

$$p_n = \begin{cases} \frac{\lambda^n}{n!\mu^n} p_0 & \text{for } 1 \leq n < Ns. \\ \frac{\lambda^n}{Ns^{n-Ns}Ns!\mu^n} p_0 & \text{for } n \geq Ns. \end{cases} \tag{20}$$

Similarly, since the sum of the probabilities must be equal to 1, we obtain

$$p_0 = \left(\sum_{n=0}^{Ns-1} \frac{\lambda^n}{n!\mu^n} + \sum_{n=Ns}^{\infty} \frac{\lambda^n}{Ns^{n-Ns}Ns!\mu^n} \right)^{-1}. \tag{21}$$

To simplify the expressions we introduce the notation $r = \lambda/\mu$ and $\rho = r/Ns = \lambda/(Ns\mu)$. Now the expression for p_0 becomes

$$p_0 = \left(\sum_{n=0}^{Ns-1} \frac{r^n}{n!} + \sum_{n=Ns}^{\infty} \frac{r^n}{Ns^{n-Ns}Ns!} \right)^{-1}. \tag{22}$$

Since $r/Ns = \rho < 1$, the second sum above can be further simplified in the following way:

$$\sum_{n=Ns}^{\infty} \frac{r^n}{Ns^{n-Ns}Ns!} = \frac{r^{Ns}}{Ns!} \sum_{n=Ns}^{\infty} \left(\frac{r}{Ns}\right)^{n-Ns} = \frac{r^{Ns}}{Ns!} \sum_{m=0}^{\infty} \left(\frac{r}{Ns}\right)^m$$

$$= \frac{r^{Ns}}{Ns!} \frac{1}{1-\rho}. \tag{23}$$

After substitution of (23) in (22) we obtain

$$p_0^{-1} = \sum_{n=0}^{Ns-1} \frac{r^n}{n!} + \frac{r^{Ns}}{Ns!} \frac{1}{1-\rho}. \tag{24}$$

For the expected length of the queue Yq we have

$$Yq = \sum_{n=Ns+1}^{\infty} (n-Ns)p_n = \sum_{n=Ns+1}^{\infty} (n-Ns)\frac{r^n}{Ns^{n-Ns}Ns!}p_0 = \frac{r^{Ns}p_0}{Ns!} \sum_{i=1}^{\infty} i\rho^i$$

$$= \frac{r^{Ns}\rho p_0}{Ns!} \sum_{i=1}^{\infty} i\rho^{i-1} = \frac{r^{Ns}\rho p_0}{Ns!} \frac{d}{d\rho}\frac{1}{1-\rho} = \frac{r^{Ns}\rho p_0}{Ns!(1-\rho)^2}. \tag{25}$$

Again, using Little's formula we obtain the mean waiting time of a call in the queue:

$$Tq = \frac{Yq}{\lambda} = \frac{r^{Ns}}{Ns!\, Ns\, \mu(1-\rho)^2} p_0. \tag{26}$$

Now, we can find the expected number of call attempts in the queuing system (Y_{s+q}). First we notice that

$$T_{s+q} = Ts + Tq = \frac{r^{Ns}}{Ns!\, Ns\, \mu(1-\rho)^2} p_0 + \frac{1}{\mu}. \tag{27}$$

From the Little's formula we have $Y_{s+q} = \lambda T_{s+q}$. Therefore

$$Y_{s+q} = r + \frac{r^{Ns}\rho}{Ns!(1-\rho)^2} p_0. \tag{28}$$

Recall that

$$r = \frac{\lambda}{\mu} = \frac{ofr.Fq\,Ys}{crr.Fs + Fis + Fns + Fbr + Far + Fac} \tag{29}$$

and

$$\rho = \frac{r}{Ns} = \frac{ofr.Fq\,Ys}{(crr.Fs + Fis + Fns + Fbr + Far + Fac)Ns}. \tag{30}$$

After substitution of (29) and (30) in (24), (25), (26), (27) and (28) we obtain the following expressions for the parameters of the queue:

$$Yq = \left(\frac{ofr.Fq\,Ys}{crr.Fs + Fis + Fns + Fbr + Far + Fac}\right)^{Ns}$$
$$\cdot \frac{\frac{ofr.Fq\,Ys}{(crr.Fs + Fis + Fns + Fbr + Far + Fac)Ns}}{} \cdot p_0$$
$$\cdot \frac{1}{Ns!\left(1 - \frac{ofr.Fq\,Ys}{(crr.Fs + Fis + Fns + Fbr + Far + Fac)Ns}\right)^2}, \tag{31}$$

where

$$p_0^{-1} = \sum_{n=0}^{Ns-1}\left(\frac{ofr.Fq\,Ys}{crr.Fs + Fis + Fns + Fbr + Far + Fac}\right)^n \frac{1}{n!}$$
$$+ \left(\frac{ofr.Fq\,Ys}{crr.Fs + Fis + Fns + Fbr + Far + Fac}\right)^{Ns} \frac{1}{Ns!}$$
$$\cdot \frac{1}{1 - \frac{ofr.Fq\,Ys}{(crr.Fs + Fis + Fns + Fbr + Far + Fac)Ns}}. \tag{32}$$

$$Tq = \left(\frac{ofr.FqYs}{crr.Fs + Fis + Fns + Fbr + Far + Fac}\right)^{Ns}$$

$$\cdot \frac{Ys}{Ns!Ns(crr.Fs + Fis + Fns + Fbr + Far + Fac)}$$

$$\cdot \frac{1}{\left(1 - \frac{ofr.FqYs}{(crr.Fs + Fis + Fns + Fbr + Far + Fac)Ns}\right)^2} \, p_0. \qquad (33)$$

$$T_{s+q} = \left(\frac{ofr.FqYs}{crr.Fs + Fis + Fns + Fbr + Far + Fac}\right)^{Ns}$$

$$\cdot \frac{Ys}{Ns!Ns(crr.Fs + Fis + Fns + Fbr + Far + Fac)}$$

$$\cdot \frac{1}{\left(1 - \frac{ofr.FqYs}{(crr.Fs + Fis + Fns + Fbr + Far + Fac)Ns}\right)^2} \, p_0$$

$$+ \frac{Ys}{crr.Fs + Fis + Fns + Fbr + Far + Fac}. \qquad (34)$$

$$Y_{s+q} = \frac{ofr.FqYs}{crr.Fs + Fis + Fns + Fbr + Far + Fac}$$

$$+ \left(\frac{ofr.FqYs}{crr.Fs + Fis + Fns + Fbr + Far + Fac}\right)^{Ns}$$

$$\cdot \frac{ofr.FqYs}{(crr.Fs + Fis + Fns + Fbr + Far + Fac)Ns}$$

$$\cdot \frac{1}{Ns!\left(1 - \frac{ofr.FqYs}{(crr.Fs + Fis + Fns + Fbr + Far + Fac)Ns}\right)^2} \, p_0. \qquad (35)$$

Finding Parameters of the Queuing System M|M|Ns|Ns + Nq|FIFO.
Finally, we consider the queuing system which is used in the conceptual model
of overall telecommunication system with queue in the switching stage. The
difference between this queuing system and the one from the previous section is
that the buffer has finite length denoted by Nq. This sets a limit on the total
number of call attempts in the queuing system – they cannot be more than
$Nq + Ns$. Although often used, we could not find in literature expressions for
all parameters of the queuing system in one source. There are partial results
in [8,9]. Here, by analogy with the previous types of queuing systems we find
analytical expressions for the parameters of the queue. First, we notice that the
arrival rate λ_n is equal to 0 when $n \geq Ns + Nq$. The probability for the system
to be in state n is now given by

$$p_n = \begin{cases} \frac{\lambda^n}{n!\mu^n} p_0 & \text{for } 1 \leq n < Ns. \\ \frac{\lambda^n}{Ns^{n-Ns}Ns!\mu^n} p_0 & \text{for } Ns \leq n \leq Ns + Nq. \end{cases} \qquad (36)$$

Again, the condition that the sum of the probabilities p_n should be equal to 1, gives us the following expression for p_0:

$$p_0 = \left(\sum_{n=0}^{Ns-1} \frac{\lambda^n}{n!\mu^n} + \sum_{n=Ns}^{Ns+Nq} \frac{\lambda^n}{Ns^{n-Ns}Ns!\mu^n} \right)^{-1}. \tag{37}$$

In order to simplify the expression we set $r = \lambda/\mu$ and $\rho = r/Ns$. For the second sum in (37) we have

$$\sum_{n=Ns}^{Ns+Nq} \frac{\lambda^n}{Ns^{n-Ns}Ns!\mu^n} = \frac{r^{Ns}}{Ns!} \sum_{n=Ns}^{Ns+Nq} \rho^{n-Ns}$$

$$= \begin{cases} \frac{r^{Ns}}{Ns!} \frac{1-\rho^{Nq+1}}{1-\rho} & \text{for } \rho \neq 1. \\ \frac{r^{Ns}}{Ns!}(Nq+1) & \text{for } \rho = 1. \end{cases} \tag{38}$$

After substitution in (37) we obtain

$$p_0^{-1} = \begin{cases} \sum_{n=0}^{Ns-1} \frac{r^n}{n!} + \frac{r^{Ns}}{Ns!} \frac{1-\rho^{Nq+1}}{1-\rho} & \text{for } \rho \neq 1. \\ \sum_{n=0}^{Ns-1} \frac{r^n}{n!} + \frac{r^{Ns}}{Ns!}(Nq+1) & \text{for } \rho = 1. \end{cases} \tag{39}$$

For the expected length of the queue in this case we have

$$Yq = \sum_{n=Ns+1}^{Ns+Nq} (n-Ns)p_n = \frac{p_0 r^{Ns}}{Ns!} \sum_{n=Ns+1}^{Ns+Nq} \frac{(n-Ns)r^{n-Ns}}{Ns^{n-Ns}}$$

$$= \frac{p_0 r^{Ns} \rho}{Ns!} \sum_{n=Ns+1}^{Ns+Nq} (n-Ns)\rho^{n-Ns-1} = \frac{p_0 r^{Ns} \rho}{Ns!} \sum_{i=1}^{Nq} i\rho^{i-1}$$

$$= \frac{p_0 r^{Ns} \rho}{Ns!} \frac{d}{d\rho} \left(\frac{\rho - \rho^{Nq+1}}{1-\rho} \right) = \frac{p_0 r^{Ns} \rho}{Ns!(1-\rho)^2} [(1-\rho^{Nq}(Nq+1))(1-\rho) + \rho - \rho^{Nq+1}]$$

$$= \frac{p_0 r^{Ns} \rho}{Ns!(1-\rho)^2} [(\rho-1)\rho^{Nq}(Nq+1) + 1 - \rho^{Nq+1}]. \tag{40}$$

The above holds for $\rho \neq 1$.

To obtain the number of call attempts in the system Y_{s+q} we notice that a part p_{Ns+Nq} of the incoming flow of call attempts are blocked because the buffer has finite length $Nq + Ns$. This probability in the conceptual model is equal to Pbq. Therefore, the incoming rate becomes $\lambda(1 - Pbq)$ and as in (28) we have

$$Y_{s+q} = Yq + Ys = \frac{p_0 r^{Ns} \rho}{Ns!(1-\rho)^2} [(\rho-1)\rho^{Nq}(Nq+1) + 1 - \rho^{Nq+1}] + \frac{\lambda(1-Pbq)}{\mu}$$

$$= \frac{p_0 r^{Ns} \rho}{Ns!(1-\rho)^2} [(\rho-1)\rho^{Nq}(Nq+1) + 1 - \rho^{Nq+1}] + r(1-Pbq). \tag{41}$$

With the Little's formula we obtain

$$T_{s+q} = \frac{Y_{s+q}}{\lambda(1-Pbq)}. \tag{42}$$

and

$$Tq = T_{s+q} - \frac{1}{\mu} = \frac{Yq}{\lambda(1 - Pbq)}$$

$$= \frac{p_0 r^{Ns} \rho}{Ns!(1 - \rho)^2} \frac{[(\rho - 1)\rho^{Nq}(Nq + 1) + 1 - \rho^{Nq+1}]}{\lambda(1 - Pbq)}. \tag{43}$$

Finally, the probability of blocked queue (Pbq) is equal to the probability that the system is in state $Ns + Nq$ and from (36) we have

$$Pbq = \frac{\lambda^{Ns+Nq}}{Ns^{Nq}Ns!\mu^{Ns+Nq}} p_0. \tag{44}$$

Recall that

$$r = \frac{\lambda}{\mu} = \frac{ofr.FqYs}{crr.Fs + Fis + Fns + Fbr + Far + Fac} \tag{45}$$

and

$$\rho = \frac{r}{Ns} = \frac{ofr.FqYs}{(crr.Fs + Fis + Fns + Fbr + Far + Fac)Ns}. \tag{46}$$

After substitution in (40)–(44) we obtain

$$Yq = p_0 \left(\frac{ofr.FqYs}{crr.Fs + Fis + Fns + Fbr + Far + Fac}\right)^{Ns}$$

$$\cdot \frac{ofr.FqYs}{(crr.Fs + Fis + Fns + Fbr + Far + Fac)Ns} \cdot \frac{1}{Ns!}$$

$$\cdot \frac{1}{[1 - \frac{ofr.Fq.Ys}{(crr.Fs + Fis + Fns + Fbr + Far + Fac)Ns}]^2}$$

$$\cdot \left[\left(\frac{ofr.FqYs}{(crr.Fs + Fis + Fns + Fbr + Far + Fac)Ns} - 1\right)\right.$$

$$\cdot \left(\frac{ofr.FqYs}{(crr.Fs + Fis + Fns + Fbr + Far + Fac)Ns}\right)^{Nq} (Nq + 1) + 1$$

$$\left. - \left(\frac{ofr.FqYs}{(crr.Fs + Fis + Fns + Fbr + Far + Fac)Ns}\right)^{Nq+1}\right], \tag{47}$$

where

$$p_0^{-1} = \sum_{n=0}^{Ns-1} \frac{(ofr.Fq.Ys)^n}{n!(crr.Fs + Fis + Fns + Fbr + Far + Fac)^n}$$

$$+ \sum_{n=Ns}^{Ns+Nq} \frac{(ofr.FqYs)^n}{Ns^{n-Ns}Ns!(crr.Fs + Fis + Fns + Fbr + Far + Fac)^n}. \tag{48}$$

$$Y_{s+q} = p_0 \left(\frac{ofr.FqYs}{crr.Fs + Fis + Fns + Fbr + Far + Fac} \right)^{Ns}$$

$$\cdot \frac{ofr.FqYs}{(crr.Fs + Fis + Fns + Fbr + Far + Fac)Ns} \cdot \frac{1}{Ns!}$$

$$\cdot \frac{1}{[1 - \frac{ofr.Fq.Ys}{(crr.Fs + Fis + Fns + Fbr + Far + Fac)Ns}]^2}$$

$$\cdot \left[\left(\frac{ofr.FqYs}{(crr.Fs + Fis + Fns + Fbr + Far + Fac)Ns} - 1 \right) \right.$$

$$\cdot \left(\frac{ofr.FqYs}{(crr.Fs + Fis + Fns + Fbr + Far + Fac)Ns} \right)^{Nq} (Nq + 1) + 1$$

$$\left. - \left(\frac{ofr.FqYs}{(crr.Fs + Fis + Fns + Fbr + Far + Fac)Ns} \right)^{Nq+1} \right]$$

$$+ \frac{ofr.FqYs}{crr.Fs + Fis + Fns + Fbr + Far + Fac}(1 - Pbq). \qquad (49)$$

$$T_{s+q} = \left[p_0 \left(\frac{ofr.FqYs}{crr.Fs + Fis + Fns + Fbr + Far + Fac} \right)^{Ns} \right.$$

$$\cdot \frac{ofr.FqYs}{(crr.Fs + Fis + Fns + Fbr + Far + Fac)Ns} \cdot \frac{1}{Ns!}$$

$$\cdot \frac{1}{[1 - \frac{ofr.Fq.Ys}{(crr.Fs + Fis + Fns + Fbr + Far + Fac)Ns}]^2}$$

$$\cdot \left[\left(\frac{ofr.FqYs}{(crr.Fs + Fis + Fns + Fbr + Far + Fac)Ns} - 1 \right) \right.$$

$$\cdot \left(\frac{ofr.FqYs}{(crr.Fs + Fis + Fns + Fbr + Far + Fac)Ns} \right)^{Nq} (Nq + 1) + 1$$

$$\left. \left. - \left(\frac{ofr.FqYs}{(crr.Fs + Fis + Fns + Fbr + Far + Fac)Ns} \right)^{Nq+1} \right] \right.$$

$$+ \frac{ofr.FqYs}{crr.Fs + Fis + Fns + Fbr + Far + Fac}(1 - Pbq) \Bigg] \cdot \frac{1}{ofr.Fq(1 - Pbq)}. \qquad (50)$$

$$Tq = p_0 \left(\frac{ofr.FqYs}{crr.Fs + Fis + Fns + Fbr + Far + Fac} \right)^{Ns}$$

$$\cdot \frac{ofr.FqYs}{(crr.Fs + Fis + Fns + Fbr + Far + Fac)Ns}$$

$$\cdot \frac{1}{Ns! \left(1 - \frac{ofr.FqYs}{(crr.Fs + Fis + Fns + Fbr + Far + Fac)Ns} \right)^2}$$

$$\cdot \left[\left(\frac{ofr.FqYs}{(crr.Fs + Fis + Fns + Fbr + Far + Fac)Ns} - 1 \right) \right.$$

$$\cdot \left(\frac{ofr.FqYs}{(crr.Fs + Fis + Fns + Fbr + Far + Fac)Ns} \right)^{Nq} (Nq + 1)$$

$$\left. + 1 - \left(\frac{ofr.FqYs}{(crr.Fs + Fis + Fns + Fbr + Far + Fac)Ns} \right)^{Nq+1} \right]$$

$$\cdot \frac{1}{ofr.Fq(1 - Pbq)}. \tag{51}$$

$$Pbq = \frac{(ofr.FqYs)^{Ns+Nq}}{Ns^{Nq} Ns!(crr.Fs + Fis + Fns + Fbr + Far + Fac)^{Ns+Nq}} \cdot p_0. \tag{52}$$

5 Conclusion

The conceptual model of overall telecommunication system with queue described here in details is a base for the development of analytical model of the network. The analytical model can be used to solve important teletraffic tasks such as dimensioning and redimensioning of the network and predicting the QoS. The analytical expressions obtained in Sect. 4 for the parameters of the queuing system are the first step in the development of the analytical model.

In our future work, we shall use the conceptual model described in the present paper and the expressions for the parameters of the queuing system to obtain a system of equations for the dynamic parameters. We shall propose numerical methods for solving the resulting non-linear system.

Acknowledgements. The work of V. Andonov and A. Otsetova was partially funded by the Bulgarian NSF Project DM 12/2 – "New Models of Overall Telecommunication Networks with Quality of Service Guarantees".

The work of S. Poryazov was supported by the National Scientific Program "Information and Communication Technologies for a Single Digital Market in Science, Education and Security (ICT in SES)", financed by the Bulgarian Ministry of Education and Science.

References

1. Haverkort, B.R.: Performance of Computer Communication Systems: A Model-Based Approach. Wiley, New York (1998)
2. ITU E.600, ITU-T Recommendation E.600: Terms and Definitions of Traffic Engineering (Melbourne, 1988; revised at Helsinki, 1993)
3. Iversen, V. B.: Teletraffic Engineering Handbook. ITU-D SG 2/16 & ITC. Draft, December 2003. http://www.tele.dtu.dk/teletraffic/. Accessed 11 Dec 2004
4. Poryazov, S.A., Saranova, E.T.: Some general terminal and network teletraffic equations for virtual circuit switching systems. In: Nejat Ince, A., Topuz, E. (eds.) Modeling and Simulation Tools for Emerging Telecommunication Networks, pp. 471–505. Springer, Boston (2006). https://doi.org/10.1007/0-387-34167-6_24

5. Poryazov, S., Saranova, E.: Models of Telecommunication Networks with Virtual Channel Switching and Applications. Academic Publishing House "Prof. M. Drinov", Sofia (2012)
6. Poryazov, S., Andonov, V., Saranova, E.: Comparison of four conceptual models of a queuing system in service networks. In: Proceedings of the 26th National Conference with International Participation TELECOM 2018, Sofia, 25–26 October, pp. 71–77 (2018)
7. Poryazov, S., Saranova, E., Ganchev, I.: Conceptual and analytical models for predicting the quality of service of overall telecommunication systems. In: Ganchev, I., van der Mei, R.D., van den Berg, H. (eds.) Autonomous Control for a Reliable Internet of Services. LNCS, vol. 10768, pp. 151–181. Springer, Cham (2018). https://doi.org/10.1007/978-3-319-90415-3_7
8. Schneps, M.: Systems for Distribution of Information. Svyaz Publishing House, Moscow (1979). (in Russian)
9. Vishnevskiy, V.M.: Theoretical Foundations Of Computer Networks Planning. Tehnosfera, Moscow (2003). (in Russian)

On-Site Measurements of TETRA Standard Emission Disturbing Interference

Eugen Stancu$^{(\boxtimes)}$, Simona V. Halunga, Octavian Fratu, and Valerică Bîndar

Telecommunications Department, Electronics, Telecommunications and Information Technology Faculty, University "Politehnica" of Bucharest, Bucharest, Romania eugenixstancu@yahoo.com, shalunga@elcom.pub.ro

Abstract. In this paper a simple test-bed to evaluate the effect of an unmodulated disrupting signal on a TETRA π/4-DQPSK (Differential Quadrature Phase-Shift Keying) signal has been developed and implemented, such that the transmitted signal does not affect other communication system existing in the same area. An unmodulated disrupting signal, with increasing amplitude, has been overlapped on the transmitted data and the parameters of the received signal has been evaluated with an Agilent Vector Signal Analyzer model 89600. Based on the results obtained, several interesting conclusions have been highlighted at the end.

Keywords: Disturbing signal · Interferences · Phase modulation · Signal quality parameters · TeTRa

1 Introduction

TETRA is a Professional Mobile Radio (PMR) standard that offers a wide range of services, starting with security services and ending with space-based modes of work [1]. A great advantage of the system is the large coverage using a single frequency, without the need to implement complex radio frequency re-use schemes. Another major advantage is the possibility of providing services to several institutions on the same infrastructure. Mobile stations (MS) communicate via TETRA standard base stations. Also, MS can communicate between them without base stations in situations where the network is unavailable or base stations are stopped for various reasons. The major application of TETRA is group dial mode [2]. The structure of the network is shown in Fig. 1.

The most important interface specification is the ETSI TETRA air interface, which ensures interoperability between radio terminals and base stations that allows a basic communication mode commonly referred to as Trunked Mode Operation (TMO). Even though the TETRA system has been developed and standardized during the 90 s, there is still recent research that aims to develop the system and to find new applications for it. In [3, 4] the authors proposed a positioning method of tram vehicles by combining positioning data from satellite positioning system, the interconnection between the vehicles being performed using TETRA; the system benefits thus of reduced costs, high accuracy positioning preserving also the continuity, reliability and maintainability of

V. Poulkov (Ed.): FABULOUS 2019, LNICST 283, pp. 263–270, 2019.
https://doi.org/10.1007/978-3-030-23976-3_23

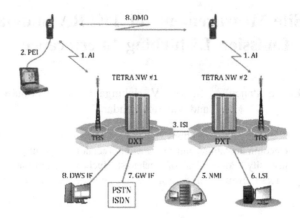

Fig. 1. Tetra network interfaces [3]

the TETRA system. In [5] is presented an innovative signalling compression method for the Mission-critical push-to-talk over LTE call service introduced in LTE release 16, with limited capacity of carrier aggregated broadband system and proposed an architecture that hosts compression proxies for the network and user without the changing the core network of LTE system. During the last couple of years patent applications have been also been made. In [6] the authors presented a system and a methodology developed for reducing the interference between two communication entities based on a determined geographical proximity of the two mobile stations, while in [7] an authentication method and the associated structure has been presented.

The remainder of the paper is organized as follows in the second chapter are described the signal quality parameters that are evaluated and the mathematical background that stands behind them. Chapter three presents the measurement setup, the location, the resources used, and the simulation algorithm, as well as the results obtained under different disrupting parameters, the way in which the modulation quality parameters are affected. In the final part some interesting results are highlighted.

2   Measurement and Evaluation of TETRA Signal Parameters

The data is transmitted digitally, by the Tetra base station, through a channel affected by noise, fading and other disturbances and, in order to evaluate their effect, a vector analyser is used at the receiver end. This represents each received symbol as a vector, compares it with a reference, and evaluates several parameters [8, 9] that reflect the quality of the received signal, as follows. The *Measured Error Vector*, EVM, denoted by [*n*] is the Euclidean distance between the measured point and the ideal reference point, given by

$$EVM[\text{n}] = \sqrt{Ierr[\text{n}]^2 + Qerr[\text{n}]^2} \qquad (1)$$

where $Ierr[n]$ and $Qerr[n]$ are the in phase and quadrature components of the error vector. The mean square value of EVM (% EVM) is determined as

$$\%EVM = \frac{\frac{1}{N}\sum_{k=1}^{(N-1)}\sqrt{Ierr[k]^2 + Qerr[k]^2}}{[peak\ reference\ vector]} \tag{2}$$

where N is the number of measured points considered for calculating EVM root mean square and the [peak reference vector] is the amplitude of the most important (highest power) point in the reference signal constellation. The IQ Magnitude Error is determined as the difference between the magnitudes of the measured signal and reference the one

$$IQ\ Magnitude\ Error = \sqrt{IMeas^2 + QMeas^2} - \sqrt{IRef^2 + QRef^2} \tag{3}$$

The Phase Error represents the phase difference between the reference signal and the measured one and is determined as

$$Phase\ Error = \arctan\left(\frac{QMeas}{IMeas}\right) - \arctan\left(\frac{QRef}{IRef}\right) \tag{4}$$

The Frequency Error (Freq Err) is the difference between the frequency of the signal and the central frequency of the analyser, and shows the bearer frequency shift with respect to the local oscillator. The IQ Offset - represents an evaluator of the rotation of the constellation points due to channel effect and it is determined as.

$$IQ\ Offset = 20\log_{10}\left(\frac{signal}{offset}\right), \tag{5}$$

where signal and offset represents the ratio of the power from the central frequency to the average power of the signal.

The Amplitude Droop is a measure of the degree of change in the signal amplitude during a burst (temporal slot), measured in dB/symbol. The IQ Gain Imbalance compares the magnitudes of the in phase and quadrature components and is expressed in dB.

$$IQ\ gain\ imb = 20\log_{10}\left(\frac{Imag}{Qmag}\right) \tag{6}$$

Finally, the Quadrature Error (Quad Err) quantifies the deviation from orthogonality between the in phase and quadrature components, that usually indicates a problem on the transmitter side [6].

Maximal dynamic and static reference sensitivity levels for a BS receiver under normal and extreme conditions are stated in Table 1 [7].

Table 1. Maximum sensitivity levels for a base station receiver

Normal	−106 dBm	−115 dBm
Extreme	−100 dBm	−109 dBm

The limit values for phase modulation specifies the minimum reference interference ratio performances (C/Ic for co-channel, and C/Ia for adjacent channel), that depends on the channel type, modulation, channels state and receiver class. For $\pi/4$-DQPSK the reference interference ratios imposed by specifications are

- for co-channel interference, $C/Ic = 19$ dB for both mobile and base stations;
- for adjacent channel interference, below 700 MHz $C/Ia = -40$ dB for the mobile station and $C/Ia = -45$ dB for the base station while over 700 MHz $C/Ia = -40$ dB for both mobile and base stations.

3 Case Study

As more and more radiocommunication services emerges, radio interference becomes a phenomenon that increasingly affects the quality of TETRA services. These licenses include military, aeronautical, governmental and emergency services, which use the 380–385 MHz and 390–395 MHz bands. In addition to these, there are also many low-power, unlicensed radio transmissions from wireless microphones, Wi-Fi spots, video cameras, alarm systems, and more. Bucharest has over 2 million inhabitants, but, with the commuters, they can be twice as many, therefore, the discovery of the source of interference on a TETRA radio frequency is an important critical activity. In order to achieve this goal, several steps have to be performed.

In order to identify the disturbing signal, one has to see what are the signals that reach the device that might have problems, or behaves in an unusual manner. For example, a base station antenna is its first item checked. For digital transmissions, such as cellular ones, interferences manifests themselves by a decreased coverage, a blockage or a loss of conversions, or even a transfer rate lower than the usual one. That familiar cascade sound from the cellular phone or cellular station indicates a poor reception and a large bit error rate that can be caused by interference. A second interference indicator is the noise level that reflects into a larger bit error rate in the receiving channel. Other performance indicators, such as call set-up time, latency time, will suffer.

The measurements were performed in Bucharest and a Tetra base station was used for testing. The cell emission power was reduced to 10 W (40 dBm) in order to avoid disturbing other communications in the same area. Base Station Broadcasting Frequency was 394.587,5 MHz and the receiver frequency were 384.587,5 MHz. With the *Rohde & Schwarz SME 03* signal generator, a disturbance non-modulated signal with the power levels increasing from 3 mW (5 dBm) to 10 mW (10 dBm) and then 79 mW

(19 dBm) was generated successively on the base station's emission frequency (394.587,5 MHz). Evaluation of the received signal was made with the *Agilent Vector Signal Analyzer 89600*, tuned on the base station frequency (394.587,5 MHz). The distance between the generator antenna and the Tetra cell broadcast antenna was 30 m and the one between the signal generator's antenna and the receiving antenna of the Agilent analyser was 10 m. The block diagram of the test-bed setup is shown in Fig. 2.

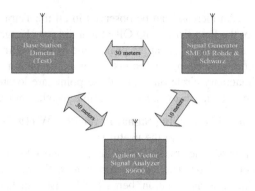

Fig. 2. Block diagram of the test bed

Case 1 Disturbing Signal Level 3 mW (5 dBm) - This level of the disturbing signal is still below the useful signal level, but, even though, the number of errors increase, and the Error Vector Magnitude value reaches the maximum admissible value of the standard (10% rms). The Freq Err and IQ Offset parameters do not change significantly with respect to the measurements without the disturbing signal. The results are presented in Fig. 3, which shows the six graphs that highlight the Tetra emission parameters, namely IQ Time Measurement, Spectrum, Error Vector Spectrum, Symbols/Errors, IQ Ref Spec, IQ MeasSpec, Vector Time Error and IQ Error.

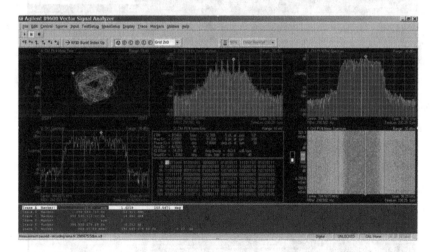

Fig. 3. Disturbed emission representation at 3 mW (5 dBm)

Case 2 Disturbing Signal Level 10 mW (10 dBm) - At this level of the disturbing signal (below the useful signal), the diameter of the constellation points decreases significantly, as shown in Fig. 4, thus the resistance of the π/4-DQPSK signal to noise reduces significantly, and so does the error probability.

An increase can be observed in all the Tetra transmission error parameters, except for the Freq Err and IQ Offset that did not change significantly. It can also be observed a sudden increase in the peak value of Phase Error, as well as the fact that some of the lines connecting the points of the constellation are passing through the centre of the imaginary circle on which these points are located increasing thus the dynamic range and making it even more sensitive to other noise, fading and other disturbances.

Case 3 Disturbing Signal Level 79 mW (19 dBm) - For this value of the disturbing signal is equal to the useful signal level, a significant increase of all the transmission error parameters, including Freq Err and IQ Offset, as it can be seen from Fig. 5. The constellation deteriorates importantly, the constellation points move and rotate from their original position, being barely distinguished (Table 2).

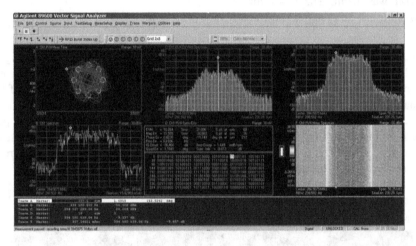

Fig. 4. Disturbed emission representation at 10 mW (10 dBm)

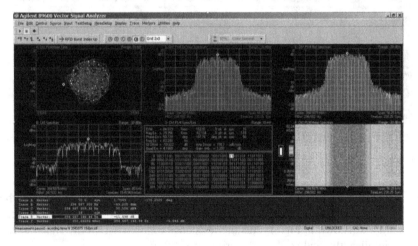

Fig. 5. Disturbed emission representation with 79 mW (19 dBm)

Table 2. Centralization of results from simulations

Disturbing signal level	EVM % rms	Mag err % rms	Phase error deg	Freq Error Hz	IQ Offset dB	Quad Err deg	Amp Droop mdB/sym	Gain Imb dB
undisturbed	1.4	0.9	0.62	64.1	−35.1	0.1	4.1	0.18
3 mW (5 dBm)	9.5	6.6	3.9	62.6	−34.9	−1.3	−463.6	−0.01
10 mW (10 dBm)	16.2	11	6.6	63.6	−36.4	−1.1	1.6	−0.07
79 mW (19 dBm unmodulated)	84.5	29	50.7	83.2	−19.9	4.1	150.7	1.28

4   Conclusions

All the measurements presented in this paper had been performed to highlight the changes in the modulation constellation accuracy and the overall quality parameters of the received signal when an unmodulated disrupting signal is affecting a standard TETRA communication system. The measurements were performed in real conditions in Bucharest and a Tetra base station had been used as receiver.

Based on those results, the following conclusions have been drawn, as follows:

1. The Agilent Vector Signal Analyzer 89600 analyser detects based on the Error Vector Spectrum graph low-level disrupting signals under the TETRA cell finger-print in all cases.
2. In the case studied, at the value of 5 dBm of the disturbing signal, the Error Vector Magnitude reaches the maximum permissible value of the standard (10% rms).
3. When the disrupting signal equals to the level of the useful signal, a significant increase in all transmission error parameters has been observed, including the Freq Err and IQ Offset, that had not changed significantly so far. Also, the constellation deteriorates, the received signal points move from their initial position and can no longer be distinguished.
4. In comparison to other phase-modulated transmissions, the π/4-DQPSK (Differential Quadrature Phase-Shift Keying) proved to be more efficient, but also more sensitive to disturbing signals and less robust to variations in transmission channel parameters.
5. When the disrupting signal exceeds 10 mW, some of the lines connecting the constellation points are passing through the centre of the imaginary circle on which they are located, increasing thus the dynamic range and making it even more sensitive.
6. The error transmission parameters increase with the level of the disrupting signal, until it reaches the level of the useful signal, then the increase of the level of the disturbing signal no longer causes the increase of the errors.

According to the standard, the traffic can no longer be performed at a disturbing signal 19 dBm higher than the useful signal; no evidence has been made in this respect, but it has been found that at this level of disrupting signal, the errors are very high and the whole constellation deformed.

Acknowledgment. This work was supported by a grant of the Ministry of Innovation and Research, UEFISCDI, project number 33PCCDI/01.03.2018 within PNCDI III, Platform of multi-agent intelligent systems for water quality monitoring on Romanian sector of Danube and Danube Delta (MultiMonD2), and partially funded under contract no. 5Sol/2017 within PNCDI III, Integrated Software Platform for Mobile Malware Analysis (ToR-SIM) and contract no. 213PED/2017, OFDM System based on FFT with non-integer argument (FractOFDM).

References

1. Ferrús, R., Sallent, O.: Mobile broadband communications for public safety: the road ahead through LTE technology. Wiley, New Jersey (2015)
2. Dunlop, J., Girma, D., Irvine, J.: Digital Mobile Communications and the TETRA System. Wiley, New York (2000)
3. Yongmei, S., Fuzhang, W., Yishun, Z.: Vehicle positioning method of modern tram based on TETRA communication system. In: Balas, V.E., Jain, L.C., Zhao, X. (eds.) Information Technology and Intelligent Transportation Systems. AISC, vol. 454, pp. 147–154. Springer, Cham (2017). https://doi.org/10.1007/978-3-319-38789-5_25
4. Järvinen, T.: Location System solution in Terrestrial Trunked RAdio (TETRA) Professional Mobile Radio (2010)
5. Niu, Z., Li, H., Xu, C.: A signaling compression method for MCPTT trunking communication system based on carrier aggregated broadband system. In: 2017 7th IEEE International Conference on Electronics Information and Emergency Communication (ICEIEC), pp. 215–218. IEEE, July 2017
6. Bercovici, M.S., Koren, E., Kugman, E., Shemesh, Y.A.: Method and apparatus for mitigating interference between mobile devices in a wireless communication system. U.S. Patent 9,615,299. Motorola Solutions Inc. (2017)
7. ETSI EN 300 392-2 V3.1.1 (2006-09), Terrestrial Trunked Radio (TETRA); Voice plus Data (V+D); Part 2: Air Interface (AI)
8. http://www.lightwaveonline.com. Accessed 28 June 2018
9. Terrestrial Trunked Radio (TETRA): http://www.etsi.org s.l.: ETSI, 2001. ETSI EN 300 392-2 V2.3.2 (2001-03)

An Overview of Methods of Reducing the Effect of Jamming Attacks at the Physical Layer of Wireless Networks

Dimitriya Mihaylova[(✉)]

Faculty of Telecommunications, Technical University of Sofia,
8 Kl. Ohridski Blvd, 1000 Sofia, Bulgaria
dam@tu-sofia.bg

Abstract. Jamming as a form of denial-of-service is a commonly-used attack initiated against security at the physical layer of a wireless system. This paper starts with an overview of various types of jamming and measures for its detection. Then, a number of methods for jamming mitigation that can be used at the physical layer are discussed and compared according to their main advantages and drawbacks.

Keywords: Jamming · Denial-of-Service · Physical layer security

1 Introduction

Interference is a major issue in modern-day wireless networks. As a consequence of their easily accessible air interface, wireless systems are impacted by interference emanating from a number of sources. Intra-cell interference, coming from other legitimate users (LUs) in the cell, is usually avoided by using orthogonal frequency division multiple access (OFDMA), meaning that the resources allocated to the users in the cell are orthogonal to one another. On the other hand, frequency reuse in neighbouring cells results in inter-cell interference, which is a big challenge in multi-cell systems. The amount of inter-cell interference depends on numerous parameters, namely the suppression and frequency reuse factors, the antenna gain of the receiver, the transmit power of interfering users and the attenuation (which emanates from small-scale fading, shadowing and path loss). The effect of inter-cell interference can be reduced by collaboration and coordination among cells or by an intelligent management system that regulates the transmission rates and powers.

In order to be successfully decoded at the base station (BS), the received signal's power must exceed the overall power of interference plus ambient noise. In other words, the signal-to-interference-plus-noise-ratio (SINR), which is a quantitative limitation of the channel capacity according to the Shannon-Hartley theorem, must exceed zero decibels. For this reason, an effective attack that an adversary can mount against the security of a wireless system involves deliberately increasing the level of interference in the transmission channel. When the source of interference is not a valid user of the network but rather a malicious user intentionally generating interfering signals in order to disrupt legitimate communication, this type of intervention is called jamming.

© ICST Institute for Computer Sciences, Social Informatics and Telecommunications Engineering 2019
Published by Springer Nature Switzerland AG 2019. All Rights Reserved
V. Poulkov (Ed.): FABULOUS 2019, LNICST 283, pp. 271–284, 2019.
https://doi.org/10.1007/978-3-030-23976-3_24

Jamming can be initiated during the transmission of either data or pilot signals, or both. The uplink pilot transmission phase is typical for time division duplex (TDD) systems, whose channel state information (CSI) is obtained at the BS based on the information about the sent and received pilots. Therefore, jamming the pilots' exchange may result in erroneous computation of the channel gain which, similarly to data transmission jamming, destroys the legitimate communication. A special subcase of jamming the pilot phase is the so-called pilot contamination attack, in which the jammer interferes with the same set of pilots which are used for legitimate channel estimation [1].

The intentional interference may have a significant positive effect on the network performance as well. An interesting opportunity employed by the physical layer security (PLS) comprises interference transmissions from legitimate parties, known as artificial noise (AN) [2], aiming to prevent message decoding from attackers that eavesdrop on the information exchange.

Numerous research works have focused on the different aspects of interference. However, in the scope of this paper, only the interference originated from jamming attacks is considered. In [3] the authors examine the downlink data transmission in a massive MIMO system and demonstrate that unless the jamming attack is initiated during the training phase, it does not have significant impact on the system's performance. Several strategies for jamming the MIMO CSI at the data link layer are presented in [4], such as opposite waterfilling, channel inversion and channel rank attacks. Uplink massive MIMO jamming is discussed in [5] together with investigation of the optimal jamming energy allocation for data and training phases when the number of antennae at BS is much larger than the number of users served by the network. Although many other studies are directed to massive MIMO improvements against jamming, many of the emerging wireless networks are not capable of supporting such a large number of antenna elements, due to hardware restrictions and computational and energy limitations. The physical layer security approaches against jamming, which are discussed in this paper, are extremely beneficial to this type of network.

The paper is organized as follows: in Sect. 2, the topic of jamming attacks on the physical layer and different studies related to their mitigation are discussed. Existing methods that can be used on the physical layer to reduce the effect of a jamming attack are described and several of their main features are compared in Sects. 3 and 4, respectively.

2 Related Studies

The open nature of emerging wireless systems exposes them to the risk of different types of malicious intervention. One possible attack that can be launched against the security of a wireless network is the so called DoS (Denial-of-Service) attack. With the DoS underway, the intruder aims to make the system's resources and services unavailable to its legitimate users and thus disable normal system operation. Depending on the functions performed, each layer of the network architecture is vulnerable to certain types of DoS attack. The authors of [6] describe several possible types of DoS attacks at the various layers of WSNs (Wireless Sensor Networks), whose security enhancement attracts significant scientific interest with the development of CPSs (Cyber-Physical Systems) and IoT (Internet of Things). A schematic representation of DoS attacks on the levels of the TCP/IP stack is given in Fig. 1.

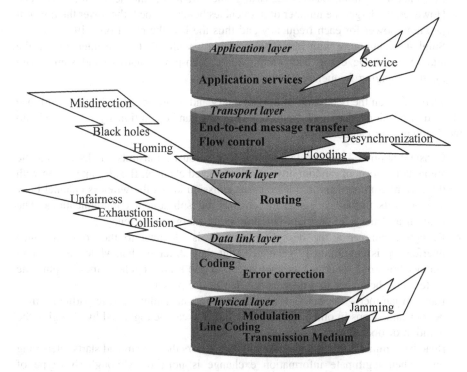

Fig. 1. Possible Denial-of-Service attacks on the TCP/IP layers

Though each level of the protocol stack is vulnerable to specific types of DoS attacks, as illustrated in Fig. 1, the focus of this paper is solely on the physical layer when threatened by a jamming attack.

The jamming attack on the physical layer represents a deliberate generation of radio signals by an adversary with the intent to interfere with the signals transmitted between legitimate parties and thus degrade the quality of legitimate communication. Moreover, as the intruder occupies the resources of the wireless channel, it impedes the users of the network from accessing the channel, leading to DoS at the physical layer. In order to increase their impact on the system's performance, the adversary can undertake various jamming strategies in accordance with his capabilities, the desired effect and the characteristics of the network. Different classifications of jamming are available in the literature but the main types are briefly described here:

1. Wideband jamming – this active attack can be achieved by sending an electro-magnetic signal over the entire radio frequency spectrum, resulting in the obstruction of all ongoing transmissions [7].

2. Single-tone jamming – the adversary emits a narrowband signal within the specified bandwidth of the channel being jammed.
3. Multi-tone jamming – as described in [8], the jammer can interfere on multiple frequencies simultaneously, decreasing the SINR of the legitimate receivers. However, the larger the number of frequencies being jammed, the lower the transmit jamming power for each frequency and thus the less the effect on it [9].
4. Single-tone jamming with frequency hopping – with this type of intervention, the attacker jams the entire bandwidth with a high-power narrowband signal with rapidly-changing frequency [9].

Depending on the behaviour of the adversary and, more specifically, the recurrence of his transmissions, the single-frequency jamming can be additionally subdivided into the following six categories [7, 9, 10]:

- Constant jammer – the constant jammer continuously transmits an electromagnetic signal in the form of random bits over the selected channel. Besides interfering with the current communication, the constant emission keeps the wireless channel busy and prevents further access to the channel for subsequent communications. The main disadvantage of constant jamming is its energy inefficiency.
- Deceptive jammer – the deceptive jammer, is identical to the constant, since interference is continuously generated, but they differ in that while the constant jammer transmits random bits, the deceptive one sends regular fames, duping the system into believing that there is no illegitimate presence.
- Random jammer – the random jammer transmits at random during particular time periods and sleeps in others. Its energy efficiency can be regulated by changing the duration of operation and sleep.
- Reactive jammer – this is a jammer which monitors the system and starts interfering only when legitimate information exchange is noticed. Although this type of intrusion surpasses the previous ones in energy efficiency, its effectiveness is reduced as it degrades the SINR of the current transmissions but cannot be used to prevent access to the system resources. As the authors of [10] emphasise, the successful performance of the reactive jammer is closely bound by its capabilities to sense legitimate communication. In certain cases, the adversary can listen for specific activity on the channel, which defines a special subtype of reactive jamming. Examples of this include the node-specific and message-specific jamming attacks in [11] and the IEEE 802.15.4-specific interruption, described in [12].
- Adaptive jammer – the adaptive jammer employs the best jamming strategy in terms of energy efficiency but, as described in [10], represents an unrealistically optimal attack scenario. The adaptability of this intruder consists in adjusting their transmit power in accordance with the CSI of the legitimate channel. When the legitimate users experience good channel conditions, the jammer has to increase its power to deteriorate the communication. Conversely, if the legitimate channel is poor enough to prevent normal information exchange, no jamming is needed and the attacker can stay silent. What makes the use of adaptive jamming impractical is the time-varying fading of the wireless medium which constantly changes the RSS (Received Signal Strength) at the intended receiver. Furthermore, the legitimate channel's CSI is not available to the malicious user.

- Intelligent jammer – the intelligent jammer attacks the system in using the knowledge of certain instabilities of the upper-layers protocols. Several examples of DoS by an intelligent jammer include flooding with TCP/UDP packets, MAC (Medium Access Control) control frames or Smurf attack. As a result, this type of intrusion mostly affects the data link, network, transport and application layer, rather than the physical layer, and is therefore outside the scope of this work.

The authors of [13] discuss different detection techniques that can be used to reveal the presence of the jammer depending on the perceived behaviour. The commonly used approach is based on an analysis of the statistic of the signal received at the legitimate user, expressed by the RSS, CST (Carrier Sensing Time) or PER (Packet Error Rate).

The presence of a constant, deceptive, random and reactive jammer can be revealed through comparison of the RSS of the currently received signal to the one collected during previous transmissions. Since jamming alters the energy of the received signal, a variation in RSS demonstrates the interference's origin.

Monitoring the CST is another way to detect malicious intervention, as the DoS on the physical layer occupies the wireless channel and generates an unusual increase in CST. This could indicate the existence of a constant, deceptive or random jammer. Due to their nature, reactive and adaptive jammers transmit signals only when legitimate communications take place, therefore they do not have the effect of keeping the system busy. For that reason, the CST is not a criterion that can be used to decide whether there is a reactive or adaptive jammer in the network.

An analysis of PER can also indicate the presence of interference induced by jamming as the corruption of legitimate communication significantly enlarges the number of undecodable packets, leading to abnormal values of PER. This method is appropriate for exposing constant, random and reactive jamming, which increase the number of erroneously received packets at the destination. Since the deceptive jammer transmits regular frames, it does not affect the value of PER, hence this statistic is not suitable for detecting this type of jamming.

The unrealistic scenario of the adaptive jamming represents a great challenge from the point of view of detection because its constantly altering power can make the use of RSS or PER statistics inadequate for jamming detection. However, a combination of both the methods is a promising solution [10]. Where both RSS and PER are relatively high, the adaptive jammer can be successfully revealed.

Unlike the physical layer jammers, the intelligent one impacts the upper-layer protocols and analyses of the physical characteristics such as RSS, CST and PER, cannot be used to disclose its presence.

When a jammer is detected, measures to mitigate its influence on the system performance must be considered. Various approaches to counter jamming exist in the literature but most of them rely on complex algorithms and protocols from upper layers, which makes them unsuitable for resource-constrained applications.

A swarm intelligence conception of an ant system is suggested for use against WSN jamming in [8], where the transmission route between source and destination changes depending on parameters such as number of hops, energy and distance, SNR (Signal to Noise Ratio), BER (Bit Error Rate), packet delivery and packet loss, some of which relate to the upper layers of the protocol stack. Another study [14] proposes several

MAC layer mechanisms, including frame masking, packet fragmentation and redundant encoding, for combatting different types of jammers whose capabilities are identical to those of legitimate users. Limiting factors for their implementation are the induced overhead, computational complexity and power consumption. The authors in [15] propose a mapping protocol to inform the network about the location and shape of the jammed range so that routing management can be applied on upper layers to avoid the attacked nodes of the network. In [16] the channel surfing method for jamming avoidance is proposed, which switches to another link layer channel if jamming is detected. Another commonly used strategy to suppress the effect of jamming attacks relies on game theory. A taxonomic survey of the available game theoretic methods to defend against jamming in the literature is given in [17], where the authors draw attention to the growing number of such approaches. Nevertheless, the resource allocation problem in game theory is again solved at the MAC or data link layer, which makes it more complicated than the physical layer security techniques.

3   Jamming Mitigation Techniques Used at the Physical Layer

3.1   Spread Spectrum as a Jamming Defence Mechanism

One conventional method to counteract jamming attacks at the physical layer is by using spread spectrum techniques, which expand the spectrum of the original signal into a wider frequency band. The effect of spread spectrum modulation is twofold: on the one hand, it helps to hide the fact that communication is in progress from unauthorized parties, referred to as low probability of intercept (LPI). On the other hand, spreading the signal over the entire frequency band of the channel makes it more resistant to natural noise and interference as well as jamming and eavesdropping attacks. The various spread spectrum approaches include direct sequence spread spectrum (DSSS), frequency hopping spread spectrum (FHSS), time hopping spread spectrum (THSS), parallel sequence spread spectrum (PSSS), chirp spread spectrum (CSS), and different hybrids between them. However, the most widely used in wireless communications are DSSS and FHSS, which are outlined in the following two subsections.

Frequency Hopping Spread Spectrum. Frequency hopping (FH) is a modulation technique in which the carrier frequency changes repeatedly in order to prevent narrowband jamming [18, 19]. The algorithm according to which the frequency is shifted over the entire spectrum follows a pseudo-random sequence and must be available at both the transmitter and the receiver but has to be kept secret from non-authorised users. Otherwise, if the jammer gets access to the hopping pattern, he can simply alter the central frequency of the jamming signal following the one used in legitimate transmission, thus making FHSS modulation impractical.

For the demodulation purposes, perfect synchronisation is needed between the spreading sequences of the legitimate parties, which represents a major problem of the FHSS technique. The pseudo-random sequence agreement can be realized by using cryptography mechanisms on the upper layers of the system model, inducing high system complexity. However, a lightweight PLS key generation algorithm can be implemented instead, by which the hopping pattern can be negotiated using the random radio characteristics of the wireless propagation environment.

Another FHSS drawback concerns the inefficient use of the frequency band. Although narrowband signals, which occupy small parts of the entire spectrum for very short periods of time, are transmitted, the large number of frequencies needed for reliable FH modulation demands the availability of a wideband frequency spectrum.

Direct Sequence Spread Spectrum. Direct sequence spread spectrum is another modulation technique widely used as a measure against interference and jamming [20]. The approach consists in expanding the transmitted signal into a wider frequency band by simple multiplication to a pseudo-noise (PN) sequence, which is again random. The PN represents a sequence of rectangular pulses with values 1 and -1, also called chips. Since the PN frequency is much higher than that of the transmitted signal, the resultant spectrum of the modulated signal is similar to the spectrum of noise. Thus the narrowband jamming signal, whose power is concentrated over a small bandwidth, affects only a negligible part of the frequency spectrum of the transmitted signal. Moreover, spreading the original signal into a wider bandwidth distributes its entire power over a large number of frequency components so that its power spectral density is significantly reduced and may even fall under the white noise level. In this way, secure legitimate transmission can be carried out without being detected by a malicious user trying to intercept the communication, i.e. privacy enhancement is another advantage of DSSS application.

The larger the frequency of the PN sequence, the wider the spectrum occupied and hence the lower the power spectral density and the influence of jamming interference are. Nevertheless, spreading restrictions must be taken into account for bandwidth efficiency purposes.

The DSSS demodulation at the receiver, called de-spreading, again represents multiplication of the received signal by the same pseudo-random noise sequence used in the transmitter for spreading modulation. In order to obtain reliable results, the PN sequences of both the transmitter and receiver must be negotiated in advance, meaning that synchronization is a major challenge in DSSS, as it is in FHSS. The other disadvantage of FHSS, namely the spectrum utilization problem, also concerns DSSS, as wide bandwidth needs to be occupied for each transmission.

3.2 Jamming Filtering at the Receiver

RZF Receive Filter. An approach proposed in [21] aims to reduce the radio jamming induced by an adversary through special construction of the receive filter at the BS. The method employs the idea introduced in [22] to design the filter in a regularization manner, so as to be adjustable and able to obtain optimal results. It can be applied when the jammer attacks both the training and data transmission phases. The algorithm followed to design the receive filter, called regularized zero-forcing (RZF) and explained in Algorithm 1, uses the channel estimates of both legitimate and jamming channels – $\hat{h}$ and $\hat{g}$, correspondingly. In order to obtain $\hat{g}$, a zero-forcing technique is used. When using RZF for the estimation of jamming channels, it is assumed that at least one pilot sequence exists that is orthogonal to those of LU and remains unused during the pilots' transmission. The jamming channel is estimated by nulling the LU's training sequence through projection of the received signal onto the unused pilot sequence, which is orthogonal to the sequences assigned to LU.

After the process of channel estimation of both legitimate and non-legitimate channels, a linear RZF receive filter is constructed.

Algorithm 1: RZF algorithm

1: Uplink transmission of a training sequence and receiving its corresponding jammed signal at the BS;

2: Obtaining an estimate of the legitimate and jamming channels – $\hat{h}$ and $\hat{g}$, at the BS through zero-forcing;

3: Construction of a regularized linear receive filter, based on both $\hat{h}$ and $\hat{g}$.

The MMSE-type receiver uses conventional MMSE (Minimum Mean Square Error) estimation for filter design. Optimal performance of the MMSE-type receiver is observed when $\hat{h}$ and $\hat{g}$ are calculated with no errors from channel estimation.

The ZF-type receiver aims at eliminating the jamming signal by orthogonal projection of $\hat{h}$ onto $\hat{g}$. It reduces the complexity of the MMSE-type receiver as no matrix inversion is needed for its computations. Moreover, as the numerical results in [21] demonstrate, the ZF-type receive filter improves the rate achieved by the MMSE-type receive filter for the same levels of transmit power used by LU and the jammer. The ZF-type receiver is an RZF filter whose regularization factor converges to zero.

BJM Receive Filter. A promising approach for the mitigation of jamming attacks, that can be used at the physical layer of a MIMO wireless system, is proposed in [23]. The strategy involved consists in the construction of a jamming-resistant receiver based on a blind jamming mitigation (BJM) algorithm. The BJM algorithm can overcome the effect of jamming induced by multiple malicious devices as long as the number of receive antennae at the MIMO receiver exceeds the total number of antennae at the jammer. A main advantage of the BJM receiver is that no channel knowledge is needed to resist an attack, since the receive filter is designed using only the information about the pilot signals sent and received during the training phase. The BJM algorithm is represented in Algorithm 2.

Algorithm 2: BJM algorithm

1:   Uplink   transmission   of   a   training   sequence
$[\tilde{X}(1), \tilde{X}(2), ..., \tilde{X}(L)]$ composed of L number of pilot signals
and receiving its jammed values $[\tilde{Y}(1), \tilde{Y}(2), ..., \tilde{Y}(L)]$ at the
BS;

2: Computation of expected values $E[\mathbf{Y}\mathbf{Y}^H]$ and $E[\mathbf{Y}X^H]$ at the
BS, where X is the uplink signal at the LU, $\mathbf{Y}$ is its corresponding received signal at the BS and $(\cdot)^H$ denotes a Hermiti-
an matrix;

3: Construction of an optimal linear spatial filter P by setting
the MSE of the decoded signal at the BS to zero.

The BJM algorithm aims at designing an optimal linear spatial filter **P** using solely
the knowledge of the training signals. For that reason, the MSE (Mean Squared Error)
of the estimated pilot signals must be minimized by setting its derivative with respect to
P to be zero.

Digital Filter for IEEE 802.15.4. A method for jamming avoidance in IEEE 802.15.4
communication networks, working in the 2450 MHz frequency band, is proposed in
[24]. At the physical layer, the 802.15.4 standard incorporates the DSSS technique for
jamming mitigation. After the message is de-spread at the receiver, a MAC layer 2-byte
cyclic redundancy check (CRC) is performed. The CRC is computed at both the
transmitter and receiver ends and its value is sent together with the payload data. If both
the CRC computations differ from one another, the transmission of the packet is not
considered successful and it has to be retransmitted. This procedure represents an
opportunity for the attacker, since corruption of a symbol per packet results in denial of
service. For that reason, although DSSS is applied in the standard, the system is not
secure against jamming attacks. As interfering with only one symbol per packet is
enough to disrupt the communication, a successful jammer can take advantage and
reduce its energy consumption by undertaking random jamming attack.

For counteracting such a type of intervention, initiated at the centre frequency of a
legitimate signal, the authors of [24] suggest the use of an additional high-pass digital
filter to eliminate the narrowband jamming component. While the low-pass filter
conventionally incorporated in 802.15.4 is capable of suppressing the inter-cell interference and noise, it is not able to affect jamming at the baseband. In contrast, as the
experimental results in [24] show, jamming mitigation is achieved when an additional
high-pass finite impulse response (FIR) filter of low order is added. The operation
sequence of 802.15.4 together with the implementation of the proposed filter is summarized in Algorithm 3.

Two major problems with the proposed filtering are emphasized in [24]. The first relates to SNR degradation when no jamming is present in the system. The other weakness of this technique is in the assumption that the centre frequencies of the legitimate and jamming signals coincide, which is not a realistic scenario. To cope with these drawbacks, in [25], algorithms for filter selection in an adaptive manner are proposed. However all the algorithms explore information about the packet delivery ratio (PDR), which is a parameter computed at the MAC layer and takes the approach out of the scope of this paper, where solely physical layer security methods are discussed.

Algorithm 3: 802.15.4 algorithm with high-pass filter implemented

---

1: Transmission of a signal, spread by DSSS;

2: Signal's de-spreading at the receiver;

3: Filtering of noise and inter-cell interference by low-pass filter and jamming mitigation by high-pass digital filtering;

4: Comparison of the CRC received in the packet with the one calculated at the receiver and raising a flag if they are different.

---

4 Comparison of the Jamming Mitigation Techniques Discussed

This section comprises a comparison of several essential advantages and drawbacks of the methods discussed which can influence their implementation in different types of networks depending on the infrastructure and resources available. The results of the comparison are summarized in Table 1.

As is shown in the table, all the methods discussed need some additional processing to be conducted at the receiver – in FHSS and DSSS the signal is de-spread at the receiver, while all types of filtering are also performed there. Whereas spreading of the signal in a larger frequency band is realized at the transmitter before the message to be sent, none of the filtering methods rely on processing at the transmitter, which makes them advantageous from the ease of implementation point of view. Two more features that are in the favour of the filters proposed as distinct from the spread spectrum approaches relate to the efficient utilization of the available bandwidth and the lack of necessity for time and frequency synchronization to ensure reliable performance.

Although the digital filter design suggested for IEEE 802.15.4 networks is the easiest to be implemented, as only a simple FIR filter of low order must be additionally applied, its main drawback consists in the increased error rates in non-jamming environments. The reason for this is that the resultant band-stop filter attenuates the legitimate signal at the centre frequency when no attack is initiated.

MMSE receive filter, FHSS and DSSS are the three methods that are inappropriate to be used for networks with memory and power constraints, due to their high computational complexity.

The major disadvantage of the two RZF receive filters – MMSE and ZF, is that channel estimation is needed for them to perform successfully. Moreover, the CSI of not only the legitimate but also of the jamming channel must be obtained. For that reason, a purposely unused pilot sequence and large number of training signals are needed. Though the BJM receive filter also explores the training phase with multiple pilots, its operation does not concern any CSI which makes it more accurate in scenarios when jamming is also present in the training phase.

Summarizing the results of the properties compared in Table 1, it can be observed that the digital filter proposed for IEEE 802.15.4 networks is superior to the others from a computational complexity point of view, since only processing at the receiver, which is much simpler than in the other filtering approaches, needs to be applied. Furthermore, as no CSI is needed for its implementation, this technique is not dependent on the channel training phase and can achieve reliable results for jamming mitigation during the pilots' transmission session. Despite its inefficient performance in the absence of jamming, the aforementioned characteristics of the IEEE 802.15.4 digital filter make it the recommended method, particularly in scenarios of resource-constrained wireless systems, where operations are restricted due to computational and power limitations.

Table 1. Comparison of the jamming mitigation techniques at the physical layer

No	Features compared	Jamming mitigation technique					
		Spread spectrum approaches		Receive filter approaches			
		FHSS	DSSS	MMSE	ZF	BJM	Digital filter for IEEE 802.15.4
1	Additional processing at the receiver	✓	✓	✓	✓	✓	✓
2	Additional processing at the transmitter	✓	✓	✗	✗	✗	✗
3	Synchronization needed	✓	✓	✗	✗	✗	✗
4	Increased bandwidth needed	✓	✓	✗	✗	✗	✗
5	Performance loss in non-attack scenarios	✗	✗	✗	✗	✗	✓
6	High computational complexity	✓	✓	✓	✗	✗	✗
7	CSI needed	✗	✗	✓	✓	✗	✗
8	Large number of pilots needed	✗	✗	✓	✓	✓	✗
9	Purposely unused pilot sequence needed	✗	✗	✓	✓	✗	✗

5   Conclusion

In this paper several physical layer security methods for jamming mitigation are described and analysed based on substantial features for their implementation. Observing the main characteristics of the solutions in the comparison, in summary it could be said that a filter that does not rely on channel estimations and can adaptively change its centre frequency, using only physical layer parameters, will be a promising strategy for jamming mitigation.

A topic worthy of further investigation concerns a review of receive filter approaches that can be used in wireless systems to mitigate the effect of a jamming attack whose frequency is variable in time. Such a novel filtering method with tunable bandwidth and central frequency will be proposed in a future work. In order to be applicable in resource-constrained systems, the filter will be of low order and have low computational complexity and high efficiency. Moreover, the adaptive properties of the filter will avoid degradation of the signal in non-jamming environments and in this way will improve the performance of the digital filter proposed for IEEE 802.15.4. Such an approach is proposed in [26] and will be experimentally evaluated in the presence of jamming attacks in a future study.

Acknowledgment. The paper is published with the support of the project No BG05M2OP001-2.009-0033 "Promotion of Contemporary Research Through Creation of Scientific and Innovative Environment to Encourage Young Researchers in Technical University - Sofia and The National Railway Infrastructure Company in The Field of Engineering Science and Technology Development" within the Intelligent Growth Science and Education Operational Programme co-funded by the European Structural and Investment Funds of the European Union.

References

1. Wu, Y., Schober, R., Ng, D.W.K., Xiao, C., Caire, G.: Secure massive MIMO transmission with an active eavesdropper. IEEE Trans. Inf. Theory **62**(7), 3880–3900 (2016)
2. Bash, B.A., Goeckel, D., Towsley, D., Guha, S.: Hiding information in noise: fundamental limits of covert wireless communication. IEEE Commun. Mag. **53**(12), 26–31 (2015)
3. Basciftci, Y.O., Koksal, C.E., Ashikhmin, A.: Securing massive MIMO at the physical layer. In: 2015 IEEE Conference on Communications and Network Security (CNS), Florence, pp. 272–280 (2015)
4. Miller, R., Trappe, W.: On the vulnerabilities of CSI in MIMO wireless communication systems. IEEE Trans. Mob. Comput. **11**(8), 1386–1398 (2012)
5. Pirzadeh, H., Razavizadeh, S.M., Björnson, E.: Subverting massive MIMO by smart jamming. IEEE Wirel. Commun. Lett. **5**(1), 20–23 (2016)
6. Sinha, P., Jha, Rai, A.K., Bhushan, B.: Security vulnerabilities, attacks and countermeasures in wireless sensor networks at various layers of OSI reference model: a survey. In: 2017 International Conference on Signal Processing and Communication (ICSPC), Coimbatore, pp. 288–293 (2017)
7. Amin, Y.M., Abdel-Hamid, A.T.: Classification and analysis of IEEE 802.15.4 PHY layer attacks. In: 2016 International Conference on Selected Topics in Mobile & Wireless Networking (MoWNeT), Cairo, pp. 1–8 (2016)

8. Muraleedharan, R., Osadciw, L.: Jamming attack detection and countermeasures in wireless sensor network using ant system. In: 2006 SPIE Symposium on Defense and Security, April 2006 (2006)

9. Mpitziopoulos, A., Gavalas, D., Konstantopoulos, C., Pantziou, G.: A survey on jamming attacks and countermeasures in WSNs. IEEE Communications Surveys Tutorials 11(4), 42–56 (2009). Fourth Quarter

10. Zou, Y., Zhu, J., Wang, X., Hanzo, L.: A survey on wireless security: technical challenges, recent advances, and future trends. Proc. IEEE 104(9), 1727–1765 (2016)

11. O'Flynn, C.P.: Message denial and alteration on IEEE 802.15.4 low-power radio networks. In: 2011 4th IFIP International Conference on New Technologies, Mobility and Security, Paris, pp. 1–5 (2011)

12. Jokar, P., Nicanfar, H., Leung, V.C.M.: Specification-based Intrusion Detection for home area networks in smart grids. In: 2011 IEEE International Conference on Smart Grid Communications (SmartGridComm), Brussels, pp. 208–213 (2011)

13. Pelechrinis, K., Iliofotou, M., Krishnamurthy, S.V.: Denial of service attacks in wireless networks: the case of jammers. IEEE Commun. Surv. Tutor. 13(2), 245–257 (2011). Second Quarter

14. Wood, A.D., Stankovic, J.A., Zhou, G.: DEEJAM: defeating energy-efficient jamming in IEEE 802.15.4-based wireless networks. In: 2007 4th Annual IEEE Communications Society Conference on Sensor, Mesh and Ad Hoc Communications and Networks, San Diego, CA, pp. 60–69 (2007)

15. Wood, A.D., Stankovic, J.A., Son, S.H.: JAM: a jammed-area mapping service for sensor networks. In: 24th IEEE Real-Time Systems Symposium, RTSS 2003, Cancun, Mexico, pp. 286–297 (2003)

16. Xu, W., Wood, T., Trappe, W., Zhang, Y.: Channel surfing and spatial retreats: defenses against wireless denial of service. In: Proceedings of the 2004 ACM Workshop on Wireless Security (WiSe), NY, USA, pp. 80–89 (2004)

17. Vadlamani, S., Eksioglu, B., Medal, H., Nandi, A.: Jamming attacks on wireless networks: a taxonomic survey. Int. J. Prod. Econ. 172, 76–94 (2016)

18. Navda, V., Bohra, A., Ganguly, S., Rubenstein, D.: Using channel hopping to increase 802.11 resilience to jamming attacks. In: IEEE INFOCOM 2007 - 26th IEEE International Conference on Computer Communications, Barcelona, pp. 2526–2530 (2007)

19. Bloch, M., Barros, J.: Physical-Layer Security: From Information Theory to Security Engineering. Cambridge University Press, Cambridge (2011)

20. Liu, Y., Ning, P., Dai, H., Liu, A.: Randomized differential DSSS: jamming-resistant wireless broadcast communication. In: IEEE INFOCOM, pp. 1–9 (2010)

21. Do, T.T., Björnson, E., Larsson, E.G.: Jamming resistant receivers for massive MIMO. In: 2017 IEEE International Conference on Acoustics, Speech and Signal Processing (ICASSP), New Orleans, LA, pp. 3619–3623 (2017)

22. Peel, C.B., Hochwald, B.M., Swindlehurst, A.L.: A vector-perturbation technique for near-capacity multiantenna multiuser communication-part I: channel inversion and regularization. IEEE Trans. Commun. 53(1), 195–202 (2005)

23. Zeng, H., Cao, C., Li, H., Yan, Q.: Enabling jamming-resistant communications in wireless MIMO networks. In: 2017 IEEE Conference on Communications and Network Security (CNS), Las Vegas, NV, pp. 1–9 (2017)

24. DeBruhl, B., Tague, P.: Digital filter design for jamming mitigation in 802.15.4 communication. In: 2011 Proceedings of 20th International Conference on Computer Communications and Networks (ICCCN), Maui, HI, pp. 1–6 (2011)

25. DeBruhl, B., Tague, P.: Mitigation of periodic jamming in a spread spectrum system by adaptive filter selection. In: Proceedings of the International Symposium on Photonic and Electromagnetic Crystal Structures, pp. 431–439 (2012)
26. Nikolova, Z., Stoyanov, G., Iliev, G., Poulkov, V.: Complex coefficient IIR digital filters. In: Márquez, F.P.G. (ed.) Digital Filters, Chapter 9, April 2011, pp. 209–239. InTech (2011). ISBN: 978-953-307-190-9

The Analysis of Key Performance Indicators (KPI) in 4G/LTE Networks

Fidel Krasniqi[1], Liljana Gavrilovska[1], and Arianit Maraj[2,3(✉)]

[1] Ss. Cyril and Methodius University in Skopje, Skopje, Republic of Macedonia
[2] Kosovo Telecom, Prishtina 10000, Republic of Kosovo
arianit.maraj@kosovotelecom.com
[3] Faculty of Computer Sciences, AAB College,
Prishtina 10 000, Republic of Kosovo

Abstract. The main challenge of MNOs (Mobile Network Operators) is providing multimedia services with high performance. The 4G/LTE technology has been developed to meet user requirements and provide high network performance. In order to monitor and optimize the network performance, there is a need of using Key Performance Indicators (KPIs). The KPIs can control the quality of provided services and achieved resource utilization. These indicators are categorized into the following subcategories: accessibility, retainability, mobility, integrity and availability. The presented analysis is performed on real network implemented by Telecom of Kosovo (TK) that is the main mobile Operator in Kosovo. Measurements and analysis are focused on a 24-cell cluster of 4G/LTE TK.

Keywords: Multimedia · Mobility · Integrity · Availability · 4G/LTE

1 Introduction

We are living a digital revolution where information is mostly presented in a multimedia context. Costumers do not use only voice and data services, but they are keen to use multimedia services as well. Mobility, supported by mobile communication systems and necessity to communicate at any time and from everywhere, add additional requirements to networking paradigms. In order to meet these growing requirements, mobile technologies have passed through a number of generations from the first generation (1G) to nowadays fourth generation (4G) [1–9], and future 5G and beyond.

A tremendous demand for mobility and higher data rates has resulted in development of more reliable mobile networks. To support these demand,, Telecom of Kosovo (TK) offers different services to its customers, such as voice and data services through various mobile systems, such as 2G, 3G and 4G/LTE [2].

The 4G/LTE technology is still facing some problems such are uninterrupted communication, security and high performance [10–18]. Moreover, the QoS (Quality of Service) and security issues are critical for some basic services, such as VoIP [19–26] and IPTV services [2, 27–30]. The TK also aims to address these issues with high attention, in order to provide services with high quality to its users.§

© ICST Institute for Computer Sciences, Social Informatics and Telecommunications Engineering 2019
Published by Springer Nature Switzerland AG 2019. All Rights Reserved
V. Poulkov (Ed.): FABULOUS 2019, LNICST 283, pp. 285–296, 2019.
https://doi.org/10.1007/978-3-030-23976-3_25

This paper focuses on performance analyses of TK's 4G/LTE network, based on the main KPI performance indicators. More specifically, it is focused on analyzing the following key indicators: *mobility, integrity* and *availability*. The measurements are performed on a segment of the TK's 4G/LTE network in Pristina, consisting of 24 base stations. The notified indicators are measured at network level.

The paper is organized as follows: the next section presents a literature review related to KPI performance analysis in 4G/LTE technology; Sect. 3, delves into general aspects and explains the 4G/LTE network architecture; Sect. 4 and Sect. 5 introduce the KPI performance indicators and demonstrate the importance of their analysis in offering services with high quality in 4G. Section 6 provides analysis of the KPI parameters in TK and Sect. 7 gives concluding remarks.

2   Literature Review

Recently, we are witnessing growing interest in research focusing on KPI performance analysis in 4G/LTE networks. Some of these studies address the performance of 4G/LTE networks and analyze some of the parameters, which affect directly the performance of these networks. Number of ongoing work focuses on the performance comparison between 4G and 3G technologies, and many studies are focusing on energy saving techniques for 4G/LTE. The authors in [2] address some of the main parameters, which affect the network performance (KPI indicators), such as: accessibility and retainability in real network. But, according to our knowledge, none of these studies has addressed jointly the *mobility, integrity* and *availability* in a real and active network.

Authors in [1] analyze the performance and power characteristics of 4G/LTE in comparison with 3G/Wi-Fi networks. They designed a tool for android devices called *4Gtest* attacking more than 3000 users within a two months period of time. They also observed the network performance of LTE networks. Using a comprehensive data set consisting of 5-month traces of 20 smartphone users, the authors in [1] investigate also the energy usage in 3G, LTE, and Wi-Fi networks and evaluate the impact of configuring LTE-related parameters.

Authors in [2] address the KPI performance indicators in order to monitor and optimize the mobile network performance. They are focusing only on two parameters, such as accessibility and the retainability. Measurements and analysis are performed for a 24-cell cluster of real 4G/LTE network. The authors found out that the performance of the 4G/LTE network stays within the recommended values of 3GPP standard and manufacturers. Our work will be a continuation of this work and will analyze some different parameters, which are very important for quality optimization in 4G/LTE networks.

Knowing that one of the main challenges of 4G is security that can prevent a network to be entirely compromised by malicious devices, the authors in [3] are focusing on security aspects of 4G networks. They identify the vulnerability of the handover key management as so called desynchronization attacks. Such attacks jeopardize secure communication between users and mobile networks and are influencing the entire network performance. They explore how the network operators can determine an optimal interval for updates that minimizes the signaling load, while protecting the security of user traffic. The analytical and simulation studies demonstrate the impact of the key update interval on performance criteria such as network topology and user mobility.

The authors in [4] study the security issues and the impact on the performance of 4G/LTE. In 4G networks, the forward key separation plays a vital role in handover process and it can be vulnerable due to the presence of rogue base stations. The periodic update of the root key stored in the base stations can reduce the consequences from different attacks. But, the selection of the best possible key update interval is a vague issue and therefore it is difficult to achieve stability between the degree of the exposed messages and the signaling load. The competitors can sign up into the website multiple times and degrade the performance of a certain web server in 4G network. This paper proposes a method that maintains history/status tables to keep a record of the media access control address in an intranet environment. The performance analysis shows that this proposed system provides better security and significant reduction in latency, and thus improves the overall quality of the 4G.

Authors in [5] observe the performance analysis and optimization of LTE key features. They conclude that the current deployment of the LTE system involves several levels of optimizations and enhancements offered to the users. Authors in [5] focus mainly on LTE features of 3GPP's Release 8 and 9 standards. The performance aspects explain in details the following features/enhancements: LTE connected mode Discontinuous Reception (C-DRX), which is used to conserve the battery of mobile devices, the circuit switch fallback solution (CSFB, a protocol which allows voice to be transmitted over LTE) used to support voice calls over LTE, and multi-input–multiple-output (MIMO) techniques.

Recently, a lot of studies addressed the performance analysis of the 5G networks [6–13]. However, since the 5G era still is not completely standardized and tested, this paper focuses on the most advanced features and performance improvement in 4G/LTE systems, since they will be present for some years from now, especially in the developed countries. The aim in this paper is to analyze the key performance indicators in the real TK's 4G/L network. Moreover, we are focusing on optimizing network parameters in order to offer high perceptual quality to the end users.

3   General Aspects and Network Architecture of 4G/LTE

Due to the continuous increase in requirements for higher capacity and QoS, UMTS technology has faced some design constraints, similar to the limitations that GSM and GPRS faced a decade ago. The 3GPP (Third Generation Partnership Project), decided to redesign two segments of the system; the radio and the backbone segments [2].

The results in today's LTE (Long-Term Evolution) system. The development of the network from the perspective of data rates is presented in Fig. 1. A key requirement for LTE was to facilitate a smooth transition from the current mobile communications systems to the new systems. This is enabled by reusing the current spectrum of previous technologies, resolving interaction between the current and the future systems and the reusing of the existing network infrastructure. All 4G/LTE network interfaces are based on IP (Internet Protocol).

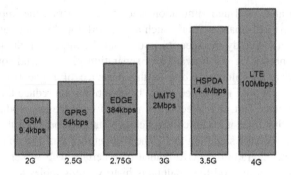

Fig. 1. Network development from GSM to LTE from the perspective of data traffic rates [17]

The overall architecture of the LTE network is similar with the GSM and UMTS networks. In principle, the network is divided on radio network part and central network part, as shown in Fig. 2. However, the number of logical network nodes has been reduced to simplify the architecture leading to flat architecture design. That reduces the implementation cost and the overall delays in the network [2, 18, 26]. Figure 2 presents the general LTE architecture. The tasks of each element is clarified below:

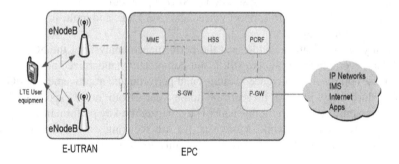

Fig. 2. General LTE architecture according to 3GPP release 8

- *E-UTRAN:* Is responsible for establishing radio communications between the EU (User Equipment) and the Evolved Packet Core (EPC) network. The E-UTRAN consists of eNodeBs, which are base stations (similar to BTS in 2G or NodeB in 3G) that connects and controls the EU's activities with the EPC [2].
- *P-GW (Packet Data Network Gateway):* P-GW is responsible for allocating IP addresses to the UE, QoS implementation and traffic-based charging.
- *S-GW (Serving Gateway):* All IP packets are transmitted via S-GW. Also, the S-GW is used to hold information for carriers when the UE is in idle state.
- *MME (Mobility Management Entity):* MME is considered as the control node that is used to process signaling between the UE and CN.

4   The KPI (Key Performance Indicators) in 4G/LTE Network

The 4G/LTE optimization process is very complex task for the Mobile Network Operators (MNOs). This process includes the effects of multiple factors, which should be considered separately. Today, the MNOs are facing many challenges such as dynamically changing service requirements, technologies, competition, etc. In some ways, this has changed the MNOs' business model and new tools are required not only to manage the network, but also the subscribers. The KPI indicators are used to measure the network performance. These indicators should be selected in a way that they measure end-user performances and the resource utilization [2].

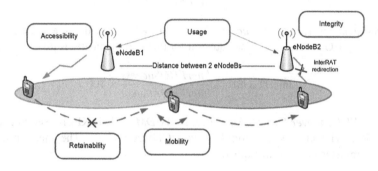

Fig. 3. 4G/LTE Key performances indicators

The main optimization target is to maximize the KPI performances while minimizing the resource utilization [14]. These indicators can be also used to detect unacceptable performances features. In most states, regulatory authorities publish target levels of the KPIs values and the MNOs are obliged to meet them. The 3GPP standardized 4G/LTE networking KPIs are presented in Fig. 3 and are categorized as follows: accessibility, retainability, mobility, integrity and availability [2, 15–17].

5   Key Performance Analysis in 4G/LTE Network; Mobility, Integrity and Availability

The process of optimization of the 4G/LTE network includes the *effects of multiple factors*, which should be considered carefully. The KPI indicators should be selected in a way that they can measure end users' performance [14]. The KPIs can be used for monitoring and optimization of the radio network performances in order to provide better QoS in the 4G/LTE network. In this section, we analyze only three parameters: *mobility, integrity* and *availability*.

5.1 Mobility

Mobility is one of the fundamental functionalities, which enables continuous services for the mobile users inside one particular zone, when they are mobile. Mobility KPIs are related to Handover (HO). The measurements include the number of HOs inside the E-UTRAN (intra HOs) and between the different radio technologies (interRAT HOs). These measurements should be performed on the cell level or for group of cells. The relevan KPIs are:

- *Intra-frequency Handover Success Rate:* This KPI is used to evaluate the intra-frequency HO success rate. This parameter is shown better with the Eq. (1) below:

$$\text{IntraFHOSR} = \frac{IntraFHOSuccess}{IntraFHOAttempt} \times 100\% \tag{1}$$

- *Inter-frequency Handover Success Rate:* This KPI is used for evaluating inter-frequency HO success rate. The equation for this KPI parameter is given in Eq. (2):

$$\text{InterFHOSR} = \frac{InterFHOSuccess}{InterFHOAttempt} \times 100\% \tag{2}$$

- *Inter-RAT Handover Success Rate (LTE to WCDMA):* This KPI is used to evaluate inter-RAT HO success rate from LTE to WCDMA network. The equation for this KPI parameter is given in Eq. (3).

$$\text{IRATHO}_{\text{L2W}_{\text{SR}}} = \frac{IRATHO\_L2W\_success}{IRATHO\_L2W\_Attempt} \times 100\% \tag{3}$$

- *Inter-RAT Handover Success Rate (LTE to GERAN):* This KPI is used to perform the Inter-RAT HO success rate from LTE network to GERAN (Eq 4).

$$\text{IRATHO}_{\text{L2G}_{\text{SR}}} = \frac{IRATHO_{L2G_{success}}}{IRATHO_{L2G_{Attempt}}} \times 100\% \tag{4}$$

5.2 Integrity

The integrity KPI parameters show the impact of E-UTRAN in the quality of service. The following parameters are calculated on the level of cells or clusters:

- *Service Downlink Average Throughput:* This parameter has some indicators, which could be used for actual downlink traffic during the busy hours.
- Service Uplink Average Throughput: This parameter is used to evaluate the uplink traffic during the busy hours.
- *Cell DL Average Throughput:* This parameter evaluates downlink data rate in kbps.
- *Cell UL Average Throughput:* This parameter evaluates uplink data rate in kbps

- *Cell DL Maximum Throughput:* This parameter is calculated based on the maximal bitrate in downlink, measured every second.

$$CellDLMaThp = \frac{CellDLMazTrafVolforEach1s\,(\text{bit})}{1000\,(\text{ms})} \tag{5}$$

- *Cell UL Maximum Throughput:* This parameter is calculated based on the maximal bitrate in uplink, measured every second.

$$CellMaTh = \frac{CellULMazTraffVolforEach1s(bit)}{1000(ms)} \tag{6}$$

5.3   Availability

The availability KPIs measure the percentage of time during which the network cells have not been available. According to 3GPP, one cell is considered to be available when eNodeB can offer E-RAB services in that particular cell.

The E-UTRAN Cell Availability measures the percentage of time in order to evaluate the service degradation and the network performance. This parameter can be measured in the cluster level (eq. 7).

$$Availability = \frac{meas. - \sum RRU.CellUnavailableT}{Meas_{period}} \times 100\% \tag{7}$$

6   Case Study: Analysis of KPI Parameters in TK

This section analyze some of the main KPI indicators in 4G/LTE network implemented in TK: *mobility, integrity* and *availability*. These indicators are measured at the cluster level, whereas the measurements have been performed in a cluster in Pristina City that includes the neighborhoods like "Dardania", "Ulpiana" and part of the "Sunny Hill" [31]. Drive testing are performed using the Swiss Qual Diversity Ranger and Free Rider III equipment. This cluster consists of 24 eNodeB (sites) with a total of 63 cells. The details for a cluster created for measurements in TK network are shown in Table 1.

Table 1. The cluster created for measurement purposes in TK 4G/LTE network [31]

Technology	Sites	Cells
2G	41	115
3G	24	63
4G	24	63

The data is derived from the terminals installed in TK by different manufacturers. The results of the drive test for quality of radio coverage are shown in Fig. 4. They present average values for the entire measurement cluster. The results in Fig. 4 show that generally the value of 67.7% of moderate coverage and quality is achieved and that we are dealing with good coverage and quality in 15.7% of measured samples. Poor coverage areas have been identified also in 15.7% of the measured samples, whereas poor quality and interference in 0.9% of the measured samples.

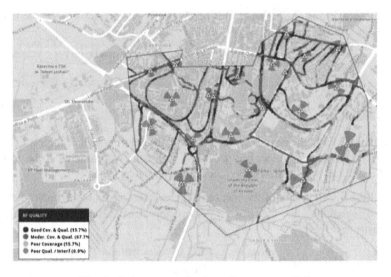

Fig. 4. Drive test results for radio coverage [31]

The results for the measured metrics (number of 4G-4G handovers, number of 3G-4G handovers, number of location update, etc.) in the selected 4G/LTE TK cluster are presented in Table 2. Based on these activities we calculate the 4G network's KPIs (mobility, integrity and availability) for this cluster.

Table 2. Drive Test measurements in the considered cluster [31]

Ping Delay Avg (ms)	53.40
Ping Delay Max (ms)	53.81
Ping Delay Min (ms)	52.99
Call attempt	140
Call reselection from UTRAN	119
Location area Update	254
Handover 4G-4G	978
Handover 3G-4G	289

Based on the technical specification for 3G and 4G networks, the measurements were performed in several TK's clusters. The measured results for mobility are presented in Table 3.

Table 3. Main KPIs for 4G/LTE network in TK for mobility [31]

QoS Area	4G KPI	TK KPIs
Mobility	Intra LTE inter-cell HO SR	–
	Intra eNB HO SR (Src cell)	LTE_5043a
	Intra eNB HO SR (Target Cell)	–
	Inter eNB X2 HO SR (Src C)	LTE_5058b
	Inter eNB X2 HO SR (Tar Ce)	–
	Inter eNB S1 HO SR (Sr. Cell)	LTE_5084a
	Inter eNB S1 HO SR (Targ.C)	–

Mobility: For the TK's 4G observed clusted, according the Table 3, the main KPI parameters that define the mobility are: Intra eNodeB Handover Success rate and Inter E-nodeB X2 HO success rate. The measurement results for these indicators are shown in the Fig. 5.

Fig. 5. Results after measurements in TK network for mobility [31]

For the indicator eNodeB HO success rate, the threshold have been set to 98%, which means that the lower values are reflected in quality, because the performance is degraded. Whereas the values higher than 98% mean that the quality is good. During our measurements, we measured very good values, which are from 99.35% till 99.97%. This means that the mobility from one cell to another is within the recommended values. For the indicator Inter E-nodeB X2 HO, the manufacturer have set the threshold in 96%. Our results show that the values for this indicator in TK network are from 98% to 99.84%.

Throughput (Integrity): In 4G/LTE TK network the main indicators which measure the bit rate in downlink are: Max App DL throughput (kbps) and Avg App DL throughput (kbps), whereas for uplink Max App UL throughput (kbps) and Avg App UL throughput (kbps). The obtained values for Uplink and Downlink for this TK network are the following:

- Max App DL throughput = 60 Mbps
- Avg App DL throughput = 47 Mbps
- Max App UL throughput = 34 Mbps
- Avg App UL throughput = 30 Mbps

These values are achieved using the following transmission environment: bandwidth in LTE TK network is 200 MHz for uplink and downlink, multiplexing used is FDD, mobile devices of CAT 3 Samsung S5, the speed of the car is about 20 km/h. The measurements have been performed during busy traffic hours in Pristina City. Even under these conditions, the measurements show a great network performance.

Availability: The availability is analyzed in the TK's 4G/LTE TK segment. The results are presented in the Table 4.

Table 4. Availability for 4G/LTE network in TK [31]

4G	KPI	Availability
June 2018	ALU	96.92%
	NOKIA	97.68%
	Total	97.21%
	Threshold	>99%

The results presented in Table 4 show that the availability depends on the different manufacturers. These availability's values are lower than the threshold (>99%). Analyzing the entire network, we found that in the network designed and covered by ALCATEL, the indicator that measures availability is 96.81%, whereas in the Nokia part the indicator that measures availability is 97.53%. The average of this indicator (for Alcatel and Nokia) for the entire network is 97.17%.

The KPI indicators allow us to indicate the network performance. The results clearly show that availability has lower values than the threshold (threshold > 99%).

7 Conclusions and Future Work

The innovations of multimedia technologies and services are affecting the way of doing businesses in everyday life. Managing QoS/QoE, attracting and retaining customers, improving user satisfaction and understanding the subscriber base, can significantly contribute to access successful telecommunication services.

In this paper we presented a case study performed over the TK's 4G/LTE network segment.. We analyze three of the main KPI indicators: *mobility, integrity* and *availability*. The data obtained from the measurements and analysis show high performance of the 4G/LTE TK network. The only KPI indicator, which is not within the recommended 3GPP and manufacturers' values, is *availability*. The results shows that the average value of this indicator, for both manufacturers (Nokia and Alcatel), is below the required threshold (higher than 99%). This problem is due to the power shortages in some zones, transmission problems, and hardware defects. The *mobility* and *integrity* are within the recommended values.

The results of this study shows that the main challenge for this real network is the huge increase in the demand for access to 4G/LTE services and the rapid growth in the volume of data traffic that affects the network performance. The possible degradation of the analysed KPIs directs TK to increase the network coverage of 4G/LTE, especially in some areas where coverage does not meet the criteria in accordance with standards and manufacturers. From measurement results and analysis, we have learned that the TK needs to make greater efforts and investments to cover with signal these problematic areas, particularly with 3G and 4G, as the only alternative for having access to Internet and other multimedia services. It is recommended to have particular tools for optimization, that can be implemented on both hardware and software upgrade systems. The constant checking of the KPIs should enable adaptation to increasing data traffic.

Our future work will be focused on analyzing the QoS and QoE in the overall 4G/LTE network implemented in TK. Also, we will try to address the main challenges that the Operators will face during the transition process from 4G to 5G technologies.

References

1. Huang, J., et al.: A close examination of performance and power characteristics of 4G LTE networks. In: Proceedings of the 10th International Conference on Mobile Systems, Applications, and Services. ACM (2012)
2. Krasniqi, F., Maraj, A., Blaka, E.: Performance analysis of mobile 4G/LTE networks. In: 2018 South Eastern European Design Automation, Computer Engineering, Computer Networks and Social Media Conference (SEEDA-CECNSM), Kastoria, Greece, 22–24 September 2018. IEEE/Scopus (2018)
3. Han, C., Choi, H.: Security analysis of handover key management in 4G LTE/SAE networks. IEEE Trans. Mob. Comput. 13(2), 457–468 (2014). https://doi.org/10.1109/tmc.2012.242
4. Krishnamoorthy, V., Mathi, S.: Security enhancement of handover key management based on media access control address in 4G LTE networks. In: 2015 IEEE International Conference on Computational Intelligence and Computing Research (ICCIC), Madurai, pp. 1–5 (2015). https://doi.org/10.1109/iccic.2015.7435819
5. ElNashar, A., El-saidny, M.A., Sherif, M.: Performance analysis and optimization of LTE key features: C-DRX, CSFB, and MIMO. In: Design, Deployment and Performance of 4G-LTE Networks: A Practical Approach. Wiley (2014). https://doi.org/10.1002/9781118703434.ch4
6. Aryanti, D.R., Haryadi, S.: Analysis of Harmony in Gradation index on 5G cellular network: quantitative analysis. In: 2017 11th International Conference on Telecommunication Systems Services and Applications (TSSA), Lombok, pp. 1–5 (2017). https://doi.org/10.1109/tssa.2017.8272912
7. Ding, Z., et al.: On the performance of non-orthogonal multiple access in 5G systems with randomly deployed users. arXiv preprint arXiv:1406.1516 (2014)
8. Bae, J.S., et al.: Architecture and performance evaluation of MmWave based 5G mobile communication system. In: 2014 International Conference on Information and Communication Technology Convergence (ICTC). IEEE (2014)
9. Lei, L., et al.: Prototype for 5G new air interface technology SCMA and performance evaluation. China Commun. 12(Supplement), 38–48 (2015)
10. Wang, Y., Jing, X., Jiang, L.: Challenges of system-level simulations and performance evaluation for 5G wireless networks. IEEE Access 2, 1553–1561 (2014)
11. Tesema, F.B., et al.: Mobility modeling and performance evaluation of multi-connectivity in 5G intra-frequency networks. In: 2015 IEEE GLOBECOM Workshops (GC Wkshps). IEEE (2015)

12. Fan, W., et al.: A step toward 5G in 2020: low-cost OTA performance evaluation of massive MIMO base stations. IEEE Antennas Propag. Mag. **59**(1), 38–47 (2017)
13. Zhang, J., et al.: Mobility enhancement and performance evaluation for 5G ultra dense networks. In: 2015 IEEE Wireless Communications and Networking Conference (WCNC). IEEE (2015)
14. Reunanen, J., Salo, J., Luostari, R.: LTE key performance indicator optimization, November 2015. https://doi.org/10.1002/9781118912560.ch12
15. GPP Technical Specification 24.301, 'Non-Access-Stratum (NAS) protocol for Evolved Packet System (EPS); Stage 3', June 2011
16. GPP Technical Specification 32.450 v9.1.0, KPIs for E-UTRAN (Release 9) (2010)
17. GPP Technical Specification 36201 v8.3.0, LTE Physical Layer general Description (Release 8) (2009)
18. Er Sh, A.: LTE Network Architecture. Link: http://ershoeb.blogspot.nl/2016/03/lte-network-architecture.html. Accessed 11 Jan 2018
19. Maraj, D., Sefa, R., Maraj, A.: QoS Evaluation for different WLAN standards. In: 2015 23rd International Conference on Software, Telecommunications and Computer Networks (SoftCOM), Split, pp. 190–194 (2015). https://doi.org/10.1109/softcom.2015.7314115
20. Maraj, D., et al.: Performance analysis of WLAN 802.11G/N standards using OPNET (Riverbed) application. In: 2015 57th ELMAR, Zadar, pp. 129–132 (2015). https://doi.org/10.1109/elmar.2015.7334513
21. Shatri, B., Maraj, A., Imeri, I.: Broadband Wireless Access (BWA) implementation in NGN network. In: Communication Theory, Reliability, and Quality of Service, CTRQ 2008 (2008)
22. Kryvinska, N., Strauss, C., Auer, L.: Next Generation applications mobility management with SOA - a scenario-based analysis, pp 415–420. IEEE (2010)
23. Kryvinska, N., Strauss, C., Collini-Nocker, B., Zinterhof, P.: A scenario of service-oriented principles adaptation to the telecom providers service delivery platform, pp 265–271. IEEE (2010)
24. Kryvinska, N., Strauss, C., Collini-Nocker, B., Zinterhof, P.: A scenario of voice services delivery over enterprise W/LAN networked platform, p 332. ACM Press (2008)
25. Maraj, A., Imeri, I.: WiMAX integration in NGN network, architecture, protocols and Services. WSEAS Trans. Commun. **8**(7), 708–717 (2009)
26. Kryvinska, N., Strauss, C., Collini Nocker, B., Zinterhof, P.: Enterprise network maintaining mobility – architectural model of services delivery. Int. J. Pervasive Comput. Commun. **7**, 114–131 (2011). https://doi.org/10.1108/17427371111146419
27. Maraj, A., Shehu, A., Miho Mitrushi, R.: Studying of different parameters that affect QoS in IPTV systems. In: 9PthP WSEAS International Conference on Telecommunication and Informatics (TELE-INFO 2010), Catania, Italy, 29–31 May 2010 (2010). ISSN: 1790-5117, ISBN: 978-954-92600-2-1
28. Arianit, M., et al.: Bandwidth allocation for multiple IPTV users sharing the same link: a case study of Telecom of Kosovo. Turk. J. Electr. Eng. Comput. Sci. **25**(4), 3227–3239 (2017)
29. Shehu, A., et al.: Analysis of QoS requirements for delivering IPTV over WiMAX technology. In: Conference on Software, Telecommunications and Computer Networks (SoftCOM), vol. 2, no. 1, pp. 380–385 (2010)
30. Maraj, A., Rugova, S.: Analysis of routing metrics for offering IPTV over WiMAX using fuzzy logic. WSEAS Trans. Commun. **9**(7), 439–451 (2010), ISSN: 1109-2742
31. Blaka, E.: Analiza e performances se rrjetave mobile 4G/LTE-rast studimi VALA. Mater thesis, AAB College, Faculty of Computer Sciences, under supervision of Prof. Arianit Maraj Prishtina (2018)

A Novel MAMP Antenna Array Configuration for Efficient Beamforming

Dimitra D. Kalyva$^{(\boxtimes)}$, Dimitrios K. Ntaikos, and Constantinos B. Papadias

Athens Information Technology, 44 Kifissias Ave., 15125 Athens, Greece
{dkal,dint,cpap}@ait.gr

Abstract. Multi-Active Multi-Passive (MAMP) antenna arrays with reduced number of active elements are studied, for matching the patterns of all-active uniform linear arrays. Based on previous work on MAMP antenna arrays, we present a novel configuration, namely a circular one. By jointly calculating the PEs' loads and baseband weights of the proposed MAMP array, we can produce a radiation pattern similar to that of a ULA with accuracy up to 97.5%, while the number of AEs is reduced by 33% and in some cases with suppressed side lobes. Moreover, a reduction in the width of the array by 3 times is achieved. Thus, the complexity, compactness and cost of the antenna array can be reduced without compromising the quality of the resulting beam.

Keywords: Multi-active multi-passive (MAMP) arrays ·
Hybrid antenna arrays · Load and weight optimization

1 Introduction

Multi-active multi-passive (MAMP) antenna arrays are RF devices that consist of a small number of active elements (AE) where each AE is surrounded by multiple passive elements (PEs). The PEs are connected to variable loads, usually capacitors. Adjusting these load values leads to changes in the far field radiation pattern of the MAMP antenna. This enables the implementation of adaptive control techniques on the antenna. To this end, a MAMP antenna system of n active elements can shape a directive beam in such a way that it matches the beam of a conventional m-element uniform linear array (ULA), where $m > n$. The efficiency of this methodology is identified not only in the gain of the transmission, but also in the number of RF chains used, which is considerably smaller. In this paper, we are investigating a circular MAMP (C-MAMP) layout. The logic behind the creation of the C-MAMP antenna array lies in the theory of parasitic antennas [1].

While the single-active multi-passive (SAMP) antenna arrays, consisting of a single AE and multiple PEs, have been thoroughly studied, little has been said about the MAMP antenna arrays. This paper is based on and is an extention of the study presented in [2]. While in classical all-active arrays beamforming involves baseband signal processing, so that the gain is maximized or minimized

© ICST Institute for Computer Sciences, Social Informatics and Telecommunications Engineering 2019
Published by Springer Nature Switzerland AG 2019. All Rights Reserved
V. Poulkov (Ed.): FABULOUS 2019, LNICST 283, pp. 297–305, 2019.
https://doi.org/10.1007/978-3-030-23976-3_26

depending on the desired directions, in parasitic antenna arrays beamforming is achieved through the control of the loads of the passive elements. This adaptive control is implemented via the *Alternating Optimization Stochastic Beamforming Algorithm* (AO-SBA), which is rigorously explained in [2].

This work is organized as follows: in Sect. 2 we present the considered MAMP architecture; a short summary and the state-of-the-art methods are presented in Sect. 3; Sect. 4 is devoted to the presentation of our simulation results; finally, Sect. 5 summarizes the findings.

2   MAMP Antenna Arrays

In this paper we introduce a new circular topology of the MAMP antenna array, which differs from the previously studied rectangular MAMP (R-MAMP), in the way the parasitic elements are placed. More specifically, while the AEs remain parallel to the z-axis, with their centers lying on the x-axis at a distance $l_a = \lambda/2$ from one another, the PEs are positioned in such a way that each cluster forms a circle around its corresponding AE, of radius $l_p = 0.22\lambda$, lying in the x-y plane, as it is presented in the following Fig. 1. Hence, should the position of an AE be: $(x_a, 0)$, then the corresponding positions of the N_p PEs of its cluster would be given by the expression:

$$x_{pi}(i = 1 : N_p) = x_a + l_{pi} \cdot cos(\theta_i)$$
$$y_{pi}(i = 1 : N_p) = l_{pi} \cdot sin(\theta_i)$$

where θ_i denotes the angle between the $x - axis$ and the line segment with edges $(x_a, 0)$ and (x_{pi}, y_{pi}).

It is noted that since the PEs are placed symmetrically around the AE, angle θ_i will vary depending on the number of PEs selected each time.
We denote:

$$N_a : \text{the number of AEs}$$
$$N_p : \text{the number of PEs (constituting each AE cluster)}$$

And so it will be:

$$\theta_i(i = 1 : N_p) = \frac{360}{N_p} \cdot (i - 1)$$

However, the topology described in this paper, is vulnerable to present overlaps between the PEs of neighboring clusters belonging to neighboring AEs. In order to avoid such phenomena, the two distances l_a and l_p must satisfy the following condition:

$$l_a > 2 \cdot l_p$$

As far as the antenna elements are concerned, they are considered to be linear and ideal cylindrical dipoles of length $l = \lambda/2$ and of radius $r = \lambda/100$.

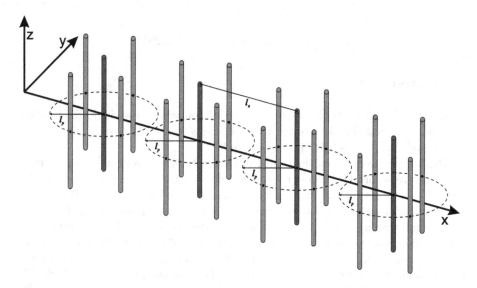

Fig. 1. Layout of the proposed C-MAMP antenna array with 4AEs (red dipoles) and 4PEs (blue dipoles) per AE. (Color figure online)

In order to compute the impedance matrix Z, all mutual effects that appear among all the side-by-side dipoles are taken into account, regardless of the fact that the inter-element distance might be large enough for it to be omitted.

The radiation intensity of the antenna, α, the complex normalized current vector on the antenna elements, i, and the voltage vector, v, are described through the expressions:

$$\alpha(\phi) = i^T \cdot s(\phi)$$
$$i(X, v) = (Z + X)^{-1} \cdot v$$

where: $s(\phi)$ is the respective steering vector at a given azimuth angle ϕ_0, X is the load reactance matrix that adjusts the radiation pattern of the antenna array and Z is the matrix representing the mutual impedance between each and every pair of the antenna elements.

The analytical expressions of the matrices X and Z for our case, where $N_a = 4$ and $N_p = 6$, are then given as:

$$X_i = \begin{vmatrix} x_i(1) & 0 & 0 & 0 & 0 & 0 & 0 \\ 0 & x_i(2) & 0 & 0 & 0 & 0 & 0 \\ 0 & 0 & x_i(3) & 0 & 0 & 0 & 0 \\ 0 & 0 & 0 & R_a & 0 & 0 & 0 \\ 0 & 0 & 0 & 0 & x_i(4) & 0 & 0 \\ 0 & 0 & 0 & 0 & 0 & x_i(5) & 0 \\ 0 & 0 & 0 & 0 & 0 & 0 & x_i(6) \end{vmatrix}$$

$$X = \begin{vmatrix} X_1 & 0_{7\times7} & 0_{7\times7} & 0_{7\times7} \\ 0_{7\times7} & X_2 & 0_{7\times7} & 0_{7\times7} \\ 0_{7\times7} & 0_{7\times7} & X_3 & 0_{7\times7} \\ 0_{7\times7} & 0_{7\times7} & 0_{7\times7} & X_4 \end{vmatrix}$$

$$Z = [z_{ij}] \quad : (i,j) \in \{(1...28), (1...28)\}$$

3 State-of-the-art

Although quite a few studies have been carried concerning the single-RF ESPAR antennas, [3], little has been done when it comes to MAMPs, and therefore the bibliography on this subject is very limited.

Researchers working on the topic have presented their work in [4], where they show the cross-correlation coefficient between an estimated beam pattern and a desired one, to optimize a function that calculates the loads of a SAMP antenna. The minimization task was approached by using a steep gradient scheme based on a simultaneous perturbation stochastic approximation (SPSA) method [5]. The gradient was approximated by using the two-sided finite-difference method [6]. Additionly, in [4], the authors have incorporated a smoothing technique, which provides better convergence properties [7]. However, since only a single AE antenna was considered, the steering of the beam was mainly enabled due to the circular geometry of the proposed antenna. Thus, beam steering could not have been achieved solely by the tuning of the loads, supposing that a linear geometry had been selected. Their algorithm is known as the Stochastic Beamforming Algorithm (SBA).

One rather straightforward solution for optimizing the radiation pattern of a MAMP antenna array and enabling the rotation of the beam, is to directly extend the SBA for SAMP antennas in [4] to the MAMP arrays. In our case though, a different initialization of the non-zero voltage (weight) values proved essential. Instead of choosing unitary initial values, *the considered complex weights are given by the steering vector of the corresponding ULA* (ULA with AEs equal to those of the MAMP) at a certain direction of arrival ϕ_0.

As we will present in the numerical evaluation section, the estimation performance of this approach proved to be quite limited. After extensive experimentation, we used the following extensions of the SBA for the MAMP antenna arrays, depending on the selection of its smoothing sequence $(\beta_m)_{m=1}^{M}$:

- SBA-SS1: Stochastic Beamforming Algorithm with the *smoothing sequence 1*, as the one used in [4], i.e., $\{40, 35, 30, 20, 10, 2.8, 2.4, 2, 1.5, 1, 0.75, 0.4, 0.2, 0.1\}$.
- SBA-SS2: Stochastic Beamforming Algorithm with the *smoothing sequence 2*, $\beta_m = \beta_{m-1}/2$, $\beta_0 = 5$, $m = 1, \ldots, 13$. This selected sequence has optimal decaying, as reported in [8].

4   Numerical Evaluation

For our numerical investigation we examine the effect of the PEs on multiple active ones. More precisely, we attempt to match the radiation pattern of a 6-element ULA with the resulting beam of a C-MAMP array consisting of 4 AEs and 6 PEs. To that extend, an improvement of the radiation pattern of a 4-ULA is achieved, without adding any further active elements, but only passive ones.

As mentioned above, the algorithm presented in [2] has been used, so as to compute the optimization loads and weights (voltage vector). The parameters set in the algorithm are: $\tau = 100$, $N_m = 10.000$, $T_{er} = 10^{-6}$, $eps = 10^{-10}$, $\beta_m = \frac{\beta_{m-1}}{3}$, $\beta_0 = 3$, $m = 1, ..., 25$.

The initial topology under examination is the C-MAMP with 4 AEs and 4 PEs at an azimuth angle of $\phi_0 = 90°$, which is compared to the 4-ULA and 6-ULA. In order to validate the improvement of the resulting beam as the number of PEs increases, we also use 6 PEs, while maintaining the azimuth angle and the number of AEs. The resulting figures confirm our initial assumptions, and an improvement is observed. More specifically, not only does the steady state error decrease, but also the convergence towards it is smoother. The latter is due to the fact that, by increasing the number of parasitic elements the algorithm converges to its stable state more quickly, and therefore, the resulting curve becomes smoother for the same number of iterations m. According to Fig. 2(a) and (b), we see that the C-MAMP antenna matches quite well the pattern of the 6-ULA in both cases (the mismatch error is around 6.83% and 3.23%, respectively). In Figs. 3(a) and (b), where we present the azimuthal plane of the radiation pattern, it is obvious that the C-MAMP matches accurately the pattern of the 6-ULA.

Next, we evaluate the flexibility of our proposed C-MAMP antenna array configuration in terms of its ability to rotate the radiation pattern towards any direction, and thus we change the azimuth angle to $\phi_0 = 60°$, while the topology still has 4 PEs per AE. As depicted in Fig. 4(a), the C-MAMP array does converge to the pattern of the 6-ULA, with a matching error of around 5.86%. In order to reduce the matching error, we increase the number of the PEs to 6, and observe that it improves (in Fig. 4(b) the matching error is around 5.58%). As explained in the previous case, similarly here, apart from the error reduction, we observe more smoothness in its convergence. However, the smoothness is noted only for $m > 10$, whereas for $5 < m < 10$ there is a steep increase of the error. This may be caused by insufficient number of iterations N_m of the algorithm at that point, or by the need of a slightly different parameter, among those used in the adaptive algorithm. In any case, this doesn't affect the final result significantly, since the steady state error convergence is as expected. In Figs. 5(a) and (b) we notice the matching of the radiation patterns.

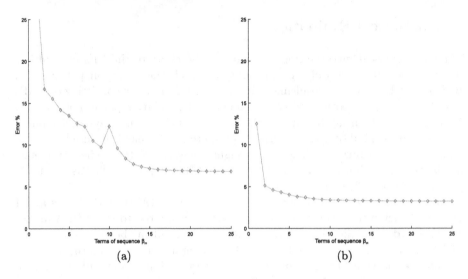

Fig. 2. Matching error at $\phi_0 = 90°$ between a 6-ULA and the C-MAMP with: (a) 4AEs and 4PEs and, (b) 4AEs and 6PEs.

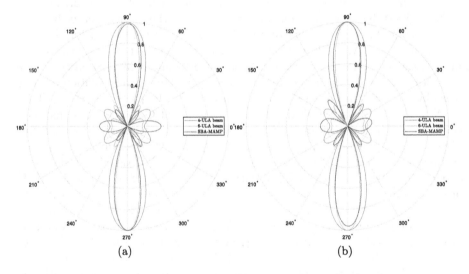

Fig. 3. Radiation pattern comparison at $\phi_0 = 90°$ between 4-ULA, 6-ULA and C-MAMP with: (a) 4AEs and 4PEs and, (b) 4AEs and 6PEs.

As a final confirmation step, we set the azimuth angle to $\phi_0 = 45°$, maintaining the number of PEs at 4. Figure 6(a) confirms the adaptability of the C-MAMP antenna array, since the resulting matching error is around 3.52%. In addition to that, in Fig. 7(a) we observe a narrower beam with a significant reduction in the side lobes. Finally, the case of $\phi_0 = 70°$ azimuth angle is considered, although, this time the number of PEs used is set to 8. Once again, the

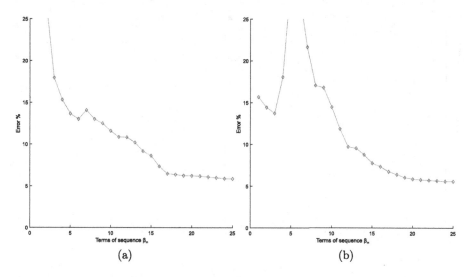

Fig. 4. Matching error at $\phi_0 = 60°$ between a 6-ULA and a MAMP antenna array with: (a) 4AEs and 4PEs and, (b) 4AEs and 6PEs.

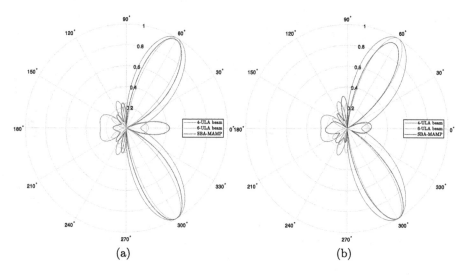

Fig. 5. Radiation pattern comparison at $\phi = 60°$ between a 4-ULA, a 6-ULA and a MAMP antenna array with: (a) 4AEs and 4PEs and, (b) 4AEs and 6PEs.

matching error in Fig. 6(b) is around 2.49% and the produced beam in Fig. 7(b) matches to a great extend, the radiation pattern of the 6-ULA. In both cases, the figures referring to the steady state errors reconfirm our above mentioned comments concerning their convergence.

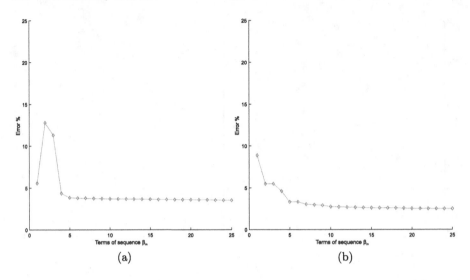

Fig. 6. Matching error between a 6-ULA and a MAMP antenna array with: (a) 4AEs and 4PEs at 45° and, (b) 4AEs and 8PEs at 70°.

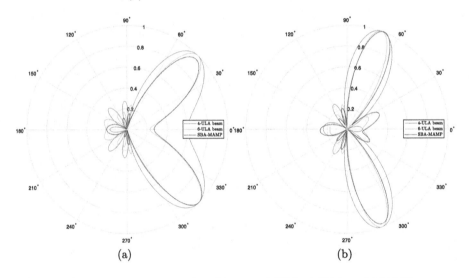

Fig. 7. Radiation pattern comparison between 4-ULA, 6-ULA and MAMP antenna array with: (a) 4AEs and 4PEs at 45° and, (b) 4AEs and 8PEs at 70°.

5   Conclusions

In this paper, an altered version of the R-MAMP antenna array with a circular topology of the passive elements was proposed. The so-called C-MAMP antenna array provides greater compactness compared to the R-MAMP topology (0.44λ compared to 1.2λ on the y-direction), which can be very useful when referring to large structures. Both the efficiency of the topology according to the number of passive elements used, and its versatility relative to pattern rotation, were examined. As evidenced by the numerical simulations, the C-MAMP can successfully replicate the radiation pattern of the 6-ULA, in various azimuth angles, by reducing the number of AEs from 6 to 4. This corresponds to a 33% reduction of the RF chains needed to create the same beam pattern, thus reducing the overall cost of operating such a MAMP antenna array. Finally, an increase in the number of the passive elements has been shown to provide greater accuracy in the results. Future expansions of the problem include the development of an actual C-MAMP antenna system, in order to compare the simulated results with measured ones. This will verify the correctness of the proposed model, as well as its efficiency in real-life problems.

References

1. Kalis, A., Kanatas, A.G., Papadias, C.B.: Parasitic Antenna Arrays for Wireless MIMO Systems. Springer, New York (2014). https://doi.org/10.1007/978-1-4614-7999-4
2. Papageorgiou, G.K., Ntaikos, D.K., Papadias, C.B.: Efficient beamforming with multi-active multi-passive antenna arrays. In: 2018 IEEE 19th International Workshop on Signal Processing Advances in Wireless Communications (SPAWC), pp. 1–5, June 2018. https://doi.org/10.1109/SPAWC.2018.8445890
3. Marantis, L., et al.: The pattern selection capability of a printed ESPAR antenna. In: 2017 11th European Conference on Antennas and Propagation (EUCAP), pp. 922–926, March 2017. https://doi.org/10.23919/EuCAP.2017.7928841
4. Barousis, V., et al.: A stochastic beamforming algorithm for ESPAR antennas. IEEE Antennas Wirel. Propag. Lett. **7**, 745–748 (2008)
5. Spall, J.C.: Introduction to Stochastic Search and Optimization: Estimation, Simulation, and Control, vol. 65. Wiley, New York (2005)
6. Wilmott, P., Howison, S., Dewynne, J.: The Mathematics of Financial Derivatives: a Student Introduction. Cambridge University Press, Cambridge (1995)
7. Styblinski, M., Tang, T.S.: Experiments in nonconvex optimization: stochastic approximation with function smoothing and simulated annealing. Neural Netw. **3**(4), 467–483 (1990)
8. Chin, D.C.: A more efficient global optimization algorithm based on Styblinski and Tang. Neural Netw. **7**(3), 573–574 (1994)

Virtual Engineering and Simulations

Design Development of a Car Fan Shroud Based on Virtual Prototypes

Konstantin Kamberov[✉] [iD], Blagovest Zlatev [iD], and Todor Todorov

Laboratory "CAD/CAM/CAE in Industry",
FIT, Technical University – Sofia, 1756 Sofia, Bulgaria
{kkamberov, bzlatev, ttodorov}@3clab.com

Abstract. The study aims to present virtual prototyping applicability for design and evaluation of complex system of automotive industry. It presents a new principle design solution and illustrates design development, based entirely on virtual prototyping. The design concept is to provide solution for radiators fan and its shroud for high speeds when the fan acts like resistance. Multiple design variants are examined using virtual prototype of radiators, fan, shroud and all engine components. Developed design variants are compared by their performance both at low and high speeds.

Keywords: Car fan · Shroud · CFD · Virtual prototype

1 Introduction

Computational fluid dynamics or CFD is the analysis of systems involving fluid flow, heat transfer and associated phenomena such as chemical reactions by means of computer-based simulation. The technique is very powerful and spans a wide range of industrial and non-industrial application areas [1, 2, 9, 10].

In the early years, the development of methods to numerically solve the equations of fluid dynamics, most research performed was of interest to the CFD community and was used mainly for research purposes. However, after a level of maturation of CFD numerical methods, practical applications of CFD analysis has been increased significantly last years because it is considered as a mature discipline now that can contribute considerably to the design, analysis and development of engineering systems involving fluid flows. CFD simulations provide insight into the details of how products and processes work, and allow new products to be evaluated in the computer, even before prototypes have been built. This is driven by the Virtual Prototyping (VP) ability to cut down developmental costs by minimizing physical testing [7] which can result in considerably reduced design cycle time and design costs [1, 2, 8].

The study aims to present CFD analyses and virtual prototyping applicability for design and evaluation of complex system of automotive industry. It should provide solution for the fan and its shroud for high speeds when the fan acts like resistance. When cooling components are combined to form a cooling package, it can be expected that interactions between the components will modify their flow resistance characteristics. Recent requirement for the motor fan of radiator cooling are the large air flow

V. Poulkov (Ed.): FABULOUS 2019, LNICST 283, pp. 309–317, 2019.
https://doi.org/10.1007/978-3-030-23976-3_27

performance and electrical power consumption reduction. Large air flow is required mainly because of current increased application of downsized engines and diesel engines with large heat generation. On the other hand, reduction of electric power consumption for each component is a significant factor for enhancement of fuel and electric power consumption efficiency in HEVs and EVs driven by electricity [3, 4, 6].

The study shows complete process, starting with building the concept of physics, detailed review of virtual prototype itself, obtained results and comparison and their analysis. The major target is to obtain design with minimal resistance at all examined three drive velocities.

2 Concept of Physics

Main idea is to use an idealized model that contains examined components – shroud, fan and engine and inlet channel. The concept is shown on Fig. 1. Main target is to reach an optimal design and explore possibility to include openings that tends to increase fluid flow passing through motor space with minimal recirculation (bypass) flows. The study is carried out at 3 drive velocities: 10 km/h, 40 km/h and 240 km/h. Fan motor rotates at 2500 min^{-1} and is to be included by its pressure/fluid flow function. Thus, several ranges are to be covered [5].

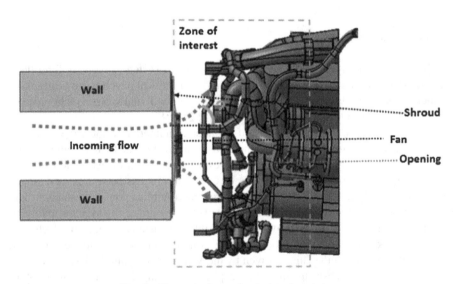

Fig. 1. Concept of examined virtual prototype

Simulation results for different design variants will be compared by some major parameters that are tracked as mass flow rate through entire model (needs to be increased) and bypass (recirculation) through air guides (negative factor).

Input data includes detailed geometry models. These models need clean-up and simplification as to obtain input model suitable for CFD optimization. Some assumptions are defined as follows: simplified models of surrounding components (side covers and rear cover) are included as to present more accurate fluid flow boundaries; all components will be simplified maximally as to fasten and facilitate optimization process. For instance, the shroud is simplified as to facilitate computational model without decreasing significantly its accuracy. Major simplifications are performed over engine components. All assumptions are shown graphically on Fig. 2.

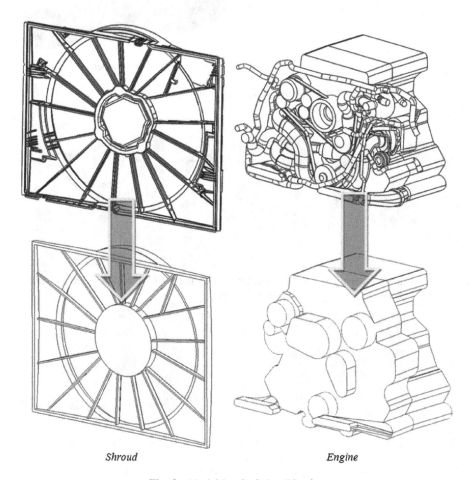

Shroud   Engine

Fig. 2. Model level of simplification

3 Virtual Prototype

The virtual prototype includes fluid volume only (all solid components are presented by their walls). CAD model of examined fluid area is shown on Fig. 3 as well as prepared mesh model.

Prepared model allows easy to implement various designs of the shroud. Examined 5 design variants are shown on Fig. 4.

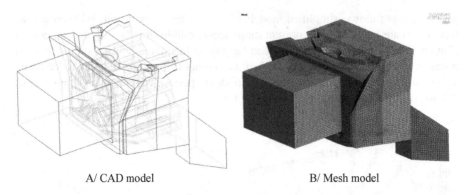

A/ CAD model   B/ Mesh model

Fig. 3. Virtual prototype used in engineering analyses

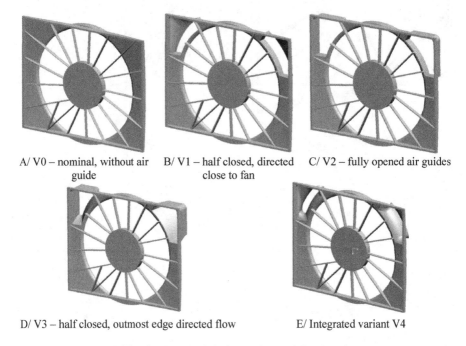

A/ V0 – nominal, without air   B/ V1 – half closed, directed   C/ V2 – fully opened air guides
guide   close to fan

D/ V3 – half closed, outmost edge directed flow   E/ Integrated variant V4

Fig. 4. Examined design variants of the shroud

The applied fluid flow boundary conditions are shown on Fig. 5. All models use velocity set on inlet – determined by incoming fluid flow. The fan is presented by its characteristic that is predefined by the manufacturer. The system is opened at the rear side where two outlets to atmosphere are defined.

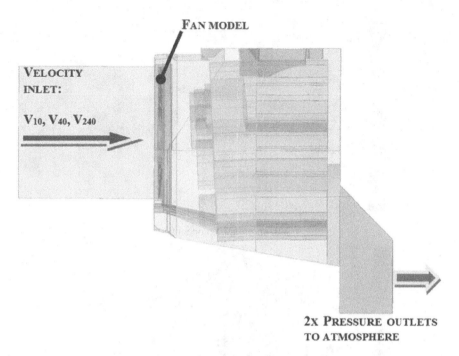

Fig. 5. Applied boundary conditions

4   Virtual Prototyping Results and Comparison

The virtual prototyping consists of 15 separate analyses performed in total and there is a large set of data to be considered. General overviews of obtained results are reported by fluid flow parameters presented by velocity vectors in vertical and horizontal planes. This is shown for all variants, for 10 km/h speed of incoming fluid flow, on Fig. 6.

All engineering analyses over four variants for shroud openings as well as initial (NO AIRGUIDE) design are presented also by the next parameters:

- Total mass flow rate (in kg/s) – represents fluid flow through entire model and is measured on its inlet;
- Mass flow rate through air guides;
- Pressure drop for entire system.

These parameters are sorted out in Table 1 for each of examined design variants.

5   Results Analysis

Initially, the presented in results are shown as graphics on Fig. 7 to allow easy comparison and to illustrate next major conclusions concerning examined variants V1 to V4 (V0 – the initial design – is not considered of interest):

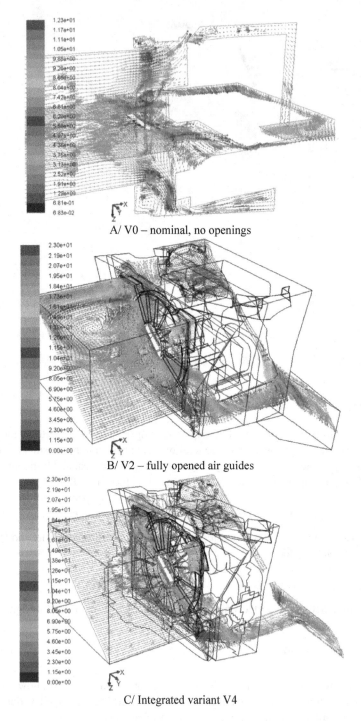

A/ V0 – nominal, no openings

B/ V2 – fully opened air guides

C/ Integrated variant V4

Fig. 6. A sample for obtained set of results: velocity vectors at 10 km/h, m/s

Table 1. Summary of calculated parameters for each design variant

Parameter	Velocity	V0	V1	V2	V3	V4
Total mass flow, q, kg/s	10 km/h	1.05	0.94	1.05	0.99	0.98
	40 km/h	4.19	4.29	4.41	4.34	4.31
	240 km/h	25.15	26.05	27.16	25.98	25.93
Mass flow rate through air guides, q_A, kg/s	10 km/h	–	−0.29	−0.52	−0.24	−0.17
	40 km/h	–	0.45	0.31	0.46	0.29
	240 km/h	–	3.16	5.79	3.14	1.96
Overall pressure drop, Δp, Pa	10 km/h	242	235	246	238	237
	40 km/h	1689	1665	1691	1647	1662
	240 km/h	65841	64544	63938	63002	64558

- Variant V2:
  - This variant has maximal opening of air guides, resulting in about 8% increase of fluid flow @ 240 km/h. It shows maximal bypass @ 10 km/h – nearly two times more than V1 and V3 – which is negative. It also shows bypassing @ 40 km/h;
  - This variant has max pressure drop for lower velocities (10 km/h and 40 km/h);
  - Its overall performance is worst;
- Variant V1:
  - Shows better performance, when comparing to V2 @ 10 km/h and @ 40 km/h, but it is worse @ 10 km/h, when comparing to V3;
  - Its total mass flow is lower than V3 @ 10 km/h and @ 40 km/h, and it has higher pressure drop @ 40 km/h and @240 km/h compared to V3;
- Variant V3:
  - It has the second performance among examined variants, when comparing them @ 10 km/h, and it shows higher fluid flow compared to V1 and V4;
  - It has also best performance as pressure drop;
- Variant V4:
  - It has best performance among examined variants, when comparing them @ 10 km/h – about 1/3 bypassing, in comparison to fully opened variant V2;
  - Has worst total mass flow among examined variants, except @ 10 km/h;
- General conclusions:
  - Variant V3 has increased total fluid flow, compared to shroud without air guides (variant V0) and it has decreased overall pressure drop;
  - Bypassing is mainly due to the under pressure before fan, which causes recirculation. Variant V4 shows minimal bypassing, but it still exists. Air guide shape does not influence bypassing;
  - Overall performance of variant V3 shows its optimal balance.

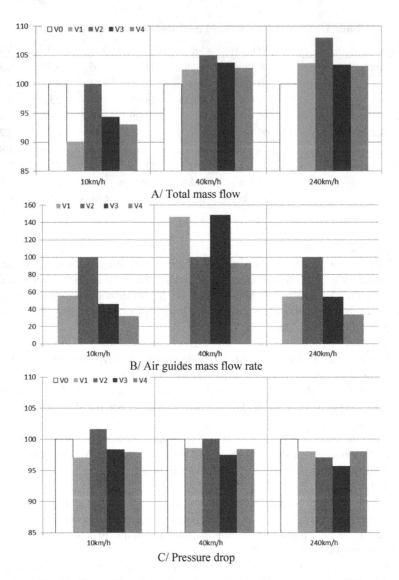

Fig. 7. Comparisons by parameters – presented in percentage to V0

6   Conclusion

A complex system of automotive industry - car fan and shroud – is studied in detail as to obtain a principally new design. Especially, a new design of the shroud is searched that will allow optimal engine cooling at low and high speeds. Design development is based entirely on virtual prototyping. Five different designs are compared on the basis of performed 15 numerical analyses. These design variants are compared by their performance both at low and high speeds, to select optimal solution.

Presented study is a good demonstration of the possibilities to use virtual prototyping at early design stage. Detailed information about various physical parameters allows the designer to change design in proper way, to generate new, better variants and finally – to reach optimal design. This example demonstrates virtual prototyping strength to give information for internal design parameters that remains "invisible" in physical prototyping.

Acknowledgment. This work was supported by the European Regional Development Fund within the Operational Programme "Science and Education for Smart Growth 2014–2020" under the Project CoE "National center of mechatronics and clean technologies "BG05M2OP001-1.001-0008- C01.

References

1. Andersson, B., et al.: Computational Fluid Dynamics for Engineers, 1st edn. Cambridge University Press, Cambridge (2012)
2. Versteeg, H.K., Malalasekera, W.: An Introduction to Computational Fluid Dynamics, 2nd edn. Pearson Education Limited, Glasgow (2007)
3. Ishikawa, M., Otsuki, Y.: Efficiency improvement of motor fan for cooling radiator. Calsonic Kansei Tech. Rev. (11), 32–38 (2014)
4. Genov, J., Kralov, I.: BEM theory adaptation taking into account the wind speed vertical gradient for wind turbines of high class part 2 numerical analysis of the aerodynamic interaction. In: AIP Conference Proceedings, vol. 2048, p. 020016 (2018)
5. Malakov, I., Zaharinov, V., Tzenov, V.: Size RANGES OPTImization. Procedia Eng. **100**, 791–800 (2015). ISSN 1877-7058
6. Mitov, Al., Kralev, J., Angelov, Il.: Investigation of model-based tuning of PI regulator for electrohydraulic steering system. In: The 9th International Congress on Ultra-Modern Telecommunications and Control Systems (ICUMT), Germany (2017). ISSN 2157-023X
7. Atanasov, V., Kovatchev, G.: Study of the cutting power in longitudinal milling of oak wood. In: 29th International Conference on Wood Science and Technology, ICWST 2018: Implementation of Wood Science – Proceedings, pp. 27–34 (2018). ISBN: 978-953292059-8
8. Tonchev, K., Balabanov, G., Manolova, A., Poulkov, V.: Personalized and intelligent sleep and mood estimation modules with web based user interface for improving quality of life. In: Arai, K., Kapoor, S., Bhatia, R. (eds.) SAI 2018. AISC, vol. 858, pp. 922–935. Springer, Cham (2019). https://doi.org/10.1007/978-3-030-01174-1_71
9. Todorov, G., Sofronov, Y., Petkov, A.: Innovative joystick virtual prototype ergonomy validation methodology by physical 3D printed functional model. In: International Conference on High Technology for Sustainable Development, HiTech 2018 – Proceedings, Article number 8566241 (2018). ISBN: 978-153867039-2
10. Todorov, T., Nikolov, N., Todorov, G., Ralev, Y.: Modelling and investigation of a hybrid thermal energy harvester. In: MATEC Web of Conferences, vol. 148, Article number 12002 (2018). ISSN: 2261236X

Implementation of Piezoelectric Actuators for Pilot Valve of High Response Hydraulic Servo Valve

Ilcho Angelov, Konstantin Kamberov$^{(\boxtimes)}$, Alexander Mitov, and Tsvetozar Ivanov

Technical University of Sofia, 8 Kl. Ohridski Blvd., 1680 Sofia, Bulgaria
{ilangel, kkamberov, a_mitov}@tu-sofia.bg,
tsivanov@3clab.com

Abstract. The high degree of automation in the use of electronic control in all industrial and mobile applications is most often done by hydraulic proportional control devices, where the regulating element changes remotely in proportion to the electrical signal. This provides the possibility to change the parameters of the hydraulic energy – flow rate and pressure – a realization of adaptive control by proportional electric control. The focus of this study is set on piezoelectric actuators that are electromechanical transducers, suitable for driving and controlling high-speed hydraulic actuators and relatively small insensitive zones. Detailed analysis of various existing designs is performed prior to development of conceptual model. Further, a design exploration is performed through virtual prototypes that helps studying in high level of detail various work parameters. It is of great importance for successive design development as some of the controlled parameters (as deformations) are very sensitive and has great influence over device performance.

Keywords: Hydraulics · Pilot valve · Piezoelectric · Virtual prototyping

1 Introduction

Hydraulic proportional control valves are devices in which the position of the regulating element changes remotely in proportion to the electrical signal. This provides the possibility to change the parameters of the hydraulic energy – flow rate and pressure, during the production process and realization of adaptive control of the machine itself. The most widely used application is the hydraulic valves with proportional electric control, that are divided into two main types: proportional valves and servo valves. Servo valves differ from conventional proportional valves with higher performance and overlapping close to zero. They have better static and dynamic characteristics than proportional valves and they are mainly used in electrohydraulic closed-loop systems to control the speed and position of hydraulic machines (hydro cylinders and hydro motors). The main directions of design improvements are oriented towards their dynamic behavior, reduction of hydraulic losses, improved performance and providing other advantages (egg. low cost) over conventional directional control valves and

© ICST Institute for Computer Sciences, Social Informatics and Telecommunications Engineering 2019
Published by Springer Nature Switzerland AG 2019. All Rights Reserved
V. Poulkov (Ed.): FABULOUS 2019, LNICST 283, pp. 318–326, 2019.
https://doi.org/10.1007/978-3-030-23976-3_28

conventional pilot operated valves. Recently, the development of hydraulic valves is directed to novel methods for actuate the regulating element (the most common of spool type). Modern technical solutions in this area are using stability piezoelectric transducers built into the hydraulic control devices for industrial and mobile applications [1–3] (Fig. 1).

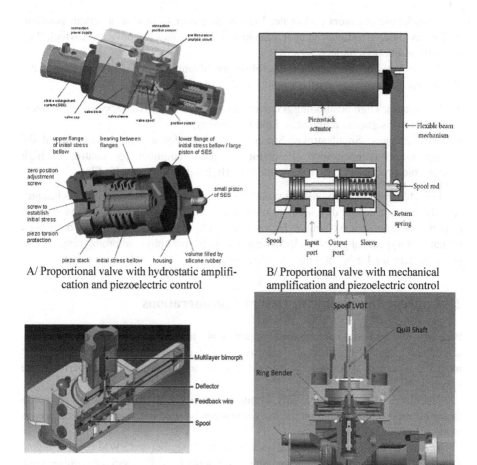

A/ Proportional valve with hydrostatic amplification and piezoelectric control

B/ Proportional valve with mechanical amplification and piezoelectric control

C/ Servo valve with hydraulic amplification type "nozzle-wall" and piezoelectric control

D/ Proportional valve with "disk" type piezoelectric control

Fig. 1. Different types of valve control design [1, 3–5].

The piezoelectric actuators are electromechanical transducers that, thanks to their dynamic characteristics, are suitable for pilot control of high response hydraulic valve with small dead-band. There are two basic types of piezo transducers, according to the class of electro-mechanical actuators to which they belong, they are named: axial and disk.

The impossibility of using piezoelectric transducers as an effective actuator in direct-operated hydraulic devices is a result of both the small working stroke and the presence of steepness in the force characteristic as a function of the working range of stroke. It is therefore more appropriate to use them in control valves of small size to serve for pilot electrohydraulic control of the basic regulating element in a proportional valve.

Piezoelectric actuators do not need electrical power to hold in a certain position, unlike any other electromechanical transducers. This makes the devices in which they are built an energy-efficient.

On the basis of this analysis, the following advantages and disadvantages of the piezoelectric transducers can be summarized:

- Advantages: High positioning accuracy in dynamic mode; High speed performance; No control signal is required to hold in position;
- Disadvantages: Small stroke; Strangeness of the force characteristic; Need for temperature compensation; Powerful electronic amplifier for control of high dynamic processes; Low robust stability; High self-sufficiency [5, 6].

This study aims to demonstrate possibilities to apply virtual prototyping techniques at early stage of design development of piezoelectric actuators for pilot valve of high response hydraulic servo valve. Engineering analyses are applied using developed virtual prototypes that gives results close to expected from physical prototyping [7] and provides data for further design considerations.

2 Concept Development. Design Considerations

Based on the fact that conventional proportional valves have limited dynamic characteristics, in terms of insufficient sensitivity, precision and high production costs, in most cases makes them not the best choice for applications in high performance systems.

Therefore, a new type of highly dynamic, stability and relatively low cost manufacturing valves are required on the market that can be used in the control of devices in modern hydraulic drive systems.

The use of two-way cartridge valves connected in parallel and PWM (Digital Signal Pulse) (PCM) is one possible alternative to the unconditionally specified requirements, but this is not always appropriate for large linear drives. For this, in the last decade, in parallel with the rapidly developing digital hydraulic devices and systems, the direction of the piezoelectric controlling hydraulic valves has been shaped.

An application of this type of control devices can also be found in more unpretentious hydraulic valves with pilot (indirect) control of the spool shown in Fig. 2. The device has pilot stage that includes four pilot valves, each of 2/2-way type, which is proportionally driven by a piezoelectric actuator. The direct coupling to the actuator provides high stiffness of the pilot stage and thus – a high response of the valve [1, 6].

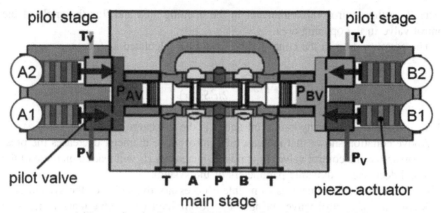

A/ Proportional valve with "disk" type piezoelectric control [1]

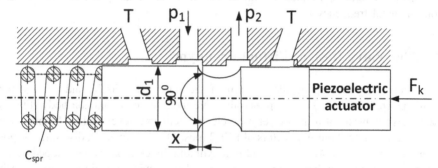

B/ Principal design of control valve with disk piezoelectric actuator

Fig. 2. Schematic presentation of hydraulic valves with pilot (indirect) control

The flow rate through the control valve when the spool valve is fully opened is

$$q = \frac{\Delta V}{\Delta t},$$

where $\Delta V = A_{sp}s$ is a valve displacement and Δt is a switching time. Taking into account that the effective area of the spool is

$$A_{sp} = \pi \frac{d_{sp}^2}{4},$$

where d_{sp} is a spool diameter.

The opening section in function of the stroke of control valve x could be representation as follows

$$S_{sp}(x) = \pi d_1 x \sin\left(\frac{\theta}{2}\right),$$

where d_1 is the control valve diameter in the opening area and θ is the angle of the control valve in the opening area.

The pressure drop in the control valve could be calculated as follows

$$\Delta p_{Loss} = \frac{\rho q^2}{2\mu^2 S_{sp}^2(x)},$$

where ρ is the density of hydraulic oil and μ is the discharge coefficient.

Above equation shows that increase of control valve diameter decreases the pressure drop across the control valve. In opposite, increasing d_1 will lead to increase of the mass and decrease of dynamic parameters of the system.

An additional requirement as to maintain necessary dynamics of the system concerns constant of control valve spring – c_{spr}. Combined with valve mass it needs to assure high operating frequency with maximum force of the piezo actuator F_k and control signal frequency f.

3   Pilot Valve Design. Virtual Prototype

Next step is to develop detailed design of the pilot valve itself, and – its virtual prototype (refer to Fig. 3). Two pilot valves are mounted in a common body (Fig. 3). Each valve consists of a multilayer piezoelectric actuator, developed by Siemens and used in common-rail diesel injectors of PCR2 (pos. 1), valve (pos. 2), disc springs (pos. 3) and set screw (pos. 4), all mounted in a hydraulic block (pos. 5). Developed design has relatively low number of components, but they require specific production technology, especially coating of moving parts as to decrease friction and wear [8].

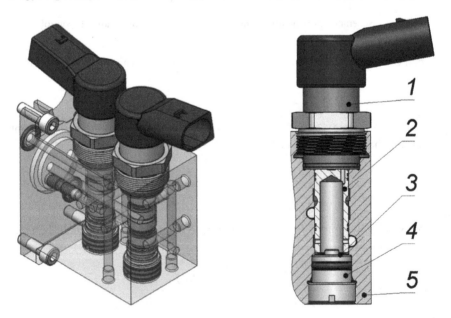

Fig. 3. Design and virtual prototype of the pilot valve.

Prepared virtual prototype is used further for two engineering analyses – under thermal and under pressure – using Finite Element Method (FEM), as to determine maximal deformations of valve and hydraulic block. Relative displacement of these bodies is decisive parameter for pilot valve functionality.

3.1 Engineering Analysis at Thermal Loads

Entire structure is set on temperature of 60 °C and is fixed on its mounting flange, as it is shown on Fig. 4.

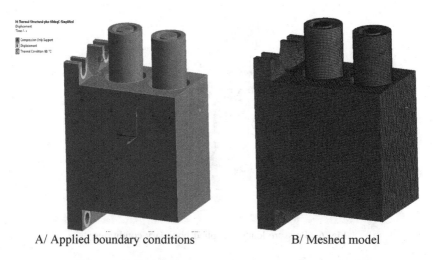

A/ Applied boundary conditions   B/ Meshed model

Fig. 4. Simulation model used for structural analysis at thermal loads

Simulation results are presented by total deformation distribution fields on Fig. 5.

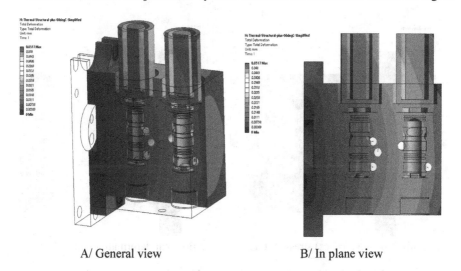

A/ General view   B/ In plane view

Fig. 5. Total deformation distribution fields, mm.

It is clearly seen that there is some difference in valve and block dilatations. An additional calculation shows that this difference is allowable (under 8 μm axially and under 3 μm radially) and thermal loads will not influence significantly work parameters and functionality of examined device.

3.2   Engineering Analysis at Pressure Loads

Next engineering analysis is to check influence of pressure loads. It uses the same meshed model, but different boundary conditions applied (refer to Fig. 6).

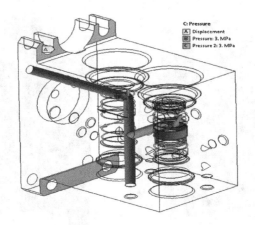

Fig. 6. Pressure loads – applied boundary conditions.

Simulation results are shown for the hydraulic block as it is the major component of interest – on Fig. 7.

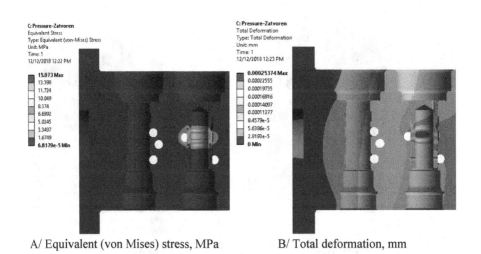

A/ Equivalent (von Mises) stress, MPa   B/ Total deformation, mm

Fig. 7. Results for hydraulic block, subjected on pressure loads

This design check shows that there are no critical zones that could be found. The deformations are ~ 1 μm and the stresses are insignificant.

3.3 Summary of Engineering Analyses

Both performed engineering analyses – under thermal and under pressure loads – shows sufficient rigidity of the structure that will withstand applied work loads without changing its functional parameters. Developed virtual prototypes are suitable for design optimization as to explore various size ranges [9, 10, 12]. Further design development will be based on physical prototyping and tests, as it is usual in such cases [11].

4 Conclusions

Based on the review and analysis of existing technical solutions concerning the control of hydraulic devices with piezoelectric actuators, as well as on performed engineering analyses over developed virtual prototypes, the following can be summarized:

1. Based on the advantages and disadvantages of the relatively new, for the hydraulic drive equipment, a type of actuators, they are suitable for use in pilot electro-hydraulic control of spool type proportional hydraulic devices (in particular hydraulic valves).
2. To date, the construction of proportional valves and servo valves with piezoelectric actuators includes the presence of a position feedback ("LVTD" type) of the main regulating element therein. This makes them applicable in closed control systems to which systems have high accuracy and performance requirements for executive hydraulic cylinders (motors).
3. The development of hydraulic control devices with piezoelectric control without internal feedback of the main regulating element (spool) implies the introduction of feedback in the executive hydraulic cylinders (motors), which makes them applicable in systems without high requirements for dynamic qualities. However, the practice shows that this leads to complications in the control algorithm.
4. Developed concept for piezoelectric actuators for pilot valve of high response hydraulic servo valve has its design solution and prepared virtual prototype could be used for further technical documentation and physical prototyping.
5. Performed engineering analyses show acceptable results that is not expected to interfere work parameters of the device, and especially – overlapping and opening of the valves. These results are good basis for further product development and are expected to be validated through physical tests.

Acknowledgment. This work was supported by the European Regional Development Fund within the Operational Program "Science and Education for Smart Growth 2014 - 2020" under the Project CoE "National center of mechatronics and clean technologies" BG05M2OP001-1.001-0008-C01.

References

1. Rechert, M.: High response hydraulic servovalve with piezo-actuators in the pilot stage. O+P Oelhydraulik und Pneumatik **12**, 64–81 (2006)
2. Schugt, M.: Piezo forte. Neue Verstaerkerkonzepte fur Hochleistungs-Piezoaktoren. F&M Mechatron. **111**, 23–31 (2003)
3. Persson, J., Plummer, A., Bowen, C., Elliott, P.: Non-linear control of a piezoelectric two stage Servovalve. In: The 15th Scandinavian International Conference on Fluid Power, SICFP 2017, Linköping, Sweden, 7–9 June (2017)
4. Changbin, G., Zongxia, J.: A piezoelectric direct-drive servo valve with a novel multi-body contacting spool-driving mechanism: design, modelling and experiment. Proc. IMechE Part C J. Mech. Eng. Sci. **228**(1), 169–185 (2014)
5. Lindler, J.E., Anderson, E.H.: Piezoelectric Direct Drive Servovalve. SPIE Paper 4698–53, Industrial and Commercial Applications of Smart Structures Technologies, San Diego (2002)
6. Han, C., Choi, S.-B., Han, Y.-M.: A piezoelectric actuator-based direct-drive valve for fast motion control at high operating temperatures. Appl. Sci. **8**, paper 1806 (2018)
7. Gieva, E., Ruskova, I., Nedelchev, Kr., Kralov, I.: COMSOL numerical investigation of acoustic absorber. In: 9th National Conference with International Participation, ELECTRO-NICA 2018 – Proceedings (2018)
8. Kandeva, M., Karastoyanov, D., Ivanova, B., Dimitrova, A., Sofronov, Y., Nikolov, N.: Friction and wear of Ni coatings with nanosize particles of SiC. In: 5th World Tribology Congress, WTC 2013, vol. 3, pp. 2569–2572 (2014)
9. Malakov, I., Georgiev, T., Zaharinov, V., Tzokev, A., Tzenov, V.: Demand modeling for the optimization of size ranges. In: Annals of DAAAM and Proceedings of the International DAAAM Symposium, pp. 435–444 (2015)
10. Semov, P., Koleva, P., Dandanov, N., Poulkov, V., Asenov, O.: Performance optimization in heterogeneous wireless access networks based on user heat maps. In: 2018 41st International Conference on Telecommunications and Signal Processing, TSP 2018 (2018). ISBN 978-153864695-3, Article number 8441319
11. Todorov, G., Sofronov, Y., Petkov, A.: Innovative joystick virtual prototype ergonomy validation methodology by physical 3d printed functional model. In: International Conference on High Technology for Sustainable Development, HiTech 2018 – Proceedings (2018). ISBN 978-153867039-2, Article number 8566241
12. Todorov, T., Nikolov, N., Todorov, G., Ralev, Y.: Modelling and investigation of a hybrid thermal energy harvester. In: MATEC Web of Conferences, vol. 148 (2018). ISSN 2261236X, Article number 12002

Design Considerations Through Study of Thermal Behaviour of Smart Poles

Konstantin Kamberov[✉], Mario Semkov, and Blagovest Zlatev

Laboratory "CAD/CAM/CAE in Industry", FIT, Technical University – Sofia,
1756 Sofia, Bulgaria
{kkamberov,msemkov,bzlatev}@3clab.com

Abstract. This paper demonstrates implementation of virtual prototyping approach in early stage of design concept evaluation. Examined structure is of contemporary smart pole design with integrated telecommunication equipment. The combination of integrated design (inside poles) and contemporary electronic equipment thermal management leads to the need of careful examination of thermal behaviour of entire structure. Most important issue is connected to the problem how to transfer generated heat to the environment. Presented study is performed through multiphysics analyses – thermal CFD (Computational Fluid Dynamics) – using virtual prototyping techniques to assess several design variants performance parameters. Used virtual prototypes enable to view in detail heat transfer process and to reach a better solution for cooling components placement. Each design parameter is assessed and further recommendations are formed for design improvement. Final design uses fans placed on the top of the pole structure leading to allowable thermal loads over electronic equipment.

Keywords: Smart pole · Telecommunication · Virtual prototyping · CFD · Heat transfer improvement

1 Introduction

1.1 Study Organization

The first chapter serves as an introduction to the problem at hand and the study focus.

The second chapter presents the methodology used for evaluating the thermal behaviour of a smart pole by virtual prototypes.

The third chapter presents the creation of the virtual prototype and the results from the performed calculations.

The fourth chapter presents general conclusions based on the performed study.

1.2 Study Objective

Commercial cellular networks are handling more traffic than ever as society embraces broadband mobility. Along with macro cellular towers to build out coverage across countryside, carriers and infrastructure providers are deploying smaller equipment to bring antennas closer to the end user. In some cases, these deployments can take place using pole facilities, including utility poles, street lights and traffic signals. A lot of

© ICST Institute for Computer Sciences, Social Informatics and Telecommunications Engineering 2019
Published by Springer Nature Switzerland AG 2019. All Rights Reserved
V. Poulkov (Ed.): FABULOUS 2019, LNICST 283, pp. 327–338, 2019.
https://doi.org/10.1007/978-3-030-23976-3_29

examples are available in today's infrastructure that some author defines them as "visual pollution" [1]. Thus, in some cases, new poles can be effective in providing wireless coverage for small-cell networks. When integrated into the network deployment strategy from the start, these "smart" poles can be designed as structures that blend into the environment, may carry the required telecommunication equipment internally inside the pole and provide opportunities for new technologies offered in the future. In these circumstances, existing available infrastructure may not be accessible or in the right location or height to properly position the telecommunication equipment. In other cases, the existing pole infrastructure may be impractical to reinforce, requiring new pole structures. Smart poles can be deployed to supplement or replace existing poles and conform to the existing infrastructure. Smart pole designs must take into consideration the telecommunication equipment to be deployed today and any known future technology requirements [2, 3].

Smart poles require integrated design of electronic equipment through usually built-in solutions. Additionally, the trend for densely populated printed circuit boards (PCB) and high processing speeds of power electronics and telecommunication systems has created a real challenge to develop sustainable thermal management solutions. Electronic equipment should operate within a limited temperature range for acceptable reliability. A large number of research studies in thermal management of electronics have been conducted [4–7].

The combination of an integrated design (inside poles) and a contemporary electronic equipment thermal management leads to the need of a careful examination of thermal behaviour of the entire structure. A major point is to transfer the generated heat to the environment. Among all the available cooling methods, the forced convection air cooling is the most common approach. In this direct heat removal approach, a fan is installed to a heat sink forming an assembly [8]. Air is forced through the heat sink by the fan; thus, the heat is directly transferred to the final heat transfer medium - air [9]. Natural convection or buoyancy-driven heat transfer and fluid flow in enclosures are an important subject in engineering applications such as double pane windows, semiconductor production, nuclear reactor cores, electronic equipment cooling, solar energy technologies, etc. [10]. In the literature, numerous research studies have been undertaken on whether to use natural convection and several research works have revealed that it could have a significant effect on both the thermal performance and of energy consumption cost [11].

1.3   Study Focus. Used Technology

Main focus in this study is set on the decision whether to use *natural convection or forced convection* for thermal management of integrated design of telecommunication equipment and pole. The specifics of examined case are also geographic area of application – a country with tropical climate and high average temperatures.

The aim of the current study is to quantify thermal behaviour of installed inside pole electronics in two major cases – natural (case A) and forced convection (case B).

Another important feature to be considered is the position of outlet – top of the pole or through side vents. This design decision is also important for reaching optimal electronics cooling effect.

Virtual Prototyping (VP) allows to evaluate design at its earliest stage and to check different variants. Its application involves engineering analysis tools that offers possibilities for higher level of exploration of physical processes. This allows to review ongoing processes in detail and to direct design changes in right direction. The numerical simulation gives a better understanding of the underlying physics and allows the user to check rapidly the influence of specific parameters. Another advantage is the cost for a "numerical test" that is significantly lower than for a physical test [12]. VP is very useful in design since they allow the influence of modifications and different parameters to be assessed, directly, without spending time on prototype manufacturing [13].

Examined engineering problem – cooling of installed inside pole electronic equipment – requires to solve a thermal fluid task, or a multiphysics simulation. Fluid flow simulations are known as Computational Fluid Dynamics (CFD) analysis and it has been employed usually to solve the air-side flow and heat transfer. Several tools for multiphysics simulation are already widely used in practice and this facilitates further application of this technique [14–16].

2   Methodology for Pole Mounted Telecommunication Equipment Thermal Behaviour Evaluation Using Virtual Prototyping

The methodology is based on two sets of engineering analyses, based on planned two variants of convection transfer – natural and without active heat sources (type A) and forced (type B). Another option is explored – the placement of exhaust opening of the pole. Variant 1 is oriented to top side of the pole placement of exhaust opening, while variant 2 explores side opening.

Main target is to increase heat transfer to environment. The methodology is shown in general on Fig. 1.

Methodology consists of the following stages:

- **S1: Simulation Model of Physical Process:** This stage examines the possibilities for various designs and ends with generated geometry models;
- **S2: Virtual prototypes simulation:** Separate simulation model are built for each generated geometry of design model. Combinations of convection transfer type (A or B) and opening placement (1 – top and 2 – side) are examined forming 4 simulation models in total.
- **S3: Comparison:** Examined variants are compared by their maximal temperatures for components. Additional review of fluid flow is performed for each variant as to analyse reasons for thermal results. This stage final result is the decision whether an optimal variant could be selected or there is a need for further design improvement.
- **S4: Additional variant(s) virtual prototyping:** This stage is optional and depends on performed comparison and analysis results in stage 3.
- **S5: Final recommendations for design:** Concluding stage of the design improvement process where final design solution is chosen and certain technical recommendations are formed.

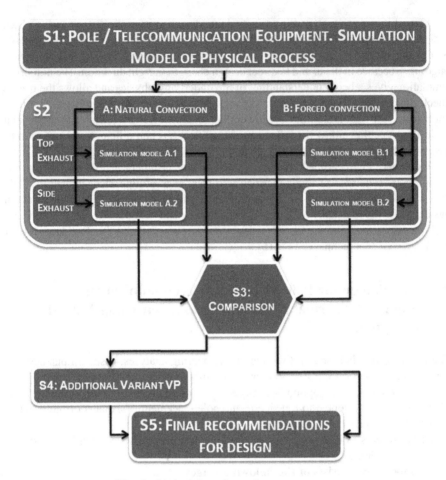

Fig. 1. Methodology for variants assessment.

3   Pole Mounted Telecommunication Equipment Thermal Behaviour Evaluation

3.1   Stage 1: Simulation Model of Physical Process

A simplified geometry model is prepared, based on the initial CAD model of preliminary design and telecommunication equipment placement. Simplification consists of removing small geometric objects that could increase solution complexity without adding any significant accuracy to the results.

Prepared geometry contains also the fluid volume as well as any unnecessary solid bodies are removed – subtracted from fluid volume – as their power losses will be set up through their boundary walls.

Generally, the included solid bodies are: bamboo, steel pole (with detailed ventilation grid) and battery insulation. This model will be used as a basis for all examined cases as the fans are included too. Resultant geometry model is shown on Fig. 2 bellow. Important feature is that due to its symmetry, the design is presented by a half model. The materials used in the design have properties as are listed in Table 1 below, according to parts designation on Fig. 2.

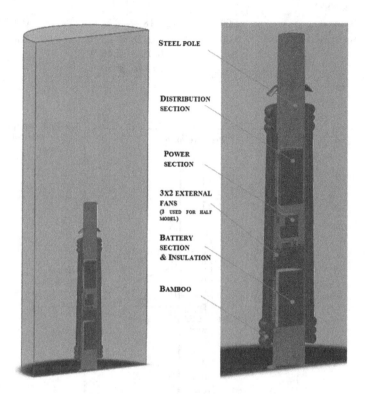

Fig. 2. Simplified geometry model and modelled fluid zone

Thermal CFD analysis explores the contained in assembly fluid as well as solid bodies. Thus, numerical simulation model contains fluid zones – surrounding zone and internal zones, as well as the included three solid bodies (steel pole, battery insulation and bamboo). The model contains approximately 2 220 000 cells and 660 000 nodes.

All applied fluid flow boundary conditions and general view of meshed structural components are shown on Fig. 3.

All fans of power section use common parameters, and especially having work point of:

$$p = 0.32 \, \text{in} - \text{H}_2\text{O} \, (80 \, \text{Pa}) \tag{1}$$

$$q = 2.21 \, \text{m}^3/\text{min}. \tag{2}$$

Table 1. Materials, used in simulation models

Mat #	Name	Density, ρ, kg/m^3	Thermal conductivity, λ, W/m*K	Emissivity, ε
1	STEEL S355 (USED FOR POLE)	7850	50	0.5
2	BAMBOO	900	0.18	0.9
3	BATTERY INSULATION	2000	0.0328 @ 23 °C; 0.0383 @ 46 °C; 0.0416 @ 50 °C	0.8

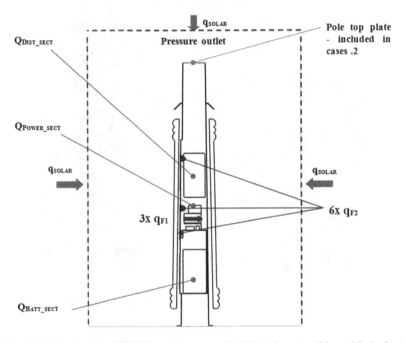

Fig. 3. Multiphysics (thermo-CFD) analyses – applied boundary conditions. Meshed model

Sun direction vector, used in simulations, corresponds to global position of: longitude: 25° and latitude: 20°, and for date 01-July, time: 13:00 h relative to the pole axis.

Power losses in the major components are included according to the received technical specification:

- Battery Section: 120 W;
- Power Section: 350 W;
- Distribution Section: 625 W.

Included boundary conditions for each examined case are summarized in Table 2 below.

Table 2. Summary of applied BCs

Parameter	Case A		Case B	
	A.1	A.2	B.1	B.2
AMBIENT TEMPERATURE, °C	55			
EXHAUST SURFACE	Top of pole	Between bamboo and pole	Top of pole	Between bamboo and pole
Heat transfer BCs				
SOLAR IRRADIATION, q_{SOLAR}, W/M^2	325			
POWER LOSS IN DISTRIBUTION SECTION, Q_{DIST_SECT}, W	0	0	625	625
POWER LOSS IN POWER SECTION, Q_{POWER_SECT}, W	0	0	350	350
POWER LOSS IN BATTERY SECTION, Q_{BATT_SECT}, W	0	0	120	120
Fluid flow BCs				
FLUID FLOW OF POWER SECTION FAN, q_{F1}, M^3/MIN	0	0	0.27	0.27
FLUID FLOW OF EXTERNAL FAN, q_{F2}, M^3/MIN	0	0	2.83	2.83

3.2 Stage 2: Virtual Prototypes Simulation

The results from the examined four separate analyses are presented by fluid flow and by temperatures. These presentations aim to have direct visual comparison among examined cases and to qualify potential of each variant. Fluid flow parameter of velocity is used as representative for intensity of heated air transport and temperature distributions are used for observation of critically loaded components for further design improvement.

The velocity fields are shown as contours on Fig. 4 for both "no load, natural" case A and for "forced convection" case B – with exhaust through pole top (cases with indices 1) and between bamboo and pole (cases with indices 2).

Temperature distributions are shown on Fig. 5 – over symmetry plane – again using common scale between 55 °C and 100 °C and by examined cases – "no load, natural" case A and for "forced convection" case B.

3.3 Stage 3: Comparison

Obtained results are analysed and next comments are formed as listed below:

- Major parameter, object of this study, is the temperature for each of the examined components. All results by components are merged and shown in percentages, where subcase A.1 (no internal heat sources, no fans active, open pole top) is used as basis (values for components are shown as 100%). This is shown on Fig. 6 below.

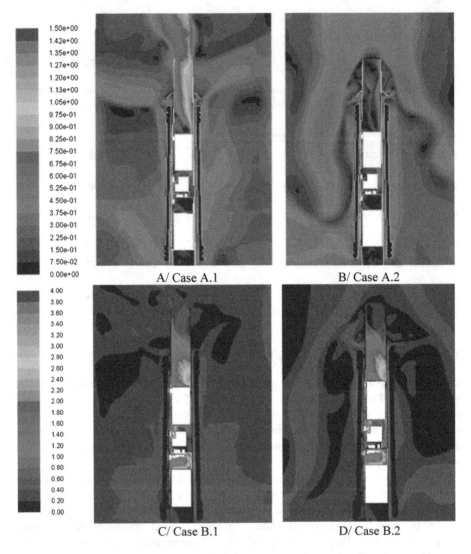

Fig. 4. Contours of velocity magnitude in symmetry plane – for all variants, m/s

- Studying the effect of closing top of the pole, it is seen that distribution section shows major rise of temperature – by 20–30%. Battery section shows also rise of temperature, especially in the case when internal heat flux is added – more than 30%;
- Power section shows no significant rise in any case;
- Studying the effect of switched on fans and internal heat sources, it is seen that most affected components are distribution (up most) and battery section;
- Fans near distribution section (upper pair) are too close to it and are practically ineffective;

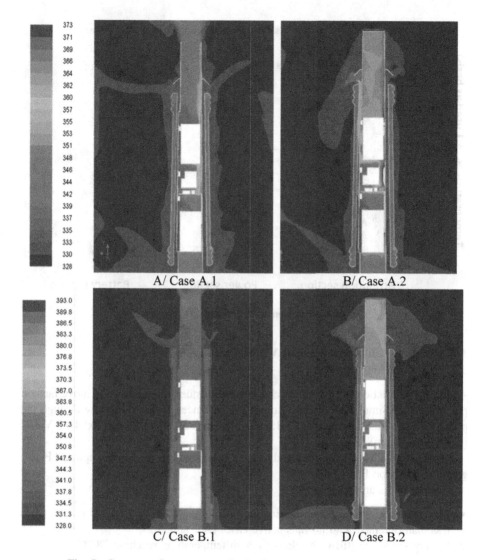

Fig. 5. Contours of temperature distribution fields on symmetry plane, K

- Fans near power section (middle pair) have some effect as it is seen also by temperature comparison on Fig. 6;
- Fans near battery section (bottom side pair) have negative effect as they redirect the flow downwards as form a closed loop inside;
- Exhaust through top of the steel tower is recommended;
- Fans position near the grid is ineffective (all electronic sections are modelled as not porous bodies);
- Improvement could be reached by positioning a group of fans at the top plate of the pole. This will reinforce stack effect and will decrease inside temperature.

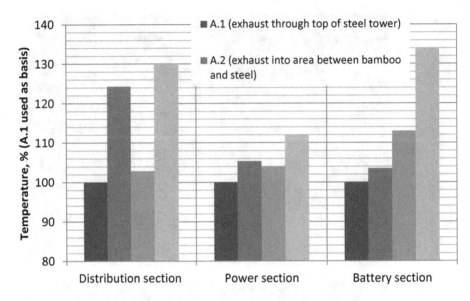

Fig. 6. Comparison among variants by components

3.4   Stage 4: Additional Variant Virtual Prototyping: Fans on Pole Top Plate

Additional simulation is provided to check recommended modification to move fans on pole top plate. Simulation model assumes, for instance, certain fluid flow through the pole top plate, that corresponds to 12 mounted fans HE910028, Fan axial 48 V DC (120X120X38mm)-R Type.

Obtained results for cases C.1 and C.2 are compared together on the updated Fig. 6 graph – shown on Fig. 7.

Several notes are listed below:

- Both distribution and power sections temperatures are decreased and reach values less than obtained with no fans active cases (A.1 and A.2);
- Battery section is still with relatively high temperature, reaching 78 °C.

3.5   Stage 5: Final Recommendations for Design

Examined additional variant shows definitive improvement of overall thermal behaviour of the structure. Components does not reach 80 °C and this design could be further developed in detail. Later improvement could be searched in direction to optimize battery section dissipated power.

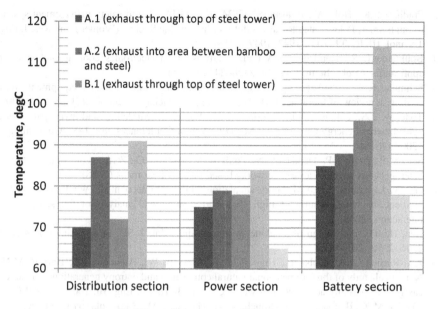

Fig. 7. Comparison among variants by components

4   Conclusions

An innovative design of a pole with integrated telecommunication equipment is developed, based on virtual prototyping. Main outcomes from performed study are:

- Design evaluation at conceptual stage and major decisions based on engineering analyses results. Earlier prediction of functionality and behaviour has major effect to reduce product development cost and time to market;
- Reduction of number of physical prototypes – additionally increases effectiveness of virtual prototyping;
- Direct quantification of physical properties of design and detailed view of physical processes. This is specific advantage of virtual prototyping against physical.

Acknowledgements. This work was supported by the European Regional Development Fund within the Operational Programme "Science and Education for Smart Growth 2014 - 2020" under the Project CoE "National centre of mechatronics and clean technologies" BG05M2OP001-1.001-0008-C01.

References

1. Nagle, J.C.: Cell phone towers as visual pollution. Notre Dame J. Law Ethics Public Policy **23**, 537–568 (2009)
2. Lockwood, J., de Grasse, A., Hild, R., Kaczmarek, K., Kelly, M., Lau, P.: Small cells on pole facilities: a primer on how utility poles, street lights and traffic signals will help drive next-generation mobile broadband networks. Wireless Infrastructure Association (2017)

3. Pradhan, S.K., Holo, V., Bhusan, S.: GSM and ADHAR based safety management system through Smart Poles: a step towards safety for humanistic Society (Women). Int. Res. J. Eng. Technol. (IRJET) **05**(03), 1943–1947 (2018)
4. Boukhanouf, R., Haddad, A.: A CFD Analysis of an electronics cooling enclosure for application. Appl. Therm. Eng. **30**, 2426–2434 (2015)
5. Schmidt, R.R., Shaukatullah, H.: Computer and telecommunications equipment room cooling; a review of literature. EEE Trans. Compon. Packag. Technol. **26**(1), 89–98 (2003)
6. Todorov, T.S., Nikolov, N.L., Todorov, G.D., Ralev, Y.: Modelling and investigation of a hybrid thermal energy harvester. In: MATEC Web of Conferences, vol. 148, Article number 12002 (2018)
7. Semov, P., Koleva, P., Dandanov, N., Poulkov, V., Asenov, O.: Performance optimization in heterogeneous wireless access networks based on user heat maps (2018)
8. Genov, J., Kralov, I.: BEM theory adaptation taking into account the wind speed vertical gradient for wind turbines of high class part 2 numerical analysis of the aerodynamic interaction (2018)
9. Ren, H.: Thermal design of a cabinet with heat sinks. Int. J. Sci. Eng. Technol. Res. **4**(7), 2346–2350 (2015)
10. AAl-Rashed, A.A., Kolsi, L., Hussein, A.K., Hassen, W., Aichouni, M., Borjini, M.N.: Numerical study of three-dimensional natural convection and entropy generation in a cubical cavity with partially active vertical walls. Case Stud. Therm. Eng. **10**, 100–110 (2017)
11. Cherier, M.K., Benouaz, T., Bekkouche, S.M., Hamdani, M.: Some solar passive concepts in habitat through natural ventilation case study: Dry climate in Algeria Ghardaia. Case Stud. Therm. Eng. **12**, 1–7 (2018)
12. Atanasov, V., Kovatchev, G.: Study of the cutting power in longitudinal milling of oak wood (2018)
13. Tonchev, K., Balabanov, G., Manolova, A., Poulkov, V.: Personalized and intelligent sleep and mood estimation modules with web based user interface for improving quality of life, vol. 858 (2019)
14. Todorov, G., Sofronov, Y., Petkov, A.: Innovative Joystick Virtual Prototype Ergonomy Validation Methodology by Physical 3d Printed Functional Model (2018)
15. Todorov, T., Nikolov, N., Todorov, G., Ralev, Y.: Modelling and investigation of a hybrid thermal energy harvester, vol. 148 (2018)
16. Gieva, E.E., Ruskova, I., Nedelchev, K., Kralov, I.: COMSOL numerical investigation of acoustic absorber. In: ELECTRONICA 2018 - Proceedings, Sofia (2018)

Computer Aided Design of Customized Implants Based on CT-Scan Data and Virtual Prototypes

Georgi Todorov[1]([⊠]), Nikolay Nikolov[2], Yavor Sofronov[1],
Nikolay Gabrovski[3], Maria Laleva[3], and Todor Gavrilov[1]

[1] Laboratory "CAD/CAM/CAE in Industry", FIT,
Technical University of Sofia, 1756 Sofia, Bulgaria
{gdt,ysofronov}@tu-sofia.bg, todor.gavrilov@gmail.com
[2] Department "Theory of Mechanisms and Machines", FIT,
Technical University of Sofia, 1756 Sofia, Bulgaria
nickn@tu-sofia.bg
[3] Department of Neurosurgery,
University Hospital Pirogov, 1606 Sofia, Bulgaria
gabrovski@gmail.com, mlaleva@gmail.com

Abstract. Personal implants for reconstruction of craniofacial harms become more and more important due to their better performance than modelling titanium mesh or alloplastic material during surgical operation. This is due to the good fit in the implant area, reduced surgical time and better cosmetic results. The creating of such implants is a challenging task. In this article structured process workflow with clearly defined steps was introduced. All of the steps were evaluated with solving of clinical case. In this first article the reconstruction from CT-data and 3D modelling of custom implants for the purpose of cranioplasty were reviewed in details.

Keywords: Virtual engineering · CT-scan · 3D modelling · Custom implants ·
CAD/CAM surgery · Reconstructive surgical procedure

1 Introduction

The reconstruction of craniofacial skeleton is extremely challenging task even for the most experienced surgeon. Some of the critical factors that contribute to the complexity include anatomy, presence of vital structures adjacent to the affected part, uniqueness of each case and risks of infection. In any craniofacial reconstruction whether secondary to trauma, ablative tumour resection, infection and congenital/developmental deformities, restoration of aesthetics and function [1–3] is the primary goal and calls for precise pre-surgical planning and execution of the plan [4–7].

Craniofacial defects have complex anatomical shapes that are hard to achieve intraoperatively by carving harvested bone from same or other donor sites. Therefore, it would be very useful for the surgeon to be assisted by proven methods in mechanical engineering by virtue of which the design and production of cranioplasty implants can be planned prior to surgery with accuracy and precision.

© ICST Institute for Computer Sciences, Social Informatics and Telecommunications Engineering 2019
Published by Springer Nature Switzerland AG 2019. All Rights Reserved
V. Poulkov (Ed.): FABULOUS 2019, LNICST 283, pp. 339–346, 2019.
https://doi.org/10.1007/978-3-030-23976-3_30

2 State of the Art

Cranioplasty is a procedure for treatment of cranial defects, usually caused by trauma, tumour removal or decompressive craniotomy. The main goal of cranioplasty is to protect the brain and improve the quality of life and especially the social functioning of patients. Therefore, the ideal skull implant would adapt to the cranial defect and would achieve complete closure, being radiolucent – for post-operative imaging, resistant to infections, biomechanical-resistant, easy to fit on place, inexpensive, and easy to use.

Surgeons have adapted to enhanced visualization and even today this is an advancing field. Advantages of virtual reality can be totally beneficial only when transferred to the clinical practice and help the surgeons to achieve better results. Development of computer aided design (CAD) and computer aided manufacturing (CAM) systems that adapt to the surgeons needs has resulted in a gamut of the armamentarium for computer assisted processes in surgery. Such systems specifically focus on enhanced visualization tools – 3D modelling or better termed as virtual reality and gives the surgeon the ability for precise preoperative planning and perform virtual osteotomies resections and design patient specific implants preoperatively. These virtual models can be imported into an intraoperative navigation system for precise placement of different implants and medical devices.

Advances in image processing and manufacturing technologies have made it possible for the surgeons to have hand held models for a tactile perception of the defect. The next level of automation has brought in fabrication of custom designed implants as the best option for reconstruction of craniofacial defects. Custom implants for the reconstruction of craniofacial defects have recently gained importance due to their better performance over their generic, standardized counterparts. This is attributed to, the precise adaptation to the region of implantation, that reduces surgical times, in turn leading to fewer chances for infection, faster recovery and better cosmetic results [8–10].

Advances in manufacturing technology and material science has led to the possibility of turning such virtual model or design into reality as physical replica models, surgical guides or cutting jigs or splints for intraoperative use and patient specific implants.

This paper explores the process chain to derive individual design variants and to create patient-specific custom skull implants for the facial bones, frontal and temporal regions by using innovative reverse engineering and manufacturing methods based on CT-data, CAD and CAM. For this interdisciplinary project, technical scientists, medical scientists and engineers at the university work together.

The presented study is focused on the implementation of innovative technologies of Digital and Virtual engineering in the field of Medicine. It reviews the steps in 3D modelling of custom implants for the purpose of craniofacial reconstruction from CT scan data to 3D models. Steps and technics for physical prototyping will be presented in next article.

3 Conventional Restoration

The most preferred way for surgeons is the removed during the surgical procedure bone to be returned back for the patient's cranioplasty. This bone has the advantage of fitting to the skull defect. In all other cases alloplastic materials, such as PMMA, hydroxyapatite, titanium mesh, etc, are used. All of them, however, are subject to some kind of processing during surgical intervention, such as preparation, adaptation, modelling and contouring, which prolongs the time of the intervention and sometimes does not achieve the desired result, especially for large and complex defects.

The use of pre-made alloplastic implants for the specific patient and cranial defect, based on 3D bio-modelling and printing, overcomes these inconveniences.

4   Process Workflow

The aim of this study combines engineering methods for rapid reconstruction of stranded geometric information with modern production methods to achieve efficient construction of personal implants. The developed complete process flow for CAD/CAM generated implants is shown in Fig. 1, tested in real case scenario and is described briefly below.

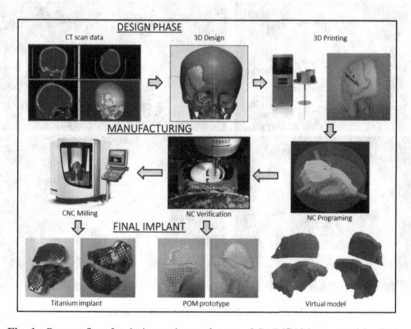

Fig. 1. Process flow for design and manufacture of CAD/CAM generated implants.

The process is known as "reverse engineering" in the engineering world and it starts with acquiring computerized tomography (CT) scan data or magnetic resonance imaging (MRI) 2D image data as DICOM (Digital Imaging and Communications in Medicine) files. The DICOM data is then processed using software as MIMICS, Bio-build or other to create a 3D model of the anatomy depicting the defected area. The 3D model file is then imported into 3D design software which could be either a haptic based environment as Freeform Geomagic or CAD based one as 3-matic to create the final implant design.

This article will review the process workflow and the latest achievements in custom implants in the cranial, skull base, maxillary and face-related treatments, and in particular the connection between applications for CAD/CAM technologies in the craniofacial reconstruction.

5   CT Scan Data

Special software (Mimics) for the image processing was used. A set of stacked 2D cross-sectional images is first imported. These 2D images shown on Fig. 2, in DICOM format, come from medical scanning equipment. Once the stacked images are imported, they can be viewed and edited using the tool box available in Mimics. The quality of 3D images that Mimics can create directly correlates to the slice thickness and pixel size of the 2D images.

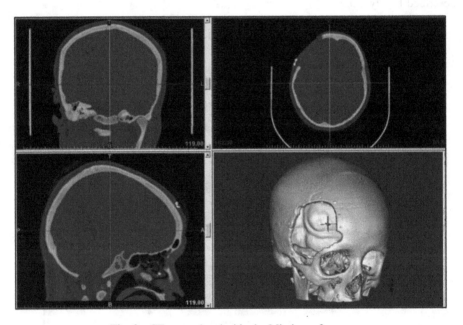

Fig. 2. CT scans data inside the Mimics software.

The medical images coming from CT or MRI scanners consist of grayscale information. By grouping together similar grey values, the image data can be segmented, and models created. The first step in creating a 3D image from 2D data is segmentation. Mimics have several tools to segment, or section, regions of interest.

After thresholding, a mask may need to be separated into numerous objects. Mimics create a mask based off of how surrounding pixels compare to a selected data point's grey value, automatically determining threshold values. This tool proves very useful for segmenting structures such as bone structures [11]. As final result from Mimics there is a 3D model of segmented bone structures.

The 3D models created in Mimics are in STL file format. STL became as standard for rapid prototyping systems, commonly known as 3D printers, and can describe very complex geometries (such as medical geometries) as triangle mesh. Because the STL models match the patient data, the models are useful in communication and clinical work planning. The RP models allow surgeons and engineers to test the shape, fit, function, and validation of projects before implement them on actual patient.

The next step is to use the software "3-matic".

6 3D Design

Typically the design of an individual cranioplasty implant is a very complex and time consuming task, since it requires the integration of anatomical structures into the design. The flanges need to fit perfectly on the patient's head. In this case challenge was the designing of proper eye orbit restoration. This entails incorporating scanned anatomical data into the design. The first phase of preparing the model, after importing, is creating the outline for the cranial plate with the defected area (Fig. 3), however the skull needs to be smooth enough. It is important to reduce the number of triangles, which makes the model easier to work with. It is important to define the curve close to the defect, but in a low curvature area, so that tangency is maintained between the skull and the implant. 3-matic has a tool that helps with identifying areas of high tangency. This will project a colour map of the surface curvature on the skull model.

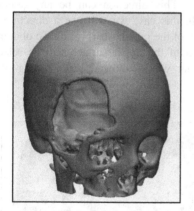   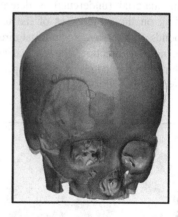

Fig. 3. Creating the outline.   **Fig. 4.** Matching the mirrored skull.

The next step in the creation of the cranioplasty implant is to mirror the healthy geometry (Fig. 4) and create a guiding line. These lines can be used for surface construction operation to 'guide' the new surface. This makes the implant to fit perfectly in the skull and results in a smooth skull-implant transition.

The intersection of the defect curve will serve as the starting/ending point for the guiding curve. The goal is to match the mirrored skull as closely as possible, and use the imported points as beginning and ending points.

The next step is creating the cranioplasty implant using the curve as "Defect outline", and the mirrored side of the skull as a reference (Fig. 5). After creating the Implant, additional software procedures can be done to further improve the design of the implant.

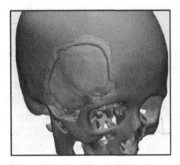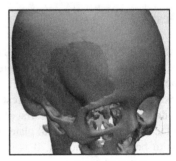

Fig. 5. Creating the implant.

The fitting direction of the prosthesis is defined as the direction in which the prosthesis should be taken in or out. Depending on this direction the exact area of blocking material (undercuts) is determined. This direction can be any direction, depending on the preferences of the user. In this case we will use a direction that corresponds with the average normal direction of the prosthesis (Fig. 6). To obtain this average normal direction, the surface normal of the upper surface will be selected. Smoothing of the edges is also applied, that would allow a better fitting of the prosthesis.

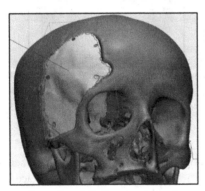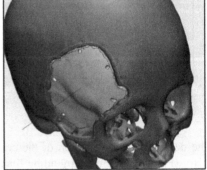

Fig. 6. Creating the fitting direction and offset.

Finally the implant goes to several operations to ensure a better fit, which include an offset in the inner direction. It leaves a clearance around the implant which would give the structure enough room to adjust and heal correctly. The final shape of the implant is shown on Fig. 7. It follows head's natural shape and has very good eye orbit restoration with relatively simple design and enough thickness to fulfil production constraints. With the implant fully prepared in the 3-matic software, the next stage of model preparation can begin.

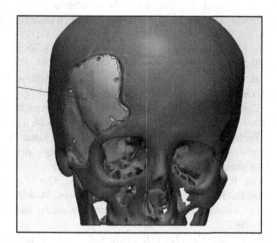

Fig. 7. The final shape of the implant in 3-matic.

At the end of this stage the goal is to ensure that the implant is suited for 3D printing. Because of the many transition stages performed, the STL file fixing of flipped triangles, bad edges, holes and other defects is required.

7 Conclusion

In the current study a structured process workflow chain which requires good knowledge of medical imaging and of various specialized software products for CT reconstruction and 3D modelling was presented. Creation of this model is a milestone for next stages of manufacturing customized implant which will be presented in details in next article.

Designing of a custom cranioplasty implant is a difficult procedure which requires the collaborative work of experienced team composed of surgeons and engineers who should discover a common solution from different perspectives.

Acknowledgements. This work has been supported by the National Science Fund of Bulgaria under the Project DH-17-23 "Developing an approach for bone reconstruction and implant manufacturing through virtual engineering tools".

References

1. Parthasarathy, J.: 3D modeling, custom implants and its future perspectives in craniofacial surgery. Ann. Maxillofac. Surg. **4**(1), 9–18 (2014). Department of Engineering, Director Engineering MedCAD Inc. Dallas TX 75226, USA

2. Shimko, D.A., Nauman, E.A.: Development and characterization of a porous poly (methyl methacrylate) scaffold with controllable modulus and permeability. J. Biomed. Mater. Res. B Appl. Biomater. **80**, 360–369 (2007)

3. Schlickewei, W., Schlickewei, C.: The use of bone substitutes in the treatment of bone defects-the clinical view and history. In: Macromolecular Symposia, vol. 253, pp. 10–23 (2007)

4. Lane, J.M., Sandhu, H.S.: Current approaches to experimental bone grafting. Orthop. Clin. North Am. **18**, 213–225 (1987)

5. St John, T.A., et al.: Physical and monetary costs associated with autogenous bone graft harvesting. Am. J. Orthop. (Belle Mead NJ) **32**, 18–23 (2003)

6. Silber, J.S., et al.: Donor site morbidity after anterior iliac crest bone harvest for single-level anterior cervical discectomy and fusion. Spine (Phila Pa 1976) **28**, 134–139 (2003)

7. Parthasarathy, J., Parthiban, J.K.: TP08PUB117 Lake Buena Vista, FL, USA: Society of Manufacturing Engineers. Rapid Prototyping in Custom Fabrication of Titanium Mesh Implants for Large Cranial Defects. RAPID, 20–22 May 2008

8. Connell, H., Statham, P., Collie, D., Walker, F., Moos, K.: Use of a template for custom cranioplasty. Phidias EC Funded Netw. Proj. Rapid Prototyp. Med. **2**, 7–8 (1999)

9. D'Urso, P.S., et al.: Custom cranioplasty using stereolithography and acrylic. Br. J. Plast. Surg. **53**, 200–204 (2000)

10. Lee, M.Y., Chang, C.C., Lin, C.C., Lo, L.J., Chen, Y.R.: Custom implant design for patients with cranial defects. IEEE Eng. Med. Biol. Mag. **21**, 38–44 (2002)

11. Mimics Lesson 2: Basic. https://www.researchgate.net/file.PostFileLoader.html?id=5686aa597dfbf9d5458b458b&assetKey=AS%3A313124089991168%401451666008906. Accessed 08 May 2017

Additive/Subtractive Computer Aided Manufacturing of Customized Implants Based on Virtual Prototypes

Georgi Todorov[1]([✉]), Nikolay Nikolov[2], Yavor Sofronov[1],
Nikolay Gabrovski[3], Maria Laleva[3], and Todor Gavrilov[1]

[1] Laboratory "CAD CAM/CAE in Industry", FIT,
Technical University of Sofia, 1756 Sofia, Bulgaria
{gdt,ysofronov}@tu-sofia.bg, todor.gavrilov@gmail.com
[2] Department "Theory of Mechanisms and Machines", FIT,
Technical University of Sofia, 1756 Sofia, Bulgaria
nickn@tu-sofia.bg
[3] Department of Neurosurgery, University Hospital Pirogov,
1606 Sofia, Bulgaria
gabrovski@gmail.com, mlaleva@gmail.com

Abstract. Using of personal implants for reconstruction of craniofacial harms become more and more important due to the better performance, good fit in the implant area, reduced surgical time and better cosmetic results then traditional mesh. Although creating of such implants is a complex task, but in this article structured process workflow with clearly defined steps was introduced. All of the steps were evaluated with solving of clinical case. In this second article using innovative manufacturing methods based on 3D Reconstruction/Modelling and final result were explored in details.

Keywords: Virtual engineering · 3D modelling · Craniofacial surgery · Patient specific implants · CAD CAM surgery · Reconstructive surgical procedure

1 Introduction

In any craniofacial reconstruction whether secondary to trauma, ablative tumour resection, infection and congenital/developmental deformities, restoration of aesthetics and function is the primary goal and calls for precise pre-surgical planning and execution of the plan [1–7].

Development of computer aided design (CAD) and computer aided manufacturing (CAM) systems that adapt to the surgeons' needs has resulted in a gamut of the armamentarium for computer-assisted surgery. Advances in manufacturing technology and material science have led to the possibility of turning such virtual model or design

V. Poulkov (Ed.): FABULOUS 2019, LNICST 283, pp. 347–360, 2019.
https://doi.org/10.1007/978-3-030-23976-3_31

into reality as physical replica models, surgical guides or cutting jigs or splints for intraoperative use and patient-specific implants.

The success and longevity of implants depend upon factors like material characteristics, the design of the implant and the surgeon's experience. This new level of automation gave the opportunity to fabricate custom designed implants which fulfil all of previously defined requirements for reconstruction of craniofacial defects. Custom implants for the reconstruction of craniofacial defects have gained importance due to their better performance over their generic, standardized meshes and plaques. This is attributed to, the precise adaptation to the region of implantation, that reduces surgical times, in turn leading to lesser chances for infection, faster recovery and better cosmetic results [8–10].

CAD/CAM systems have enabled the ability to design and manufacture custom implants at an acceptable cost in a reasonable time. Additive manufacturing technologies as stereolithography (SLA), polyjet, fused deposition modelling; 3D printing, selective laser melting (SLM), selective laser sintering (SLS), electron beam melting (EBM) and direct metal deposition (DMD) made possible for manufacturing of anatomic parts with high level of complexity without any significant design and technology constraints. These technologies also opened completely new field of designs with best strength to weight ratio and that are lattice structures. Best advantage for SLS, SLM and EBM methods is the direct production with well-known biocompatible materials like titanium alloy Ti6Al4V and CoCr. Growing importance of polymers as materials for implants like polyetheretherketone (PEEK) is possible due to FDM facilities.

2   Process Flow

The complete process workflow for generating custom implants is shown in Fig. 1 and the design steps were described in previous article "Creation of custom implants using 3D modelling based on CT-scan data and virtual prototypes (part 1)".

The result from the 3D modelling process is the final shape of the implant, shown on Fig. 2. It follows head's natural shape and has very good eye orbit restoration with enough thickness to fulfil production constraints.

Aim of this article is to present production steps from process workflow to derive individual design variants and to create patient-specific custom skull implants for the facial bones, frontal and temporal regions by using innovative reverse engineering and manufacturing methods based on CT-data.

The implant could be produced by adding material layer by layer additive manufacturing, commonly known as "3D printing", or by machining – subtractive manufacturing [11].

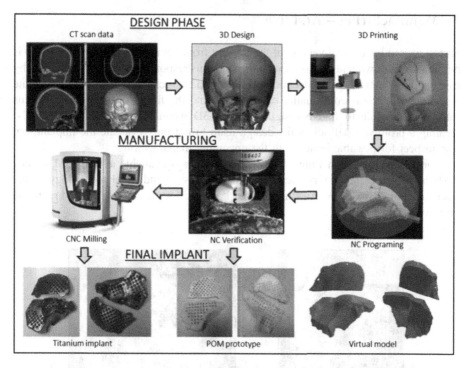

Fig. 1. Process flow for design and manufacture of CAD/CAM generated implants.

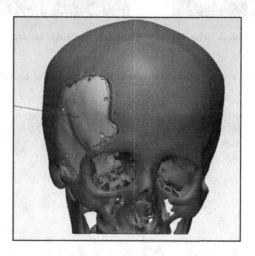

Fig. 2. The final shape of the implant in 3-matic.

3 Manufacturing – Additive

Fastest way to have a real version of the implant from computer 3D model with who is possible to sit down and discuss it with the surgeons responsible for the operation is by using additive manufacturing technology. This step is crucial as it serves as an accurate assessment for the overall quality of the shape and the fitting of the implant. In this step, it is possible to find oversights that on 3D weren't noticeable. Additionally, creating a prototype will allow the design team to not only evaluate the implant, but also inspect for possible issues with the upcoming manufacturing.

The FDM Dimension Elite 3D printer by Stratasys available at the "CAD/CAM/CAE in industry" laboratory located in the Faculty of industrial technology at the Technical university of Sofia - Bulgaria and it is used for the creating of the first phase prototype shown on Fig. 3.

 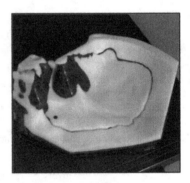

Fig. 3. The 3D printed implant inside the printer.

After cleaning the support material, the implant takes the shape shown on Fig. 4.

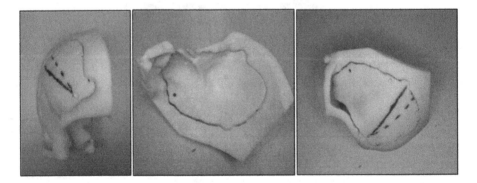

Fig. 4. The 3D printed implant with part of the skull.

Main advantage of the 3D printed design is that it allows final development stages to be planned with surgeons as attachment, holes and cut-outs.

Additive technology as SLM with certificated biocompatible titanium alloy TiAl6V4 could be used for direct production of the implant, but especially for this case balance was not on this side, because as shown on Fig. 3 support structures are commensurable with the volume of the implant. That increases the material consumption, build time, post-processing time and finally cost price. It's important to put into account possible process failures that cause loss of material and most valuable time.

4   Manufacturing – Subtractive

For manufacturing of the implant several steps have been taken:

- Choosing the equipment and workpiece
- Preparing the model for manufacturing
- Creating the NC program using Powermill
- Virtual verification of the tool paths using Vericut
- Physical verification of the tool paths using POM workpieces
- Manufacturing the implant from titanium
- Post-processing and finishing.

4.1   CNC Milling

The DMG Ultrasonic 20 (Fig. 5) milling centre is used for the manufacturing of the prototype, it is available at the "CAD/CAM/CAE in industry" laboratory located in the Faculty of industrial technology at the Technical university of Sofia – Bulgaria.

With the Ultrasonic technology developed in collaboration with SAUER, DMG MORI has for many years now been offering high-performance machine tools for the high-precision 5-axis machining of complex workpieces made of advanced materials. The tool holders with adapted actuator technology are changed into the milling spindle simply and automatically. Each of these holders contains so-called piezo elements, which are activated by a program-controlled inductive system with a high frequency of between 20 and 50 kHz. The actual tool rotation is thus superimposed with an additional tool movement in the longitudinal direction so that a defined amplitude, which can be programmed in the NC-program, in the range of up to more than 10 μm is generated on the cutting edge of the tool or on the grinding layer. During grinding, drilling and milling this Ultrasonic superimposition of vibrations has a direct, positive impact on process forces, metal removal performance and tool service life and thus on the machining result in the form of cost efficiency and a accuracy.

The Ultrasonic results in a higher removal rate, accurate edge machining and up to 40% reduced process forces in the machining of advanced materials such as glass, ceramics, titanium, composite materials and hard metal. Deflections are minimized while workpiece accuracy and process reliability are increased [12].

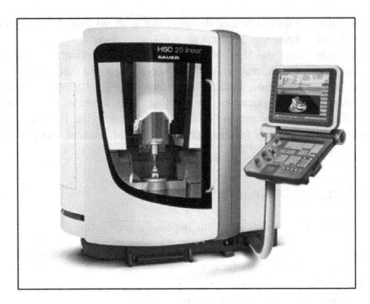

Fig. 5. DMG MORI Sauer Ultrasonic 20 milling center.

Milling Titanium

Titanium milling is a highly time-intensive process. A major portion of the costs of titanium products are associated with the complexity and time spent machining them, rather than the scarcity of the metal. The arc of engagement of the cutter has a direct impact on its cutting speed. If the arc of engagement of the cutter is larger, it will take more time to cut.

Since machining titanium components represents roughly 40% to 50% of cost, companies continuously concentrate on finding new approaches to improve speed and lower cost. Nevertheless, extreme care is essential to maintain the quality of the product and ensure the tools remain in good condition. Since titanium is a heat-resistant material, the heat generated during the cutting process is not dissipated in the metal, as it would be in aluminium or steel. Instead, the cutting tool absorbs the heat. Excessively aggressive milling could cause combustion due to the low thermal conductivity of titanium. Moreover, although the hardness of titanium may not be as good as other materials, titanium is abrasive in nature, thus causing further tool damage. The edge of the tool is required to be protected by dissipating the heat generated during the milling process through the use of coolants.

Tools are subjected to wear and tear when used in any type of metal machining. However, extra precautions need to be taken in the case of titanium to have a longer tool life without compromising a sustainable and profitable cutting speed. Special tools designed for titanium machining are necessary, even the higher price range, in the case of manufacturing only a single part, in the case of an implant, it is recommended.

Titanium 6AL4V and 6AL4V ELI, alloys made of 6% Aluminium and 4% Vanadium, are the most common types of titanium used in medicine. Because of its harmonizing factor with the human body, these titanium alloys are popularly used in medical procedures, as well as in body piercings. Also known as Gr. 5 and Gr. 23, these are some of the most familiar and readily available. The workpiece is in the shape of a disk (Fig. 6).

Composition (Mass-%):		Properties		
Ti	89,8	Type		5
Al	6	Vicker's hardness	HV 10	353
V	4	Coefficient of thermal expansion	25 - 500°C	9,8 x 10-6K-1
Fe	< 1	Density		4,43 g/cm3
		0,2% Elongation limit	Rp 0,2	828 MPa (N/mm2)
		Tensile strenght	Rm	895 MPa (N/mm2)
		Ductile yield	A5	10%

Fig. 6. Interdent medical titanium material specification.

Milling titanium requires specialized tools as well. Due to the low thermal conductivity of the titanium, the heat dissipates in the cutting tool instead of the workpiece. This leads to the requirement for specialized equipment. A set of milling tools specifically designed for titanium machining are prepared. With the workpiece and machining tools selected, the next stage of preparing the model for manufacturing can begin.

4.2 Virtual Model

Due to the limitations of the titanium disk, the implant is separated into two pieces that are tied together with medical titanium thread and then connected to the skull. A set of holes are also added which serve as the connection points between the implant and the skull. The first step of editing the 3D geometry of the implant is to separate the 2 pieces using a flat surface within the Materialise Magics software as shown on Fig. 7.

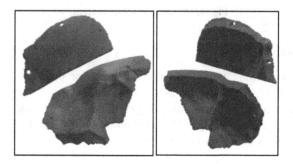

Fig. 7. Separating the 2 pieces using a flat surface.

A set of bulges and indentations are added (Fig. 8) that are positioned on the same flat surface that was used for the separation. Their purpose is to not only connect the two parts of the implant, but also to ensure a better fit and prevent any unwanted movement of the pieces.

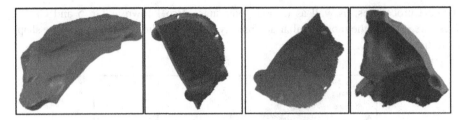

Fig. 8. Creating a set of bulges and indentations.

A set of support square rods is also added to the model. They serve as holders that keep the implant connected to the workpiece after the machining is finished as shown on Fig. 9. They will be partially milled allowing the implant to be manually removed from the workpiece after the machining is finished. With this step completed, the next stage of creating the NC program can begin.

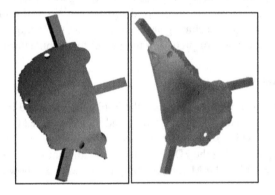

Fig. 9. Creating a set of bridges.

4.3   NC Programing

PowerMill CAM software provides many strategies for optimizing tool paths and reduce tool load in high-speed and 5-axis milling machines.

The NC program begins with a roughing operation on both sides (Fig. 10) of the implant with a 3 + 2 axis strategy. This operation removes most of the material but leaves a rough surface finish on the implant.

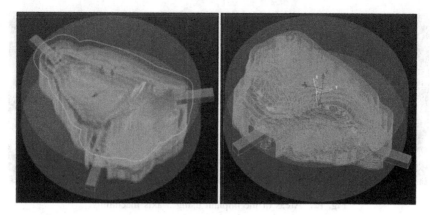

Fig. 10. Rough milling of the implants.

The value for step over, or the vertical distance travelled between each transition, defines the quality of the surface. In the next operation of fine milling the value is lower in order to achieve a better surface finish but machining time increases. Powermill visualizes the contours and they can be seen on Fig. 11.

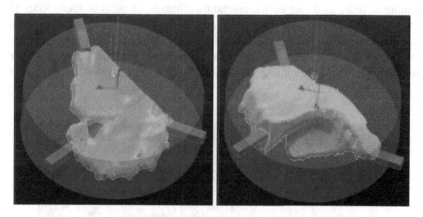

Fig. 11. Fine milling of the implants.

The process of rough and fine machining is repeated for both pieces of the implant. Because of the complex geometrical shape, that is common in cranioplasty implants, some areas of the implants require a more advanced approach to manufacturing and the use of 5 axis milling. It involves simultaneous coordinated movement of all 5 axis of the machine. The milling process is shown on Fig. 12.

With the NC program completed for both pieces the next stage of verification can begin. It is separated into Virtual verification using NC simulation software and subsequent physical verification using a POM workpiece.

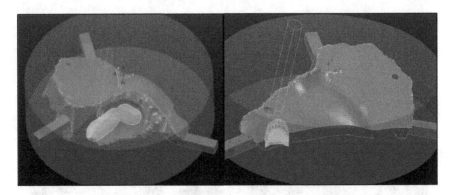

Fig. 12. Areas of the implant using 5-axis machining.

5 NC Verification

5.1 Virtual NC Verification

After the NC programs are finished a verification of the machine movements is necessary. In this case it is done using the software Vericut.

The Vericut software, has become the industry standard for simulating CNC machining in order to detect errors, potential collisions, or areas of inefficiency [14].

One of the features of the Vericut software is that it allows the use of a pre-made work environment for the machine. In this case the DMG Ultrasonic 20 layout is loaded (Fig. 13a). Afterwards the workpiece is positioned in the holder with the correct coordinate system and the milling simulation can begin (Fig. 13b).

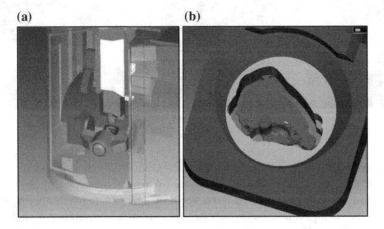

Fig. 13. (a) DMG Ultrasonic 20 layout, (b) The milling simulation process.

After multiple validation checks the simulation goes through. The program verifies the tool paths and the next stage of physically testing the NC program can begin.

5.2 NC Physical Verification

A second verification of the NC programs completed and verified with Vericut was performed using plastic workpiece to evaluate manufacturing quality and accuracy. A POM workpiece is prepared with the same dimensions as the titanium disks only difference was feed and speeds. Achieved result is shown on Fig. 14.

Fig. 14. Milling of a POM workpiece.

With the second verification test completed the results are inspected. The two implant pieces, shown on Fig. 15, verify the NC program, the desired surface quality and overall shape.

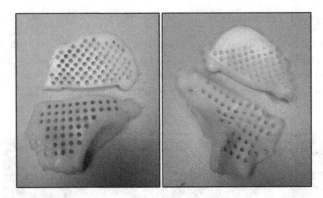

Fig. 15. The machined POM implants.

After two verification, one virtual and one physical, the machining of the titanium alloy could begin. The machining of each piece takes approximately 6 h and the resulting pieces can be seen in the next paragraph.

5.3 Post-processing of the Implant

Each step in the process workflow for producing medical devices presents particular challenges. At the final step surface finishing that removes any sharp edges or corners which could damage the patient or surgeon during and after the surgery should be done. Because of the complex geometrical shapes of the implant the process is quite delicate and time consuming, but of equal importance since any leftover sharp deformations could have an impact on the overall success of the implanting operation.

The finishing procedure is done manually by hand and the final shape of the implant can be seen on the Fig. 16. The 2 implant pieces weight a total of 85 g (respectively 30 and 55 g).

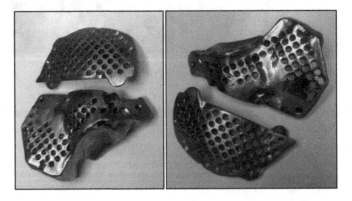

Fig. 16. The two pieces of the implant after finishing procedures.

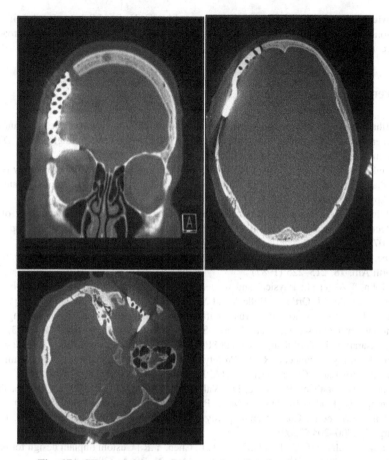

Fig. 17. CT scan of the patient several weeks after the operation.

6   Conclusion and Post-surgery

In conclusion the creation of a custom cranioplasty implant is a complex multistep procedure, requiring the collaborative work between doctors and engineers. It mixes the knowledge of additive and subtractive manufacturing technologies and material science with tomographic imaging and medical knowledge in terms of implants for the reconstruction of craniofacial injuries.

The results from the implanting procedure in real patient are shown on Fig. 17 and demonstrate how the advances in medicine and engineering allow the creation of biocompatible human spare parts with increased precision despite the complex shapes present in the human body. The images show the curve of the implant is following the curve of the skull. The patient showed very quick recovery and fast accommodation to the implant, due to the high level of achieved geometrical accuracy.

Acknowledgements. This work has been supported by the National Science Fund, Ministry of Education and Science of Bulgaria under the Project DH-17-23 "Developing an approach for bone reconstruction and implant manufacturing through virtual engineering tools".

References

1. Parthasarathy, J.: 3D modeling, custom implants and its future perspectives in craniofacial surgery. Ann. Maxillofac. Surg. **4**(1), 9–18 (2014). Department of Engineering, Director Engineering MedCAD Inc. Dallas TX 75226, USA
2. Shimko, D.A., Nauman, E.A.: Development and characterization of a porous poly (methyl methacrylate) scaffold with controllable modulus and permeability. J. Biomed. Mater. Res. B Appl. Biomater. **80**, 360–369 (2007)
3. Schlickewei, W., Schlickewei, C.: The use of bone substitutes in the treatment of bone defects-the clinical view and history. In: Macromolecular Symposia, vol. 253, pp. 10–23 (2007)
4. Lane, J.M., Sandhu, H.S.: Current approaches to experimental bone grafting. Orthop. Clin. North Am. **18**, 213–225 (1987)
5. St John, T.A., et al.: Physical and monetary costs associated with autogenous bone graft harvesting. Am. J. Orthop. (Belle Mead NJ) **32**, 18–23 (2003)
6. Silber, J.S., et al.: Donor site morbidity after anterior iliac crest bone harvest for single-level anterior cervical discectomy and fusion. Spine (Phila Pa 1976) **28**, 134–139 (2003)
7. Parthasarathy, J., Parthiban, J.K.: TP08PUB117 Lake Buena Vista, FL, USA: Society of Manufacturing Engineers. Rapid Prototyping in Custom Fabrication of Titanium Mesh Implants for Large Cranial Defects. RAPID, 20–22 May 2008
8. Connell, H., Statham, P., Collie, D., Walker, F., Moos, K.: Use of a template for custom cranioplasty. Phidias EC Funded Netw. Proj. Rapid Prototyp. Med. **2**, 7–8 (1999)
9. D'Urso, P.S., et al.: Custom cranioplasty using stereolithography and acrylic. Br. J. Plast. Surg. **53**, 200–204 (2000)
10. Lee, M.Y., Chang, C.C., Lin, C.C., Lo, L.J., Chen, Y.R.: Custom implant design for patients with cranial defects. IEEE Eng. Med. Biol. Mag. **21**, 38–44 (2002)
11. Rotaru, H., et al.: Cranioplasty with custom-made implants: analyzing the cases of 10 patients. J. Oral Maxillofac. Surg. **70**, e169–e176 (2012)
12. Complete machining with enhanced ULTRASONIC. https://en.industryarena.com/dmgmori/news/complete-machining-with-enhanced-ultrasonic–6301.html. Accessed 26 May 2017
13. Chrzan, R., Urbanik, A., Karbowski, K., Moskała, M., Polak, J., Pyrich, M.: Cranioplasty prosthesis manufacturing based on reverse engineering technology. Med. Sci. Monit. **18**, MT1–6 (2012)
14. Machine Simulation and Optimization: Production Machining. https://www.productionmachining.com/products/machine-simulation-and-optimization. Accessed 29 May 2017

Miscellaneous

ANN Modelling of Planar Filters Using Square Open Loop DGS Resonators

Marin Nedelchev[1]([✉]), Zlatica Marinkovic[2], and Alexander Kolev[1]

[1] Faculty of Telecommunications at Technical University of Sofia,
8 Kl. Ohridski Blvd, 1000 Sofia, Bulgaria
mnedelchev@tu-sofia.bg
[2] Faculty of Electronic Engineering, University of Niš,
Aleksandra Medvedeva 14, 18000 Niš, Serbia
zlatica.marinkovic@elfak.ni.ac.rs

Abstract. This paper presents a novel modelling method for planar defected ground structure (DGS) square open loop resonator filters. The increased complexity of the coupling mechanism between the resonators and the impossibility to analytically calculate the coupling coefficients created the need of accurate modelling of the coupled resonators. Design process requires to calculate the filter dimension for the given coupling coefficient. A novel method based on artificial neural networks (ANNs) is proposed in this paper. ANNs are used to develop the filter forward and inverse models aimed to calculate the spacing between the resonators for predetermined coupling coefficients from the approximation. An example filter is designed, simulated and measured. A very good agreement between the measurements and the filter requirements is observed.

Keywords: Defected ground structure · Planar filter · Coupling coefficient · Artificial neural network · Inverse model

1 Introduction

Microstrip filters are important components in microwave systems and their synthesis is a matter of persistent development and research. They must meet the stringent requirements for low passband loss and high rejection in the stopband, while suppress the harmonics spurious passbands. Planar filters are attractive to implement, because of their ease of manufacturing, adjustment and variety of topologies that offer realization of cascaded or cross-coupled filters with quasi-elliptic response. One of the most adopted microstrip resonators are the half-wave resonators and their derivatives - hairpin resonator, square open loop resonator, miniaturized hairpin resonator [1–3]. Increasing the order of the filter in order to achieve better suppression in stopband leads to increase of the sizes of the entire filter. Consequently, the main purpose is to reduce the size of the filter in order to implement it in modern compact systems in the low microwave band. The benefit of the square open loop filter is the compact topology, but it suffers from realization of wide bandwidths, that require smaller gaps between the resonators. The synthesis of microstrip filters can be improved by intentionally

© ICST Institute for Computer Sciences, Social Informatics and Telecommunications Engineering 2019
Published by Springer Nature Switzerland AG 2019. All Rights Reserved
V. Poulkov (Ed.): FABULOUS 2019, LNICST 283, pp. 363–371, 2019.
https://doi.org/10.1007/978-3-030-23976-3_32

implementing slots in the ground plane of the microstrip line. These slots are known as defected ground structures (DGS) and can be used as resonators combined to the microstrip line. The advantage is that no manufacturing constraints exist as the DGS and the microstrip line can overlap. The DGS resonators are investigated in [4] as the coupling coefficient is investigated and curve fitting formulas are derived. Also, it is possible to derive the formulas for the inverse relationship, i.e. for calculating the filter dimensions for the given value of the coupling coefficients. However, the accuracy of these formulas can be improved and additional tuning in a simulator is necessary. Having in mind good fitting abilities of the artificial neural networks (ANNs), which has qualified them as a good modeling tool in the field of RF and microwaves [5–15], this paper presents an alternative approach for design of planar filters using coupling coefficients derivation based on the ANNs. An example filter with DGS square open loop resonators is synthesized using the ANN for calculation of the coupling coefficients and the external coupling factor. The filter response is simulated in Ansys Electronics Desktop and the filter is manufactured and its response is measured. The measured and simulated results coincide in order to prove the validity of the proposed approach.

The structure of the paper is as follows. After this introductory section, in Sect. 2 the considered model of DGS resonator and coupling structure is given. The ANN based design approach is described in Sect. 3. Section 4 contains the numerical results and discussion and the final conclusions are given in Sect. 5.

2   Model of DGS Resonator and Coupling Structure

In this paper, all the simulations and design procedures are performed for dielectric substrate FR-4 with height $h = 1.5$ mm, relative dielectric constant $\varepsilon_r = 4.4$ and loss tangent $tg\delta = 0.02$ and center frequency $f_0 = 2.4$ GHz. The square open loop resonator considered in this paper is etched in the ground plane of the microstrip line and appears to be dual to the standard microstrip square open loop resonator described in [4]. It is shown in Fig. 1, where a denotes the side of the square, w is the width of the slot and g is the gap between the arms.

Fig. 1. DGS resonator etched in the ground plane

The resonator consists of a slot line nearly half wavelength long. The etched resonator is symmetrical around the axis and the open end is in the middle of the main transmission line. The magnetic field is stronger at the both ends of the line and the electric filed is at its maximum near the middle of the resonator.

For the further simulations and design procedures, the width of line is equal to the 50Ω microstrip line for specified FR-4 substrate. The resonance frequency can be found using the topology shown in Fig. 1 with a feeding line on the top side of the substrate. Once, the resonance frequency is found by the simulation, the filter design process continues with realization of the coupling coefficients with proper coupling topologies.

The most common coupling topology used is shown in Fig. 2. It consists of two closely positioned resonators with their sides.

Fig. 2. Coupling topology of DGS resonators etched in the ground plane

The nature of the coupling is mixed as neither the electric, nor the magnetic field is dominating over. The sign of the coupling coefficient is positive and this topology can be used in cascade topologies of microstrip filters. The resonance frequency and the coupling coefficients are extracted from the performed simulations and following the methods described in [1]. The obtained values are used for training and test of the ANN.

3   ANN Application in Microwave Filters Design

The proposed approach is based on two ANNs, one for forward model modeling the coupling coefficient dependence on the spacing between resonator, Fig. 3(a), and the other for modeling the inverse dependence, i.e., the dependence of the spacing between resonators on the coupling coefficient, Fig. 3(b).

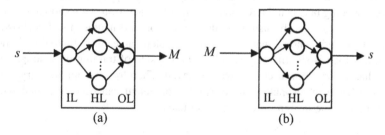

Fig. 3. ANN model of the filter coupling: (a) forward model and (b) inverse model

Multilayered ANNs with one hidden layer are used. The ANNs have one neuron in the input layer (IL) corresponding to the input parameter and one neuron in the output layer (OL) corresponding to the modeled parameter. Between the input and output layer, there is a hidden layer (HL), consisting of neurons having a sigmoid transfer function. The number of hidden neurons is determined during the model development. The input layer has a buffer role, and therefore the input neuron has the unitary transfer function. The neuron for the input layer has a linear transfer function. Connection between neurons from adjacent layer are weighted. The connection weights and biases of transfer functions are the ANN parameters which are optimized in order to train the ANN to learn the dependence between the input and output parameters, which is represented by a dataset of the input-output parameter combinations. There are several different training algorithms, such as the Levenberg-Marquardt algorithm [5] which is used here. The input-output pairs used for the ANN training are obtained in a full-wave simulator.

The trained ANN gives accurate response not only for the input values used for the ANN training but also for any other input value from the considered range of values. It should be noted that the range of the validity of this model, regarding to the input range, is determined by the range of the values of the training input data.

Once ANNs has been properly trained, the modeled parameters can be calculated accurately in a very short time by finding the response of the corresponding ANN, avoiding need for simulations or optimizations and tuning in full wave-simulator.

4   Numerical Results

The described modeling approach was applied to the resonators having the physical dimensions $a = 14.5$ mm, $g = 1$ mm, $w = 2.71$ mm, which is tuned to the center frequency of $f_0 = 2400$ MHz. For several different values of the spacing between the resonators the coupling coefficient was calculated. Further, the ANNs for the forward and inverse model were developed. In both cases the ANNs with different number of hidden neurons were trained and the ones giving the best modeling results were taken as the final models. For the both cases the ANNs having five hidden neurons gave the best accuracy.

To illustrate the modeling accuracy, in Fig. 4 the coupling coefficient was plotted against the spacing between the resonators. The reference values are shown as symbols, and the values simulated by using the developed forward neural model is shown as a solid line. It should be noted that the shown simulated values were plotted with the step of 0.1 mm, which is significantly smaller than the step of training data sampling. It is obvious that a very good accuracy was achieved. Therefore, for an arbitrary value of the spacing between resonators the coupling coefficient can be determined within a moment making the design process more efficient.

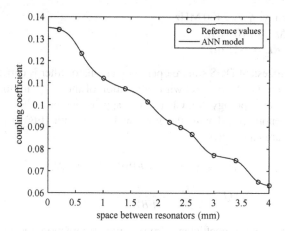

Fig. 4. Filter coupling coefficient versus the space between resonators

As far as the inverse model is considered, the spacing between resonators obtained by the chosen ANN is plotted in Fig. 4 with the step of 0.001 and compared with the reference data used for the model development. As for the forward model, a very good modeling accuracy was achieved. It is much better than the previous models based on the exponential approximation of the modeled dependence [16] (Fig. 5).

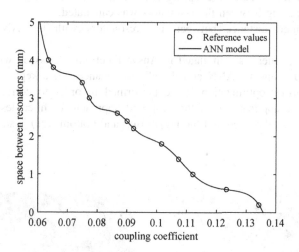

Fig. 5. Spacing between the resonators vs. coupling coefficient

Further the inverse model is used to synthesize a third order filter.

In order to prove the proposed approach, a third order filter is synthesized. The filter specifications are:

- Center frequency: $f_0 = 2400\,\text{MHz}$
- Bandwidth: $\Delta f_0 = 270\,\text{MHz}$
- Return Loss: $RL = -15\,\text{dB}$

The design process of DGS square open loop resonator filter is carried out using the method described in [1, 4]. It starts with calculation of the coupling matrix $[k]$ for low pass canonical filter topology for Chebyshev approximation. Then all the coupling coefficients are renormalized with the fractional bandwidth (FBW) and the external coupling factors are calculated as:

$$M_{12} = M_{23} = k_{12}.FBW = k_{23}.FBW,$$
$$Q_e = \frac{k_{S1}}{FBW} = \frac{k_{3L}}{FBW} \tag{1}$$

where k_{ij} are the coupling coefficients from the approximation and Q_e is the external quality factor.

The calculated values of the coupling coefficients from the Chebyshev approximation are $M_{12} = M_{23} = 0.099$ and the external quality factor is $Q_e = 8.4027$. For the realization of the computed coupling coefficients the topology of mixed coupling was used.

Following the simulations of the coupling topology, the coupling coefficient was extracted.

Further, for the calculated coupling coefficient of 0.099 (which is for the ANN training), the spacing between the resonators was calculated.

The computed distance between the resonators with the ANN is $s_{ANN} = 1.8948\,\text{mm}$.

The designed filter was simulated in Ansys Electronics Desktop with the dimensions computed using the ANN and the all the distances were kept as they are calculated. No further optimizations were performed in order to correctly prove the accuracy and the applicability of the proposed approach for filter design. The synthesized filter was fabricated and the layout (top and bottom side) is shown in Fig. 6.

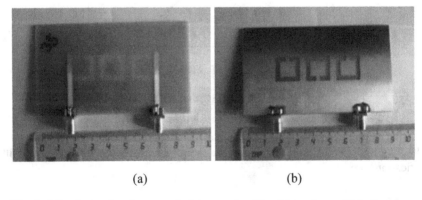

(a)   (b)

Fig. 6. Manufactured and measured slot resonator filter (a) top layer, (b) bottom layer

The measured and simulated results are presented on a common plot on Fig. 7. As it is seen, there is a very good agreement between the simulated and measured results.

Table 1 summarizes the main parameters of the design requirements, the simulation and measured results. f_{low} and f_{high} denote the low and high cut-off frequency in the filter response.

Table 1. Simulation and measurement parameter comparison

	f_0 [MHz]	f_{low} [MHz]	f_{high} [MHz]	BW [MHz]
Design	2400	2265	2535	270
Simulation	2438	2272	2552	280
Measurement	2402	2228	2525	297

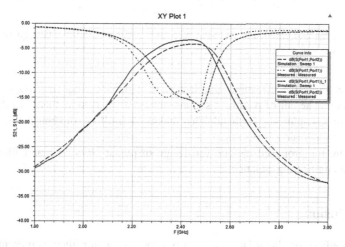

Fig. 7. Measured and simulated narrowband response of the third order DGS square open loop resonator filter

The minimum measured return loss in the passband is −13.6 dB and the simulated value is −14 dB. The minimum passband loss is −4 dB due to the high dielectric losses in the substrate FR-4. It is seen from Fig. 7 that there is very good agreement between the simulated and measured results.

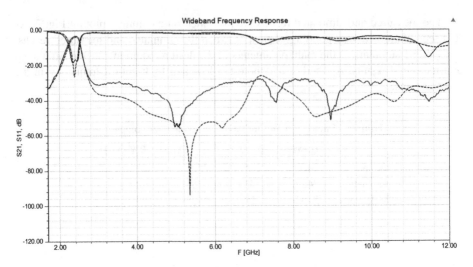

Fig. 8. Measured and simulated wideband response of the third order DGS square open loop resonator filter

Figure 8 show the measured simulated and wideband frequency response of the designed filter. The out-of-passband suppression up to $5f_0$ is more than -25 dB with no well pronounced spurious passband. This makes such filters convenient for use where harmonics' suppression is necessary.

Therefore the proposed method for design of planar DGS resonator filters can be used in the engineering practice.

5 Conclusion

A design method for planar DGS square open loop resonator filters is presented in this paper. The method is based on developing the ANN aimed to calculate the coupling coefficient for the given spacing between resonators (forward model) as well as the spacing between the resonators for predetermined coupling coefficients of the filter (inverse model). The numerical results showed, that very good modeling accuracy was achieved. Furthermore, that this method enables calculating of the spacing between the resonators which will results in the filter characteristics according to the design requirements, which was not the case when simple curve fitting exponential formulas are used, when it was necessary to perform additional tuning of the spacing value. The filter with the dimensions calculated by the proposed approach was fabricated and the filer was measured. The simulation and measurement results show very good agreement and prove the applicability of the proposed method for the filter dimensions calculation.

Acknowledgment. Development of the neural model has been supported by the Serbian Ministry of Education, Science and Technological Development under the project TR 32025. The design procedure development, filter fabrication and measurements have been supported by the Ministry of Education, Republic of Bulgaria and Bulgarian National Science Fund under contract number DN 07/19/15.12.2016 "Methods of Estimation and Optimization of the Electromagnetic Radiation in Urban Areas".

References

1. Hong, J., Lancaster, M.J.: Microstrip Filters for RF/Microwave Applications. Wiley, Hoboken (2001)
2. Carg, M.K.: A review of defected ground structures (DGS) in microwave design. Int. J. Innov. Res. Electr. Electron. Instrum. Control Eng. 2(3), 1285–1290 (2004)
3. Parui, S.K., Das, S.: A new defected ground structure for different microstrip circuit applications. Radioengineering 16(1), 16 (2007)
4. Vagner, K.: A novel bandpass filter using a combination of open-loop defected ground structure and half-wavelength microstrip resonators. Radioengineering 19(3), 392–396 (2010)
5. Zhang, Q.J., Gupta, K.C.: Neural Networks for RF and Microwave Design. Artech House, Boston (2000)
6. Christodoulou, C., Gerogiopoulos, M.: Applications of Neural Networks in Electromagnetics. Artech House, Inc., Norwood (2000)
7. Rayas-Sanchez, J.E.: EM-based optimization of microwave circuits using artificial neural networks: the state-of-the-art. IEEE Trans. Microw. Theory Tech. 52(1), 420–435 (2004)
8. Kabir, H., Zhang, L., Yu, M., Aaen, P., Wood, J., Zhang, Q.J.: Smart modelling of microwave devices. IEEE Microw. Mag. 11, 105–108 (2010)
9. Michalski, J.: Artificial neural networks approach in microwave filter tuning. Prog. Electromagn. Res. 13, 173–188 (2010)
10. Marinković, Z., Marković, V., Caddemi, A.: Artificial neural networks in small-signal and noise modelling of microwave transistors. In: Kwon, S.J. (ed.) Chapter 6 in Artificial Neural Networks, pp. 219–236. Nova Science Publishers Inc. (2011)
11. Agatonović, M., Stanković, Z., Doncov, N., Sit, L., Milovanović, B., Zwick, T.: Application of artificial neural networks for efficient high-resolution 2D DOA estimation. Radioengineering 21(4), 1178–1185 (2012)
12. Agatonović, M., Marinković, Z., Marković, V.: Application of ANNs in evaluation of microwave pyramidal absorber performance. Appl. Comput. Electromagn. Soc. J. 27(4), 326–333 (2012)
13. Marinković, Z., et al.: Neural approach for temperature-dependent modeling of GaN HEMTs. Int. J. Numer. Model. Electron. Netw. Devices Fields 28(4), 359–370 (2015)
14. Marinković, Z., Kim, T., Marković, V., Milijić, M., Pronić-Rančić, O., Vietzorreck, L.: Artificial Neural network based design of RF MEMS capacitive shunt switches. Appl. Comput. Electromagn. Soc. J. 31(7), 756–764 (2016)
15. Đorđević, V., Marinković, Z., Marković, V., Pronić-Rančić, O.: Extraction of microwave FET noise wave temperatures by using a novel neural approach. Int. J. Comput. Math. Electr. Electr. Eng. COMPEL 35(1), 339–349 (2016)
16. Nedelchev, M., Marinkovic, Zl., Kolev, Al.: ANN based design of planar filters using square open loop DGS resonators. In: ICEST 2018, Nis, Serbia, pp. 89–93 (2018)

Ground Sky Imager Based Short Term Cloud Coverage Prediction

Stefan Hensel[1][(✉)], Marin B. Marinov[2] [iD], Raphael Schwarz[1], and Ivan Topalov[2]

[1] Department for Electrical Engineering, University of Applied Sciences Offenburg, Badstraße 24, 77652 Offenburg, Germany
stefan.hensel@hs-offenburg.de
[2] Department of Electronics, Technical University of Sofia, 8, Kliment Ohridski Blvd., 1756 Sofia, Bulgaria
mbm@tu-sofia.bg

Abstract. The paper describes a systematic approach for a precise short-time cloud coverage prediction based on an optical system. We present a distinct pre-processing stage that uses a model based clear sky simulation to enhance the cloud segmentation in the images. The images are based on a sky imager system with fish-eye lens optic to cover a maximum area. After a calibration step, the image is rectified to enable linear prediction of cloud movement. In a subsequent step, the clear sky model is estimated on actual high dynamic range images and combined with a threshold based approach to segment clouds from sky. In the final stage, a multi hypothesis linear tracking framework estimates cloud movement, velocity and possible coverage of a given photovoltaic power station. We employ a Kalman filter framework that efficiently operates on the rectified images. The evaluation on real world data suggests high coverage prediction accuracy above 75%.

Keywords: Cloud coverage · High dynamic range images · Prediction algorithms · Short term irradiance prediction

1 Introduction and Motivation

Load forecasts have been an essential part of the management of electrical energy infrastructure and markets for decades. The integration of solar energy in the classical energy supply structures reduces the cost of generating power from other resources but at the same time introduces its own challenges and costs. Those challenges are mainly caused by the unstable conditions of regenerative energy sources. Main factor for the varying solar energy is the dynamic change of the sky conditions. Clouds are considered as one of the key elements in the sky which cause fluctuation in solar energy. A precise and short-term cloud coverage prediction is needed for a variety of applications primarily for the photovoltaic electrical power generation or for the alternative solar power plants whose electricity yield depends heavily on the cloud coverage of the sky. Light cloud cover of the sun already reduces generated power by up to 30% as

© ICST Institute for Computer Sciences, Social Informatics and Telecommunications Engineering 2019
Published by Springer Nature Switzerland AG 2019. All Rights Reserved
V. Poulkov (Ed.): FABULOUS 2019, LNICST 283, pp. 372–385, 2019.
https://doi.org/10.1007/978-3-030-23976-3_33

compared to cloudless conditions. If the light of the sun is dimmed by dense clouds, the yield could decrease by more than 75% [1].

The numerical weather prediction and the state-of-art geostationary satellite-based forecast approaches are restricted by their spatial and temporal resolution and are too rough for very short-term forecast applications. In this context, forecast approaches based on ground based sky imager are very promising as they provide high temporal and spatial resolution hemispherical information of the cloud cover [2, 3].

The choice of solar radiation forecast method depends strongly on the time periods which may vary from the perspectives of a few days in advance (intraweek), a few hours (intraday) or a few minutes (intrahour). Depending on the forecasting application different time horizons are relevant.

For very short time period of about 5–30 min, a number of techniques based on sky images have been developed for both Global Horizontal Irradiance (GHI) and Direct Normal Irradiance (DNI) prediction using cloud positioning information and deterministic models [2, 4].

For time horizons of 1–2 h, forecasting applications tend to be more statistical approaches such as autoregressive integrated moving averages [3].

One of the main advantages of sky imaging using large, ground based sensor network is that with only one or with a couple of cameras positioned in the zone of interest the actual cloud coverage can be determined with high resolution. The imaging systems can track cloud movements and can be used to reconstruct the spatial specificity of the clouds. With the current distribution and motion field, for about 5–30 min, future cloud configurations with high temporal and spatial resolution inside the forecast window can be predicted.

In contrast, a sensor network must be configured with a sufficiently close spacing throughout the zone of interest so that there is enough lead-time in the direction of cloud movement.

In most cases this scenario cannot be achieved due to cost reasons. Long-term, high-quality solar radiation data from ground sensors are vital for applications such as resource estimation and performance modelling. However for short-term forecasts, sky-imaging systems are more promising [3].

Short-term prediction of cloud coverage can generally be divided in two steps. The first involves the detection and the segmentation of clouds using available images. This one is of great importance since the quality of the second step, the actual prediction, depends on the most detailed representation of the clouds possible.

2   Approach and Tools

2.1   Camera

In this study, a ground-based sky camera is used to monitor the sky. It is mounted on the roof of the University of Applied Sciences Offenburg (Fig. 1).

Fig. 1. The camera system mounted on the roof of the University of Offenburg [5]

The sky camera is based on basic SkyImager-Designs as for example in [6] or [7, 8], and is pointed directly at the sky. A CCD sensor from Kodak and a 180° circular fisheye lens from Sigma Lens are used. As part of a testbed system, temperature and solar irradiance are measured [5]. This camera uses a fisheye lens with an angle of view of 185°. This results in a distortion of the imaged objects as shown in Fig. 2.

The lens curves the lines of the chessboard which in reality are straight. Similarly the actual straight path of a cloud is curved by the lens which makes subsequent tracking and cloudiness prediction much more difficult. Furthermore the movement of a cloud in the edge area of the shot in reality corresponds to a significantly greater distance compared to the same movement in the center of the picture. It is therefore useful to perform a distortion correction of the used images in a further pre-processing step and thus facilitates the subsequent prediction.

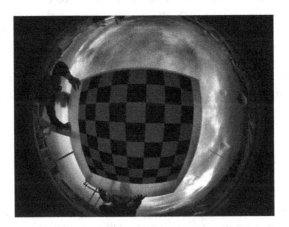

Fig. 2. Distortion of a chessboard by the fisheye lens

2.2 Calibration Principles

The principle of calibration is based on the Unifying Theory for Central Panoramic Systems of Geyer and Daniilidis [9] which states that any catadioptric and perspective projection can also be produced by imaging a three-dimensional sphere centered in the effective pixel.

The search for the transfer function of the lens connecting the three-dimensional coordinates of a point in the object space with the coordinates of its image in the plane of the image sensor is crucial for the image conversion algorithm. The task of finding the transfer function is solved by calibrating the omnidirectional optical system.

There are many methods for calibrating omnidirectional optical systems. One of the more detailed comparisons of these methods is given in [9, 10]. Out of the many methods of calibration, considered by the authors, a group of four methods available in the form of open source tools was highlighted.

1. Use of a spherical model of the camera; several images of a two dimensional test object are needed for calibration [11].
2. Use of a spherical model of the camera; A three-dimensional test object, consisting of three perpendicular test objects in the form of a chessboard is used for calibration [12].
3. A spherical camera model is also used. One camera image containing at least 3 lines is taken for calibration [13].
4. Omnidirectional images are considered distorted, the parameters must be calculated. Objects in the form of a chessboard are used for calibration [14].

The third technique, however, does not work with super-wide fisheye lenses. The rest three methods have approximately the same indicators of the calibration accuracy which are sufficient for solving the problem.

A technique is needed that would not require special technical equipment and could also be performed by unskilled personnel (or user of the system). In view of this the Scaramuzza method was chosen as the simplest and most convenient one for practical use.

The technique is implemented in the form of "OCamCalib" toolkit for MATLAB environment. To perform the calibration it is necessary to take several images of the test object in the form of a chessboard using a calibrated optical system. A further calibration process is practically completely automated. The calibration results are the calculated parameters (such as center coordinates and polynomial coefficients) for two functions defining a direct connection between the three-dimensional coordinates of the point in the object space and the coordinates of its image in the coordinate system of the image sensor $((u', v')) = world2cam(x, y, z)$ and $((x, y, z)) = cam2world(u', v')$. The calibration process is described in detail in [13–15].

The underlying model does only the reposition of the pixels on the image plane with an assumed distortion function. Additionally a vector $(x, y, z)^T$ is computed radiating from the single viewpoint to a picture sphere pointing in the direction of the incoming light ray for each pixel position $(u, v)^T$. This reference frame originates in the center of the image.

The radial distortion is defined as a Taylor polynomial with Function F(ρ) given as

$$F(\rho) = a_0 + a_1\rho + a_2\rho^2 + a_3\rho^3 + \ldots + a_n\rho^n \qquad (1)$$

$$\rho = \sqrt{u^2 + v^2}. \qquad (2)$$

The coefficients a_i define the intrinsic parameters and the Euclidean distance of the pixel position $(u, v)^T$ from the image center and is defined by Eq. (2). The latter is needed to make use of the spherical projections properties so that a point in camera coordinates can always be represented as a point on a specific ray. This is expressed in Eq. (2) with c being an arbitrary scaling factor.

$$\begin{pmatrix} x \\ y \\ z \end{pmatrix} = c \begin{pmatrix} u \\ v \\ F(\rho) \end{pmatrix} \qquad (3)$$

To project a point from camera coordinates onto an image the parameters of Eq. (3) has to be determined in order to get u and v. The calculation is based on a least squares criterion and is done for the overdetermined system with singular value decomposition.

2.3   Distortion Correction by Interpolation

Once the parameters have been determined for the camera in use the distorted images can now be transformed to an area-consistent perspective. This is achieved with a simple interpolation [16]. With this function the input image V at the coordinates of the distorted fisheye sampling points in X and Y is interpolated to the coordinates of the undistorted equirectangular points in Xq and Yq. The result Vq is the undistorted image. X and Y correspond to the pixel coordinates of the image used. The two matrices Xq and Yq are determined with the help of a function that needs as input a three-dimensional point as well as the calibration parameters of the camera.

Each 3D point is composed of X and Y image coordinates of the point to be undistorted and the negative Z coordinate N_Z where N_Z corresponds to the assumed focal length of the camera.

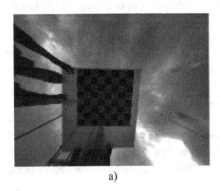 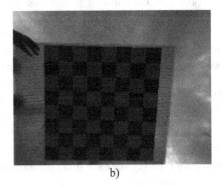

a)   b)

Fig. 3. Distortion correction of the image from Fig. 2, with (a) $N_Z = -300$ and (b) $N_Z = -600$

Figure 3 shows the result of the interpolation for two different values of N_Z. The distorted lines of the chessboard in the input image are straight lines on the output images as desired. Higher values of N_Z increase the close-up details but restrict the field of view as shown in Fig. 3(b). Values that are chosen smaller increase the distortions of the equirectangular transformation in the areas towards the image borders which can be seen in Fig. 3(a). The proposed procedure is fast and completely automatic as the user is only asked to collect a few images of a checker board and to click on its initial corner point. The only assumption is that the lens can be modeled by a Taylor series expansion of a unified spherical perspective model (For further details we refer to [17]). It should be noted that distortion correction is performed for each of the three RGB channels independently and then the channels are recombined into the undistorted RGB image.

The aim of the pre-processing step is to prepare the images of the fisheye camera for subsequent detection of the position of the sun, then to perform segmentation of the clouds and finally to determine the movement of the clouds in order to predict a possible reduction in solar power generation. If the lens parameters are known the transformation from fisheye images to an equirectangular representation shifts the problem of trajectory estimation from a non-linear motion model of changing radial patterns of the clouds to a *linear system* that can be tackled with efficient algorithms, e.g. the Kalman Filter.

3   Sun Path Calculation and Cloud Segmentation

3.1   Sun Position Calculation

The zenith and the azimuth angles of the sun at a particular time can be calculated using the longitude, latitude and altitude of the desired location as well as any date and time [18, 19]. A zenith angle of $0°$ corresponds to the maximum possible zenith, $90°$ sunrise or sunset. If these two angles are known the sun's XY position on the distorted HDR image, when these two angles are known, can be calculated using the following formulas:

$$x_{sun} = r_{sun} \cdot cos(\varphi_{sun}) + \frac{width_{pic}}{2} \tag{4}$$

$$y_{sun} = r_{sun} \cdot sin(\varphi_{sun}) + \frac{height_{pic}}{2} \tag{5}$$

The azimuth angle of the sun is presented with the angle φ. The orientation of the camera should be taken into consideration and thus the computed value based on the Sun Position function should be shifted producing next correction for the images used here:

$$\varphi_{sun} = -Azimuth_{sun} + 164.2484 \tag{6}$$

The required radius r_{sun} can be determined by the calculated zenith angle for this purpose - the corresponding distance in pixels of the sun to the center of the image is measured several times at every possible zenith angle. For a given zenith angle the corresponding radius can be read out via this table.

Figure 4 shows the calculated sun path for the months of January, March, May, July, August and October. As expected, the position of the sun is much lower in the winter months than, for example, as shown in the figures. Going to the image edges leads to a bigger sun distortion in the rectified HDR images. For the upcoming steps it would be more difficult to separate the sun from the cloud shapes which would rely on rectified images.

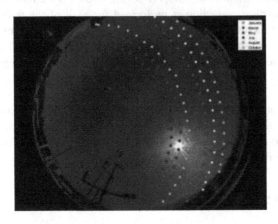

Fig. 4. Sun path during the year over the Offenburg University

3.2 Segmentation of Clouds and Sky

To segment clouds from clear sky we use the so-called Red-Blue Ratio (RBR) which only relies on the red and blue color channel [13]. In addition to the RBR with fixed parameters a dynamic and local thresholding scheme analogue to [14] is used.

1. **RBR value and Clear-Sky Image (CSI).** The physical scattering of wavelengths is the source for the RBR and this is the reason that the skies are colored in blue and clouds in different shades of gray. The ratio is calculated with

$$RBR = \frac{R}{B} = 1 + \frac{R - B}{B}. \tag{7}$$

The segmentation of thick clouds from clear sky is easy. But the common case of thin layered or wispy clouds, so called cirrus clouds, or the combination of thick and thin clouds against the sky is a hard task only relying on a single threshold. The problem is depicted in Fig. 5 coverages from thick to thin, emphasizing the problem of choosing a sensible threshold for segmentation. Besides cloud thickness, the inhomogeneity of the sky poses the biggest problem for thresholding methods. The RBR value of a clear sky, when reaching the sun and horizon, increases. In order to escape incorrect detection of sky pixels as clouds the clear sky RBR_{CSI} value is subtracted from the current value of RBR of the HDR image RBR_{HDR}.

$$RBR_{diff} = RBR_{HDR} - RBR_{CSI}. \tag{8}$$

This renders the resulting RBR spectrum independent of the actual influence of sky illumination. A prerequisite for the subtraction is the availability of clear sky images for every time of the year. Since this is hard to come by (except in some desert regions), we choose to generate the ideal clear sky image based on a physical model.

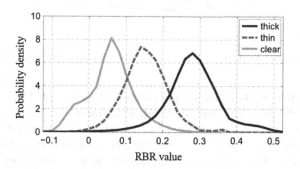

Fig. 5. Typical RBR values (image adapted from [3])

2. **Calculation of CSI values.** In order to have a calculated CSI image we used the methods described in [3]. Based on the CIE Standard Clear Sky model [20], the color intensity L of the clear sky is calculated as a function of the sun pixel angle (SPA) and the pixel zenith angle (PZA) using the following formula:

$$I_p(PZA, SPA) = \alpha_1 \cdot \underbrace{\left[1 + exp\left(\frac{a_3}{cos(PZA)}\right)\right]}_{=f_1(PZA)} \cdot \underbrace{\left[a_4 + a_5 \cdot SPA^{a_6} + a_7 \cdot cos(SPA)^2\right]}_{=f_2 SPA} \tag{9}$$

The luminance and subsequently the color values of the presumed clear sky could be computed if the parameters a_1 to a_7 are known. With the help of this the PZA and SPA values are converted from the x-y-coordinates. The PZA, denoted by Z in Fig. 6, is determined as the distance of the pixel to the center of the fisheye image.

The CSI for each pixel can be computed only when all seven parameters for the three color channels have been calculated using Eq. (10):

$$CSI = \left(a_1 PZA^2 + a_2 PZA + a_3\right) \cdot \left(a_4 SPA^3 + a_5 SPA^2 + a_6 SPA + a_7\right) \tag{10}$$

A model of a Clear Sky Image has been created by computing a function for the intensity of each pixel based on its position. This CSI image is used for the separation of the clouds from the sky.

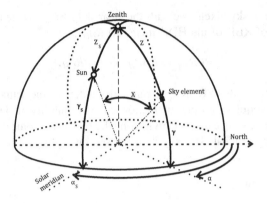

Fig. 6. Angle definitions for object positioning in the sky [20]

For cloud discovery two diverse approaches have been used. The first one is *fixed red blue ratio threshold* and the second one is a *dynamic gray scale threshold*. All images are sharing the same determined RBR threshold. A universal threshold for the given image is calculated with the help of the algorithm for gray scales values of the difference between HDR image and CSI. Extremely adequate results are obtained from both algorithms for diverse scenarios: the method based on RBR obtains good results in separating ticker and darker clouds while the gray scale method obtains weaker results. For improving the output of thinner clouds, the results are inverted and the gray scale threshold performs better than the RBR method. For the occasion when there are different parts of clouds both methods are used which produce reasonable results.

The described process of cloud separation should be considered as a middle step of short time solar power forecast. A throughout calibration and tuning should be done of the camera and the HDR images. After this process, an algorithm for prediction of the movement of the clouds should be used, in our case a model-based estimation in a multi assumption domain. The gray value algorithm was chosen for our research although both processes produce proper results because its separation results are good and the output of the separation deliver the information for the clustering and separate cloud movement forecast using monocular camera images. Further details and exemplary results are shown in [21].

4 Tracking

In this chapter the final short-term prediction of the before segmented cloud coverage is explained.

For the detection and tracking of multiple objects on a motionless background in the video stream of a stationary camera for personal or traffic monitoring, a multiple object tracking (MOT) method is often used. In this method an individual trajectory (track) is created for each newly detected object on an image or frame. On the next frame, the objects are detected again but are now assigned to the existing tracks of the previous frame. The time between two frames for our camera system is limited to last 30 s, to allow for the taking of four exposure rows.

If one or more detected objects cannot be assigned to existing tracks, a new track will be created for them. The assignment is done exclusively through the position and movement of the objects and their center of gravity using the Kalman filter as model based estimator. The Kalman filter estimates the velocity and position of the object based on previous states. The underlying physical model allows the prediction of the actual and following time step and the actual cloud position which is then used to assign the detections in a more robust manner.

We assume the constant velocity model for the prediction and correction steps which proved the best correspondence with the actual observed cloud movement.

4.1   Kalman Filter

To reliably track an object through a series of images, its position for the current image must be estimated from previous positions and observations. A well-established approach for estimation and prediction of moving objects is the Kalman filter which estimates the current position of an object based on former states and associated observations that are combined based on a physical motion model. For this contribution several motion models were evaluated and the constant motion model was chosen heuristically matching actual cloud movement. The equirectangular projection of the fisheye image results in a linear cloud movement along the sky which allows the employment of the basic Kalman filter without the need of designing a non-linear motion model and henceforth using the non-linear filter derivatives as an unscented Kalman filter or particle filter.

The Kalman Filter is a twostep algorithm based on the predictor corrector scheme. In the first step, the current position of the object is estimated from the previous positions and the corresponding error covariance. Then, in the second step, the estimated position and the error covariance are corrected by measurement. The advantage here is that even if the position cannot be corrected one or more times by observations, the corrections are still performed using the information from previous states and motion model. The predictions are thus becoming more inaccurate the further in time the actual state is predicted. New measurements then correct the state and covariance again. The results of the filter estimation are shown exemplary in Fig. 7 for two consecutive frames. All detected cloud objects are numbered and indicated by a yellow box. The estimated position is shown by the red centroid and the blue vector visualizes the velocity, albeit scaled by a factor of ten.

Since each segmented and detected cloud is treated as an independent object, one instance of a Kalman filter is created for each cloud leading to a multi hypothesis approach for object tracking. As cloud position we define the centroid (center of gravity) of the object which yields a higher distance to neighboring clouds and lies within a relatively homogeneous area of the cloud; velocity is determined in multitudes of pixels as the shift of the centroid between the frames. The correction step of the tracker framework uses the velocity as observation giving rise to the question of appropriate data association for the cloud objects between the frames.

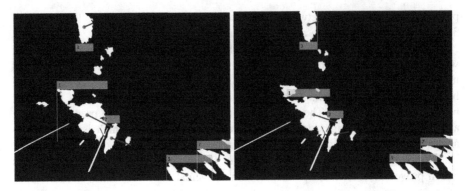

Fig. 7. Estimation of cloud position and velocity by multiple Kalman filters. Position of object is determined by the red dot, the estimated velocity by the blue vector, scaled with a factor of ten. (Color figure online)

4.2 Tracking Routine Implementation

For the tracking routine, management of the detected tracks is of utmost importance. To prevent misdetections, the tracks must be detected on a minimum number of frames before they are defined as a reliable object. At the same time, tracks that exist too long without updated measurements in the form of an associated detection must be deleted. As a result, the clouds that dissolved or left the image area are no longer pursued.

The software framework consists of two main parts. The first part initializes and manages tracks based on detected centroids.

Therefore each Kalman filter uses a detected centroid as starting position to initialize the track. Each filter has an associated lifetime indicating the frames in which its object was visible and an associated counter that determines whether a track has not been detected for too long and thus can be deleted.

The second part of the program is cyclically repeated for each new high dynamic range image from the exposure series. A binary cloud mask is created for the rectified HDR image as described in Sect. 3 and the current position of the Sun is calculated.

In the following data association step, all current detections are assigned to already existing tracks. The subsequent assignment is implemented as a Hungarian assignment method based on the variant described in [22].

Exemplary results for the Track management of diverging or appearing cloud objects are shown in Fig. 8. The larger cloud numbered 11 on the left side of the image is dividing and assigned two new objects on the right side namely 10 and 11.

4.3 Experimental Results

The presented algorithm was tested on several hundred images taken from different sequences containing individual weather conditions. Segmentation and initialization of the multi hypothesis tracker works reliable in all considered conditions. A demonstrative example is shown in Fig. 9. The framework is presented with two frames and associates the detected cloud centers. In the third frame all tracks are initialized with an individual Kalman filter indicated by the yellow bounding boxes and the corresponding centroid.

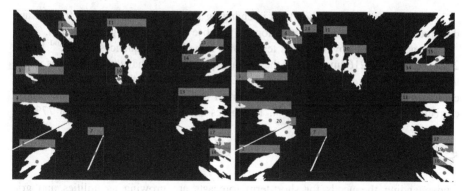

Fig. 8. Track management for diverting clouds. The cloud object 10 on the left side dissolves whereas the cloud object 11 on the left side splits up into two new objects, 10 and 11, on the right side.

Fig. 9. Initialization of Kalman filters for a given detection sequence. All cloud objects are kept by data association in the first two frames indicated on the left and in the middle. Each tracked object is shown on the right image given by its bounding box and centroid.

Short Time Cloud Coverage Prediction

An example for the prediction of the cloud object is shown in Fig. 10. The blue object in the right image indicates the predicted position after 12 frames which corresponds to six minutes. The considered object is numbered with the bounding box five.

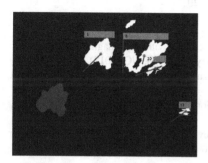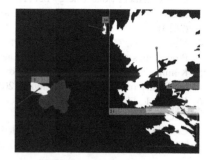

Fig. 10. Short time prediction of cloud objects. The blue shape indicates the predicted position of cloud number five of the left image. After six minutes the shape has changed but the prediction was quite accurate. (Color figure online)

Although the shape of the cloud is changing noticeably it is robustly tracked and the prediction is relatively accurate for the purpose of sun coverage prediction.

The accuracy of coverage was tested with two cloudy sequences from 2nd March 2017, comprising 216 images. For the given sequences there have been 47 cases where the sun became covered by a moving cloud. We predicted the time of five minutes and evaluated prediction with real coverage. From the 48 coverage events 37 have been correctly predicted and 11 were not. This gives an accuracy of prediction of 77%.

5   Conclusion

Understanding the needs for short-term forecasts are growing as utilities and grid operators gain experience in managing solar-power sources. The use of sky images for providing forecasts over a local spatial area has the potential to provide, at a competitive price, an accurate, high-resolution, short-term forecast needed for efficient power generation, transmission and distribution.

In this paper we present a novel approach of short time cloud coverage prediction for the purpose of solar power optimization. Our approach is based on two stages where at first the clouds are segmented from clear sky by using rectified HDR images in combination with a color based thresholding and model based clear sky simulation. In the second stage, we use a multi hypothesis Kalman filter framework to track each segmented cloud estimating current position and velocity. With this information, a short time prediction within roughly ten minutes can be given to assess the possibility of clouds moving over the sun and thus shorten the photovoltaic power output.

Acknowledgments. This paper has been produced within the framework of the ERASMUS + project Geothermal & Solar Skills Vocational Education and Training (GSS-VET).

References

1. Sun, S., et al.: Short term cloud coverage prediction using ground based all sky imager. In: IEEE International Conference on Smart Grid Communications (2014)
2. Chow, C.W., et al.: Intra-hour forecasting with a total sky imager at the UC San Diego solar energy testbed. Solar Energy 85(11), 2881–2893 (2011)
3. Kleissl, J.: Solar Energy Forecasting and Resource Assessment. Academic Press, Oxford (2013)
4. Marquez, R.; Coimbra, C.: Short term DNI forecasting with sky imaging techniques. In: Proceedings of the American Solar Energy Society, Rayleigh, NC (2012)
5. Kömm, T.: Entwicklung einer Wolkenkamera zur Kurzzeitvorhersage von Solarenergie. University of Offenburg, Offenburg (2016)
6. Kleissl, J., Urquhart, B.: Sky imager cloud position study field campaign report. University of California, San Diego (2016)
7. Cazorla, A., Olmo, F.J., Alados-Arboledas, L.: Development of a sky imager for cloud cover assessment. J. Opt. Soc. Am. A 25(1), 29–39 (2008)

8. Gauchet, C., Blanc, P., Espinar, B., Charbonnier, B., Demengel, D.: Surface solar irradiance estimation with low-cost fish-eye camera. In: Workshop on Remote Sensing Measurements for Renewable Energy, Risoe, Denmark (2012)

9. Geyer, C., Daniilidis, K.: A unifying theory for central panoramic systems and practical implications. In: Vernon, D. (ed.) ECCV 2000. LNCS, vol. 1843, pp. 445–461. Springer, Heidelberg (2000). https://doi.org/10.1007/3-540-45053-X_29

10. Paniagua, C., Puig, L., Guerrero, J.J.: Omnidirectional structured light in a flexible configuration. Sensors **13**(10), 13903–13916 (2013)

11. Mei, C., Rives, P.: Single view point omnidirectional camera calibration from planar grids. In: Proceedings of IEEE International Conference on Robotics and Automation, ICRA 2007, Rome, Italy (2007)

12. Puig, L., Bastanlar, Y., Sturm, P., Guerrero, J.J., Barreto, J.: Calibration of central catadioptric cameras using a DLT-like approach. Int. J. Comput. Vis. **93**(1), 101–114 (2011)

13. Barreto, J.P., Araujo, H.: Geometric properties of central catadioptric line images and their application in calibration. IEEE Trans. Pattern Anal. Mach. Intell. **27**(8), 1327–1333 (2005)

14. Scaramuzza, D., Martinelli, A., Siegwart R.: A flexible technique for accurate omnidirectional camera calibration and structure from motion. In: Proceedings 4th IEEE International Conference on Computer Vision Systems, ICVS 2006, NY, USA (2006)

15. Scaramuzza, D., Martinelli, A., Siegwart, R.: A toolbox for easily calibrating omnidirectional cameras. In: Proceedings of IEEE International Confernce on Intelligent Robots and Systems, IROS 2006, Beijing, China (2006)

16. Corke, P.: Robotics: Vision and Control: Fundamental Algorithms in MATLAB, 2nd edn. Springer, Cham (2017). https://doi.org/10.1007/978-3-319-54413-7

17. Hensel, S., Marinov, Marin B., Schwarz, R.: Fisheye camera calibration and distortion correction for ground based sky imagery. In: Proceedings of XXVII International Scientific Conference Electronics – ET 2018, Sozopol, Bulgaria, 13–15 September 2018 (2018)

18. Reda, I., Andreas, A.: Solar position algorithm for solar radiation application, Technical report, National Renewable Energy Laboratory (2008)

19. Asparuhova, K., Djamiykov, T., Spasov, I.: Research and design of effective positioning algorithm for solar tracking system. In: IX National Conference with International Participation (ELECTRONICA), Sofia (2018)

20. Kittler, R., Darula, S.: Cie general sky standard defining luminance distributions. In: Proceedings of Conference eSim 2002. The Canadian Conference on Building Energy Simulation (2002)

21. Hensel, S., Marinov, Marin B., Schwarz, R., Ganev, B.: Algorithms for cloud segmentation with ground-based camera images. In: Proceedings of International Conference Balkan Light 2018, Varna, Bulgaria, 20–22 September 2018 (2018)

22. Munkres, J.: Algorithms for the assignment and transportation problems. J. Soc. Ind. Appl. Math. **1**(5), 32–38 (1957)

GPU Extended Stock Market Software Architecture

Alisa Krstova$^{(\boxtimes)}$, Marjan Gusev, and Vladimir Zdraveski

Faculty of Computer Science and Engineering,
University Ss. Cyril and Methodius, Skopje, Macedonia
krstova.alisa@gmail.com

Abstract. We propose a stock market software architecture extended by a graphics processing unit, which employs parallel programming paradigm techniques to optimize long-running tasks like computing daily trends and performing statistical analysis of stock market data in real-time. The system uses the ability of Nvidia's CUDA parallel computation application programming interface (API) to integrate with traditional web development frameworks. The web application offers extensive statistics and stocks' information which is periodically recomputed through scheduled batch jobs or calculated in real-time. To illustrate the advantages of using many-core programming, we explore several use-cases and evaluate the improvement in performance and speedup obtained in comparison to the traditional approach of executing long-running jobs on a central processing unit (CPU).

Keywords: Stock market · GPU · Parallel programming · CUDA

1 Introduction

As more and more people become interested in getting familiar with and investing into the stock market, more research efforts are devoted for its analysis. The stock market is a complex platform which acts like an intermediary between the sellers of shares of stocks and the interested buyers. There are many details connected to the stock trading process that can be perplexing for the average investor or to a person who is just entering the market.

A good starting point to learn the intricacies of stock trading are web applications that simulate the stock market dynamics and offer an up-to-date overview of the stock market with all the relevant information (stock indexes, daily stock returns, volatility, Sharpe ratio etc.) being updated a few times per day. These web applications often act like a virtual stock market, where the users can learn how to build their investment portfolio, i.e. how to buy and sell shares in the most profitable way [1]. A crucial step in facilitating the process of making an

© ICST Institute for Computer Sciences, Social Informatics and Telecommunications Engineering 2019
Published by Springer Nature Switzerland AG 2019. All Rights Reserved
V. Poulkov (Ed.): FABULOUS 2019, LNICST 283, pp. 386–399, 2019.
https://doi.org/10.1007/978-3-030-23976-3_34

informed decision would be providing valuable insights about the situation on the stock market with the following use-cases:

- calculating daily/monthly/yearly stock returns,
- grouping together stocks that exhibit high correlation in returns and
- ranking stocks in terms of relevant metrics.

Note that some of these features have been integrated as part of the ByteWorx Contest, http://www.byteworx.eu/stock-contest/. Integrating such a module into the aforementioned virtual stock market system would help investors improve their risk management strategies.

Performing statistical analysis on a stock market dataset is different from applying these techniques in other fields, mostly due to the large amounts of collected data and the complex interactions between companies and individuals. This implies that constructing a web-based system that would offer all the relevant metrics re-computed in regular intervals from a stream of raw stock market data would come at a high computational cost. We aim to remedy this issue by proposing a prototype of a system which would harness the power of graphics processing units (GPUs) and the parallel programming paradigm in order to find patterns in a large stock market dataset obtained from Kaggle [2]. This dataset provides the full historical daily price and volume data for all US-based stocks and exchange-traded funds (ETFs) trading on the New York Stock Exchange (NYSE) and NASDAQ stock market and represents a good starting point for building our system.

The rest of the paper follows the following structure. Section 2 presents the related work. In Sect. 3 we describe the proposed solution to the problem of long-running tasks and the high computational cost that accompanies them. The parallelization approach this solution is based on is discussed in Sect. 4. The testing methodology used to validate the suggested concepts is described in Sect. 5 and an overview of the obtained results is demonstrated in Sect. 6. Finally, a summary of the evaluation process and concluding remarks are given in Sects. 7 and 8.

2   Related Work

The literature documents several attempts to analyze and extract knowledge from large stock market datasets using different techniques. Golan and Ziarko [3] employ a model based on the variable precision model of rough sets to acquire new knowledge from market data. There are also various stock market simulators which illustrate the principles of share trading in the form of interactive games, such as MarketWatch [4]. Many of these web applications support up to tens of thousands of users that can interact with the updated stock market data.

As we have already mentioned, a high number of users and large data volumes introduce the need for more compute-intensive operations, such as calculating user statistics, stock market indicators or identifying clusters of related stocks.

Much effort has been invested into attempting to discover meaningful relationships in data of such nature - the research presented by Gariney [5] describes several statistical measures whose integration into our system would accelerate the overall process of understanding stock market data.

Within the context of developing models for statistical analysis of data using a GPU/CUDA approach, some of the most interesting approaches include implementing the computation of pairwise Manhattan distance and Pearson correlation coefficient between data points presented in the work of Chang et al. [6]. Although not referring specifically to stock market data, the authors show that it is possible to obtain a speedup of up to 38 times when calculating this metric in comparison to the central processing unit implementation. We aim to test this claim in a stock market environment.

The hybrid approach of combining CUDA and the Message Parsing Interface (MPI) to compute the Pearson correlation coefficient described by Kijsipongse et al. in [7] offers valuable guidelines for implementing this kind of module in a distributed, possibly web-based environment. The research we propose, however, goes one step further by identifying relevant use cases for the integration of parallel computation in modern web development and testing the feasibility of this objective.

3   Proposed Solution

We propose a new web system architecture in order to decrease the load time of the virtual stock market web application by speeding up the underlying computations of relevant metrics. This section describes the extension of the traditional web architecture and the advanced use-cases that the improved web application model can be efficient for.

3.1   GPU Extended System Architecture

With large amounts of stock data being collected every day, the size of the problem at hand is scaled up, mostly due to the increased demand for web applications that deliver fast performance in analyzing this data. Web application speed is becoming more and more important for providing the impression of a fluid website experience and ultimately increasing user conversion rate. Handling thousands, sometimes even millions of records of stored or streamed stock market data to provide near real-time answers to user queries is challenging due to several factors, such as network strength, load distribution, traffic size and the nature of the computation itself. While the first factors are performance-indifferent, the problems we are trying to solve are susceptible to parallelization and thus allow room for performance improvements.

We propose extending the traditional monolithic web application architecture where the entire application is deployed onto several servers/containers by equipping each of these servers with a GPU.

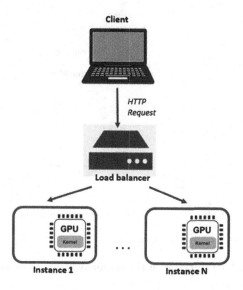

Fig. 1. Traditional monolithic architecture extended with GPU

Figure 1 presents how a HTTP request initiated by the client is first intercepted by a load balancer, which directs it to one of the available web server instances (e.g. Tomcat). This instance performs the requested computation using a CUDA kernel function which employs massively parallel computing on the built-in GPU and returns the result to the client.

3.2 Advanced Use-Cases

The aim of the proposed prototype of GPU-extended stock trading software architecture is to provide the user with an advanced, accurate and clean overview of her portfolio as well as the situation on the stock exchange of interest. The system contains several modules (functionalities):

- *Performance overview* - keeps track of the percentage change of the portfolio value for the current day, the total portfolio cost and value;
- *Transaction management* - tracks individual buy and sell transactions;
- *Visualization module* - provides stock charts for a chosen company illustrating price and volume trends for a given period of time (1 day, 1 week, 1 month etc.) and
- *Additional metrics* - determines volatility and Sharpe ratio for a given portfolio; calculates correlation coefficient of chosen company with any other company on the stock market based on past data.

We seek to optimize the computations which constitute the last module for displaying additional metrics.

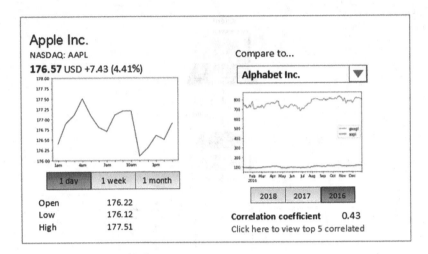

Fig. 2. User interface of the company comparison module

Figure 2 displays all relevant statistics the company view offers to the users, such as opening, closing, high and low prices for the chosen time period. The right side of the view enables the user to choose another company to compare to - a chart illustrating the closing prices across a given period for the two companies is given and the correlation coefficient is computed. The link at the bottom of the screen gives a list of the 5 companies with the closest correlation coefficient to the base choice company. The described concepts can be expanded to include other relevant metrics.

4   Parallelization Approach

We identify three scenarios related to stock market analysis that can be included as part of the *Additional Metrics* functionality illustrated in Sect. 3. More precisely, we propose computing metrics such as the Pearson correlation coefficient between stocks and the Sharpe ratio by exploiting the highly parallelizable nature of these problems. In addition, we describe a parallel CUDA approach to ranking/sorting stocks based on a metric like the Pearson correlation coefficient.

4.1   Identifying Related Stocks Using the Pearson Correlation Coefficient

From a user's perspective, the ultimate goal of buying shares is to make profit by buying stocks in companies that are expected to do well on the market, i.e. whose share price would rise. Upon inspecting current and past trends of the performance of a specific company, it can be useful to see whether another company exhibits similar or different behavior. One way to do this is by calculating the Pearson correlation coefficient between two variables, in this case two populations of stock market data for two companies. This coefficient can help to determine how well a mutual fund is behaving compared to its benchmark index, or how a mutual behaves in relation to another fund or asset class. It is also a useful tool for building a portfolio and mitigating risk - by adding a low or negatively correlated mutual fund to an existing portfolio, diversification is increased.

Assume X and Y hold the closing prices of CompanyX and CompanyY. A Pearson correlation coefficient $r_{X,Y}$ is defined by (1), where n is the number of samples, $\bar{X}$ and $\bar{Y}$ are the means of X and Y, respectively and σ_X and σ_Y are their standard deviations.

$$r_{X,Y} = \frac{\sum_{i=1}^{n}(X_i - \bar{X})(Y_i - \bar{Y})}{\sigma_X \sigma_Y} \tag{1}$$

The value for the correlation coefficient can range from -1.0 to 1.0, where -1.0 means perfect negative correlation, whereas 1.0 indicates perfect positive correlation.

Parallel reduction is used as a common data parallel primitive to speed up the computation of the mean and standard deviation. Although perhaps not evident at first sight, according to (2), computing the standard deviation can be treated partially as a reduction problem - computing sum of squares in the numerator can be done in parallel using reduction, which is one of the basic data parallel primitives. Also, calculating the mean of the input array can be implemented using parallel summation followed by division by the length of the array, n.

$$\sigma = \sqrt{\frac{\sum_{i=1}^{n} X_i^2}{n} - \bar{X}^2} \tag{2}$$

Processing large arrays which can have up to millions of elements means that multiple thread blocks must be used. The PyCUDA implementation [8] uses interleaved addressing to avoid bank conflicts and the shared memory to reuse intermediate results and data that has already been pulled from global memory.

4.2 Ranking Stocks Based on Correlation Coefficient

In addition to being able to find the degree to which two companies' shares movements are associated, another practical use-case would be to offer the user a list of most or least correlated companies with the one she is currently analyzing. For this purpose, we need to compute the Pearson correlation coefficient (1) between all pairs of company stock market data. This can be executed as a scheduled batch-job in a predefined time period, for example once a day.

The proposed approach would allow the resulting array of correlation coefficients for a given company to be constructed faster compared to a serial approach.

Upon a user request to display the most or least correlated companies for a certain company, a sorted array of correlation coefficients using the bitonic sort algorithm is implemented in CUDA [9,10]. We opt for this algorithm because it is highly parallelizable, i.e. the data to be sorted can be efficiently distributed among the threads in the GPU.

4.3 Parallel Computation of Sharpe Ratio

The Sharpe ratio is the average return earned in excess of the risk-free rate per unit of volatility or total risk. One way to better understand this metric is by observing a "zero-risk" portfolio which has a Sharpe ratio of exactly zero. The greater the value, the more attractive the risk-adjusted return. This metric can be computed by (3), where n is the number of business days used in the calculation for and d is the daily return as a vector for the given period.

$$Sharpe = \frac{\sqrt{n} \cdot \bar{d}}{\sigma_d} \tag{3}$$

We make use of the Pandas library in Python to compute the daily returns on a closing price series for a given portfolio and reuse the aforementioned parallelized code for determining the mean and standard deviation of the returns vector.

5   Testing Methodology

In order to illustrate the discussed concepts and identify the scenarios which might result in an improvement over the traditional methods of computation, we perform several experiments to compare the proposed parallelized approach with a serial solution.

The testing environment is a desktop computer using an Intel Core i5-4200M 2.5 GHz CPU for testing the sequential implementation of the programs. An NVIDIA GeForce GT 820M graphics card is used for the CUDA-based testing. This GPU configuration allows the utilization of CUDA with compute capability of 2.1, which implements concepts like atomic functions, 3D grids of thread blocks, surface functions etc. [11].

The software tools used as part of the testing methodology were Numpy, one of the most powerful and fast libraries for scientific computing with Python for the serial CPU implementation and PyCUDA, a fast Python wrapper for the CUDA parallel computation API, which integrates seamlessly with the Flask micro web framework. We chose PyCUDA for its robustness, automatic memory management and error checking, and near-zero wrapping overhead. Wise exploitation of these concepts, as well as the massively parallel hardware offered by the GPUs can lead to the time needed for a user to receive an HTTP response being determined only by the speed of the communication channel rather than the complexity of the request.

Kaggle dataset [2] is used in the experiments. Figure 3 gives an overview of how the stock market data is distributed over the years. The x-axis represents the year the data is collected for and the y-axis gives the corresponding number

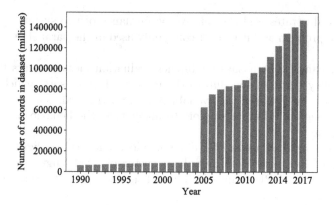

Fig. 3. Distribution of part of the records in the available dataset over the years

of available records for that year. The dates of the records in the dataset range from the beginning of 1962 until October 2017 and it can be seen that the amount of collected data has grown significantly in the period between 2005 and 2017[1], reaching a maximum of 1405977 records for 2017. The records are distributed unevenly among 7197 companies on the US stock market and provide enough data to experiment with finding correlations between older and newer data.

Our experiments aim at measuring the execution time of three different metrics. We consider the implementation, computation and evaluation of each of these metrics as three separate logical units, i.e. modules (M) denoted by:

- $M1$ to calculate the Pearson correlation,
- $M2$ to calculate the Sharpe ratio, and
- $M3$ to calculate the stocks ranking.

The response time for the sequential execution is denoted by $T_s(M)$ and for parallel $T_p(M)$, where M refers to either $M1, M2$ or $M3$.

Afterwards, we evaluate the possible speedup obtained by the parallelization approach for each identified module, calculated by (4).

$$S(M) = \frac{T_s(M)}{T_p(M)} \qquad (4)$$

The speedup is defined as the ratio of the sequential execution time to the parallel execution time, i.e. it measures the improvement in speed of execution of the specific task when using a parallel as opposed to a sequential method of processing. The larger the value of $S(M)$, the more significant the difference between the two measured times. The advantages of using this evaluation approach are several:

---

[1] The author of the dataset does not provide reasons for the very sharp increase in collected data between 2004 and 2005.

- Speedup illustrates well the relative performance of two systems processing the same problem and it is most commonly used in the parallel programming world.
- Speedup can also be a base for further evaluation measurements like parallel efficiency (ratio of speedup to the number of processors) which provides information on how well the available resources are used.
- We can generate informative plots to understand the behavior of the parallelized code.
- By computing the speedup for different block and grid configurations for a problem of fixed size (for example, a vector of fixed length) we can identify the optimal GPU setup which would significantly outperform sequential processing.

The experiments consist of test cases with different block sizes - we compare the efficiency of the program when using 32, 64, 128, 256, 512 and 1024 threads per block (block sizes). The blocks are launched in a grid of blocks with dynamically determined dimensions, depending on the size of the array.

Different aspects of the dataset are taken into consideration for modules $M1$ to $M3$. For $M1$, as input (the x-axis on Fig. 4) we take two arrays of equal length consisting of closing prices for two companies over the same period of time. For $M2$, the computations are also performed over a single array of closing prices, however the daily returns are calculated first. Finally, for $M3$ as input we take an array of values for the Pearson correlation coefficient between N pairs of companies.

The size of the input also varies in each module. In $M1$ for a given company, the number of available information about the closing prices ranges from 16 thousand to 1.6 million. For $M2$, in order to obtain a noticeable improvement in performance, a bigger dataset was needed and the experiments were conducted on several dataset sizes ranging from 16 thousand to 11.6 million records. Finally, for $M3$ the number of values to be sorted goes up to 1.4 million.

6   Evaluation of Results

This section describes the obtained results and evaluates the performance of the proposed parallelized approach for calculating metrics as opposed to using standard methods and libraries.

To illustrate the benefits of parallel computing we artificially extend the available dataset for the query companies by replicating and applying minor transformations to the closing prices. More specifically, we replicate the original vector to reach the desired size and add a random number between 0 and 2 to every value except the original ones. The random number added to the replicated closing prices conforms with the volatile nature of the stock market (if we exclude major political or economic events, the closing prices usually do not vary dramatically from day to day).

Figure 4 compares the execution time needed to calculate the Pearson correlation coefficient on vectors with variable number of elements. For a given

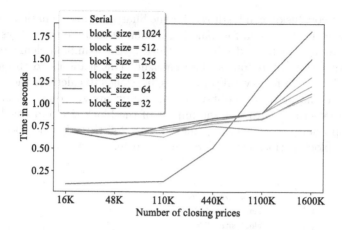

Fig. 4. Performance evaluation of $M1$ module for Pearson correlation coefficient calculation.

company, the number of available information about the closing prices ranges from 16 thousand to 1.6 million (as shown on the x-axis is a logarithmic scale of the number of closing prices, and y-axis the execution time (in seconds) of computing the $M1$ module of Pearson correlation coefficient.

One can observe that for vectors with a relatively small number of instances, the CPU version significantly outperforms our PyCUDA implementation. This is because a lot of time is lost on initializing the kernel function, copying the input vectors to and from the GPU etc. The benefit of using the parallel approach becomes evident for arrays larger than 400 thousand elements - the relatively constant CUDA execution time (around 0.7 s) is a better result than the growing value for Numpy's execution time.

After performing experiments with several different block sizes, as explained in Sect. 5, we can see that most block sizes yield similar results in performance. The block size that stands out with lowest execution time is 256 threads per block, as shown in Fig. 4.

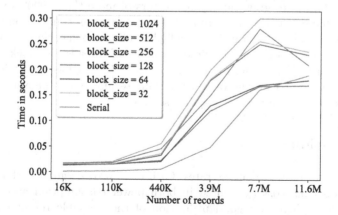

Fig. 5. Performance evaluation of $M2$ module for Sharpe ratio calculation.

A similar conclusion can be drawn for the Sharpe ratio calculation - the standard way is efficient enough for handling moderate to large-size arrays (Fig. 5). The performance starts to decline after hitting the 7-million-elements mark - this is when PyCUDA becomes more efficient. This leads us to the idea that we can combine data for several companies/portfolios to calculate the respective values for the Sharpe ratio to obtain a more significant speedup. We have again run several experiments to test the impact of the block size and conclude that the most optimal performance is achieved with 256 threads per block, with 64 threads per block performing insignificantly worse.

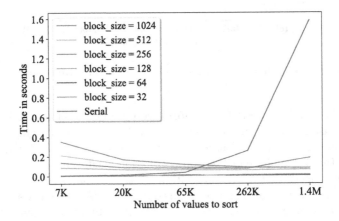

Fig. 6. Performance evaluation of $M3$ module for sorting of correlation.

Finally, we evaluate the performance of the bitonic sort algorithm on the Pearson correlation coefficient vectors computed using the parallel approach. Once again we compare the time of execution of the PyCUDA implementation and the standard Python sorting method. There is a negligible difference between the two approaches in processing vectors of moderate size. The gap in performance starts to grow rapidly on vectors of more than 20000 values - the parallel bitonic sort performs more than 4 times faster in comparison to sorting on the CPU. Figure 6 illustrates the negligible difference in execution time when running the bitonic sort with a different number of threads per block. Although the concept of implementing bitonic sort with PyCUDA has been tried out on sorting correlation coefficient values, the same technique can be applied to any other stock market metric that requires sorting.

7 Discussion

As the previous section demonstrates, GPUs can provide good performance at low computational cost (measured in both power consumption and execution time) provided there is a good utilization of the available resources. Thread block size is a key factor in determining kernel occupancy. Kernel occupancy can be defined as the ratio of active warps on a Streaming Multiprocessor (SM) to the maximum number of active warps supported by the SM [12]. This metric is important as it provides information as to how well the parallel kernel is using the allocated GPU resources.

Multiple grid and thread block sizes can provide high kernel occupancy, however different configurations can lead to differences in execution time. We seek to explore the effect of specifying different combinations of grid and block sizes to optimize the parallelized approach for each module. In particular, we are interested to apply the hypothesis that larger block sizes lead to better results, as noted by Connors and Qasem [13].

Our experiments show that different configurations affect the performance of the CUDA implementation for the three discussed problems differently. For instance, the most optimal thread block size for computing the Pearson correlation coefficient has been shown to be 256 threads per block, leading to a speedup of 2.6 times compared to the serial implementation. The same holds for the calculation of the Sharpe ratio for a vector of stock market records - performance is best when we use 256 threads per block, yielding a speedup of up to 1.2 times.

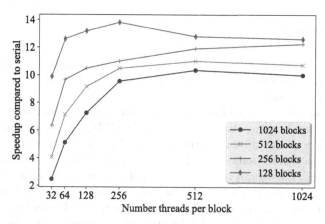

Fig. 7. Speedup diagram - bitonic sort

We conduct additional trials for the last use-case, that is sorting records using the bitonic sort algorithm. Figure 7 illustrates the dependency between using different grid and block sizes and the resulting speedup. We perform 4 series of experiments with 4 different grid sizes, i.e. 128, 256, 512 and 1024 blocks. The respective block sizes (threads per block) are given on the x-axis and the resultant speedup is shown on the y-axis. We conclude that it is best to use a grid size of 128 blocks and 256 threads per block; this allows the sorting task to execute up to 13.8 times faster than the sequential version of the program. As can be seen from the plot, for grid sizes larger than 256, a bigger number of threads in each block leads to better performance compared to using less threads for the same grid size.

It can be noticed that 256 threads per block has proven to be optimal in all three cases, which means that larger block sizes do lead to satisfactory results.

In spite of CUDA's superior performance in processing very long sequences of data, there is a lower bound to the vector size for which the parallel approach becomes more efficient than the sequential. This lower bound is different for the three problems. For the Pearson correlation coefficient, the CPU is faster in processing sequences of up to 400 thousand elements. The Sharpe ratio has an even higher threshold - the GPU accelerated version of the computation starts to outperform for sequences longer than 7 million elements. This is because Python libraries like Numpy are specifically designed to utilize the CPU resources in the most optimal way. However, this result leads us to the conclusion that in order to make the most out of the GPU execution environment, we should either increase the complexity of the problem, while still allowing room for parallelization or combine multiple simple computations in one. We show that sorting is a good example of the first concept, where the GPU accelerated bitonic sort algorithm is superior to the CPU sorting technique even for moderately large arrays of 20 thousand elements. With an optimal resource distribution, the maximal speedup is 14 times compared to the sequential version.

8   Conclusion

In this paper, we described several use-cases for a stock market software system and proposed a parallel-programming approach to optimize the computations these use-cases include.

We proposed a system architecture which has the advantage over traditional web architectures in a way that it incorporates a GPU to speed up computations. The lower time needed for calculating the result requested from the user would lead to a decrease in response time. This means that if the relevant computations are fast enough, the overall response time will depend only on the speed of the communication channel. The paper also provided a view on the user interface which encompasses the use-cases. Finally, we evaluated the performance of the parallel approaches to compute the desired metrics compared to the traditional CPU methods.

Our current research efforts are directed towards applying the described concepts to other relevant metrics, such as ranking users by their performance, identifying related stocks by means of clustering analysis etc. We also seek to explore the approach of having a single GPU thread block allocated per user in order to speed up individual computations. Furthermore, we are interested in evaluating the effect of breaking down the monolithic architecture into dedicated microservices which would also incorporate GPU-accelerated computations and then comparing the two architectures.

References

1. Peachavanish, R.: Stock selection and trading based on cluster analysis of trend and momentum indicators. In: Proceedings of the International MultiConference of Engineers and Computer Scientists, vol. 1, pp. 317–321 (2016)
2. Marjanovic, B.: Huge stock market dataset. https://www.kaggle.com/borismarjanovic/price-volume-data-for-all-us-stocks-etfs. Accessed 02 May 2018
3. Golan, R.H., Ziarko, W.: A methodology for stock market analysis utilizing rough set theory. In: Computational Intelligence for Financial Engineering: Proceedings of the IEEE/IAFE 1995, pp. 32–40. IEEE (1995)
4. Marketwatch - an online virtual stock market simulator. https://www.marketwatch.com/game. Accessed 02 May 2018
5. Gariney, V.: Statistical analysis for daily forecast of stock prices (2002)
6. Chang, D.-J., Desoky, A.H., Ouyang, M., Rouchka, E.C.: Compute pairwise Manhattan distance and Pearson correlation coefficient of data points with GPU. In: 2009 10th ACIS International Conference on Software Engineering, Artificial Intelligences, Networking and Parallel/Distributed Computing, pp. 501–506 (2009)
7. Kijsipongse, E., Suriya, U., Ngamphiw, C., Tongsima, S.: Efficient large Pearson correlation matrix computing using hybrid MPI/CUDA. In: 2011 Eighth International Joint Conference on Computer Science and Software Engineering (JCSSE), pp. 237–241, May 2011
8. Klöckner, A., Pinto, N., Catanzaro, B., Lee, Y., Ivanov, P., Fasih, A.: GPU scripting and code generation with PyCUDA. In: GPU Computing Gems Jade Edition, pp. 373–385. Elsevier (2011)
9. Mu, Q., Cui, L., Song, Y.: The implementation and optimization of Bitonic sort algorithm based on CUDA, CoRR, vol. abs/1506.01446 (2015). http://arxiv.org/abs/1506.01446
10. Ionescu, M.F., Schauser, K.E.: Optimizing parallel Bitonic sort. In: Parallel Processing Symposium: Proceedings, 11th International, pp. 303–309. IEEE (1997)
11. NVIDIA Corporation: Compute capabilities. https://docs.nvidia.com/cuda/cuda-c-programming-guide/index.html#compute-capabilities. Accessed 12 May 2018
12. NVIDIA Corporation, Gameworks Documentation, "Achieved occupancy". https://docs.nvidia.com/gameworks/content/developertools/desktop/analysis/report/cudaexperiments/kernellevel/achievedoccupancy.htm. Accessed 12 May 2018
13. Connors, T.A., Qasem, A.: Automatically selecting profitable thread block sizes for accelerated kernels. In: 2017 IEEE 19th International Conference on High Performance Computing and Communications; IEEE 15th International Conference on Smart City; IEEE 3rd International Conference on Data Science and Systems (HPCC/SmartCity/DSS), pp. 442–449, December 2017

Providers and Consumers Mutual Benefits in Energy Efficiency Model with Elements of Cooperative Game Theory

Igor Bimbiloski[✉], Valentin Rakovic, and Aleksandar Risteski

Faculty of Electrical Engineering and Information Technology,
Univ. Ss. Cyril and Methodius, Skopje, Macedonia
igor.bimbiloski@gmail.com,
{valentin, acerist}@feit.ukim.edu.mk

Abstract. Energy efficiency is a process under development and execution in all levels of society and economy, mostly driven by the environment protection interests. One of dilemmas in this process is the interest of the electricity provider companies, what kind of model to use in order to secure their profitability and benefits from energy efficiency projects deployment? This paper is presenting an ICT model for energy efficiency, model with scalable development, starting on a level of fundamental and currently available resources. The model is consumer centric and integrates communication tools. Using the approach of cooperative game theory, we are analyzing if this model is beneficial for all stakeholders in energy efficiency chain, the providers and the consumers. Having in mind the diversity of markets for electricity, in our case we deal with the simplest scenario, considering provider – consumer relation in two regimes of electricity network stage, peak and normal load, as the baseline from where the specific commercial cases could be further developed.

Keywords: Energy efficiency model · Electricity providers' interests ·
Cooperative approach · Game theory

1 Introduction

Game theory is the theory of "strategic thinking" [1]. It is recently gaining ground in systems and control engineering, mostly in engineered systems involving humans, where there is a trend to use game theoretic tools to design protocols that will provide incentives for stakeholders to cooperate. For instance, scientists tend to use game theoretic tools to predict or avoid blackouts in power networks.

Utility companies as suppliers (providers) of the electricity are implementing DSM (Demand Side Management) programs to control the energy consumption at the customer side of the meter [2]. These programs are deployed to use the available energy more efficiently without installing new generation and transmission infrastructure, i.e. without significant investments.

Different DSM programs include diversity of approaches: conservation and energy efficiency programs, fuel substitution programs, demand response programs, and residential or commercial load management programs. Residential load management

V. Poulkov (Ed.): FABULOUS 2019, LNICST 283, pp. 400–412, 2019.
https://doi.org/10.1007/978-3-030-23976-3_35

programs usually aim at one or both of the following objectives: reducing consumption and shifting (migrating) consumption. This can be achieved among users by encouraging energy-aware consumption patterns and by constructing more energy efficient buildings.

Also, there is a need for practical solutions to shift the high-power household appliances to off-peak hours to reduce the peak-to-average ratio (PAR) in load demand. Moreover, unbalanced conditions resulting from an increasing number of electric appliances (e.g. electric cars) may lead to further degradation of the power quality, voltage problems, and even potential damage to utility and consumer equipment if the system is not properly reinforced.

In this paper, we will consider the topic of consumer behavior and consumption patterns change as a driver for the electricity efficiency. On the DSM side, we will consider the scalable model with minimum investments for achieving energy efficient management. We will consider cooperative game theory approach as a beneficial for both provider and consumer side.

In next chapter, we are presenting the model development in 3 (three) levels. The first level, the basic level is about building the interactions between utility company and each user with current electricity infrastructure and communication devices. Actually, we present the usage of the smart devices connected to the mobile telecom infrastructure and mobile applications as a main tool for handling the consumer behavior. The next level is deployment of smart meters and real time follow up of the electricity load by user individually, which will personalize the communication among utility and consumer. And the last level, third level is about full automation of the process, using M2 M, IoT and AI tools for control and management of electricity consumption and network load.

The third chapter is explaining the model for the communication on the first and basic level, the main architecture and the flows. In the next chapter, we use the game theory to prove that the usage of this model is beneficial for all the stakeholders of the ecosystem: providers, consumers and environment protection goals.

2 Developing the Model

The development of the model is considering few aspects of the electricity industry and the technical ecosystem around. It considers the aspect of current interest of the stakeholders in the industry, investments and financial implications, environment protection targets, and consumer behavior and interests. The purpose of this model is to be applicable in the current environment of the electricity (energy) industry, and ready to be extended according to the expected technical extensions.

2.1 Basic Idea of the Model

In this model, the end user i.e. the consumer is in the center of the energy ecosystem and consequently the proposed model is consumer-oriented model. The assumption is that the consumer can be in 3 (three) types of state (state of movement, at home and at work, as shown in Fig. 1), according to which the appropriate energy efficiency model is determined [3].

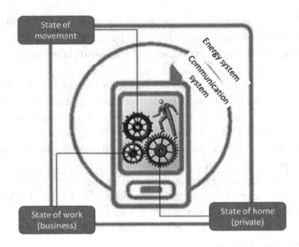

Fig. 1. The states of the energy consumer in a user-oriented model for energy efficiency

The model includes the use of smart phones as a tool to identify the state of the consumer, while at the same time it will also serve as a communication tool through which directions and advices (messages, information, etc.) will be received about the behavior of the consumer. Considering the everyday use of smart phones and mobile applications, as well as user dependency and time of use, it is expected that their use will strongly affect energy efficiency habits.

One group of EU-related interventions concerns the commutation and engagement of users, information and promotions, training, personal advice, etc. The concept that is dealt with in this paper should contribute to energy savings initiatives by changing user behavior with information and engagement of users by applying smart phones and mobile applications.

2.2   Structure and Elements of Model

The draft model will use the two common basic elements: consumer and supplier.

The first element - the consumer i.e. man will be identified through the smartphone and it can be located in three states: state of work, a state of home and a state of movement, as shown in Fig. 1.

- State of movement (Movement mode) - It is a condition where the user uses a transport. Upon entering the user in the vehicle, the mobile phone enters a special "driving mode", using micro-localization through an existing communication PAN network. In this mode, the mobile device starts communicating with a special central application "Traffic application". This application provides information on the user's route, whether it is in private or public transport. It is a central application that collects data from all users.

- State of work (Working Mode) - Each office and office space is equipped with a network device and micro-localization of the employees via the mobile phone can be performed. According to these data, algorithms for monitoring and managing the habits of employees can be made.
- State of home (Home mode) - If there is a wireless private network in the home (e.g. a Wi-Fi network connected to the Internet), then the user with a mobile device when entering the home will be registered that enters a private area. If this is to be linked to a central application, it can thus have an insight into the electricity consumption and can automatically send messages to the user about the amount of energy consumed, the price, and dynamics of consumption or activities that should be taken. Also, this opens up the possibility of creating separate tariff packages for different types of users, similar to the example of telecom operators.

The second element is the supplier, who will be identified through the facility and the electric meter in business or private facilities or vehicles for transporting energy consumers. Accordingly, we will have three forms of suppliers of metering energy: a supplier of business facilities, a supplier of private facilities and a supplier of consumer transport (Fig. 2).

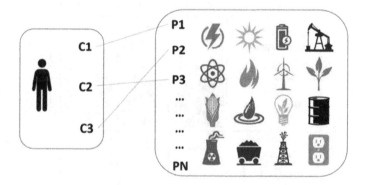

Fig. 2. Connection of the consumer state with the energy supplier

2.3 Scalability and Applicability of the Model

The purpose of the model is to be a universal model, applicable to all situations of the energy environment, starting from the very basic energy supply in under developed regions, but extendable to the state of the art technology environment in a highly developed and competitive environment.

The first level of applicability of the model, the basic level is the environment with basic supply energy infrastructure, consisting mostly on electricity distribution with no developed other energy supply (Fig. 3). This is the case that actually exists in the developing areas e.g. Macedonia, where there is still a monopoly of the electricity distribution, and very limited heating and gas supply infrastructure.

The second level considers deployment of the smart meters on the energy distribution system, which is the basic and essential step in a way towards smart grid. This is already under deployment in many countries, but still need time and investments to achieve the final level of a smart grid.

And the third and final stage considers the usage of advanced ICT tools, like IoT systems at home, in office in transport, and usage of big data analytics and Artificial Intelligence. In this phase, the full automation of the energy system is expected, where the consumer behavior will be completely followed by the ICT systems and no consumer intervention – action will be needed for the control and monitoring of the systems.

In this paper, we will start with the basic model prediction about the potential savings in energy, mostly on the electricity saving at home (Fig. 3, scope of this paper). Our goal is to examine if this model is beneficial to be used by electricity providers to implement it and use it, especially for the purpose of the load balancing and to predict or avoid blackouts in power networks.

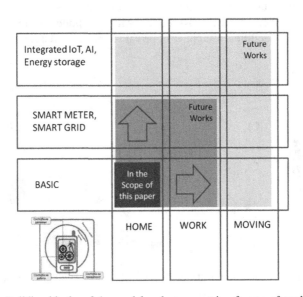

Fig. 3. Building blocks of the model and cross-matrix of areas of applicability

3 Provider's and Consumer's Benefits in Cooperative Game Theory Approach

3.1 Element of the Game Theory and the Nature of the Environment

Game theory is more frequently used as a tool for analysis and strategy definition in energy systems [4–9].

The elements of the game theory that is used in the proposed model and accordingly in this paper are:

- Provider of the electricity, and
- Consumer of electricity at home.

The motives and consequently the strategies of these elements are opposite one to another: provider motive is to maximize the profitability by optimum consumption and distribution in time, and consumer motives to reduce the consumption but in a reasonable manner which will fulfill life standards. One of the important elements in this story is environmental protection, which means reduction and effectiveness in energy consumption.

The assumption is that the provider has live information (real time info) of the total consumption of the electricity that it's provided on the predefined area with definite number of consumers. The timeframe (resolution) of measurement of electricity consumption is predefined by the provider (seconds, minutes, or hours). The main goal of the provider is to avoid picks in the electricity consumption, because the price he pays for the pick electricity towards the electricity production is higher than the regular price, but not compensated by the end users. We assume that the end users have the flat price for the electricity in the time, and they do not have any info about the consumption of electricity, neither for its own home, and neither for the total consumption.

The model that we are proposing, predicts the use of the mobile platform which consists of few elements (Fig. 4):

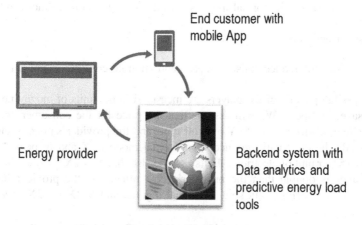

Fig. 4. Mobile platform system architecture

- Storage and processing unit, with modules for predicting electricity consumption. The modules will be based on machine learning and AI predictive algorithms, according to the available info in the provider database and from consumers. The collection of the data will use IoT systems and smart grid technologies.
- Administrative Unit for notifications towards the end consumers, manage by provider. Based on the load of the network and price deviations of electricity, provider could request appropriate actions from the consumers.
- Mobile app, used by the end users for receiving information about electricity savings and efficiency. Mobile app is sending real time notification to consumers with a request to act (reduce or migrate the energy consumption in other time frame). Consumers could download the app from Google and iOS for free.

- Also, the system is using available 3G/4G or Wi-Fi networks and applications for localization of the smartphone i.e. consumer and its state (work, home or movement).

There are 2 (two) states of the environment that the ecosystem (nature) is working, the normal state when the electricity consumption is usual one and there are no expected abnormal changes, and the second stage of the ecosystem (nature) is when there are predicted extraordinary deviations in electricity consumption, like extreme temperature change, events (music, sport, meetings,), natural disasters…

The provider P, can have two actions to choose: a) to send an info to the end consumer C and ask him to reduce or shift the electricity consumption whet it is in normal mode of loading b) to send request to reduce or shift the consumption from peak to normal time. The option not to send request or info, considers that there is no action on consumer side anyhow. The consumer C has 3 (three) options to choose, (a) to accept the request of provider and take an action for reduction (b) to shift the consumption (c) not to take any action.

Provider action set:

$$A_P = \{\text{send info in normal mode}, \text{send info in overload mode}, \text{not send}\} \quad (1)$$

Consumer action set:

$$A_C = \{\text{act and reduce consuption}, \text{act and migrate consuption}, \text{not act}\}. \quad (2)$$

The possible payoffs of the players are measured in the units of money i.e. money that are saved or spent. We will assume that the price for the consumer per unit of electricity (e.g. kWh) is equal to Y over all time, and the provider's price of electricity cost (towards the electricity producers) in normal mode is X and in peak (overload regime) is 4X per unit of electricity. Let's assume also that Y = 2X, i.e. that the price of the consumer is double than the provider's cost price, and the provider has profit Y-X = X for each energy unit sold in normal regime, and Y-4X = −2X loss in peak regime.

In Table 1, we will assume that the average volume of the electricity which is the subject of request for reduction or shift is 1 unit of electricity (e.g. 1 kWh) in some definite period of time (e.g. 1 h).

In normal regime, the interest of the provider is to keep the higher level of consumption and earn maximum revenue from consumers within the planed limits of total network load. If the provider sends a request for reduction of the consumption and the consumers accept it, the provider will have a lost opportunity of −X profit, and the consumer will benefit of +2X savings. Or, payoff in this scenario will be $\prod$(P, C) = (−1X, +2X), where $\prod$(P, C) shows the payoffs of the provider (P) and the consumer (C), respectively (Table 1). So, this is the regime that is not beneficial for the provider to take any action for reduction of consumption. But, when the providers ask the consumer to allocate the consumption in another time slot, than payoff of the provider is neutral $\prod$(P, C) = (0, 0). Also, if the consumer does not take action, the effect on both sides is neutral $\prod$(P, C) = (0, 0).

Table 1. Game theory for Provider-Consumer

		Consumer		
		Act to reduce	Act to migrate	Not acting
Provider	Normal regime	Reduce units (−1, −1)	Migrate units (1, 1)	
		Payoff (−1X, +2X)	Payoff (0, 0)	Payoff (0, 0)
	Peak regime	Reduce units (−1, −1)	Migrate units (1, 1)	
		Payoff (+2X, +2X)	Payoff (+4X, 0)	Payoff (−2X, 0)

What is very important case for the provider is the peak regime of the network. In this case, when the provider has an outspending for extra load (4X price payment for extra electricity from producers) it is beneficial to request the consumer to reduce the energy. For the provider, is more beneficial to shift the consumption of the energy from the peak to normal regime in other time slot. The provider will generate losses of -2X if the consumer do not take any action $\prod(P, C) = (−2X, 0)$. So, when the provider enters (or predict) the overload of the network, then it's beneficial to take an action. If the consumer reduce the consumption, the payoff is equal on both sides $\prod(P, C) = (+2X, + 2X)$, or when the consumer shift the consumption from pick to normal regime the provider has the maximum payoff of +4X, $\prod(P, C) = (+4X, 0)$.

For the consumer, any scenario is either beneficial or neutral, so there are no doubts that the consumers will benefit of deployment of the model. The provider overall will benefit, if he manages the load of consumption on appropriate way by using proposed model.

3.2   Game Theory Tree

Figure 5 is showing the game theory tree, where we can see the moves and payoffs of provider and consumer. We have seen from the table before that the highest interest of the provider is to use the system for shifting of consumption, because its interest is to improve profitability. That's why we are considering that for this purpose the provider will use the system most frequently, with probability of 50%. But in the same time, the provider need to balance with the consumer interest, and considering that consumer is neutral in shift scenario and positive in reduce scenario, the provider should use the system for the purpose of reduction of consumption, too. In the reduction scenario, provider is negative in payoff in the neutral regime, but positive when he is working in peak mode. So, in other to balance the interests of both sides, considering the providers leading role in management of the platform, we assume the probability for migration on 50% of the cases, little less but still in the balance of 40% for the reduction, and 10% of non-interest.

If we follow the assumptions from above, and the probabilities for the provider requests as it is explaining in Fig. 5, we could calculate the payoff of the provider of the usage of the system. The total payoff of the provider is:

$$2X * 0.4 * 0.4 + 4X * 0.4 * 0.5 + (−2X) * 0.05 * 0.1 = 1.11\ X \text{ (units of money)} \quad (3)$$

PAYOFF

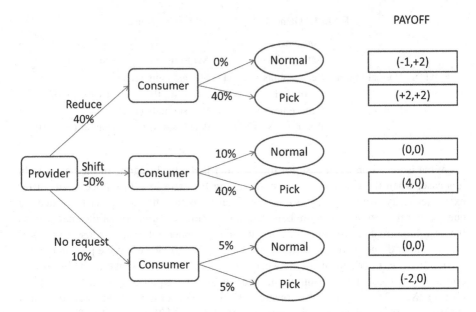

Fig. 5. Game theory tree for provider – consumer actions

We see that with this model the payoff of the provider on the profitability level with above assumptions is 1.11 X units of money, per request for 1 unit of electricity change in definite time. The consumer side is beneficial anyhow, so the model is acceptable for all stakeholders in the electricity market.

Figure 6 shows that the breakeven of profitability of the provider using this model with the assumptions from Fig. 5, is achieved on level of peak price 1.5 X, which is lower than the consumer price of Y = 2X. Also, we could see that the benefit of the provider is higher than the consumer one when the peak price is 2.7 or higher than the normal price of production.

3.3   The Model with Two Pricing Tariffs on Consumer Side

The pricing model on the consumer side could include more than one tariff, which means that the price for consumer is not equal over the whole time as we have analyzed above. Further on, we will analyze 2-tariff price model on the consumer side, where the cheap tariff Z = X, meaning that the profit on provider side in this regime is Z-X = 0. This is the case where the regulation is imposing social support for some segments of the community. The analysis with this assumption is presented below in Table 2. The other inputs in the model are the same as before for the peak and normal regime of work.

If the consumer is in the cheap regime, it means that the reduction of electricity will produce payoff on the consumer side as X as a saving, and the provider payoff will be 0 as profit neutral, $\prod(P, C) = (0, +X)$. So, for the provider, any kind of activity in cheap regime is neutral.

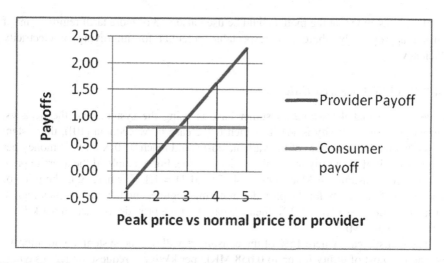

Fig. 6. Provider payoff as function of cost of electricity in peak load (consumer price is Y = 2X, normal provider cost for electricity production is 1X)

Table 2. Payoffs for Provider-Consumer in 2 tariff consumer pricing model

		Consumer			
		Act to reduce	Act to migrate		Not acting
Provider	Cheap regime (Y = X)	Reduce units (−1, −1)			
		Payoff (0, +1X)	Payoff (0, 0)		Payoff (0, 0)
	Normal regime (Y = 2X)	Reduce units (−1, −1)	Migrate units (1, 1) to cheap	Migrate units (1, 1) to normal	
		Payoff (−1X, +2X)	Payoff (−1X, +1X)	Payoff (0, 0)	Payoff (0, 0)
	Peak regime	Reduce units (−1, −1)	Migrate units (1, 1) to cheap	Migrate units (1, 1) to cheap	
		Payoff (+2X, +2X)	Payoff (+3X, +1X)	Payoff (+4X, 0)	Payoff (−2X, 0)

If the environment is in the normal regime, and we have a migration of the consumption from normal to cheap regime, than the provider has a profit losses of −X, $\prod(P, C) = (-X, +X)$. In the other cases in this regime, the situation is as in the Table 1. This shows that the provider has no interest to shift the usage of the electricity from normal to cheap regime, which is understandable considering that this is usually the regime of work for social support of vulnerable social categories. But, when the network is in the peak regime of work, the provider has an interest to migrate the consumption to the cheap regime, $\prod(P, C) = (+3X, +X)$. So in general, the model could produce more benefit if it is appropriately used even in the 2-tariff price regime.

We can assume that the model could be used also in 3 or more tariff regimes, and if it used appropriately, there is a respectable potential for improving of electricity efficiency.

3.4   Realistic Localized Case

If we assume that the whole consumer base is using the system, and the peak vs. normal price of electricity is +20% (which is the case in Macedonia [10]), the system shows that the improvement of the variable cost could reach 0.10 X units of money per action per unit of electricity in definite period of time. For example, if the average price per kWh for consumer in Macedonia is 4,731 MKD = 1,1 X, where X is the price of production of electricity for the provider in normal regime, and the price in pick regime for the provider is +20% or 1.2 X, then the payoff of the provider per action per kWh is 0.09 X or 0.387 MKD.

The realistic case where 15% of the consumers will use the system, could improve the variable cost of utility for up to 0.058 MKD per kWh per request, or 1.2% savings could be achieved from the total cost of the provider (Fig. 7).

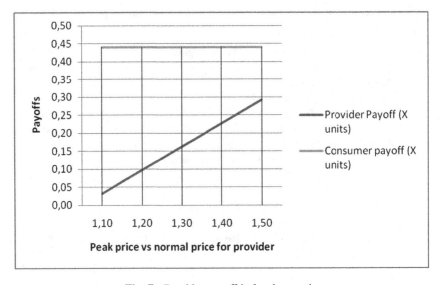

Fig. 7. Provider payoff in local scenario

4   Summary and Future Works

The success of the energy efficiency initiatives depends on the interests of the involved stakeholders, starting from the environment protection institutions, consumers, electricity providers, technology developers, regulatory bodies. One of the key stakeholders in the chain are electricity providers, who are the main pillar for successful deployment of energy efficiency initiatives, starting from the building of awareness and engagement of their consumer base, up to the smart grid technology deployment. The key element for providers is benefits on profitability that the energy efficiency models will deliver.

In this paper, we analyze the benefits of deployment of the proposed ICT model for electricity providers and consumers. The proposed model is scalable from development perspective, and also it is applicable on different levels depending from the market situation. In order to find whether the model is beneficial for electricity providers, we have analyzed the basic relation provider-consumer, and we have proved that the model is beneficial for both, by using approach of cooperative game theory. Actually, in this model, we assume that the provider-consumer communication is used for reduction and shift of the individual consumer electricity load, from one to the other regime: shifting the load from pick to normal and reducing the load from normal regime. Separately, these scenarios are not beneficial for provider, but in a combination and appropriate management, the total benefit of the usage of the model shows positive results for the provider.

The diversity in the market of electricity consumption should be considered with different assumptions adapted to the market circumstances, and accordingly the benefits for the provider and consumer could vary case by case, but in general it produces a positive payoff for both players. There is a breakpoint where the benefits of the provider could be even higher than the consumer benefits, and also there is another breakpoint where the provider has negative payoff.

The future works should consider different scenarios in different markets and should search for the best balance of provider-consumer benefits. Also, considering that the model in this paper is analyzed only for home environment, it should be further analyzed within extended levels 2 and 3, including smart grid and IoT effects, where the consumer behavior will be minimized and M2M steering of the energy consumption will be deployed. We believe that the payoff effects in the new scenarios will be higher for both consumer and provider players.

References

1. Bauso, D.: "Game Theory: Models, Numerical Methods and Applications" - Dipartimento di Ingegneria Chimica. Gestionale, Informatica, Meccanica, Università di Palermo, Foundations and Trends R in Systems and Control 1(4), 379–522 (2014)
2. Mohsenian-Rad, A.H., Wong, V.W., Jatskevich, J., Schober, R., Leon-Garcia, A.: Autonomous Demand-Side Management Based on Game-Theoretic Energy Consumption Scheduling for the Future Smart Grid. Paper no. TSG-00045-2010 (2010)
3. Bimbiloski, I., Risteski, A.: Draft Concept for Energy Efficiency Improvements with usage of Smart Phones and Artificial Neural Networks. ETAI 2018, Struga, Macedonia (2018)
4. Han, S., Lu, Y., Yang, S., Mu, X.: Game Theory-Based Energy Efficiency Optimization in Multi-User Cognitive MIMO Interference Channel. School of Information Engineering, Zhengzhou University, Zhengzhou 450001, China, 2016 IEEE MTT-S International Wireless Symposium (IWS) (2016)
5. Wei, F., Liu, J.Q., Yang, Z.H., Ni, F.: A game theoretic approach for distributed energy trading in district energy networks. In: 2017 IEEE Conference on Energy Internet and Energy System Integration (EI2)

6. Mohsenian-Rad, A.-H., Wong, V.W.S., Jatskevich, J., Schober, R.: Optimal and Autonomous Incentive-based Energy Consumption Scheduling Algorithm for Smart Grid. Department of Electrical and Computer Engineering The University of British Columbia, Vancouver, Canada, 2010 Innovative Smart Grid Technologies (ISGT)
7. Marzband, M., Javadi, M., Domínguez-García, J.L., Moghaddam, M.M.: Non-cooperative game theory based energy management systems for energy district in the retail market considering DER uncertainties. IET Gener. Transm. Distrib. **10**(12), 2999–3009 (2016)
8. Deng, R., Yang, Z., Chen, J., Asr, N.R., Chow, M.Y.: Residential energy consumption scheduling: a coupled-constraint game approach. IEEE Trans. Smart Grid **5**(3), 1340–1350 (2014)
9. Saad, W., Han, Z., Vincent Poor, H., Basar, T.: Game theoretic methods for the smart grid. In: 2012 in IEEE Signal Processing Magazine (2012)
10. Energy Regulatory Commission of Republic of Macedonia, Electricity Prices (2016)

Parallelism in Signature Based Virus Scanning with CUDA

Andrej Dimitrioski[✉], Marjan Gusev, and Vladimir Zdraveski

Faculty of Computer Science and Engineering,
"Ss. Cyril and Methodius" University, Skopje, Republic of Macedonia
`andrej.dimitrioski@students.finki.ukim.mk`,
`{marjan.gushev,vladimir.zdraveski}@finki.ukim.mk`

Abstract. Information security is playing big role in the computer technologies. Its job is to detect unauthorized violation of the information integrity, secure it and also recover it, if the integrity was violated. One of the things that can alter an information are computer viruses. One of the task of the information security is also to detect these malicious applications and prevent their goal. This can be achieved in various techniques and one of them is signature based virus scanning. This technique uses a virus database (virus signatures) to detect if a file or application is infected with a specific virus. In this paper we are going to see in more details how is this implemented, which algorithm are mostly used and also try to improve its performance by parallelizing it on GPU by using CUDA. We are also going to see how CUDA utilizes large number of threads to solve a specific problem and use it to implement a parallel signature based virus scanner. Later we are going to see the performance benchmarks of the conducted experiments and discuss them and give a final conclusions for the usage of a GPU in signature based virus scanning.

Keywords: Virus · Scanning · CUDA · GPU

1 Introduction

Computer viruses are malicious applications that can harm the computer in various ways and they can be written in different programming languages. Their first appearance starts in 1970's and through the development of computer technologies they were getting more and more advanced and now we know a plethora of different types of computer viruses. In the early 80's computer viruses were primitive, destructive and were mostly distributed through software and transferred from a computer to a computer by using floppy disks. When the computer networking hit mainstream users it opened whole new ways of infecting computers with viruses. In that time there was the first appearance of computer worms which they are able to replicate itself and spread to other computers. This was

© ICST Institute for Computer Sciences, Social Informatics and Telecommunications Engineering 2019
Published by Springer Nature Switzerland AG 2019. All Rights Reserved
V. Poulkov (Ed.): FABULOUS 2019, LNICST 283, pp. 413–422, 2019.
https://doi.org/10.1007/978-3-030-23976-3_36

achieved through emails, hidden in attachments in a form of an application or any type of a media file. Spreading through network usually was aided by flaws in the network stack of the operating systems or flaws in software that relied on the network. This trend continued in the next years till today and it is unimaginable to encounter a virus which does not rely on the computer network. Virus scanning or namely the anti-virus software starts in the late 1980's as measure to deal with viruses. At that time anti-virus software was primitive relaying on a simpler techniques to detect and handle virus infections. These most include techniques like signature based virus scanning and they were quite effective since metamorphic viruses did not exist back then. Also its usage wasn't trivial because it had a complicated interface. As of today that has changed drastically, more detection techniques were developed which was caused from the streamlined improvement of the viruses. These include polymorphic, unusual behavior, heuristic and cloud based detection.

From the start of the development of anti-virus software till today the CPU is the main resource that is used to execute these detection techniques. The CPU mostly relies on sequential execution, though processors of this era are capable to execute several instructions in parallel in the same time due to the larger number of cores and threads. As applications get more and more demanding and techniques get more and more complex this means big performance impact in systems where can it mean more than the actual security. We know that GPUs are capable of utilizing large number of cores and that is proven to have great performance on graphical computing. The possibility to exploit the potential of these devices in more general problems was introduced with the GPGPU [6] or General-purpose computing on graphics processing unit which is extensively used in parallel programming paradigm.

Right now there are several platforms where a end-user can develop GPGPU application. CUDA [7] being the one of the most popular and developed by NVIDIA provides an API to utilize their graphic cards. Having this in consideration we can see that the problem we introduced above may be transformed in a way that we can use the large number of cores in the GPU to scan programs for a malicious code which frees the CPU and we can use it in executing other tasks.

2   Related Work

Virus detection has a wide area of development and research. Since CPU processing still has major role in virus scanning, most of the researches and related work lies on it. In a particular the specific topic about signature based detection looses its popularity because of the lack of a success rate when it comes dealing with polymorphic viruses. Because of that the shift is now towards using heuristic scanning techniques [11], [10] that can deal with self-modifying code. On other hand, related work for a GPU aided virus scanning appeared in late 2009 where NVIDIA posted [3] about Kaspersky Lab using their GPUs and CUDA. This is achieved by uploading the suspected malicious file to Kaspersky Lab data center where with the usage of NVIDIA CUDA and complex virus detection algorithm it can quickly detect if the file is really malicious and give suggestion to the user what to do next. Kaspersky is claiming that performance increase reached even 360 times over the Intel Core2 Duo processor. NVIDIA released a white-paper [4] on their GPU Gems site showing how pattern matching technique in virus scanning can provide better performance with the use of a GPU. Intel on the other hand announced [5] that their 6th, 7th, 8th and their future CPU generations will offload virus scanning from the CPU to their GPU so it will help the performance and battery life. Although this is not really related to CUDA platform, it shows that work on using the GPU for virus scanning is leaning towards a successful future. Similar work [2] on the paper's area has been done, where by using GPU and NFA [8] improved performance of virus scanning compared to open source anti-virus software ClamAV [9]. Another research on signature based detection has been done where by using highly-efficient memory compression technique and CUDA [12] showed improvement in memory usage and performance in pre-processing and run-time stage. A research [14] on virus detection by using Big Data [13] and Hadoop based comparison and pattern matching was aided by use of a GPU.

3   Architecture and Design

3.1   Specifying the Problem

The problem that we are covering here is a signature based virus scanning. In computer systems files are represented with bytes, that way it is easier for the CPU to work with them. A variable length of bytes may represent instruction, some data or something similar and also they may represent malicious segment of the a file. A old technique that is still being used is a signature based scanning. This technique searches for specific set of bytes. These specific set of bytes (sometimes named Signature) are commonly stored in a file called Virus Definition Database. These databases are updated on regular basis by the anti-virus vendors. So altogether this technique takes the file, and scans if it consists a known signature. In this paper we are going to simplify the problem, and make an assumption that programs that we are going to scan are not going to be polymorphic or in other words, no variations of a signature may end up in a file causing not to be detected by anti-virus.

3.2   Algorithm that We Are Going to Use

Solving the scanning problem on the first hand seems easy and if we consider that we have one pattern (virus definition) to scan. We will certainly have a great scanning performance. The problem gets harder if we have more than one virus definition. A brute force implementation of that will mean that we will need to do as many single searches as the number of virus definitions and that for certain will be slow if we have thousands of registered definitions in the database. We will have performance improvement if we use some known string searching algorithm as Rabin-Karp, Knuth-Morris-Pratt or Boyer-Moore but still we wont get the results that we want. So we need to find a way to search concurrently for every virus definition in one take. This gets even harder if we have different lengths in virus definitions. That's where Aho-Corasick [1] algorithm comes to play. The idea behind that algorithm is to build a finite state machine represented with a trie structure. This structure contains nodes with links between them which helps in pattern matching by fast transitions. Functions that this algorithm use are: Goto, Failure and Output function. Goto function gives us a next state for the current state and character. Failure function represents when the current character does not have an edge. And output function is used to map every pattern that ends at some state.

3.3   CUDA Programming Model

CUDA utilizes a large number of threads to run on a processor or in this case streaming multiprocessor. It achieves this by running them grouped in a thread blocks, and one or more (highly dependent on the GPU specifications) thread blocks can run simultaneously on streaming multiprocessor. These thread blocks on other hand form a grid of blocks. Having this, CUDA gives opportunity to the programmer to let him define the structure of the grid or thread blocks depending on the problem. Since we can't do computation without data, with CUDA we can also reserve space on the GPU RAM for transferring the required data from the system memory. The memory model in the GPU is divided to 3 kinds of memory: Local - used only by a single thread (also named cache), very limited and the fastest one. Shared - used only by threads defined in a thread block and it is slower than a local memory. Global - used by every thread in the grid and it is the slowest and the largest one.

3.4   Implementation and Restrictions

Aho-Corasick algorithm to work needs first to build the trie as we mentioned before. From the observation this process seems to be highly sequential as we can't simply run a multiple threads for each of the signatures and build the trie. This is because as mentioned earlier it uses all of the patterns to create the structure. But on the other hand after the state machine is built, the algorithm takes the input text (file in our case) processing character by character (byte by byte). This on the CPU will require starting from the start of the file and scanning byte by byte all the way to the end.

In previous subsection we mentioned that GPU can utilize large number of threads. So instead of using the CPU to scan through whole file, we can divide the file in section of a bytes and give each thread to pass a one section. Since we have blocks and each one has same number of threads running on it, we are actually going divide a larger section of the file to each block, and divide that section into smaller sections and give it to each thread in the block. We can see this illustratively with thread blocks and the threads in it in Fig. 1 and also with Eq. 1 we denote how much bytes each GPU thread will have to scan.

$$bytesPerThread = \frac{totalNumOfBytes}{numOfBlocks * threadsPerBlock} \tag{1}$$

$$bytesPerThread \geq max(L(vd_1), L(vd_2), ..., L(vd_n)) \tag{2}$$

Because we can have a different sizes of a files and also we can have different sizes of blocks and threads, this can vary. But we need to make sure that every thread will scan equal or more bytes than the largest virus definition. We denoted that in Eq. 2

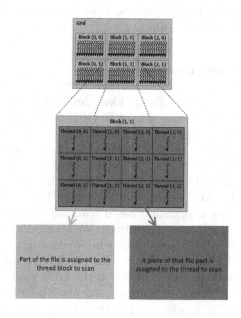

Fig. 1. GPU execution of scanning algorithm.

For the virus scanning we also need the file to reside in the memory of the GPU as well as the data structure (trie) used for scanning the file. We mentioned that the GPU uses global, shared and local memory and they have own memory limits. Keeping this in mind, we need to decide where every piece of the data will reside. Local and shared memory are extremely small so we can store the variables that are used in scanning and also some parts of the trie (Failure and Output function), so every thread will have own variables while scanning and every thread block will have own copy of the Failure and Output function. In global memory we are going to store the Goto function and the file since their size is pretty larger than the rest of the data. Every thread on the GPU will have access to this data. This is where we have limitations of running the scan more optimal as possible. Access to global memory is slow and even slower when more than one thread wants to access same piece of data. This although is not a problem for accessing the file since every thread has own chunk to process but Goto function since it is used by all threads can lead to high number of memory access conflicts thus decreasing the performance of the scanning. Also since shared memory is small, we cannot always store the Failure and Output functions in it because of their size which depends of the size of the virus definition file, so in some cases if the virus definition is large we have to store them in the global memory which further can decrease the performance. Another restriction we have to mention is the limit of the actual virus definitions which in this implementation is 32 because of the Integer data structure (4 bytes) used for the Output function. CUDA still does not have wide range support for more complex data structures, in our case Bitset data structure which makes it possible to use larger virus definitions.

4 Experiment and Discussion

We conducted a experiment on different files sizes, each with different number of blocks and threads and maximum size of 32 virus definitions. We need to point out that these are random files, and virus definitions were generated with random section of these files. System we used has Intel i5-5200U (up to 2.70 GHz), 8 GB of RAM and NVIDIA GeForce 940M (2 GB of RAM). We benchmarked the time that it takes the CPU and GPU to process the files on their respective algorithms. The goal of this experiment is to show how the GPU and CUDA are capable of executing a signature based scanning on multiple file sizes and comparing them with CPU scan counterpart. We scanned a files with sizes 1670, 1400, 600, 100 and 10 MB. Also we made sure we don't give a thread a number of bytes to scan which is smaller than the largest virus definition we generated.

We ran the scanning on 1670 MB file on the GPU multiple times with different configuration of blocks and threads and also on CPU for reference. The speedup started from 256 blocks and 256 threads per block and kept rising till 1024×1024 which had around 5.7 times speedup over the CPU. With 32×32 and 64×64 configurations we encountered less performance due to a threads having to scan large chunks of the file. That is because performance of a single thread on a GPU is much worse than the performance of a CPU. The results are shown in more detail in Fig. 2 and Table 1 below. The first column of the table represents the CPU result, next ones are GPU results noted by NumberOf-Blocks × NumberOfThreads.

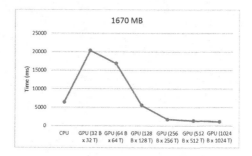

Fig. 2. Running the scan on 1670 MB file.

Table 1. Running the scan on 1670 MB file

	CPU	(32×32)	(64×64)	(128×128)	(256×256)	(512×512)	(1024×1024)
1670 MB	6430 ms	20350 ms	16879 ms	5597 ms	1750 ms	1369 ms	1126 ms

Similar results were encountered on 1400 MB file where we had around 6 times speedup over the CPU. We encountered speedup in the rest of the tests shown below, and they had better results than the CPU on every configuration we tested. The results are shown in more detail in Fig. 3 and Table 2 below.

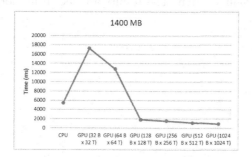

Fig. 3. Running the scan on 1400 MB file.

Table 2. Running the scan on 1400 MB file

	CPU	(32×32)	(64×64)	(128×128)	(256×256)	(512×512)	(1024×1024)
1400 MB	5433 ms	17234 ms	12784 ms	1815 ms	1533 ms	1155 ms	915 ms

In the 600 MB file scan we had steady improvement as we increased the blocks and threads peaking to maximum of 6 times speedup over the CPU. The results are shown in more detail in Fig. 4 and Table 3 below.

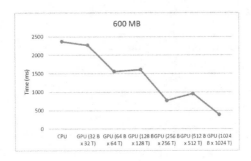

Fig. 4. Running the scan on 600 MB file.

Table 3. Running the scan on 600 MB file

	CPU	(32 × 32)	(64 × 64)	(128 × 128)	(256 × 256)	(512 × 512)	(1024 × 1024)
600 MB	2372 ms	2273 ms	1558 ms	1610 ms	773 ms	957 ms	394 ms

In the 100 MB file scan, the 32 × 32 configuration gave immediate speedup over CPU but as we started to increase them, the performance degraded till 256 × 256 as from that point again to see steady improvement but not much from the 32 × 32 configuration. The results are shown in more detail in Fig. 5 and Table 4 below.

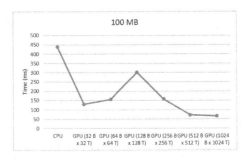

Fig. 5. Running the scan on 100 MB file.

Table 4. Running the scan on 100 MB file

	CPU	(32 × 32)	(64 × 64)	(128 × 128)	(256 × 256)	(512 × 512)	(1024 × 1024)
100 MB	439 ms	130 ms	156 ms	302 ms	158 ms	72 ms	66 ms

10 MB file scan was no different than 100 MB one, same sharing a strange degradation of a performance with 64 × 64 and 128 × 128 configurations. The results are shown in more detail in Fig. 6 and Table 5 below.

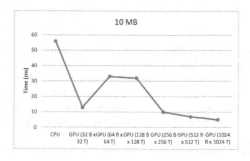

Fig. 6. Running the scan on 10 MB file.

Table 5. Running the scan on 10 MB file

	CPU	(32 × 32)	(64 × 64)	(128 × 128)	(256 × 256)	(512 × 512)	(1024 × 1024)
10 MB	56 ms	13 ms	33 ms	32 ms	10 ms	7 ms	5 ms

5 Conclusion

The implementation of the problem even if it was fairly simple and accounting the restriction for the limited usage of the faster shared memory we still managed to get better results than CPU across all of the file sizes we tested. From the experiment we can conclude two types of usages for GPU virus scanning:

(a) Use of large number of threads to scan a very large file.
(b) Use of large number of threads and distribute them across many small files.

This is because our experiment showed a improvement across all file sizes. For the larger ones we saw significant improvement if we used large number of threads. On smaller sizes even the smallest number of threads showed improvement over the CPU. We have to bear in mind that in our test bench we used a graphics card that has small VRAM (video RAM) size and also has limits when it comes storing shared data for every thread block. That gives us greater chance of having a memory access conflict while running a scan and degrading our performance and also preventing us to scan even large files. So in a scenario where it is possible to put the whole scanning data structure in shared memory (better graphics card), we can decrease the memory conflicts and yield even more performance improvements. With this we showed that signature based virus scanning is actually possible to do on GPU as it can be applicable in situations where we want to speedup the scanning of the file or just offload some work of the CPU to the GPU. We also have to mention that this is not the only scanning virus technique out there, there are several others like anomaly detection with machine learning that as well can utilize the power of a GPU. But still as of today signature based scanning is intensively used as first set of checks in the virus scanning procedures or combined with other techniques. Further development and research in this field can enable the opportunity to completely offload the virus scanning on the GPU so we can free up the CPU for the tasks where the performance is most needed.

References

1. Aho, A.V., Corasick, M.J.: Efficient string matching: an aid to bibliographic search. Commun. ACM **18**, 333–340 (1975)
2. Vicente Dias, A.N.: Detecting Computer Viruses using GPUs
3. New Virus Scanning Solution Uses NVIDIA CUDA. https://blogs.nvidia.com/blog/2009/12/15/new-virus-scanning-solution-uses-nvidia-cuda/
4. Chapter 35: Fast Virus Signature Matching on the GPU. https://developer.nvidia.com/gpugems/GPUGems3/gpugems3_ch35.html
5. Intel offloads virus scanning to the GPU for better battery life and performance. https://www.pcworld.com/article/3268985/security/microsoft-intel-virus-scanning-gpu.html
6. GPGPU. https://en.wikipedia.org/wiki/General-purpose_computing_on_graphics_processing_units
7. NVIDIA Inc.: CUDA. https://developer.nvidia.com/cuda-zone
8. NFA (Nondeterministic finite automata). https://en.wikipedia.org/wiki/Nondeterministic_finite_automaton
9. ClamAV. https://www.clamav.net/about
10. Gao, D., Yin, G., Dong, Y., Kou, L.: A Research on the Heuristic Signature Virus Detection Based on the PE Structure
11. Alberto, C., Gonzlez, N.: Polymorphic Virus Signature Recognition via Hybrid Genetic Algorithm. https://github.com/carlosnasillo/Hybrid-Genetic-Algorithm/blob/master/README.markdown
12. Pungila, C., Negru, V.: A highly-efficient memory-compression approach for GPU-accelerated virus signature matching. In: Gollmann, D., Freiling, F.C. (eds.) ISC 2012. LNCS, vol. 7483, pp. 354–369. Springer, Heidelberg (2012). https://doi.org/10.1007/978-3-642-33383-5_22. https://link.springer.com/chapter/10.1007/978-3-642-33383-5_22
13. Big Data. https://en.wikipedia.org/wiki/Big_data
14. Panigrahi, C.R., Tiwari, M., Pati, B., Prasath, R.: Malware detection in big data using fast pattern matching: a hadoop based comparison on GPU. In: Prasath, R., O'Reilly, P., Kathirvalavakumar, T. (eds.) MIKE 2014. LNCS (LNAI), vol. 8891, pp. 407–416. Springer, Cham (2014). https://doi.org/10.1007/978-3-319-13817-6_39. https://link.springer.com/chapter/10.1007/978-3-319-13817-6_39

Fabulous 2017

Optoelectronic Method for Increasing the Signal-to-Noise Ratio in Mass Spectrometry for Urinary Disulfoton Identification

Genica Caragea[1], Radu Alexandru Macovei[2,3], Paul Şchiopu[4],
Marian Vlădescu[4], Florin Grama[5], Maria Gabriela Neicu[6],
and Mihai Ionică[1,4(✉)]

[1] Military-Medical Scientific Research Centre Bucharest, Bucharest, Romania
mihaiionica56@gmail.com
[2] Clinical Emergency Hospital Bucharest, Bucharest, Romania
[3] University of Medicine and Pharmacy "Carol Davila" Bucharest,
Bucharest, Romania
[4] Optoelectronics Research Center, University "Politehnica" of Bucharest,
Bucharest, Romania
[5] Clinical Hospital "Colţea" Bucharest, Bucharest, Romania
[6] University for Medicine and Pharmacy "Carol Davila" Bucharest,
Bucharest, Romania

Abstract. Mass spectrometry is an optoelectronic method of determining organic substances by comparing their mass spectrum with mass spectra found in system libraries. In the case of biological products, substances of interest, biotic or xenobiotics, may be "hidden" from the background of the analyzed matrix noise, which alters the major aspect of the mass spectrum obtained and faces the impossibility of their identification. A gas chromatograph coupled with mass spectrometer (GC-MS) Varian was used, to develop a selected ion monitoring (SIM) method for increasing the signal-to-noise ratio for identifying the disulfoton in urine samples.

Keywords: GC-MS · SIS · Disulfoton · Urine

1 Introduction

Organophosphorus compounds is a class of substances widely used as a pesticide. These include disulfotone, which is on the list of class Ia (extremely hazardous) compounds according to the degree of toxicity [1]. Disulfotone (O,O-diethyl-S-2-ethylthioethylphosphorodithioate) known as Di-Syston, Disultex, Dimaz, Solvigran and Solvirex is a systemic insecticide used to combat plant lice (Aphide) and for seed and soil treatment. The mean toxicity value is: DL50 = 2.6–12.5 mg/kg in male rats and for female rats DL50 = 1.9–2.5 mg/kg, orally [2].

The effectiveness of organophosphorus compounds in pest control in agriculture refers to their ability to inhibit acetylcholinesterase (AChE). By inhibiting the enzyme acetylcholinesterase organophosphorus compounds has prevented proper functioning

V. Poulkov (Ed.): FABULOUS 2019, LNICST 283, pp. 425–430, 2019.
https://doi.org/10.1007/978-3-030-23976-3_37

of a nerve junction. Recovery of acetylcholinesterases in the blood is localized (0.5–1% per day), severe poisoning remaining below normal over 3 months [3, 4].

Mass spectrometer represents the relative abundance of ions resulting from the ionization process of a family of molecules. The mass spectrum characterizes the unique molecules from which it has been evidenced, which gives it the property to identify with its respective molecules, from an unknown sample. If the concentration of the substance of interest is very low, the system will also ionize the molecules that accompany the sample of interest, the spectra of these molecules overlapping the spectrum of the target molecule. For this reason, methods of increasing system signal/noise ratio must be found [5].

For urine analysis of disulfotone, various detectors for chromatographic gas analysis techniques can be used, such as flame photometric detectors that exhibit good reproducibility [6] or high specificity mass spectrometers [7], presented in Table 1. The detection limit for all samples −1 µg/kg.

Table 1. Method for determination of a disulfoton in a biological sample.

Optoelectronic method	Sample	Method of preparation	Biblio
GC/FPD	feces	Chloroform extraction, oxidation with m- chloroperbenzoic acid	[8]
GC/MS (SIM)	urine blood	Extraction with hexane, concentration, dilution with acetonitrile	[9]
GC/MS (SIM)	urine plasma	Plasma: extraction with ethyl acetate. Urine: pH adjustment of 7.4, centrifugation, extraction with ethyl acetate	[10]
GC/FPD capilar GC/MS	urine blood	Dilution with 2% saline, fractionation by column chromatography, oxidation with potassium permanganate, Fractionation by column chromatography	[11]
GC/FPD capilar	bovine liver	Extraction with methanol-methyl chloride, chromatographic column cleaning concentration	[12]

FPD - flame photometric detector

The objective of this paper is to develop an optoelectronic method for increasing the signal/noise ratio of the mass spectra obtained in determining the very low concentrations of disulfoton present in the matrices of interest. The method is developed on a gas chromatographic column chromatography system coupled with a mass spectrometer.

2   Experimental Set-up

The objective of this paper is to develop an optoelectronic method for the determination of disulfoton by capillary column gas chromatography coupled with mass spectrometry and to show the importance of the application of selected ion monitoring (SIM) method in the detection of disulfotone in the matrices of interest. Generally, disulfotone, as is the majority of organophosphorus compounds, is analyzed by gas chromatography with mass spectrometer (GC-MS) using the classical method. These analytical techniques, however, have precision problems in detecting disulfotone that may occur due to matrix-related interferences. The mass spectrometric detection method in the ionic monitoring variant contributes to the elimination of these interferences between disulfoton and other chemical compounds in the matrix that remained after separation and did not separate by gas chromatography.

2.1 Material

It was used a system GC-MS/MS Varian, consisting of a Chrompack 3800 gas chromatograph and a Saturn 2000 mass spectrometer. The gas chromatograph is equipped with a Factor Four column of 30 m length and 0.25 mm diameter. The mass spectrometer is an ion trap Paul with electron impact ionization. Electronic ionization is preferred in the analysis of compounds with low polarity and relatively low molecular weight.

The samples were collected from patients admitted to the ATI II Department of the Emergency Clinical Hospital Bucharest.

2.2 Method

To obtain the injection matrix, 50 ml of urine was used. These spiked with 100 µl disulfoton solution stock are mixed with 5 ml of phosphate buffer and 5 ml of a mixture of solvents (chloroform, dichlorethane and dichlormethane 1:1:1). For the quality control of the results it adds 300 µl internal standard (midazolam solution stock). The mixture is mixed for 10 min. Take the supernatant and repeat the procedure above. After washing the supernatant, the remaining mixture is centrifuged for 8 min at 2500 rpm. After centrifugation the supernatant is discarded and the remaining mixture is brought to dryness at 80 °C. The residue was diluted with 100 µl of the solvent mixture previously used. This represents the injection matrix.

The operating parameters of the GC: gas carrier He with flow 1.2 ml/min, split ratio 1:10, septum purge 0.5 ml/min, injection temperature 300 °C, oven program start at 140 °C, wait 1 min, increase the temperature to 290 °C with 5 °C ratio, wait 12 min at 290 °C.

The operating parameters of the MS: manifold temperature 80 °C, trap temperature 170 °C, line transfer temperature 260 °C, ionization current 10 µA, mode AGC (Automatic Gain Control), acquisition data 50–450 amu, background mass 45, 1 scan/s, for fool scan.

To increase the signal-to-noise ratio its used selected ion monitoring (SIM) method for disulfoton: 85–92; 140–145; 150–159; 272–278 amu.

The ionization current was 50 µA, background mass 80 amu, 1 scan/s.

3 Experimental Results

Following the application of the GC/MS in full scan and GC/MS selected ion monitoring (SIM) methods with established and optimized parameters to obtain a separation and subsequently a satisfactory disulfoton identification. The analysis method consists in identifying the chromatographic peaks by comparing the mass spectra obtained with the spectra in the mass spectrum spectra library (Nist98, PMW, Wiley6) and the retention time.

Molecules are ionized bombarded with energetic electrons (normally 70 eV) in a low pressure region (less than 10^{-5} torr). The heaviest loaded fragment normally observed under EI conditions is the molecular ion, M +, produced by the loss of an electron from the neutral molecule and generates fragments of the compound. The number of ions created depends on Ionization Time so as long as the ionization time is higher, the more ions are created.

The following results:

Disulfoton ($C_8H_{19}O_2PS_3$) Molecular weight: 274 Retention time: 20.335 min.

Electron ionization (EI +) generates positively charged ions.

In Fig. 1 there is presented the ion chromatograms and mass spectrum for disulfoton obtained in full scan.

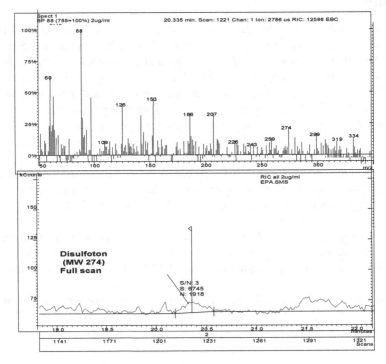

Fig. 1. The ion chromatogram and mass spectrum for disulfoton obtained in full scan.

In Fig. 2 there is presented the ion chromatograms and mass spectrum obtained from same sample for disulfoton obtained in selected ion monitoring (SIM).

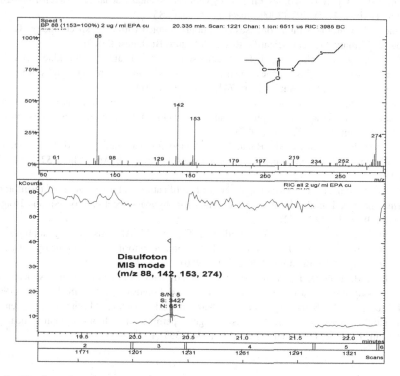

Fig. 2. The ion chromatogram and mass spectrum for disulfoton obtained in selected ion monitoring (SIM).

4 Conclusions

Peaks that have formed following the analysis of the sample by the selected ion monitoring (SIM) method, increasing the signal-to-noise ratio of disulfoton in the urine sample.

Increasing the signal/noise ratio also results in an increased sensitivity of the method for determining the disulfoton in the urine samples.

References

1. WHO IPCS: The WHO Recommended Classification of Pesticides by Hazard. IPCS (International Programme on Chemical Safety). ISBN 978 92 4 154796 3 (2009)
2. Wagner, S.L.: The acute health hazards of pesticides. In: Witt, J.M. (ed.) Chemistry, Biochemistry, and Toxicology of Pesticides. Oregon State University Cooperative Extension Service, Corvallis, OR (1989)

3. Voicu, V., Macovei, R.A., Miclea, L.: Clinical toxicology guide, 2nd edn., Brumar, Timişoara (2012)
4. Macovei, R., Dănescu, I., Ionică, M., Caragea, G.: The pattern of acute pesticide poisoning admitted in ICU II Toxicology Emergency Clinical Hospital Bucharest between 1997–2007. Clin. Toxicol. **47**(5), 507 (2009). meeting abstract 285
5. Ionică, M.: Chromatography of gases and liquids coupled with mass spectrometry. Training course. Military-Medical Scientific Research Centre Bucharest (2016)
6. Holstege, D.M., Scharberg, D.L., Richardson, E.R., et al.: Multiresidue screen for organophosphorus insecticides using gel permeation chromatography-silica gel cleanup. J. Assoc. Off. Anal. Chem. **741**, 394–399 (1991)
7. Kawasaki, S., Ueda, H., Itoh, H., et al.: Screening of organophosphorus pesticides using liquid chromatography-atmospheric pressure chemical ionization mass spectrometry. J. Chromatogr. **595**, 193–202 (1992)
8. Bowman, M.C., Beroza, M.: Rapid GLC method for determining residues for fenthion, disulfoton and phorate in corn, milk, grass and feces. J. Assoc. Off. Anal. Chem. **52**, 1231–1239 (1969)
9. Hattori, H., Suzuki, U., Yasuoka, T., et al.: Identification and quantitation of disulfoton in urine and blood of a cadaver by gas chromatography/mass spectrometry. Nippon Hoigaku Zasshi **36**, 411–413 (1982)
10. Singh, A.K., Hewetson, D.W., Jordon, K.C., et al.: Analysis of organophosphorus insecticides in biological samples by selective ion monitoring gas chromatography-mass spectrometry. J. Chromatogr. **369**, 83–96 (1986)
11. Yashiki, M., Kojima, T., Ohtani, M., et al.: Determination of disulfoton and its metabolites in the body fluids of a Di-Syston intoxication case. Forensic Sci. Int. **48**, 145–154 (1990)
12. Holstege, D.M., Scharberg, D.L., Richardson, E.R., et al.: Multiresidue screen for organophosphorus insecticides using gel permeation chromatography-silica gel cleanup. J. Assoc. Off. Anal. Chem. **74**, 1394–1399 (1991)

Integrated Software Platform for Mobile Malware Analysis – A Potential Vision

George Suciu[1,3(✉)], Laurentiu Bezdedeanu[1], Cristiana Istrate[1,3],
Mari-Anais Sachian[1], Houssam Boukoulo[2], Corentin Boscher[2],
Fabien Souleyreau[2], and Eduard-Cristian Popovici[3]

[1] R&D Department, Beia Consult International,
Peroni 16, 041386 Bucharest, Romania
{george, laurentiu.bezdedeanu, cristiana.istrate,
proiecte}@beia.ro
[2] Institut National Polytechnique de Bordeaux,
Avenue du Dr Albert Schweitzer 1, 33400 Talence, France
[3] ETTI Faculty, University POLITEHNICA of Bucharest, Bucharest, Romania
eduard.popovici@upb.ro

Abstract. With the evolution of technology, we are witnessing the development of mobile terminals that are getting closer to a personal computer in terms of features and applications. At the same time, there is an increase in the number of mobile device users, which also leads to an increase in the use of online shopping or finance management applications. Hence, mobile terminals become a target for cyber criminals. Starting from the analysis of the current situation in the world regarding cyber security technology and solutions, we aim to build an integrating software platform for mobile malware analysis. The aim of the research is to develop a software platform that integrates the malware analysis procedures for most of the existing mobile terminals. So, the main objective of this article is to analyze the quality of cyber-protective solutions for mobile devices. We present our experiments which may bring solutions for some of the major vulnerabilities like active development of mobile malware, and hacking. Moreover, in this article we discuss the issue of security on Android, making use of security platform like Kali which permits to use different kinds of security analysis programs.

Keywords: Malware · Cyber security · Integrated platform · Mobile malware · Kali

1 Introduction

Going forth in the last years, the threat to mobile phones has risen as many people are using them on a daily basis for all kind of needs. Malware is the most generic term for different kind of threats. Those threats include trojan horses, keyloggers, rootkits, viruses and worms and cybercrime [1].

To examine a malware, dynamic analysis [2] is usually used, which is a set of techniques for analyzing an application or software running in a controlled and

© ICST Institute for Computer Sciences, Social Informatics and Telecommunications Engineering 2019
Published by Springer Nature Switzerland AG 2019. All Rights Reserved
V. Poulkov (Ed.): FABULOUS 2019, LNICST 283, pp. 431–436, 2019.
https://doi.org/10.1007/978-3-030-23976-3_38

monitored environment. The idea is to observe the malware actions so we can draw conclusions about how it behaves.

An easier way to analyze the malware within the mobile device would be an integrated platform for dynamic and static analysis [3]. Mainly speaking, an integrated platform focuses on the system integration of more gentle methods used for analysis or other acts. Security is important for data protection but critical for mobile banking and intellectual property. As the mobile phones are used everyday by a lot of people and they are also connected to a lot of personal information, there is a concern to make a change in order to avoid leaks of personal information [4]. We propose a hybrid approach by developing a new software platform that enables the analysis of malware on mobile phones. The main objective is to identify the operational requirements and the capacity needed to develop this platform through a secure way. The solution that would prevent malware attacks will be presented through some tries that we made and how our integrated software platform should function and look like.

The paper is structured as follows: Sect. 2 describes related work. Section 3 shows the methodology and types of mobile threats. Section 4 analyzes research experiments and results. Finally, Sect. 5 presents the conclusions and forthcoming plans.

2   Related Work

A complete traditional anti-malware/anti-spyware software for mobile devices proactively checks applications and files for malware and viruses, scans the built-in memory and SD card, finds Potentially Unwanted Programs (PUPs) for removal and scans automatically the apps and files when accessed [5]. It also needs to automate the processes like scheduling automatic scans, updating the protection database automatically, updating over a WiFi network. It should have a privacy manager who identifies every application's access privileges in detail and breaks down access privileges by category: Contacts, Identity Information, Simple Message Service (SMS), and Security Settings. The application manager has to identify which applications are currently running, to notice installed applications and to enable custom whitelisting of approved apps. For the security audit, it identifies security vulnerabilities on the device and suggests remediation.

In [6] was proposed a system architecture for automated Android malware analysis, which is able to make predictions regarding malicious applications. The system architecture, which has a core server that runs AndroSandX server applications. For avoiding backdoor exploitation, the system has a peripheral firewall to restrict inbound connection. This system allows static, dynamic and hybrid analysis approach.

3   Methodology for Assessing Mobile Attacks

In this section we present a short classification of mobile threats and attacks, according to the NIST technology areas [7] where attacks can be exploited. Table 1 presents the assessment of attacks on hypervisors and virtualization environments running on mobile devices.

Table 1. Examples of mobile attacks

Hypervisors systems	– Hyperjacking attack – Installing system firmware rootkits – Attacking hypervisors through system firmware – Exploitation of privileged interfaces provided by the hypervisor	– Attacking hypervisor emulation of hardware devices – Management of VMs – VM sprawl – Denial of service
Virtualization environments	– VM Escape – Cache covert channel attack – VM breaking the isolation – IP or MAC address spoofing – VLAN hopping	– Traffic snooping – Resource starvation – Secure privileged/administrative guests – Unsecured VM migration

4 Experiments and Results

In this section we analyze the mobile malware experiments using Kali [8], a Linux distribution which is used for penetration, testing, and security auditing. It has been adhering completely to Debian development standards and includes many tools which are used in data security. Kali Linux provides already installed and updated penetration testing, security tools, frameworks and their updated repositories, all pre-compiled set of word-lists that is needed during penetration testing (to brute-force logins) and command line interface.

Within the experimentation work, we installed Kali Linux on the Nexus 5 smart phone and on a computer as a Virtual Machine. We used VirtualBox with the ISO that has been downloaded from the official website of Kali. Then we tried with the package air cracking, to hack the password of a WiFi network. At the end of it, we tried to find, thanks to various dictionaries, the password that was set. If the WiFi is using a WEP encryption with common words, the algorithm searches on a database of known words. Else, if it is a complicated password it would take many hours or even days, but it depends on the algorithm that it is used. For example, it can try all the French words ordered alphabetically or all the numbers starting from 0, etc. Depending on the performance of the computer it would take more or less time.

4.1 Hardware and Software Used for Installation of Kali Linux

We will describe further the installation process and the experiments made with Kali Linux to hack the WIFI password. We used the phone LG NEXUS 5X version N4F261 for installing Kali Linux Nethunter 2017. Specification of the phone is OS Android 7.1.1, Qualcomm MSM8992 Snapdragon 808 processor, Hexa-core CPU (4 × 1.4 GHz Cortex-A53 & 2 × 1.8 GHz Cortex-A57), 32 GB internal memory, 2 GB RAM, M8994F-2.6.36.2.20 network, Wi-Fi 802.11 a/b/g/n/ac, dual-band.

We used VirtualBox version 5.1.24 for the installation of Kali and it has the following performance parameters: 2048 MB of base memory, 2 processors at 2 GHz.

To experiment what a malware is, we used Kali Linux which integrates tools to create a malware and to get back, for example, some log in and password thanks to a keylogger that we can send to a pool of a computer. Firstly we created the malware with the command line presented in Fig. 1.

```
root@kali:/home/kali# msfvenom -p windows/meterpreter/reverse_tcp LHOST=172.23.5
6.199 LPORT=8080 -f exe -e x86/bikata_ga_nai -i 12 -o Bureau/malware.exe
```

Fig. 1. Creation of the malware.

Then we configured the host and the port that we are going to capture using the following command lines:

```
set payload windows/meterpreter/revers_tcp
set LHOST 172.23.56.199
set LPORT 8080
exploit -j
```

Furthermore, we launched the malware on the target computer and then we connected it to the session on Kali Linux with the following command line:

```
session -i
```

Finally, we connected to the session on Kali Linux with the previous command line. The final result is a malware which has the following repository:/home/kali and takes screenshots from the user desktop (as presented in Fig. 2).

Fig. 2. Screenshot of the target computer.

4.2   Hacking a WiFi

The first attempt at securing these access points was termed Wired Equivalent Privacy (WEP). This encryption method has been around for quite a while and a number of weaknesses have been discovered. It has been largely replaced by WPA (Wi-Fi Protected Access) and WPA2.

First, the motivation to hack someone's Wi-Fi router or access point (AP) was to navigate around the web anonymously, or more precisely, with someone else's IP address. Second, once the Wi-Fi router is hacked, the victim's traffic can be decrypted using a sniffing tool to capture and spy on all their traffic. Third, if their AP is compromised, it can be used as a node in the dark-net to share large files over torrent protocol, using someone else's bandwidth, rather than the attackers own, or as zombie node in malware attacks.

After installing Kali Linux into a Virtual Machine, the tool air-crack-ng was used. In order to hack the WEP Wi-Fi we used a network wireless USB card Gigaset 108 and the following command:

```
Airodump-ng -c channel -w (file name) -bssid BSSID
wlan0
```

The next step is to wait for data to be present from other legitimate stations and open another terminal, as presented in Fig. 3.

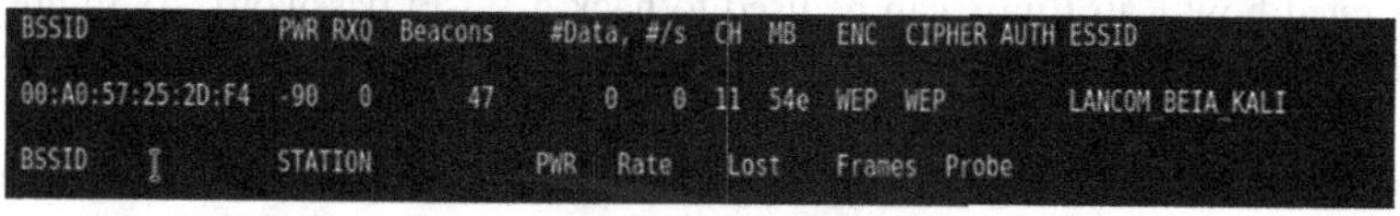

Fig. 3. Target SSID for attack.

The above command will start capturing packets from the SSID "LANCOM_-BEIA_KALI" on channel 11 and write them to file WEP crack. This command will now to capture packets in order to crack the WEP key. To do that, we will need to inject packets into the AP.

Further step is to wait for someone to connect to the AP so that we can get the MAC (Media Access Control) address from their network card. After their MAC address is captured, it can be spoofed and injected packets into their AP. To do this, the aireplay-ng command can be used. Needed are the BSSID of the AP and the MAC address of the client who connected to the AP.

The attack works by capturing an ARP packet and then replaying that ARP thousands of times in order to generate the IVs that we need for cracking the WEP, which on our setup takes approximately 1 min.

After that, the ARPs are injected into the AP, and the packets are captured in order to generate the needed airodump file WEPcrack.

If enough data is present, aircrack-ng will display the key on the platform screen, as presented in Fig. 4.

Fig. 4. The found key

5 Conclusions

In this paper, we presented related work regarding integrated software platforms for mobile malware analysis and detailed experiments we made on Kali Linux, in order to gain a better view over the platform functionalities. We demonstrated how to analyze the malware developing tools and succeeded to create a malware using Kali. Also, we demonstrated how Kali Linux can be used to hack a Wi-Fi password. As future work, we will investigate how to integrate other open source forensics tools.

Acknowledgments. This work was supported by a grant of the Ministry of Innovation and Research, UEFISCDI, project number 5 Sol/2017 and ODSI within PNCDI III.

References

1. Cristodorescu, M., Jha, S., Sanjit, A., Song, S.D., Bryant, R.E.: Semantics-aware malware detection, Carnegie Mellon University Research Showcase @CMU, p. 2 (2005)
2. Blasing, T., Batyuk, L., Schmidt, A.D., Camtepe, S.A., Albayrak, S.: An Andriod application sandbox system for suspicious software detection. In: 5th International Conference on Malicious and Unwanted Software, pp. 55–56 (2010)
3. Islam, R., Tian, R., Batten, L.M., Versteeg, S.: Classification of malware based on integrated static and dynamic features. J. Netw. Comput. Appl. **36**(2), 646–656 (2013)
4. Malhotra, A., Bajaj, K.: A survey on various malware detection techniques on mobile platform. Int. J. Comput. Appl. **139**(5), 15–20 (2016)
5. Simmonds, M.: How businesses can navigate the growing tide of ransomware attacks. Comput. Fraud. Secur. **3**, 9–12 (2017)
6. Jadhav, S.: An assistive system for android malware analysis to increase malware analysis efficiency. In: 31st International Conference on Advanced Information Networking and Applications Workshops (WAINA), pp. 370–374 (2017)
7. Chapman, C.: Network Performance and Security: Testing and Analyzing Using Open Source and Low-cost Tools. Syngress (2016)
8. Johansen, G., Allen, L., Heriyanto, T., Ali, S.: Kali Linux 2–Assuring Security by Penetration Testing. Packt Publishing Ltd. (2016)

Social Media Cloud Contact Center Using Chatbots

George Suciu[1,2(✉)], Adrian Pasat[1], Teodora Uşurelu[1],
and Eduard-Cristian Popovici[2]

[1] Research & Development Department,
Beia Consult International, Bucharest, Romania
{george,adrian.pasat,teodora.usurelu}@beia.ro
[2] ETTI Faculty, University POLITEHNICA of Bucharest, Bucharest, Romania
eduard.popovici@upb.ro

Abstract. The latest technologies advancement in NLP (Natural Language Processing) solution allows developing innovative tools that enrich customer experience with products and services. Contact Center environments gradually adopted real-time analytics solutions, and latest research is focusing on how to integrate social media channels. Based on the work made in SoMeDi and Speech2Processes projects, we propose an innovative chatbot platform that integrates data mining and sentiment analysis technologies. The aim is to offer insight into customer preferences by using DII (Digital Interaction Intelligence) and assist in mitigating several know issues in Contact Center environments.

Keywords: Chatbot · Artificial intelligence · DII · NLP · Machine learning

1 Introduction

The use of AI (Artificial Intelligence) is expected to bring major technological achievements, as computers become more human they will provide a more natural connection between people, linking their online content, and their devices, natural language will become the user interface [1]. Chatbots are created to respond quickly to user questions and obtain valuable information from large amounts of data. Recently, these intelligent personal bots grow towards ubiquity, being embedded in smartphone devices, wearables, and other IoT endpoints.

Our goal is to present an innovative chatbot platform which integrates both DII and Natural Language Processing tools, these DII technologies [2] are thoroughly presented within the SoMeDi [3] project, a research work that focused on the implementation of complex algorithms to crawl the DII data and grasp information about user needs, future trends, product development etc.

We will describe in the next section several intelligent chatbot assistants and the latest technologies used in the development process. In Sect. 3 we present our chatbot platform concept, and how the NLP and DII tools are integrated, while in Sect. 4 we correlate the innovative concepts of the chatbot platform to social media channels within contact centers. In Sect. 5 we draw the conclusions.

V. Poulkov (Ed.): FABULOUS 2019, LNICST 283, pp. 437–442, 2019.
https://doi.org/10.1007/978-3-030-23976-3_39

2   Related Work

In this section we present several data mining techniques and AI-powered chatbots, analyzing open source chatbot builder technologies.

2.1   Chatbots and Data Mining Rechniques

The recent research work for implementing better, more efficient solutions in developing data mining applications, revealed several approaches. In [4] the authors present a study for discovering frequent itemsets using HIGEN Miner (History Generalized Pattern), a technique implemented by means of the apriori-based algorithm. Also, in [5] the authors propose a topic augmented neural network to boost message-response matching.

A topic-aware convolutional neural tensor network (TACNTN) is analyzed in [6], where the topic words are obtained from a pre-trained LDA model and their weights are determined by themselves.

Chappie [7], a semi-automatic intelligent chatbot, fulfills the three important criteria of an intelligent chatbot: to understand rather than memorize, handle repetitive queries, and AIML (Artificial Intelligence Mark-up Language) based response mechanism.

Considering the expansion of messaging apps, we also documented several standalone chatbot mobile apps. First launched in 2014, Luka app [8] was thought as a mobile AI-powered social concierge service. Lark [9], a pocket coach and nutritionist, relies on the mobile device built-in sensors to track the users' activities and habits. The user can text or dictate to the chatbot what he ate or drank recently and then receive comprehensive feedback on eating, drinking, exercising, and even sleeping habits.

Penny [10], known as the most polite bank manager ever, is a free personal finance app that offers great insight into your spendings. The app can offer information about past expenses, spendings on food and medicine, income vs spending chart over the last period, by linking to the user bank accounts.

2.2   Open Source Builder Technologies

Open Source Bot Builder SDK [11] allows creating simple and sophisticated dialogues. Cognitive services enable the bot to see, hear, interpret and interact in more humane ways. Microsoft Bot Connector is a communication service that links the Bot with various communication channels such as Skype, SMS, email, and more.

We tested some of these SDK (Software Development Kit) solutions to quickly develop an intelligent application that can perceive human language and respond to user requests. The Azure [11] service accelerates the development of a Bot providing an integrated environment. The process is relatively simple, after creating a user account on Azure platform, the developer selects the programming language (C# or Node.js), and a template to build the Bot. One of the known issues related to human-computer interactions is the ability of the computer to understand what the user wants, this problem can be mitigated by training the chatbot through repetitive tests.

Testing the chatbot and adding intents, entities and utterances, are finalized over the LUIS [12] platform. By using the LUIS web interface supports creating an application with a set of intentions and entities relevant to a certain application domain. Once the application is implemented, LUIS utilizes active learning to improve. In this learning process, LUIS identifies statements about which it is relatively uncertain and asks the developer to label them according to intentions and entities.

The language is chosen when the application is created and cannot be modified later. After choosing utterances, intents, and entities, the application is tested and trained. Before publishing the chatbot on a channel, it passes through a final test on the Microsoft Azure portal. In the following section, we describe the chatbot platform architecture.

3   Proposed Chatbot Platform Architecture

A lot of the data in social media is text, granting vast possibilities for opinion mining and otherwise detecting trends and developments. Opinion mining involves analyzing people's opinions, sentiments, and attitudes expressed in written language.

So, the implementation of DII tools can advance new solutions, best suited for deployment in marketing strategies or customer care environments. Based on the research work from Somedi project, we plan to integrate:

- Development of a set of advanced mining tools for representing, analyzing and extracting meaningful patterns or topics from social media and digital interaction data;
- Development of a set of improved machine learning algorithms enabling detection, prediction, and support for automatic decision making throughout the processes;
- Improved interactive tools to visualize and manage the data.

Also, we aim to integrate enhanced natural language processing (NLP) tools from Speech2Process [13] project, and domain knowledge that changes according to the content of the dialog between the chatbot and the customer.

We propose a conceptual model (Fig. 1) of an Intelligent Chatbot Framework that supports the generation of intelligent assistant chatbot. The Platform will support the realisation of the following main functions of the chatbot: (i) sensing (ASR - Automatic Speech Recognition), (ii) thinking, that is Understanding Spoken Language (SLU) and deciding the next move of the system, (iii) acting, that is, on the one part synthesizing the specifying questions and the messages to the client, on the other part executing the wanted service.

The main components of the Platform are the following: (i) the engines, which implement the functions of the chatbot, (ii) design methodology for the technological components, based on ML (Machine Learning) technologies for UX design solutions, and, (iii) a tool-kit which supports the design and development process.

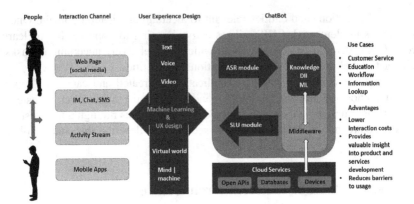

Fig. 1. ChatBot platform architecture

4   Social Media and Contact Centers

Social media is an important source of DID (Digital Interaction Data). Social media channels continuously evolve and change the way people communicate with each other and also how they interact with companies [14]. Aral et al. [15] claim that social media is "fundamentally changing the way we communicate, collaborate, consume, and create". This context is caused by the technological concept of Web 2.0, that presumes the creation and exchange of user-generated content [16]. Social media has already proved as an important marketing tool [17], and several Marketing trends rise towards structured social data (by implementing the following data mining technologies: sentiment analysis, trend analysis, pattern recognition, tagging/annotation, and toping modeling) used to improve ad targeting, based on the customers' profiles, brand mentions, topics, etc.

Also, the future of customer services lies too in social media. According to a Gartner report [18], by 2017, 50% of consumer product investments will be redirected to customer experience innovations. Gartner already stated that failure to respond via social channels can lead to a 15% increase in the churn rate for existing customers.

Regarding the industry needs, we documented several papers, and reports as in [18] and observed the financial resources to be allocated in the immediate future for this field of research. According to [19], social marketing budget will double in the next five years.

Nowadays, it is a known reality that many companies made social media channels a touch point for customer service. Contact centers are the first line of interaction with customers, and one of the urgent needs viewed from the experts' point of view is to enhance one of the key performance metrics in the contact center, First-Contact Resolution (FCR) and cover all contacts, regardless of channel. According to [20], changing the business processes within a Contact Center should start by mitigating the FCR rate (1).

$$(\text{Total Incidents Resolved} - \text{Total Incidents Reopened})/(\text{Total Incidents Opened}) = \text{FCR} \% \quad (1)$$

Integrating DII technologies will allow the analysis of repeating contacts across all the interaction channels, analysis of customer profiles for more-predictive contact patterns, and after reviewing these contact patterns and analyzing customer profiles, inefficient or ineffective processes will be revealed.

We can resemble these processes in the diagram presented in Fig. 2 with scrapping social media by using data mining and process the data with opinion mining tools, in order to reveal the hidden value from DII.

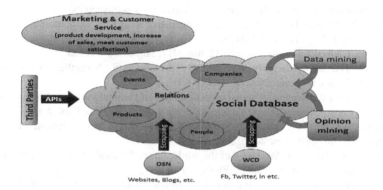

Fig. 2. Data mining and Opinion mining applied to social media platforms

5   Conclusions

The role of chatbots is to enable human machine interaction using natural language. We presented how chatbots are meeting customers expectations in social media cloud contact centers. Chatbots create a direct and close line between business and users, regardless of the service provided, offering 24/7 instant services and assistance, being always helpers and listeners. As future work we will develop a chatbot with medical knowledge for patient recovery after mobility health issues.

Acknowledgments. This work was supported by a grant of the Ministry of Innovation and Research, UEFISCDI, project number 5 Sol/2017 ToR-SIM within PNCDI III and partially funded by UEFISCDI Romania under grants Speech2Process and SoMeDi projects, and by European Union's Horizon 2020 research and innovation program under grant agreement No. 643963 (SWITCH project).

References

1. Castro, D., New, J.: The promise of artificial intelligence. Center for Data Innovation (2016)
2. McCormick, J., Little, C.: Optimize customer experiences with digital intelligence. In Forrester Report, The Digital Intelligence Playbook (2016)
3. Suciu, G., Anwar, M., Conu, R.: Social media and digital interactions using cloud services for orienting young people in their careers. ELSE Conf. **2**, 419–427 (2017)

4. Shinde, S., Mangrule, R.A.: Discovery of frequent itemset using higen miner with multiple taxonomies. Int. J. Curr. Trends in Eng. Res. **2**(6), 373–383 (2016)
5. Wu, Y., Wu, W., Li, Z., Zhou, M.: Response selection with topic clues for retrieval-based chatbots. In: Symposium for Advancement of Artificial Intelligence, pp. 1–8 (2016)
6. Lai, S., Xu, L., Liu, K., Zhao, J.: Recurrent convolutional neural networks for text classification. AAAI **333**, 2267–2273 (2015)
7. Behera, B.: Chappie-a semi-automatic intelligent chatbot. In LCPST, pp. 1–5 (2016)
8. LUKA Artificial Intelligence 12 Jun 2017. https://luka.ai/
9. LARK Care Continuum Platform 12 Jun 2017. http://www.web.lark.com/
10. Penny personal finance coach 12 Jun 2017. https://www.pennyapp.io/
11. Patil, A., Marimuthu, K., Niranchana, R.: Comparative study of cloud platforms to develop a Chatbot. Int. J. Eng. Technol. **6**(3), 57–61 (2017)
12. Language Understanding Intelligence 12 Jun 2017. https://www.luis.ai/
13. Szőts, M., Halmay, E., Gergely, T., Suciu, G., Cheveresan, R.: Semantics driven intelligent front-end. In: SpeD Conference, pp. 1–4 (2017)
14. Baruah, T.D.: Effectiveness of social media as a tool of communication and its potential for technology enabled connections: a micro-level study. Int. J. Sci. Res. Publ. **2**(5), 1–10 (2012)
15. Aral, S., Dellarocas, C., Godes, D.: Social media and business transformation: a framework for research. Inf. Syst. Res. **24**(1), 3–13 (2013)
16. Kaplan, A.M., Haenlein, M.: Users of the world, unite! the challenges and opportunities of social media. Bus. Horizons **53**(1), 59–68 (2010)
17. Houwens, B.: Machine Learning and UX. In Directed Simplicity, pp. 1–8 (2017)
18. Shaikh, F.: The benefits of new online (digital) technologies on business: understanding the impact of digital. In Digital Entrepreneurship and Global Innovation, pp. 1–4 (2016)
19. Stelzner, M.A.: Social media marketing industry report. how marketers are using social media to grow their businesses. In: Social Media Examiner (2016)
20. Oracle, An Oracle Best Practice Guide: Best Practices for Improving First-Contact Resolution in the Contact Center (2012)

Author Index

Printed in the United States
By Bookmasters